To my friend Christine,
I hope you will enjoy it
very much.

Karlee.

May 2017.

Redressing *Everyday Discrimination*

This book examines the harm that *everyday discrimination* can cause and proposes ways in which it can be redressed. Extreme forms of harmful expression, such as incitement to hatred, have been significantly addressed in law. Everyday generalised prejudice, negative stereotypes and gross under-representation of disadvantaged groups in mainstream media are, however, widely perceived as 'normal', and their criticism is regularly trivialised. In response, this book draws on critical and feminist theory in order to forge a theoretical analysis of the harm created through *everyday discrimination*. Arguing that anti-discrimination law can and should be extended as a tool to offer protection against the harm inflicted, the book goes on to consider both its limits, and possibilities, for redressing this discriminatory practice.

Karla Pérez Portilla has researched, taught and published in comparative and constitutional law, human rights and equality and discrimination themes in Mexico, England and Scotland.

Redressing *Everyday Discrimination*

The weakness and potential of anti-discrimination law

Karla Pérez Portilla

Routledge
Taylor & Francis Group

a GlassHouse book

First published 2016
by Routledge
2 Park Square, Milton Park, Abingdon, Oxon OX14 4RN

and by Routledge
711 Third Avenue, New York, NY 10017

a GlassHouse book

Routledge is an imprint of the Taylor & Francis Group, an informa business

British Library Cataloguing in Publication Data
A catalogue record for this book is available from the British Library

Library of Congress Cataloging-in-Publication Data
A catalog record for this book has been requested

ISBN: 978-1-138-91840-5 (hbk)
ISBN: 978-1-315-68853-4 (ebk)

Typeset in Baskerville
by Wearset Ltd, Boldon, Tyne and Wear

Printed and bound by CPI Group (UK) Ltd, Croydon, CR0 4YY

Contents

Acknowledgements

My interest in equality and discrimination is rooted and though I cannot be sure, I suspect began in my early childhood in Mexico, a profoundly unequal society at every level that has not managed to fully liberate itself from the injustices of a colonial past. Today it finds itself immersed in renewed forms of oppression and discrimination that are not only political and economic but also deeply ideological. I began researching and writing about equality in the year 2000 under the auspices of the Institute for Legal Research of the National Autonomous University of Mexico. My work there allowed me to attract the Chevening Scheme sponsorship for postgraduate studies in the UK. Thereafter my Masters Degree in Equality and Discrimination at the University of Strathclyde helped me identify gaps in the legal conception of discrimination and to understand that it is a multifaceted problem that exists and is maintained at many interacting levels, including the cultural. This book has benefited therefore from fifteen years of interest, study and critical debate on equality issues in Mexico, Scotland and England. It is in effect based on my PhD thesis from University College London. During my studies, sponsored by CONACYT (the Mexican Council for Science and Technology) and UCL, I presented my ideas at various legal and interdisciplinary conferences organised and co-organised by: the London School of Economics; the Faculty of Law of Cambridge University; the Faculty of Communications and Mass Media of the National Kapodistrian University of Athens, and the Institute of Communications Studies at the University of Leeds; the Centre for Law, Gender and Sexuality at the University of Kent, and Westminster University; and the British Sociological Association and Glasgow Caledonian University. Although I cannot include here all their names, I am grateful to all those who raised questions, challenged and made suggestions during my presentations. I also benefited greatly from the debates and the reactions to the debates about freedom of expression and discrimination that took place during the International Media Law Advocates Training Programme, Centre for Socio-Legal Studies, University of Oxford 2006.

Although the responsibility for everything in this book rests only with me, and indeed, not all those who have helped me along the way will necessarily agree with all its content, I am indebted to all of them. I am particularly grateful to Professor Eric Barendt and Colm O'Cinneide from UCL and to three generous and inspiring women Professors: Alison Diduck, Diamond Ashiagbor and Sandra Fredman. Alison was my PhD supervisor, she stood by me and gave me most valuable tools and advice from the day I first visited her until the day the degree was awarded. I knew I could count on her talent and wit to complete my project and make an original contribution. I want also to thank Colin Perrin (Commissioning Editor) and Gary Smith (Copy-Editor), their insightful and hugely sensible suggestions and recommendations have been invaluable in the assembly of the book.

Special thanks as always go to my parents and to my partner Andrew Johnson. Andrew has been a genuine partner in every possible way and has supported me in this and in everything I have done since the day I met him. I have benefited from his experience in equality and discrimination theory and practice at every possible level, and he is my friend, my mentor, my son's dad, my everything.

I would like to dedicate the book to Andrew and Andres O. Johnson.

Chapter 1

Introduction

1 Demeaning representation

> Black critics claim that the television industry is guilty of gross injustice in its depictions of Blacks. More often than not, Blacks are represented as criminals, hookers, maids, scheming dealers, or jiving connivers. Blacks rarely appear in roles of authority, glamour or virtue. Arab Americans are outraged at the degree to which television and film present recognizable Arabs only as sinister terrorists or gaudy princes, and conversely that terrorists are almost always Arab. Such outrage at media stereotyping issues in claims about the justice not of material distribution, but of cultural imagery and symbols.[1]

Young wrote this in 1990, focusing on the US context; however, the issues remain relevant today and are not confined to the US. In 2007 a chewing gum advert broadcast on television and cinemas in the UK depicting a black man with an exaggerated Caribbean accent and mannerisms was the object of more than 519 complaints from the public. These complaints raised a number of issues revealing that the viewers made connections between the advert and historical undervaluing, mocking and ridiculing of the accent and the mannerisms of black communities in the UK.[2] The same company produced another advert in 2011, again, allegedly 'playing with racial stereotypes' and paralleled a chocolate bar with the black model Naomi Campbell.[3] Similarly, the association of Islam with terrorism and the negative and stereotypical representation of Muslims and Arabs in western media that Young described in the 1990s continue to be matters of concern and complaint. Outrage about sexist advertising is not uncommon either; the apparently unstoppable use of women as sexual objects for decoration in advertisements and in stereotyped gender-roles is not a

1 Young (1990), p. 20.
2 See Chapter 7, II, 3.
3 *Ibid.*

practice of the past. Representations of this sort are found in 'everyday' images and messages such as advertising, tabloids and entertainment television; defining and constructing the type of society in which we live, and harming the self and social esteem of the groups they target.

Underpinning this book is the view that discrimination has many dimensions, including 'the cultural'. Demeaning and stereotypical representation in the media are 'cultural' and crucially they include 'subtle' forms of hate speech which are regularly trivialised and go unchallenged. This book examines the harm this kind of speech can cause and proposes ways in which it can be redressed. Crucially, as a part of this process, the book proposes referring to such 'speech' as *everyday discrimination* (ED), meaning the printed and audiovisual production and reproduction of images and messages that use demeaning stereotypes, ridicule, malign or disparage people on the grounds of their belonging to a disadvantaged group, where such grounds exist in conscious thought, perception, knowledge or consequence.

The book argues that the images and messages of ED are not 'just speech' but are forms of discrimination and although manifestations of disrespect and discrimination of this sort are disseminated in a variety of ways, the regulatory aspects of this book are focused on the media (television, radio, press, advertising and the internet). Different media require specific bespoke regulation. The internet, for example, is particularly difficult to regulate generally and more so is this the case with regard to content. These things said, however, despite the necessary differences in regulation, and the variety of stakeholders involved in different media; the principles derived from this book, the rationale behind the concept of ED, and the awareness-raising that naming this harm creates are all means with which to confront ED wherever it may be encountered. Ultimately, the recognition of ED as a form of injustice and discrimination is aimed at starting a process by which the public become capable of understanding the harm and start challenging it through appropriate channels where they exist or start demanding their creation where they do not.

In the main, the remedy pursued in this book is to promote 'more speech' in order to combat 'bad speech'. This should be a protected and encouraged type of speech capable of tackling prejudice and promoting understanding. This is the sort of remedy pursued because, for the most part, ED occurs as a matter of habit, it is reckless and the harm it creates is often not understood and therefore is minimised. This is not to excuse the production and reproduction of discriminatory images and messages, but to emphasise that in order to change habit and recklessness it is essential to expose the injustice these expressions engender. This implies gaining an understanding about the relations of inferiority and superiority that lie behind generalised prejudice and demeaning and stereotypical representations generated, among others, by the misogyny endemic in male-dominated societies; and the residual and renewed elements of imperialism and colonialism passed down through generations. The exposure of the economic, historical, political and ideological context where demeaning and stereotypical expressions arise has the capacity to uncover the injustice they represent and the power they have to perpetuate the same injustice. An injustice that is not only economic or political but also deeply ideological and dependent on cultural representations. This approach helps to prevent and redress generalised prejudice which indeed in many cases has the potential to generate the hatred and violence often associated with hate speech. The distinction between these two 'forms of speech' can be in many cases difficult to establish and, therefore, recognising and redressing ED prevents the free and unchallenged dissemination of expressions that cannot be proved to reach the high thresholds often established in hate speech legislation.

II Methodological considerations

Anti-discrimination law (ADL) in this book means the statutes, doctrine and case law related to equality and non-discrimination; the recognition of the harm created through ED is a project for ADL because in spite of the fact that various social science disciplines, international and regional instruments, media regulators' standards codes and indeed the targets of ED through the organised civil society, have pointed out that demeaning and stereotypical images and messages can cause harm and be discriminatory, ADL has been comparatively silent and there is no adequate analysis of the legal dimensions associated with the cultural aspects of discrimination such as demeaning stereotypical representation in the media. It is therefore appropriate and necessary to break ADL's silence and the paralysis in the legal imagination mostly created by the shields shaped by predominantly liberal freedom-of-expression law and doctrine. This book therefore offers elements to begin theorising about the concept of ED within ADL, and while recognising the centrality, value and permanent frailty of freedom of expression and indeed advocating the promotion of more speech, this book stresses the need to recognise more clearly the predicament in which ED leaves its targets and society as a whole.

The book makes use of interdisciplinary social science literature and legislation mainly from the UK, including its international and regional sources. However, the principles that can be derived from this book are useful for any other jurisdiction experiencing similar challenges. In particular, critical theory and feminist literature constitute the theoretical base of this project. This has been deemed appropriate because this material tries to project normative possibilities for ADL that are unrealised but felt as necessary in the societies analysed.[4] The ideas are propositions that arise from the problems associated with cultural aspects of discrimination in general and ED in particular. The research imagines a transformational project using ADL as a tool to offer protection against the misrecognition of harm inflicted through ED. This is to say, against the injustice of being 'routinely maligned or disparaged in stereotypic public cultural representations and/or in everyday life interactions'.[5] ADL's actual limitations, suppression and even denial of ED are explored in order to conceptualise its possibilities to redress this discriminatory practice.

The core of this book then relies on critical theory literature. In this regard it is 'critical' given its main sources, but also because of what has been done with them. The ideas in this book are propositions that arise from and challenge law's reluctance and alleged inadequacy to address the problems associated with cultural aspects of discrimination in general and ED in particular. The research imagines and proposes a project using ADL to offer protection against the 'misrecognition' harm inflicted through demeaning images and messages. Whether or not, or the extent to which, critical theory can form the foundation of any positive legal claims is debatable. However, this book does not intend to prove any such points. This book relies on critical literature because the problem it addresses has been largely ignored and/or minimised by 'mainstream legal literature/thinking' and instead, critical literature and interdisciplinary social science materials have allowed the conception of possible ways to legally address discriminatory speech. Critical theory/thinking has been used in similar ways many times before. For example, the growth, interest and subsequent political/legal enthusiasm and action in addressing the practical application of the concept of 'institutional discrimination' (Chapter 3) in law was one that grew out of what many believed 'ought' to be. This, over the years, has been fuelled by an understanding, analysis and documentation of the lived relations experienced by those now attributed with 'protected characteristic' status. This has come about because there was (and still is) a 'yearning' for things to be different and for institutional approaches to fairness and justice to be 'transformed'. There is indeed a world of ideas in critical literature from which mainstream legal thinking could benefit a great deal.

4 Critical theory, as explained by Young (1990), p. 6, is a mode of discourse which projects normative possibilities unrealised but felt in a particular given social reality. Each social reality presents its own unrealised possibilities, experienced as lacks and desires. Norms and ideals arise from the yearning that is an expression of freedom: it does not have to be this way, it could be otherwise. Imagination is the faculty of transforming the experience of what is into a projection of what could be, the faculty that frees thought to form ideals and norms.

5 Fraser (2003), p. 13.

III Research(er's) downsides, upsides and the diffusion of law

This is not a comparative law book, although it benefits from insights within different jurisdictions and locates them all in their appropriate context. Comparative law, however, is carried out for a number of purposes and often provides a 'pool of models, foreign law being used to modernise and improve the law at home ... the comparatist is led to systems that share the same problem but deal with the problem in different ways, better ways or more efficient ways'.[6] Some parts of the book on this view do benefit by drawing from different legal sources and thereby may fit some comparative law descriptions.[7] However, the specific reasons for the use of different jurisdictions' legal sources are given wherever these are referred to and always procure to be functional; aiming at showing the existence of a variety of approaches to tackling one same problem.[8] References are mainly conceptual, particularly in Chapter 6, where, given the close proximity between hate speech and ED, some hate speech concepts from different jurisdictions are referred to, showing their divergences and commonalities. Moreover, such reference indicates that there is an internationally shared problem and bringing the approaches together is functional because, although in different ways, the provisions are all performing the same task. Given the size of the undertaking, this book does not attempt to assess entire legal systems; however, it does provide the necessary elements with which to make a conceptual analysis of the harm in question and of the ways in which it has been addressed. Some level of superficiality is unavoidable; however, this has been overcome as much as possible by making explicit the purpose of referring to concepts from different jurisdictions.[9]

The analysis of the potential of ADL to address and contribute to the redress of ED takes some of its conceptual elements from Canadian and South African constitutional jurisprudence on equality and human dignity and from their emphasis on redressing disadvantage. This jurisprudence, which is presented in its appropriate context, including its pitfalls, represents only one way of understanding equality, but in foregrounding dignity is one which 'makes room' for the consideration of ED as a breach of human dignity and a form of disadvantage. These principles are offered, therefore, as an example of the conceptual ability of another aspect of the

---

6 Örücü (2006), pp. 31, 32.
7 See Zweigert and Kötz (1998), p. 11; and De Cruz (2007), p. 18.
8 Functionality means that only rules which perform the same function and address the same real problem or conflict of interests can be profitably compared. See Zweigert and Kötz (1998), p. 38.
9 On the superficiality inherent to comparative studies, see Watson (1974), p. 10.

law – here constitutional equality jurisprudence – to frame ED – harm to dignity – as a harm recognisable in law.

The conceptual analysis offers valuable insights which may then inspire new or enrich existing concepts in ADL in jurisdictions such as the UK. It is not unusual and indeed it is increasingly common that courts seek information as to how their counterparts in foreign countries resolve similar questions. Of course, this 'judicial dialogue' assumes that one court believes that the court they consult is 'right' and that both jurisdictions adhere to the same fundamental values.[10] Many elements of ADL, as indeed of all other branches of law in most jurisdictions, are the result of 'borrowing' and/or sharing in formal and informal processes, and so the UK's legislation is not free from similarities with other jurisdictions.[11] In sum, it is not extraordinary to look abroad for inspiration and both Canadian and South African jurisprudence offer valuable conceptual elements from which to draw that inspiration. However, it must be noted that even when sharing the same values, different jurisdictions may make different choices as to which competing values should be 'trumps' depending on the priorities of each jurisdiction from time to time. Given the size of the undertaking, this book does not explore these aspects of political and legal 'choice'. Instead it focuses on bringing the concept of ED to the attention of ADL theory and offering some elements with which to begin a theoretical analysis. These principles and ideas derived from the case made about ED will of course need to be 'fine-tuned' or adjusted in order to be useful for the context in which they may be applied which would necessarily be the subject of further research.[12]

This study does not, therefore, attempt law reform. It is instead a theoretical analysis that provides ideas and principles that justify the acknowledgement in law of the harm created by demeaning and stereotypical representations as a form of discrimination. Borrowing from other jurisdictions is an example of the 'movement of law', also called diffusion of

---

10 For judicial dialogue and its purposes, see Slaughter (1995), p. 524; and Markesinis (1997), pp. 195, 196.
11 The UK is, for example, deeply immersed in continental law ideas given its membership to the European Union; and indeed, 'the UK Human Rights Act, 1998 is a story of complex borrowing from theories of human rights, public international law, national laws, and the specific ideas of a British draftsman (David Maxwell Fyfe) followed by fifty years in Strasbourg, interaction with legal systems of the Council of Europe, then back to London, Edinburg and Belfast'. Twining (2009), p. 276.
12 Örücü (2002), pp. 207–208, making an analogy with music, uses the term 'transposition' when speaking of the movement of the law given that this term implies an adjustment made in order to suit the particular socio-legal culture of the recipient. Similarly, Watson (1974), p. 27, with regard to the medical analogy of 'legal transplants' explains that 'subsequent development in the host system should not be confused with rejection'.

law, legal transplants or transposition.[13] All these terms refer to a similar phenomenon, although each one makes reference to different historical contexts and social, political and economic perspectives and nuances about the movement and 'porosity' of law.[14] The term 'diffusion of law' as explained by Twining is particularly helpful in understanding the potential application of the findings of this book. Twining opts for a broader and much more complex picture and flexible methodology as a basis for studying the processes of diffusion and their outcomes. He challenges some of the assumptions ingrained in comparative studies. For example, the diffusion of law according to him is not necessarily formal, through enactment or adoption of a certain code. It can also be semi-informal or mixed: 'much diffusion is informal and protracted as when legal ideas are carried by colonists, missionaries or merchants or spread by influential legal or other writings'.[15] In this view, 'law is spread as much by literature as by legislation. Commerce, education and religion may be as important conduits as governmental action in bringing about legal change.'[16] Thus, the agent for the diffusion is not only government. It can also be commercial and other non-governmental organisations, individuals and groups: for example, writers, teachers, activists, lobbyists, colonists, merchants, missionaries, slaves, refugees and believers, who 'bring their law with them'. Another assumption often made is that it is legal rules, concepts and institutions that are 'diffused'. However, following Twining, it can also be any legal phenomena or ideas, including ideology, theories, personnel, 'mentality', methods, structures, practices, literary genres, documentary forms, symbols, rituals, etc.[17] In synthesis, what Twining urges, among other things, is to recognise the importance of informal and complex processes of interaction and movement of law and not only from a 'parent' common law or civil law system to a less developed dependent (e.g. colonial) or adolescent (e.g. transitional) system, but also from the 'less' to the 'more' developed.[18] The sources used in this book can in this view be

---

13 Other terms are reception, expansion, spread, transfer, exports and imports, imposition, circulation, transmigration, transfrontier mobility of law, grafting, implantation, re-potting, cross-fertilisation, collective colonisation, contaminants, legal irritants, layered law, hyphenated law and competition of legal systems. See, Twining (2009), p. 271; and Örücü (2002), p. 207.

14 The idea of 'legal transplants' is, however, disputed. Legrand (2001), pp. 60–63 argues that 'Given that the meaning invested into the rule is itself culture-specific, it is difficult to conceive, however, how this transfer [transplants of rules] could ever happen … At best, what can be displaced from one jurisdiction to another is, literally, a meaningless form of words … As it crosses boundaries, the original rule necessarily undergoes a change that affects it qua rule.'

15 Twining (2009), p. 24.

16 *Ibid*, p. 282.

17 See *ibid*, pp. 279–291.

18 *Ibid*, pp. 283, 284.

considered a form of diffusion of law. They help construct and introduce new ideas that allow imagining possibilities for the solution of particular problems. The propositions in this book, although primarily making reference to the UK context, should nevertheless be considered working hypotheses, this is to say, as general principles which need to be 'adjusted' and then applied to a specific legal system. Moreover, the different chapters in this book point out ways of looking at ED from different angles and propose its recognition within ADL as a possible step towards its redress. However, further research would indicate how in fact the principles suggested could be applied. Economic, political and social differences among jurisdictions may be relevant in explaining their different approaches with regard to discriminatory speech, but it is not the intention of this book to explore the reasons for those differences. Its focus is theoretical: it aims to explain *why* ED is a form of discrimination and, in drawing upon the UK as an example, to explore how it may be addressed by ADL. Indeed, ADL has been to a considerable extent fuelled by international pressure and is underpinned by norms, such as equality, which, because they have been expressed and ratified in international documents can be said to have some international normative currency. The UK then shares many international and regional commitments with other jurisdictions, it has enacted ADL and has hate speech laws. Moreover, its media regulatory bodies have standards codes which in some way have dealt with ED. These characteristics are not exclusive to the UK and, therefore, given that the harm is experienced and resisted across nations, similar principles may apply in different places for its redress. In addition, as many passages in the book emphasise, identity groups share experiences, struggles and ideas regardless of frontiers, thereby revealing the borderless existence of similar problems and the likelihood of necessarily more universal ways to redress them. Thus, despite the specificities of any individual jurisdiction, it is submitted that the principles that can be derived from this book can shed light upon the way in which existing institutions and procedures can recognise and combat ED, not only within the UK but also perhaps further afield.

There are some concerns with terminology within this book which need to be acknowledged. Referring to groups in relation to their skin colour – for example, 'black people' – may make a general political point about the injustice against 'non-whites', but 'black people' may also mean 'people of African descent', which is a distinct category, and the latter term indeed might be preferred by many.[19] People 'of colour' is another term often encountered and it may be preferred by some others over the generic 'black'. There is also some level of unease talking about BAME (black, Asian and minority ethnic people) often to refer to non-western or non-white people. The term ethnic minority is also rejected by many on the

19 See Chapter 4, IV.

grounds that it is stereotyping and pejorative because such people have often lived in Britain (for example) for several generations and anyway in many parts of Britain are certainly not in the minority. Thus none of the terms referred to is universally acceptable, probably because the terms themselves emanate from past and existing conflicts and/or injustices. It is therefore expected that the context in which these and other terms are used in the book will help determine their specific meaning and scope. Similarly, this book speaks of oppression and domination often as synonyms for 'discrimination' and the term ADL has been preferred over Equality Law or Discrimination Law.[20] Terminology, then, usually reveals its underlying ideology and its variety demonstrates that ultimately language is 'alive', dynamic and remains open to new, better ways of expressing our experiences.

IV Objectives and purpose

This book seeks overall to be a political, philosophical and legal response to the claims made by those who contest and/or are concerned with ED. Although it is primarily a legal book, it is accessible and indeed is an interdisciplinary study with the concerns of various potential readers and stakeholders in mind, including activists, students and researchers from different social science disciplines and professionals from equality commissions or bodies of that sort and media regulatory authorities.

The three main objectives pursued in this book are, first, to determine whether or not ED is a harm; second, whether it is a form of discrimination; and third, whether anything has been done about it already and if so, how effective that response has been. Chapters 2, 3 and 4 present arguments aimed at clarifying why ED is a harm. Chapter 2 provides the political and philosophical underpinnings to justify the idea that ED is a form of injustice and provides the ideological and conceptual framework within which ED needs to be understood. Chapter 3, through a multidimensional analysis of discrimination which includes the structural, institutional, personal and cultural levels, explains why ED can be understood as a form of discrimination that law is capable of addressing. Chapter 4 then focuses on demeaning stereotypical representation in the media in order to illustrate a most pervasive form of ED, and shows that it has been significantly challenged by the organised civil society working against discrimination.

Chapters 5, 6 and 7 demonstrate that discriminatory speech broadly understood has been challenged at international, regional and local levels; however, these chapters also demonstrate the need for political will and imagination to effectively balance freedom of expression with other

---

20 See Bamforth *et al* (2008), p. vi.

rights. Covering a timescale of over 30 years, Chapter 5 explores some international and regional documents that have addressed both the role of culture in discrimination generally and the role of the media in discrimination in particular, thereby revealing that ED is an unsolved old problem that cuts across nations.

Given the close proximity between hate speech and ED, Chapter 6 explores arguments of principle and international, regional and local legal initiatives addressing hate speech. It identifies flaws and forms of hate speech that go unchallenged and which should be captured by the concept of ED. Even though the discriminatory images and messages of ED can exist in private conversations and interactions, and in a variety of settings, the regulatory aspects of ED put forward in this book refer to discriminatory images and messages in the media – television, radio, press, advertising and the internet. Chapter 7 therefore explores the ways in which media regulatory bodies in the UK have addressed the issue and looks for ways for improvement, identifying principles that could be helpful for the UK and on a more general level.

Chapters 8 and 9 specify the concept of ED and the potential role of ADL in its redress. Chapter 8 brings together the findings of the previous chapters. It specifies the elements that are helpful to identify when an image or a message can be deemed discriminatory and indicates the ways in which ED is manifested. These include demeaning stereotypical representations, under-representation of disadvantaged groups, the ways in which news is reported and the human composition of the media industry itself. Chapter 9 then explores various intertwined themes, concepts and developments in ADL in the UK and elsewhere which demonstrate that the harm created through discriminatory images and messages in the media could be addressed and redressed as a specific form of discrimination. The recognition of harassment in ADL works as a precedent which reveals that ADL is capable of understanding dignitary harms which, similar to ED, create hostile environments and are reminders of relations of domination. With this last chapter, then, the book comes full circle and breaks ADL's silence about demeaning and stereotypical representation in the media; providing ground and meaning to the recurrent associations made between hate/discriminatory speech, harm to human dignity and discrimination in general.

V References

Bamforth, Nicholas, Malik, Maleiha, O'Cinneide, C. and Bindman, Geoffrey (2008), *Discrimination Law: Theory and Context*, London: Thomson, Sweet & Maxwell.

De Cruz, Peter (2007), *Comparative Law in a Changing World*, 3rd ed., London: Routledge-Cavendish.

Fraser, Nancy (2003), 'Social justice in the age of identity politics: redistribution, recognition, and participation', in Fraser, Nancy and Honneth, Axel, *Redistribution or Recognition? A Political-Philosophical Exchange*, London: Verso.

Legrand, Pierre (2001), 'What "legal transplants"', in Nelken, David and Feest, Johannes, *Adapting Legal Cultures*, Oxford: Hart.

Markesinis, Basil (1997), *Foreign Law and Comparative Methodology: A Subject and a Thesis*, Oxford: Hart.

Örücü, Esin (2002), 'Law as transposition', *International and Comparative Law Quarterly*, vol. 51.

Örücü, Esin (2006), 'Methodological aspects of comparative law', *European Journal of Law Reform*, vol. 8, no. 1.

Slaughter, Anne-Marie (1995), 'International law in a world of liberal states', *European Journal of International Law*, vol. 6.

Twining, William (2009), *General Jurisprudence*, Cambridge: Cambridge University Press.

Watson, Alan (1974), *Legal Transplants*, Edinburgh: Scottish Academic Press.

Young, Iris Marion (1990), *Justice and the Politics of Difference*, Princeton, NJ: Princeton University Press.

Zweigert, Konrad and Kötz, Hein (1998), *An Introduction to Comparative Law*, 3rd ed., Oxford: Clarendon.

Chapter 2

Locating *everyday discrimination* in a theory of justice

I Introduction

This chapter provides political and philosophical underpinnings to the idea that *everyday discrimination* (ED), meaning

> the printed and audiovisual production and reproduction of images and messages that use demeaning stereotypes, ridicule, malign or disparage people on the grounds of their belonging to a disadvantaged group, be it with such grounds in conscious thought, perception, knowledge or consequence,

is a form of harm or injustice.

There are four parts to the chapter. The first provides the ideological and conceptual framework within which ED needs to be understood. The second part is a critique of some assumptions within the distributive paradigm of justice that make it difficult to consider ED as a matter of justice that requires redress; particularly its tendency to overlook the structural, institutional and indeed the cultural arrangements that produce disadvantage.

The third part specifies the idea of *recognition* as a matter of justice, presenting ideas of authors such as Honneth, who indeed gives primacy to issues of recognition over redistribution, and therefore emphasises the need to acknowledge social injuries to one's integrity, honour and dignity as the core of social justice. The last part lays out examples of the ways in which *misrecognition* operates, the harm it causes, remedies that can be settled and some problematic themes. These examples present the context in which ED is located within the philosophical and political concept of misrecognition.

II *Everyday discrimination* as a matter of injustice

Being routinely maligned or disparaged in stereotypic cultural representations, through printed or audiovisual images and messages which are mass disseminated – for example, in advertising and tabloid reports – seems intuitively unjust. Indeed, for media regulatory bodies in the UK, these are often considered matters of discrimination (Chapter 7). The targets of these behaviours have organised themselves and condemned such practices in a variety of ways. Muslim, African, lesbian, gay and bisexual organisations have all articulated their feelings of injustice about demeaning representation (Chapter 4). They have exposed the injuries such practices have had upon their identity and opportunities, including status devaluation, disrespect, humiliation, ridicule, stigmatisation and the deterioration of the self and social esteem of the group members. The claims of these groups together with the unsatisfactory legal and media self-regulatory responses to them justify and substantiate the need to explore the topic in more detail. In order to articulate the demands of these groups, it is proposed to describe printed and audiovisual production and reproduction of images and messages that use demeaning stereotypes, ridicule, malign or disparage people on the grounds of their belonging to a disadvantaged group as 'ED', that is to say, *everyday discrimination*.

The wording *everyday discrimination* has been chosen because it has the capacity to make reference not only to annoyance and often anger about the routine use and cumulative effect of numerous individual discriminatory images and messages 'because we see them all the time', but also to their submissive acceptance created by their embedded and established normality that 'such is life', and/or resignedly, 'ah well, that's the way it is', etc. Discriminatory images are omnipresent; they can have a slow-drip, build-up effect against their targets and society as a whole. The unfairness of their routine use may trigger contestation; however, despite their pervasiveness, the harm they create is not so frequently understood. We know what it feels like and we know what the images and messages look like, but the issue has no 'recognisable' name and thus it is difficult to point it out as a problem. This is partly explained by the deep-seated nature of the issue; by the 'normality' of these images and messages; by their mainstream acceptance; and by their often unwitting, unconscious production and reproduction. *Everyday discrimination* thus gives name to a process in which 'people are just doing their jobs and living their lives without understanding themselves as agents of any oppression'.[1] Therefore, we may find ourselves drifting between stances such as the desire to act against this problem, because we believe it is unfair; and passivity, because we have simply learnt to live with ED. These stances thus serve to describe the

1 Young (1990), pp. 41, 42. This is part of Young's description of structural oppression.

intricacy and complexity of the problem and also indicate two of the essential actions that need to be taken for its redress. These are: to clearly articulate the harm and to raise awareness about ED.

In every complaint and protest against ED there is an inherent claim for justice. The questions are, however, to what conception of justice does such a claim implicitly appeal, and how does it confront or modify existing conceptions of justice?[2] Justice has been given a wide range of meanings and implications. For many years, at least since the 1970s, the distributive paradigm of justice has been the most influential. However, 'new' claims and critical views about traditional claims pose a number of challenges to its scope and underlying assumptions. The next section will explore these challenges in more detail. However, it is convenient at this point to outline a most significant problem of distributive theories vis-à-vis the inclusion of ED as a matter of justice. As explained by Young, the distributive paradigm of justice:

> tends to focus thinking about social justice on the allocation of material goods such as things, resources, income, and wealth, or on the distribution of social positions, especially jobs. This focus tends to ignore the social structure and institutional context that often help determine distributive patterns.[3]

Young then refers to other elements of justice such as decision-making power and procedures, division of labour and culture, all of which she identifies as social structures and institutional contexts that determine distributive patterns.[4] ED is not the negation of a material good; it is instead an integral part of those social structures that impact upon distributive patterns. However, because the harm of ED is not reduced solely to its negative impact on distribution but also exists in and of itself, Fraser's[5] understanding of justice as encompassing redistribution, recognition and participation is a useful supplement to Young's position.

Fraser considers the aim of justice to be participatory parity. This means that justice requires social arrangements that permit all members of

---

2 These are questions formulated by Young. She refers to the claims of 'new' group-based social movements associated with left politics, such as Feminist, Black Liberation, American Indian and Gay and Lesbian Liberation. Given that ED is a claim that does not sit comfortably in dominant theories of justice, the same questions appear apposite. See, *ibid*, p. 3.
3 *Ibid*, p. 15.
4 Institutional context includes any structures or practices in institutions of state, family, and civil society, as well as the workplace. These are relevant to judgements of justice in so far as they condition people's ability to participate in determining their actions and their ability to develop and exercise their capacities. *Ibid*, p. 22.
5 See Fraser (2003; 2005a; 2005b).

society to interact with each other as peers.[6] Participatory parity demands the *distribution* of material resources so as to ensure the participants' economic independence and voice (objective condition) and *recognition* via the institutionalisation of patterns of cultural value that express equal respect for all participants and ensure their equal opportunity to achieve social esteem (intersubjective condition).[7] *Participation* is the political dimension of justice, which concerns the nature of the State's jurisdiction and the decision rules by which it structures contestation. It tells us who can make claims for redistribution and recognition and how such claims are to be adjudicated.[8] Challenging ED requires elements of all three dimensions; however it is analytically better understood within the recognition paradigm. Recognition requires the preclusion of 'institutionalised norms that systematically depreciate some categories of people and the qualities associated with them'.[9] Indeed, Fraser considers that to be 'routinely maligned or disparaged in stereotypic public cultural representations and/or in everyday life interactions'[10] is a matter of misrecognition and thus injustice.

For Young, on the other hand, social justice means the elimination of institutionalised domination and oppression.[11] Thus, 'any aspect of social organisation and practice relevant to domination and oppression is in principle subject to evaluation by ideas of social justice'.[12] As Young understands it, the concept of justice coincides with the concept of the political. Politics as she defines it,

> includes all aspects of institutional organisation, public action, social practices and habits, and cultural meanings insofar as they are potentially subject to collective evaluation and decision-making. Politics ...

6 See Fraser (2003), p. 36. Parity means the condition of being a 'peer', of being on a par with others, of standing on an equal footing. Fraser leaves open the question as to what degree or level of equality exactly is necessary to ensure such parity. The moral requirement is that members of society are ensured the possibility of parity, if and when they choose to participate in a given activity or interaction.

7 *Ibid.*

8 See Fraser (2005a), pp. 74–76.

9 Fraser (2003), p. 36.

10 *Ibid*, p. 13.

11 Oppression consists of systematic institutional processes which prevent people from learning and using satisfying and expansive skills in socially recognised settings, or institutionalised social processes which inhibit people's ability to play and communicate with others or to express their feelings and perspective on social life in contexts where others can listen. Domination consists of institutional conditions which inhibit or prevent people from participating in determining their actions or the conditions of their actions. Persons live within structures of domination if other persons or groups can determine without reciprocation the conditions of their actions, either directly or by virtue of the structural consequences of their actions. See Young (1990), p. 38.

12 *Ibid*, p. 15.

concerns the policies and actions of government and the state, but in principle can also concern rules, practices, and actions in any other institutional context.[13]

The conceptions of justice outlined by Young and Fraser go beyond material distribution and also encompass the social structures and institutional contexts that determine distributive patterns, which includes culture. Nevertheless, Young and Fraser have disagreements, especially with regard to the distinction between redistribution and recognition. Young rejects such a dichotomy, arguing that the distinction wrongly opposes political economy to culture. Young believes that what Fraser calls recognition is 'a means to the economic and social equality and freedom that she [Fraser] brings under the category of redistribution'.[14] Young is right in the sense that misrecognition is inseparable from maldistribution (and culture is inseparable from economy). However, Fraser points out the need to address misrecognition harms as injuries in and of themselves, and it is this that provides shelter for ED claims and offers those who have complained a basis in justice to do so.

The articulation of ED as a matter of justice adopts elements of both Fraser and Young's understandings of justice. It agrees generally with Young that justice requires the elimination of oppression and domination, that is, the structural or systemic phenomena which exclude people from participating in determining their actions or the conditions of their actions,[15] but it also agrees with Fraser, that remedying misrecognition is not only a means to achieve a more just distribution, but is itself a condition of social justice. Thus, ED as a matter of justice is, in the language of Fraser, a matter of misrecognition and, when following Young, it is the injustice of cultural imagery and symbols.[16]

III Some limitations of dominant theories of justice

Multidimensional theories of justice such as those of Fraser and Young are alternatives to theories which are primarily distributive-oriented. While the latter attend to a fundamental aspect of justice, namely: securing a minimum level of material well-being, and redistributive goals have not been completely met even in many developed countries, the critique here presented is instead focused on some of the problems that addressing ED would pose for distributive-oriented theories of justice.

13 *Ibid*, p. 34.
14 Young (1997), p. 152.
15 See Young (1990), p. 31.
16 See Fraser (2003), p. 13; and Young (1990), p. 20.

1 Overlooking the social structures and institutional contexts that determine distributive patterns

Many conceptions of justice have 'equality' as a common value. Indeed, most liberal theories rely on the 'equal moral value of all' as an assumption from which redistributive ideals follow. As explained by Kymlicka:

> Part of the idea of being moral equals is the claim that none of us is inherently subordinate to the will of others, none of us comes into the world as the property of another, or as their subject.[17]

Thus, some authors such as Rawls, Dworkin and Sen have given equality a central position in their discussions.[18] The account of equality defended in

17 Kymlicka (2002), p. 61. However, having equality as a common value does not mean 'supporting an equal distribution of income'. There is a more abstract idea, that of 'treating people as equals'. This idea (commonly found in political theory, be it libertarian or indeed Marxist) suggests that a theory is egalitarian if it accepts that the interests of each member of the community matter, and matter equally. The difference in theories will therefore depend on the consequences derived from the proposition.

18 Rawls' general conception of justice relies on the idea that all social primary goods – liberty and opportunity, income and wealth, and the bases of self-respect – are to be distributed equally unless an unequal distribution of any or all of these goods is to the advantage of the least favoured. This view of justice influenced further liberal ideas of justice around aims such as respecting the moral equality of persons, mitigating the arbitrariness of natural and social contingencies, and accepting responsibility for our choices. Following this programme, Dworkin focuses on equality of resources and is generally concerned with *ex post* corrections to the inequalities generated by the market. Sen, on the other hand, acknowledges that equal distributions are not enough to secure freedom, since interpersonal variations (different endowments of inherited wealth and liabilities, together with personal characteristics such as age, sex and physical and mental abilities) determine the person's capability, that is, the freedom actually enjoyed. His approach concentrates on our capability to achieve valuable functionings that make up our lives, and more generally, our freedom to promote objectives we have reasons to value. See Rawls (1972), pp. 7, 43, 303; Dworkin (2002), pp. 5, 6, 59, 237, 238; and Sen (1995), pp. 27, 29, 33, 40. Sen takes his argument on 'capabilities' further in Sen (2009), pp. 225–320. Other authors have critiqued the usefulness of equality as a central value, particularly in the feminist agenda where, for example, instead of arguing about equality, there is a tendency to document and attack the current system of masculine advantage/privilege. See, Hunter (2008), p. 3. Many authors in this book, for example, Auchmuty (2008), offer new appraisals of a historical equality project for women, that is, the reform of married women's property laws in Britain in the second half of the nineteenth century. She demonstrates that concepts of equality provided uncertain, unstable foundations for this project, or were even disavowed by their proponents. Auchmuty argues that despite modern assumptions about the liberalism of first-wave feminists, the movement for married women's property reform in Britain was not an 'equal rights' campaign. The campaigners did not understand women to be equal to men, nor was the achievement of women's equality with men the aspiration. Rather, they adopted something more like what we would now recognise as a radical feminist analysis, concerned with men's power, domination and oppression of women, and the need to end that state of affairs.

Dworkin's book, *Sovereign Virtue*,[19] is shaped and supported by two principles of ethical individualism. First is the principle of equal importance which establishes that it is important, from an objective point of view, that human lives be successful rather than wasted. This 'requires government to adopt laws and policies that insure that its citizens' fates are, so far as government can achieve this, insensitive to who they otherwise are – their economic backgrounds, gender, race, or particular sets of skills and handicaps'.[20] The second is the principle of special responsibility which implies that 'though we must all recognise the equal objective importance of the success of human life, one person has a special and final responsibility for that success – the person whose life it is'.[21] Dworkin makes no assumption that people choose their convictions or preferences, or their personality, any more than they choose their race or physical or mental abilities; he does assume, however, an ethics which supposes that we are responsible for the consequences of the choices we make out of those convictions or preferences or personality.[22]

Even though these principles are useful in guiding the appropriateness of government intervention, they may obscure the need to ask about, identify and remedy the *causes* of the 'failure/waste' of certain people's lives (the hot potato). Likewise, while individual responsibility for one's own fate is an important and unavoidable element, it should be more clearly evaluated against the structural and institutional arrangements including the cultural context in which individual lives are immersed. For example, what Dworkin calls 'brute bad luck'[23] such as being born blind or without talents others have, can be burdens but arguably they are only so in a society whose institutions and structures have 'chosen' to provide the necessary arrangements for the success of only those who conform to a specific norm or have the talents that such a society 'decided' to appreciate. This is to say that such conditions are not necessarily bad luck in themselves but are 'bad luck' because of a particular society's failure to accommodate/work with them. So, while social justice cannot demand policy and law makers to closely follow individuals in order to make sure they make 'good choices', it can put the emphasis on social structures and institutional arrangements that we *can* actually change, influence and judge so that lives are not 'wasted'.

The choices we make – and for which we are finally responsible according to some liberal models – are, as many liberals would agree, more often than not, dependent on resources available. In other words, individuals

---

19 Dworkin (2002).
20 *Ibid*, p. 6.
21 *Ibid*, p. 5.
22 *Ibid*, pp. 6 and 7.
23 *Ibid*, p. 287.

are not independent from society or from other individuals and our 'choices' have a cultural background and a context against which they should be assessed. Communitarians, for example, would emphasise that we are partly defined by the communities and societies we inhabit and, therefore, are imbricated in the ends and purposes characteristic of them.[24] The options we have – and the choices we make – 'are not ahistorical but culturally and historically specific, inflected by the master narratives of family structure and gender roles into which each individual is thrown'.[25] Even though, Dworkin does not leave his view of individual responsibility completely without reservations; a multidimensional view of justice requires both a more pronounced emphasis on the conditions and processes that lead to more or less successful lives and their evaluation as intrinsic elements of justice. According to Baker,

> the development of emancipatory social theory requires an empirical stance, which is open-ended, dialogically reciprocal, grounded in respect for human capacity, and yet profoundly sceptical of appearances and common sense. Such an empirical stance is, furthermore, rooted in a commitment to the long-term, broad-based ideological struggle to transform structural inequalities.[26]

For example, an unreserved assessment of individual responsibility, leaving aside the so-called 'brute bad luck', would imply that women in most largely democratic countries are persistently making very bad choices. The same would be true for most minorities in developed countries. Therefore, social justice should also involve the evaluation and tackling of the causes and social contexts of apparent 'bad choices' as intrinsic elements of justice. This is not to avoid individual agency but it is to relieve individuals of burdens for which they should not unreservedly be held responsible so that:

> Although we do not choose the webs in whose nets we are initially caught, or select those with whom we wish to converse, our agency consists in our capacity to weave out of those narratives our individual life stories, which make sense for us as unique selves.[27]

In Dworkin's analysis, individuals should be relieved of consequential responsibility for those unfortunate features of their situation that are brute bad luck, but not from those that should be seen as flowing from

24 See Kukathas and Pettit (1990), p. 113.
25 Benhabib (2002), p 15.
26 Baker *et al* (2004), p. 179.
27 Benhabib (2002), p 15.

their choices.[28] Bad choices are, for example, spending money on luxury items or choosing not to work or to work at less remunerative jobs than those chosen by others.[29] While this is intuitively appealing it is also true that sometimes there can be a connection between what could be considered 'bad choices' and the choices that certain groups are inured to make as a result of the social circumstances they inhabit, including the pressures of materialist capitalist societies. Moreover, the question as to why some jobs are better remunerated than others should also be considered within social justice.[30]

On the other hand, others, such as Rawls, *have* more clearly acknowledged the importance of social structures and institutions when considering the dilemmas of inequality and injustice. For Rawls, the primary subject of justice is the basic structure of society, or more exactly, the way in which the major social institutions distribute fundamental rights and duties and determine the division of advantages from social cooperation.[31] Examples of the major institutions to which he refers are the political constitution and the principal economic and social arrangements such as the legal protection of freedom of thought and liberty of conscience, competitive markets, private property in the means of production and the monogamous family.[32] Rawls acknowledges and explains that taken together all these institutional arrangements determine individuals' positions and expectations. In his theory of justice, the individuals' chances in life can be favoured or hindered by institutions and this constitutes especially deep inequalities, 'not only are they pervasive, but they affect men's initial chances in life; yet they cannot possibly be justified by an appeal to the notions of merit or dessert'.[33]

2 Focusing on economic redistribution

For Dworkin, 'equal concern' is the sovereign virtue of political community: 'without it government is only tyranny and when a nation's wealth is very unequally distributed ... then its equal concern is suspect'.[34] Without disregarding the complexities of defining what equal concern should mean, he argues that it requires that government aim at a form of material equality that he calls 'equality of resources'.[35] Indeed, according to him, 'Equality must be measured in resources and opportunities, not in

28 See Dworkin (2002), p. 287.
29 *Ibid.*
30 See Young (1990), p. 23.
31 See Rawls (1972), p. 7.
32 *Ibid.*
33 *Ibid.*
34 Dworkin (2002), p. 1.
35 *Ibid*, p. 3.

welfare or well-being'.[36] The rationale for Dworkin's election is that we live in ethically pluralistic societies in which people disagree about how, concretely, to live well.[37] Therefore, he chooses the justice of economic redistribution since this appears to avoid the problem of imposing a particular way of life.

Inequality, however, is not only manifested in economic terms; very often, economic inequality is the result of structural and institutional arrangements, behaviours and beliefs that create second-class citizens. A 'transfer of resources' can be necessary but also of limited significance if there is no parallel transformation of the social structures and institutions that create economic inequality in the first place.

A framework of redistribution, specifically economic redistribution that does not challenge the causes of disadvantage, may have negative outcomes. For example, this omission is, in part, what makes possible a backlash against the welfare state. Its focus on redistribution of economic resources without challenging the structures that promote and sustain poverty has been accused of denying individual responsibility, stifling creativity, and reducing efficiency.[38] However, the problem is not redistribution itself but the inadequate assessment of economic problems. A solution is not cutbacks in welfare programmes (to reduce poverty and provide basic public services) as the political right would suggest, but crucially a transformation of the arrangements that create poverty.

Distributive theories, such as Dworkin's, based mostly on 'the transfer of resources', aim at responding to the critiques of the political right by being 'choice sensitive'. This is to say that people have choices and they pay for their choices. His policy recommendations focus on enabling those with resources to have more choices (e.g. allowing supplementary private health insurance), and on ensuring that the 'lazy or imprudent' do not impose the costs of their choices on others (e.g. workfare). However, focusing on choices without challenging 'unequal circumstances' can end up stigmatising the 'undeserving poor' who are seeking public subsidies for their irresponsible lifestyles. Thus, while the intention might have been to be choice-sensitive and promote a fair redistribution of economic resources, the result of not attending to the social structures and institutional contexts that maintain poverty, feeds the political right perception that some people are 'irresponsible and indolent' and therefore should be punished.[39]

36 *Ibid*, p. 237.
37 *Ibid*, p. 277.
38 See Kymlicka (2002), p. 92. These kinds of attacks come usually from the 'New Right', and were spearheaded by Reagan and Thatcher in the 1980s.
39 *Ibid*, p. 93.

3 Attending solely to post factum correction of market inequalities

Some liberal distributive theories of justice tend to see disadvantage as something inevitable in any society. There appears to be an understanding of 'unequal circumstances' as static and somehow 'natural'.[40] However, disadvantage is not a quality but a *result* of a series of practices, institutional arrangements and cultural assumptions.[41]

As Kymlicka has put it, Dworkin's system of taxing the unequal income of the advantaged and transferring it to the disadvantaged seems to 'take the existing level of inequality in the market income as a given'.[42] This order of critique was made a long time ago. Mill, for example, argued that a focus solely on *post factum* income redistributions pays attention only to the consequences of unjust power, instead of redressing the injustice itself.[43]

Existing inequalities are not given; for example, social roles and the recognition given to some jobs and not to others are the result of power relations and, indeed, depend on many people and institutions doing certain things within structural arrangements to maintain this *status quo*. This is to say that the way in which existing roles are defined matters. As Kymlicka puts it:

> People would not generally choose to enter social relations that deny these opportunities [skill development, personal accomplishment and the exercise of responsibility] or that put them in relations of domination or degradation. From a position of equality, women would not have agreed to a system of social roles that defines 'male' jobs as superior to, and dominating of 'female' jobs.[44]

This leads to the conclusion that it is not only important to redistribute income from the advantaged to the disadvantaged, but also to ensure that the advantaged do not have the power to define relations of dominance

---

40 According to Dworkin, equality of circumstances is impossible. We could try to equalise circumstances as much as possible. But that, too, seems unacceptable. Since each additional bit of money can help the 'severely retarded' person, yet is never enough to fully equalise circumstances, we would be required to give all our resources to people with such handicaps, leaving nothing for everyone else. See Dworkin (1981), pp. 242–300.

41 The notion of disadvantage is explained in detail in Chapter 9. It means in general terms a subordinated position, a devalued status and the existence of material and immaterial obstacles for the access to goods and services.

42 Kymlicka (2002), p. 82.

43 See Mill (1965), p. 953 as quoted by Kymlicka (2002), p. 82; and generally Marx (1977).

44 Kymlicka (2002), p. 90.

and servility.[45] Sen, for example, recognises that 'our diversity' impacts on our ability to achieve freedom. His emphasis is in both shifting the focus from the space of means in the form of commodities and resources to that of functionings, which are seen as constitutive elements of human well-being; and making it possible to take note of the set of alternative functioning vectors from which the person can choose. The 'capability set', as he calls it, can thus be seen as the overall freedom a person enjoys to pursue her well-being.[46] Sen's idea of justice is both modest and practical. He maintains that even though perfect justice or perfectly just social arrangements are unachievable, we *can* nevertheless identify remediable injustices. This identification is indeed what animates us to think about justice and is also central to the theory of justice.[47]

Challenging the social structures and institutional contexts that produce and maintain disadvantage requires a direct attack on the entrenched economic hierarchies of modern societies that disadvantage some people, for example 'the poor', women or 'racial minorities'. This, according to Kymlicka, might involve quite radical policies, such as affirmative action, basic income, employee self-ownership, 'stakeholding', payment to homemakers, compensatory education investment and so on.[48] Young contributes to this necessary challenge and discusses other categories of non-distributive issues of justice that distributive theories tend to ignore. These are: decision-making issues, division of labour and *culture*. Young urges the evaluation of the institutional context in which distribution occurs, thus challenging the causes of disadvantage as a matter of justice, as opposed to focusing only on *post factum* redress of market inequalities. By *decision-making issues*, Young refers to questions of who, by virtue of their positions, have the effective freedom or authority to make decisions, as well as the rules and procedures according to which decisions

---

45 Kymlicka suggests that Rawls did acknowledge that 'property-owning democracy' (a model which aims at sharply reduced inequality in the underlying distribution of property and wealth, and greater equality of opportunity to invest in human capital) would be superior to the welfare state, not only in reducing the need for *ex post* redistribution, but also in preventing relations of domination and degradation within the division of labour. However, he did not develop this idea further. *Ibid*, p. 89.

46 See Sen (1995), p. 150.

47 Sen's idea of justice brings together an evaluation but also a critique of both western and non-western thought. For him, the tackling of injustice and the shaping of progress rely on a constant, engaged public conversation, a 'government by discussion'. For this, democracy, especially in the shape of public argument and debate, plays a key role. See Sen (2009).

48 See Kymlicka (2002), p. 89.

are made.[49] Young understands *division of labour* both distributively and non-distributively. As a distributive issue, division of labour refers to how pregiven occupations, jobs or tasks are allocated among individuals or groups. As a non-distributive issue, on the other hand, division of labour concerns the definition of the occupations themselves.[50] *Culture* as a matter of justice includes the symbols, images, meanings, habitual comportments, stories and so on through which people express their experience and communicate with one another. As Young explains, the symbolic meanings that people attach to other kinds of people and to actions, gestures or institutions often significantly affect the social standing of persons and their opportunities. This includes the injustice of the cultural imperialism which marks and stereotypes some groups at the same time that it silences their self-expression.[51]

These issues are often ignored by distributive theories of justice. However, they are important since they constitute the structural, institutional and cultural context in which distributions occur and should also be liable to evaluation as matters of justice. ED is located at the cultural level following Young. Its recognition is important because it tackles injustice in areas other than the purely economic while at the same time is part of the context in which economic inequalities flourish. There is indeed a close relationship between ED and economic disadvantage. However, as we will further explain, ED is also a harm in itself that needs to be individually assessed and redressed.

4 Extending distributive principles to non-distributive issues

The distributive paradigm of justice generally assumes that justice can be achieved via the distribution of material goods (things, resources, income and wealth) and social positions, especially jobs. Nevertheless, there *are* distributive theories that extend the scope of distributive justice to

---

49 According to Young, economic domination occurs not simply because 'some persons have more wealth and income than others … [It] derives at least as much from the corporate and legal structures and procedures that give some persons the power to make decisions about investment, production, marketing, employment, interest rates, and wages that affect millions of other people. Not all who make these decisions are wealthy or even privileged, but the decisionmaking structure operates to reproduce distributive inequality and the unjust constraints on people's lives.' Young (1990), pp. 22–23.

50 Feminist claims about the justice of a sexual division of labour, for example, have been posed both distributively and non-distributively. Feminists have questioned the justice of a pattern of *distribution* of positions that finds a small proportion of women in the most prestigious jobs. However, they have also questioned the conscious or unconscious associations (not in themselves distributive issues) of many occupations or jobs with masculine or feminine characteristics, such as instrumentality or affectivity. *Ibid*, p. 23.

51 *Ibid.*

non-material goods.[52] This raises a problematic assumption; the 'goods' they include are often self-respect, opportunity, power and honour. This extension is problematic because stretching the distributive model to non-material goods misunderstands the way in which such 'goods' are used in societies.[53] These aspects of justice cannot be quantified and thus cannot be owned, possessed, exchanged or 'distributed' fairly. Cooper, for example, argues for equality of power. However, she does not see power as a commodity or a distributive matter. Equal power is instead an expression of equal value. 'Equality of power starts with the prima-facie assumption that all people should have the same capacity to impact upon their environment whether discursively, by means of resources, or in terms of participation within, recreating, or disrupting, institutional structures.'[54] Power, self-respect, opportunity and honour are all aspects of justice that need to be understood as social relationships, as functions of social relations and processes that are embedded within a culture rather than as commodities. It is those social relationships and processes which should be brought to evaluation as matters of justice; for example, the laws, cultural assumptions, institutional practices and so on that make disadvantage possible, harming the self-respect of people, rendering them less powerful vis-à-vis others and hindering their opportunities to achieve both economic and social benefits.

Rawls conceives 'primary goods' such as income and jobs as the 'social basis of self-respect'.[55] This is to say, for Rawls, distributive arrangements provide the background conditions for self-respect. However, while distributive arrangements can incidentally help, they cannot be expected to be sufficient to achieve social equality or to challenge status subordination which may not necessarily be exclusively economic. For example, Rawls' account of self-respect and self-esteem encompasses two aspects. First, it includes a person's sense of 'his' own value, 'his' secure conviction that 'his' conception of the good, 'his' plan of life, is worth carrying out. Second, for him, self-respect implies a confidence in one's ability, in so far as it is within one's power, to fulfil one's intentions.[56] The difficulty with this approach is that fairer distribution of income and jobs cannot *alone* guarantee the kind of justice necessary to impact upon our sense of our own value or the conviction that our plan of life is worth carrying out. This is so because, on the one hand, redistribution cannot on its own overcome structural and institutional injustices that are often rooted in the cultural deprecation and disrespect of certain identities; and on the other, because

52 For example, Rawls (1972); Miller (1976); and Galston (1980) as quoted by Young (1990), pp. 17–18.
53 See Young (1990), p. 15.
54 Cooper (2000), pp. 255–256.
55 See, Rawls (1972), p. 440.
56 *Ibid.*

injustice is not reduced to random maldistribution. For example, heter-onormativity in laws, policy, mass media, education and so on hinders homosexual people's conviction that their plan of life is worth carrying out. The laws, media, education and so on that send the message that homosexuality is odd, abnormal and even dangerous promote suspicion, fear, hostility and social panic against homosexuality. As a consequence, homosexual people are often disrespected and live with a socially con-tested sense of their own value. For example, according to Stonewall, lesbian, gay and bisexual people continue to live in fear of homophobic abuse. In spite of significant legal changes in recent years, Stonewall's research shows that many gay people remain subject to violence and intim-idation, with far too few reporting what they have experienced to the police.

Stonewall's *Gay British Crime Survey 2013* looks at the extent and nature of homophobic hate crimes and incidents in Britain. The polling of 2,500 lesbian, gay and bisexual adults, conducted by YouGov for Stonewall, shows that hate crime remains a serious issue across the country: one in six lesbian, gay and bisexual people have experienced a hate crime incident in the last three years; one in ten victims experienced a physical assault; and more than three-quarters of victims did not report what they had experienced to the police and two-thirds didn't report it to anyone.[57]

These findings reveal that the plan of life that lesbian, gay and bisexual people have is indeed precarious. Securing their income and jobs cannot on its own change the prejudice, hatred and violence they are facing. It is also necessary to transform the cultural, structural and institutional arrangements that contribute to the deprecation of the homosexual and bisexual identities and hinder their sense of their own and a socially accorded value.

5 Neglecting the cultural aspects of injustice

Attending to the distribution of wealth and in general material goods is certainly pressing in every society where only some people can have every-thing they need and more while others can't and live in poverty or even starve. Redistribution of material goods is therefore a priority for any justice programme.[58] However, in contemporary societies, as indeed in the past, many public appeals for justice do not primarily concern the distri-bution of material goods. For example, many transsexual, homosexual and Muslim people in British society do not necessarily live in poverty, but still

57 The survey was conducted using an online interview administered to members of the YouGov Plc GB panel of 350,000+ individuals. See Guasp *et al* (2013). Stonewall's work is further explored in Chapter 4, IV.
58 See Young (1990), pp. 15–19.

face injustice based on their group membership. Cultural representation and stereotyping can be a part of and often create for them an environment of fear, hostility, offence, abuse, humiliation, ridicule and low social- and self-esteem. If we agree that all are of equal moral value, there is something unfair or unjust about these conditions in which some live, then culture and cultural representation become aspects of injustice.

> Culture is a broad category ... it refers to all aspects of social life from the point of view of their linguistic, symbolic, affective, and embodied norms and practices. Culture includes the background and medium of action, the unconscious habits, desires, meanings, gestures, and so on that people grow into and bring to their interactions. Usually culture is just there, a set of traditions and meanings that change, but seldom as the result of conscious reflection and decision.[59]

Culture, then, is an aspect of life that cannot be understood in distributive terms only. It needs to be understood and addressed as relational social life, often as oppression and domination, disadvantaging some often at the expense of others. In this sense it is an aspect of injustice. The concept of oppression as used in the social movements of the 1960s and 1970s designates:

> the disadvantage and injustice some people suffer not because of a tyrannical power that coerces them, but because of the everyday practices of a well-intended liberal society ... oppression also refers to systemic constraints on groups that are not necessarily the result of the intentions of a tyrant. Oppression in this sense is structural, rather than the result of a few people's choices or policies. Its causes are embedded in unquestioned norms, habits, and symbols, in the assumptions underlying institutional rules and the collective consequences of following those rules.[60]

Demeaning cultural representation (ED in this study) is an aspect of injustice that contributes to oppression understood in the sense outlined above and which distributive-oriented theories of justice have ignored. It is therefore submitted that justice goes beyond the distribution of material goods; the causes of unequal distribution and the social relationships that set their context, including culture, are also aspects of justice that need to be brought to evaluation and redress.

---

59 *Ibid*, p. 86.
60 *Ibid*, p. 41. See also Frye (1983).

6 Beyond distribution and the transfer of resources

Social justice should go beyond distribution and aim as well at transforming the forces that sustain disadvantage. In this regard, Fraser distinguishes between affirmative and transformative strategies for redressing injustice. Affirmative strategies, she argues, 'aim to correct inequitable outcomes of social arrangements without disturbing the underlying social structures that generate them'.[61] This is quite close to the approach that the legislation frequently takes. More often than not, remedies are provided on an individual basis once the damage is done, as opposed to correcting unjust outcomes by restructuring their underlying generative framework. The latter is what the transformative strategies would suggest. The contrast between these two strategies is the level at which injustice is addressed, 'whereas affirmation targets end-state outcomes, transformation addresses root causes'.[62]

The question is, then, how to go beyond redistribution and transform the structural, cultural and institutional arrangements that hinder social justice? A transformational project should include a range of parallel actions at various levels. A starting point is to begin questioning the validity and alleged neutrality of existing structural arrangements and methods of valuing and assessing them. This is to say that it is necessary to transform both accepted social and legal institutions and how we evaluate their status, including, for example, the assignment of rights, duties and privileges, all of which we had previously taken for granted.[63] Challenging the injustice of heteronormativity, for example, would include re-evaluating the alleged naturalness, functionality and neutrality of the monogamous heterosexual family and its negative implications for the lives of some people. Transformation would imply, for example, a deconstruction of the institutionalised heterosexual family (in health services, adoption agencies, pension schemes and so on) in order to widen the existing family horizon. This in turn would require various changes in legislation and policies that previously excluded homosexuality from the realm of the good and consequently denied homosexual people the power to make claims and achieve legal rights. Redistribution of resources – for example, jobs and other economic rights – is necessary; however, parallel strategies specifically aimed at the examination of the cultural patterns of interpretation and communication that had previously convinced us that homosexuality was in fact 'wrong' are also needed. This requires intervention in many areas traditionally perceived as trivial and far too culturally embedded to be challenged, such as harassment in the workplace, offensive jokes and demeaning stereotypical representation in the media.

61 Fraser (2003), p. 74.
62 *Ibid.*
63 See Taylor (1994), p. 67.

IV Non-economic/material facets of justice

Social justice, then, has both economic and non-economic or material aspects. However, it has been mostly economic redistributive claims which have dominated theorising about social justice for the past 150 years.[64] In fact, the redistributive theories of liberal authors such as Rawls and Dworkin, as discussed above, successfully dominated the justice paradigm in the 1970s and 1980s. Important as it is, redistribution of wealth, income, goods and services cannot be taken in isolation. It is a part of a much bigger picture. In fact, neo-Hegelian authors such as Honneth give primacy to issues of recognition over redistribution. He attempts to 'demonstrate that even distributional injustices must be understood as the institutional expression of social disrespect or, better said, of unjustified relations of misrecognition'.[65] Disrespect and misrecognition should therefore be understood – from this point of view – as non-economic aspects of justice. To support his argument, Honneth makes reference to historical accounts that show that 'when it came to the motivational sources of resistance and protest, the experience of the isolation of locally transmitted claims to honour was much more important than economic interests'.[66] These findings bring to the discussion the idea that the core of the experience of resistance to oppression of the lower classes of capitalist societies is the social injury to 'one's integrity, honour, or dignity'.[67] Whether misrecognition is more significant than maldistribution is arguable; however, the evidence is that feelings of disrespect and misrecognition have always been present in social movements seeking justice. For example, the language used in early Feminist movements and in the African-American movement for civil rights made clear that social justice requires both redistribution and respect towards despised identities.[68]

Recognition as a matter of justice supposes an examination of the structural and institutional patterns of cultural value that sustain inequality. This means challenging the deep-seated beliefs and uncontested ideas that inform the way society operates. This challenge needs also to take into account that maldistribution or economic injustice is not exclusively an injustice of class in the conventional sense; rather, the *status subordination* of women, non-white races, homosexual, transsexual people and various

---

64 See Fraser (2003), p. 7.
65 Honneth (2003), p. 114. See also Honneth (2007).
66 Honneth (2003), p. 131.
67 *Ibid.*
68 Honneth (2003), p. 135. Consider, for example, cultural movements such as 'Black is Beautiful', which originated in the US in the 1960s, aiming at dispelling the notion that black people's natural features are inherently ugly. This sort of struggle is very much alive today in websites, blogs and charities' work, such as that of Ligali, which will be explored in Chapter 4, IV.

ethnicities reveals that the deprecation of certain identities is frequently parallel to economic injustice. That said, injustice often takes forms which cannot be redressed through strategies aimed at correcting economic injustice, such as demeaning stereotypical representation in the media and disrespect in everyday life;[69] witness the case of wealthy black football players being continuously the targets of racist chants in football matches – they do not suffer from maldistribution but misrecognition in the form of *disrespect*. This suggests that, for social justice, economic success is not enough if there is no possibility of making claims against the agents of oppression and challenging the cultural patterns of deprecation that impede parity of participation in social life. The next section offers a variety of examples of the ways in which misrecognition operates. They are all examples of processes that hinder the 'participation as peers' of the groups they affect.

V The harm done through misrecognition

Misrecognition supposes damage to one's identity, which in turn impacts upon our self and social esteem. Identity designates 'a person's understanding of who they are, of their fundamental defining characteristics as a human being'.[70] As Taylor suggests, identity, recognition and misrecognition are intricately related:

> Our identity is partly shaped by recognition or its absence, often by the misrecognition of others, and so a person or group of people can suffer a real damage, real distortion, if the people or society around them mirrors back to them a confining or demeaning or contemptible picture of themselves.[71]

Self and social deprecation are consequences of misrecognition. Their remedy is a matter of justice given their impact upon the ability of targeted groups to interact as peers – equals – in society. Such participation is not just hindered because the targeted groups have internalised a picture of their 'inferiority' and thus are less likely to take full advantage of 'equal opportunities' but because society at large has similarly gone through the same process. Examples of the deprecation of the female identity are

> sexual assault and domestic violence, trivialising, objectifying and demeaning stereotypical images in the media; harassment and disparagement in everyday life; exclusion or marginalisation in public

69 See Fraser (2003), p. 34.
70 Taylor (1994), p. 25.
71 *Ibid*, p. 67.

spheres and deliberative bodies; and denial of the full rights and equal protection of citizenship.[72]

The examples provided are what Fraser argues constitute gender-specific forms of status subordination. However, they also reveal the institutionalisation of patterns of cultural value that deprecate and disadvantage women. They can be more or less severe and dominant in different contexts. However, they all considerably hinder our pursuit of self and social esteem. When misrecognition (through the actions and processes mentioned above) is systematic and pervasively downgrades femininity, everyone, including heterosexual white men, face further obstacles when opting to pursue projects and cultivate traits that are culturally coded as 'feminine'.[73] Institutionally, for example, certain jobs are feminised, which in reality means lower status and less pay than men. This is to say that the social construction of professional fields is littered with prejudices – misrecognition – about the limits of women's capabilities,[74] which in turn leads to professions being male dominated when they are seen to require more skills and deserve more remuneration; and female when they are mainly focused on caring, which is institutionally depreciated, has lower incentives and lower remuneration.

That said, the harm done through misrecognition is not only a moral and psychological process through which one's sense of self-esteem is threatened and thus constitutes a harm in and of itself; misrecognition can also be intrinsically linked to and inseparable from specific injuries (sometimes crimes) that happen in a context of misrecognition. These can be physical such as 'gay bashing', rape, genocide, domestic violence and hate crimes. Misrecognition is therefore often cause and consequence of status subordination. There are also economic issues which are so deeply connected to misrecognition that it is impossible, for example, to distinguish whether racism is a product of the economic motives of slavery or whether slavery was motivated by racism.[75]

Even though the manifestations of misrecognition often affect individual victims, they have a considerable collective impact. The wounds of misrecognition inflict collective oppression and marginalisation on the targeted groups, which damage their sense of collective worth. Benhabib puts it this way:

72 Fraser (2003), p. 21.
73 *Ibid*, pp. 32–33.
74 See Honneth (2003), pp. 152–153.
75 According to Young, there is no separation between issues of recognition and economic struggles. Many who promote the cultivation of African-American identity, for example, do so on the grounds that self-organisation and solidarity in predominantly African-American neighbourhoods will improve the material lives of those who live there by providing services and jobs. See Young (1997), p. 148.

Collective practices can result in individual injuries: through the denigration of one's collective identity in the public sphere, individuals in a group may lose self-confidence and internalise hateful images of themselves. Known forms of collective self-hatred, particularly among members of outcast and feared minorities, like homosexuals, Jews at one time in history, and gipsies still today, come to mind here.[76]

Misrecognition is of course nothing new because relations of domination have been present throughout the history of humanity. The deprecation of certain identities can be found historically in, for example, the ideology of imperialism, colonisation and decolonisation processes and the slavery period. Neither is resistance to domination new; the women's movement dates back at least two centuries. However, even if attenuated, the ideological legacy of oppression remains in the cultural mores of contemporary societies. Likewise, there are contemporary economic, social and political events which have the potential to set the context for renewed forms of misrecognition. For example, Europe is caught today 'between the unifying and centralising forces of the European Union on the one hand and the forces of multiculturalism, immigration, and cultural separatism on the other'.[77] Increasing worldwide movement of people with different languages, physical appearances and cultural values and the partial and often manipulative standards for the evaluation of these new people in new contexts, together with competition for what are presented as scarce economic resources (that we should keep for 'our own' whomever they may be) are issues that intensify the existence of 'status battles'. Therefore, it is clear that there is a need to evaluate misrecognition as a matter of justice.

I   Manifestations of misrecognition

To speak of misrecognition is to speak of the *status order of society*. This means 'the construction, by socially entrenched patterns of cultural value, of culturally defined categories of social actors – statuses – each distinguished by the relative respect, prestige, and esteem it enjoys vis-à-vis the others'.[78] *Status subordination* occurs partly through *discrimination* via the exclusion, unfavourable treatment and/or disparagement of certain identities in both 'public' and 'private' spheres of social life (Chapter 3). In order to clarify the way in which misrecognition is manifested, some examples are provided, which complement Fraser's account of some of

---

76 Benhabib (2002), p. 51.
77 *Ibid*, p. xii.
78 Fraser (2003), p. 50.

the injustices that the recognition paradigm targets. These injustices, expressed in general terms, are: cultural domination, non-recognition and disrespect.

Cultural domination. This means to be subjected to patterns of interpretation and communication that are associated with another culture and are alien and hostile to one's own.[79] Examples of cultural domination that have not lost currency in contemporary Britain are those related to the colonisation of Africa. The dehumanisation, the marking as the 'other' and the negative stereotypic descriptions typical of colonisation remain present today. Discussions and issues can go from institutionalised racism in the police (Chapter 3) to beauty practices and standards. For example, Black girls learn from an early age that they have a 'hair problem' and the media tends to present black women in roles of virtue and power with straightened hair whereas the 'natural' look is rather associated with positions of subordination and/or lower economic or social status.[80] An example of the timeliness of the issue is the film *Beauty is . . .* (2014) by Oluwatoyin Agbetu. The film asks 'What is beauty?' and examines the answer from a philosophical position through discussions on hair, skin shade, body image and character. The film explores the risks posed by chemical straighteners and skin bleaching; it shares insights on conditions like vitiligo and alopecia while discussing the impact of biased media on children and personal relationships.

People of African descent, then, are evaluated and often evaluate themselves against standards alien and hostile to them; and as long as this continues to be the case, devalued identities will remain in the subordinated position that has been manufactured as 'their place'.

Another example which does not come without significant entanglements is related to the myriad Western positions problematising and either opposing or supporting the 'wearing of the *hijab*'. While enquiring about injustice and oppression should know no frontiers – and misogyny is found in most cultures – the identity of the speaker/commentator matters and has to be disclosed. Moreover, not having Muslim women actually leading the debate, including the debate about its necessity, as opposed to merely contributing to it, is a manifestation of cultural domination. It assumes 'knowing better' from a western point of view – including feminist stances – about what women should or should not wear. These are problems that need and have had more detailed analysis

---

79 *Ibid*, p. 13.

80 In the political thriller television series *Scandal* (2012), the African-American protagonist appears with straightened hair when in roles of power, authority and influence, as she directs a crisis management firm with strong links to the White House. Meanwhile, her natural look is only seen when she decides to escape to an island in a leisure-type lifestyle.

elsewhere; for the purposes of this example it is enough to point out issues relevant to our discussion that have been raised from a target/dominated group's point of view. In this regard, the term *Gendered Orientalism* has been put forward in order to make reference to 'the kind of feminism that centres white narratives and strips away the agency of women of color. It appropriates women's rights movements in the service of paternalism and empire.'[81] As can be noted, the term is closely related to Edward Said's powerful and influential studies of Orientalism, particularly in respect of the idea that the Orient and Islam do not represent themselves but instead are being examined and defined by the western expert.[82] And this is why, according to Julie Hall, we need intersectionality, to fight against oppressive ideologies that use and abuse the idea of justice to perpetuate injustice. Put another way, 'exploiting ideas of gender equality in order to enable racism'.[83]

Non-recognition. This implies that a person or group is rendered invisible via the authoritative representational, communicative and interpretative practices of their own culture.[84] Probably the clearest example in this regard is the social standing of women in male-dominated societies. In this sense even the most basic cultural products, such as language, render women invisible. An example of this is the male-oriented way in which language is spoken and written – say by the generic use of male pronouns and nouns. Other examples include the assimilation of women to men when it comes to rights. The fact that for many years and even in recent times maternity leave is compared to a man's illness corroborates societies' non-recognition of women, particularly in the 'public' sphere. The discriminatory implications of the non-recognition of women in male-dominated societies can thus be, for example, the denial of certain

81 See Hall (2015).
82 Said (1985).
83 See Hall (2015). The feminist theorist Kimberlé Crenshaw first utilised the term 'intersectionality' to refer to the need to address the interaction between race and gender in order to better understand and explain the relations of oppression and discrimination experienced by black women. According to her, if any real efforts are to be made to free black people of the constraints and conditions that characterise racial subordination, then theories and strategies purporting to reflect the black community's needs must include an analysis of sexism and patriarchy. Similarly, feminism must include an analysis of race if it hopes to express the aspirations of non-white women. See Crenshaw (1989), p 166.
84 See Fraser (2003), p. 50.

rights when such rights are not needed or have not been accorded to men.[85]

Disrespect. This is to be routinely maligned or disparaged in stereotypic public cultural representations and/or in everyday life interactions.[86] An example is the prejudice and ready availability of insults against homosexual people, including the use of homosexuality as an insult for those who display 'female' behaviour. Entertainment television, comedy shows, 'jokes', advertising, tabloid reports and everyday interactions even in many largely democratic and secular countries reveal 'normalised' disrespect towards gay and lesbian people. It is precisely because of these cultural products that we come to 'know' and internalise negative attitudes and stereotypes about people with a sexual orientation different from the 'normal' heterosexual. Disrespect has a double impact; demeaning ideas or beliefs harm the social- and self-esteem of homosexual people; and at the same time, these beliefs cannot be disassociated from society's attitudes and the way in which homosexual people are treated. Indeed, disrespect is directly linked to many forms of discrimination and is often both its cause and by-product (e.g. bullying, harassment and even denial of job opportunities). Remedying disrespect disseminated through the media can in fact be a justification for anti-discrimination law's incorporation of ED as a specific form of discrimination.

Frequently, cultural domination, non-recognition and disrespect interact. More often than not, they overlap and, for example, what constitutes disrespect can be rooted in cultural domination and *vice versa*. Similarly, for example, the non-recognition of women is not the only issue women face. Besides non-recognition, there is conspicuous disrespect, such as humiliating pornography and the objectification of women in advertising. The distinction is nevertheless useful to illustrate

85 Under the Equality Act 2010, s. 4., pregnancy and maternity are now protected characteristics in their own right and there is no need for a comparator. In earlier pregnancy cases it was held that since there could be no pregnant men, pregnancy was simply excluded from the protection of the sex discrimination legislation. See, for example, *Turley v Allders Stores Ltd* [1980] ICR 66 [EAT]. Thereafter, some progress was made when some jurisdictions were prepared to hold that pregnancy was equivalent to illness in its effect on the capacity to work. However, this comparison engendered a series of problems because pregnancy is not an illness and shouldn't be stigmatised in such a way; and also pregnancy should not only be protected because it may hinder the worker's ability to work for this would leave out other needs inherent to pregnancy and maternity such as breastfeeding, bonding, and its economic consequences (maternity leave and pay). At the European level the 'ill men comparator' is still a problem, particularly regarding pregnancy-related illnesses that continue after the expiry of maternity leave; and regarding pay during maternity leave which is deemed adequate if it is equivalent to sickness pay. See, Case C-179/88 *Hertz* [1990] ECR I-3979; and Council Directive (EEC) 92/85 on the protection of the safety and health at work of pregnant and breastfeeding workers [1992] OJ L348/I, art. 11(3), respectively. See generally Fredman (2011), pp. 169–171.

86 See Fraser (2003), p. 50.

that misrecognition can take various and very specific forms, all of which need to be challenged in a way appropriate for them (this book is focused only on demeaning representation in the media). Nevertheless, parallel action is needed at various levels since the measures that attend to only one aspect of the misrecognition of a group are hindered by the continuation of the others. For example, a State can recognise civil partnerships or indeed same-sex marriages through its legislation, but the misrecognition of homosexuality persists if at the same time it keeps tolerating the disparagement of homosexuality (homosexual bullying) in schools or does not pay sufficient attention to the complaints of those who identify the media as a sponsor of demeaning stereotypes. The law therefore has been capable of recognising and providing remedies for some manifestations of misrecognition which it has identified as either discrimination, harassment or indeed hate crimes. However, there remains more to be done so that existing redress mechanisms can be enriched and improved, and harms such as ED can be recognised.

2 Remedies against misrecognition

Given that misrecognition can take various forms, there are correspondingly various possible actions for its redress. The aims that such actions pursue can vary but there are common denominators, such as overcoming status subordination; de-institutionalising patterns of cultural value that hinder social participation on a 'level playing field'; and overcoming stereotypes and ascriptions in ways that can also in the end win social recognition for one's own identity, traditions and/or way of life.

Following Fraser, the aim of justice is 'participatory parity'. This means that justice requires social arrangements that permit all members of society to interact with each other as peers.[87] As already indicated, Fraser's conception of justice is three-dimensional. It requires redistribution, recognition and participation. Therefore, participatory parity demands three conditions: the removal of the political obstacles to parity, in order to make it possible for those who are poor and despised to make claims against the forces that oppress them;[88] the distribution of material resources so as to ensure the participant's economic independence and voice (objective condition); and the institutionalisation of patterns of cultural value that express equal respect for all participants and ensure equal opportunity for achieving social esteem (intersubjective condition).[89] It is

87 See *ibid*, p. 36.
88 Fraser added 'participation' as a third dimension of justice largely in response to the Keynesian–Westphalian frame on which theories of justice generally rely. See Fraser (2005a), p. 78.
89 See Fraser (2003), p. 36.

the third condition that is more specific to the recognition paradigm. It implies the preclusion of 'institutionalised norms that systematically depreciate some categories of people and the qualities associated with them'.[90] Nevertheless, the three conditions are mutually imbricated, 'just as the ability to make claims for distribution and recognition depends on relations of representation, so the ability to exercise one's political voice depends on the relations of class and status'.[91] The distinction can be said to be analytical. The question now is: what kind of strategies (or remedies) can preclude such institutional norms that depreciate some categories of people? Fraser is not very clear about what she means by 'institutionalised norms'. However, as the examples that follow will clarify, the patterns of cultural value that depreciate certain identities are often structural, in the sense that they derive from governmental decisions and are enforced through legislation; thus, structural change through legislative reform or transformation is an essential requirement. In other circumstances the norms that depreciate some categories of people operate at an institutional level; this is the case when they manage to become part of the *modus operandi* of institutions and are reinforced by institutional arrangements and procedures.

The examples laid out in the following sections are inspired by and complement Honneth, Peters and Taylor's identification of a series of objectives with a communal character that can be sought by social groups in rhetorical appeals to the concept of recognition.[92] Each of them represents a number of challenges and entails a number of problematic considerations which cannot be comprehensively discussed in this chapter. They are presented here only as examples of what appeals to recognition may theoretically include.

Resources to promote and develop a depreciated identity. This is necessary, for example, in countries where there are minority groups that have been rendered invisible and/or are disrespected. A demand can be, for example, education in the native language and adequate representation in the mass media in order to re-establish their self and social respect. The aim is recognition of a cultural identity and the resources are necessary to promote and develop the cohesion of the community. Preserving culture for its own sake is nevertheless problematic. For example, 'conservatives argue that cultures should be preserved in order to keep groups separated, because cultural hybridity generates conflict and instability ... they hope to avoid the "clash of civilisations"'.[93] Indeed, this sort of remedy can in turn promote an undesirable cultural enclavism that instead of promoting

90 *Ibid.*
91 Fraser (2005a), p. 79.
92 See Honneth (2003), pp. 163–170; and Taylor (1994), p. 65.
93 Benhabib (2002), p. 4.

parity of participation would intensify group and cultural divisions. On the other hand, a more progressive aim to protect culture claims that 'cultures should be preserved in order to rectify patterns of domination and symbolic injury involving the misrecognition and oppression of some cultures by others'.[94] This approach seems to be more in tune with the achievement of participatory parity. However, in any case, a strategy aimed at the recognition of disrespected identities should allow democratic dissent, debate, contestation, and challenge at its centre. Moreover, what is important is not merely the preservation of cultures, which ultimately are dynamic and porous, but to redress past or present disadvantages that facilitate discrimination against its members in various ambits of social life. This is to say, that no one should suffer disadvantage based on his or her real or perceived identity group.

Curricula transformation. In a context of institutionalised practices, the world of education is paramount not only for the successful achievement of social recognition but also for individuals to forge their own identity in an environment of peers. The strategies suggested are often 'to alter, enlarge, or scrap the "canon" of accredited authors on the grounds that the one presently favoured consists almost entirely of "dead white males"'.[95] In this canon, women and non-Europeans frequently receive messages about their inferiority; all they learn that counts as valuable renders their identity invisible, not worthy of attention and as having nothing important to offer to knowledge. The background premise of this in the Fanonist application is that dominant groups tend to entrench their hegemony by inculcating an image of inferiority in the subjugated. The struggle for freedom and equality must therefore pass through a revision of these images. Because

> it [colonisation] is a systematic negation of the other person and a furious determination to deny the other person all attributes of humanity, colonialism forces the people it dominates to ask themselves the question constantly: In reality, who am I?[96]

This is not to say that individuals are unable to choose the most valuable knowledge for themselves. It is to say, however, that curricula development seems to be quite reticent about the contribution that historically and to the present day subordinated cultures and identities can offer to education as a whole. Moreover, curricula transformation must be careful – again – not to induce separatism or the 'exotisation' of non-dominant authors and materials. This is also an aspect of misrecognition that can

94 *Ibid.*
95 Taylor (1994), p. 65.
96 Fanon (1990), p. 200.

only be met through the active participation of women and other despised identities in a democratic process of selection and design of incremented and modified curricula.[97]

Protection against cultural degradation, disrespect and humiliation. Examples of this are the struggle against the sexual objectification of women in the media, the prohibition or restriction of pornography and claims against harassment. Objectives of this kind 'involve an attempt to normatively reactivate the equality principle of modern law in order to present recurring experiences of degradation as the cause of group-specific disadvantage'.[98] Here, what impedes women's participation as peers in society is the violation of their dignity and a limitation of their freedom and opportunities in, for example, the workplace and at school. According to Honneth and Nickel:

> Here, depending on the constitutional order, two possibilities are generally available to those affected: depending on the facts of the case, they can define the disadvantaging effect of cultural humiliation in terms of either a violation of their dignity or a limitation of their freedom.[99]

This coincides with the rationale for the recognition of ED as a justiciable harm and is further discussed in Chapter 9.

The redress of the misrecognition harm inflicted through the images and messages of ED can take elements of all the remedies discussed above. For example, the status devaluation of a particular group as a result of discriminatory expressions could in part be redressed via resources aimed at promoting and securing such group's adequate representation in mainstream media. Curricula transformation can also help to mainstream the views and contributions of non-dominant identities and the removal and challenge to stereotypes. It is important, however, to also provide direct protection against the production and reproduction of ED in the media. The way in which this could be done is progressively built in the foregoing chapters. At this point it is convenient to anticipate that the main mechanism for the redress of ED supported in this study is, in general terms, a 'right of reply'. This sort of remedy is consistent with and fits within the multidimensional theories of justice discussed in this chapter because it promotes *participatory parity* and has the potential to rectify the status order of society. This is to say that it can contribute to cultural or symbolic change through the revaluation of disrespected identities and the cultural products of maligned groups; challenging dominant patterns of repres-

97 See Apple (1990).
98 Honneth (2003), p. 166.
99 *Ibid.* Honneth refers to Nickel's book, *Gleichheit und Differenz*, esp. ch. 3.

entation, interpretation and communication.[100] Censorship or the imposition of high fines alone does not have the capacity to redress the harm created through ED. Instead, I will argue for speech-oriented remedies. A right of reply (the opportunity to bring a counter-argument to the market place of ideas), public apologies, the modification and if necessary the removal of discriminatory images and messages, can restore and/or create 'participatory parity'; these remedies give recognition and voice to silenced and despised groups so they can use the means of expression and put forward their own definition of themselves. This fits with Young's view that culture is to a significant degree a matter of social choice:

> we can choose to change the elements of culture and to create new ones. Sometimes such change can be facilitated by passing laws or establishing policies.... A glossy magazine can establish a policy of having more articles, photographs and advertisements that depict Blacks in ordinary life activities.[101]

However, as Young herself warns us, most cultural change cannot occur by edict, we cannot regulate the expression of jokes or fantasy for the risks to liberty are too great. Therefore, the injunction 'to be just' in such matters (demeaning and stereotypical representation in the case of ED) amounts to bringing these phenomena to discussion, that is to say, to politicise them. 'The requirements of justice, then, concern less the making of cultural rules than providing institutional means for fostering politicised cultural discussion, and making forums and media available for alternative cultural experiment and play.'[102] This is what the redress of ED via conciliation processes and the remedies outlined above aims to achieve (Chapters 7–9).

This is legally possible. The right of reply finds support in European Union Recommendations (since 1997) and in the Audiovisual Media Services Directive of 2010, which includes provisions about the right of reply of natural or legal persons in relation to all TV broadcasters under the jurisdiction of a Member State.[103] Moreover, the European Court of Human

100 These are the ways in which injustice is remedied in the recognition paradigm. See Fraser (2003), p. 13.
101 Young (1990), p. 152.
102 *Ibid.*
103 See Recommendation No. R (97) 20 on 'Hate Speech'. The Appendix to this Recommendation outlines seven principles, one of which, Principle 2, 5th indent, suggests that governments examine ways to enhance the possibilities to combat hate speech through civil law, for example, providing for the possibility of court orders allowing victims a right of reply or ordering retraction; Recommendation (2006/952/EC) on 'The protection of minors and human dignity and on the right of reply in relation to the competitiveness of the European audiovisual and on-line information services industry'; and Directive 2010/13/EU, of 10 March 2010 (Audiovisual Media Services Directive), a. 28.

Rights has recognised that the imposition of a statutory obligation upon newspapers to publish a rectification is consistent with article 10.[104] Nevertheless, the right of reply is controversial; some commentators consider that it constitutes a limitation to the freedom of the press or to freedom of opinion and thus they argue that the Court has built the right of reply without proper regard to competing interests.[105] However, against this line of argument is the view of the right of reply as a legal instrument serving both the person whose rights have been violated and the public wishing to access a wide variety of information via the media. Remedying ED through a right of reply cannot escape these tensions and unsolved conundrums. Crucially, the right of reply was not tailored in order to redress ED and, therefore, what I take from it is only the principle by which people would be given the opportunity to bring counter-arguments to an otherwise biased, untrue or defamatory message. Moreover, as will be argued in the next chapters, particularly Chapter 8, contesting ED through a right of reply should be understood in the context of a dynamic, 'dissident-welcoming' version of *political deliberation* where arguments and counter-arguments need to be presented in a conciliation process that fosters the free speech of all, particularly that of the disadvantaged.

In synthesis, any strategy aimed at redressing misrecognition needs to be context-specific. It needs to be a pragmatic response to specific, existing claims for justice. In turn, this challenges the conservative bias that is focused on securing fair access to existing social goods instead of also questioning whether we need other entitlements that have not yet been recognised, such as the opportunity to pursue social- and self-esteem. Moreover, 'recognition claimants must show that the socio-cultural institutional changes they seek will supply the needed intersubjective conditions [for participatory parity] without unjustifiably creating or worsening other disparities',[106] and as the examples showed, even though economic resources are not the primary aim of recognition, they can nevertheless be necessary.

The process of determining whether or not recognition should be warranted because it is necessary for participatory parity is dialogical. It depends on the arguments and counter-arguments the actors involved provide. The whole process should remain open to interpretation and

---

104 In 2004 the European Court of Human Rights recognised a 'right to protection of reputation' under article 8. See, *Radio France v France* (App no. 53984/00) 30 March 2004; (2005) 40 EHRR29, para. 31. Similarly, an unenumerated right of reply has been recognised under article 10. See, for example, the Court's judgment in *Kaperzynoski v Poland* (App no. 43206/07), 3 April 2012, that criminalising failure to publish a reply is consistent with article 10. For a critical view on the recognition of a right of reply see, generally, O'Fathaigh (2012).

105 See, for example, O'Fathaigh (2012); and Koltay (2012).

106 Fraser (2003), p. 39.

contestation. Thus, participatory parity serves as an idiom of public contestation and deliberation about questions of justice and is, in principle, revisable, remaining open to later changes.[107] The politics of cultural dialogue involve

> the reconstruction of the boundaries of the polity through the recognition of the claims of groups that have been wronged historically and whose very suffering and exclusion has, in some deep sense, been constitutive of the seemingly unitary identity of the 'we' who constitutes the polity.[108]

There may be, of course, conflicting interests which can be very difficult to reconcile; and dialogue in a process open to contestation may not be an infallible strategy but it is nevertheless a promising means for participatory parity which assures some level of legitimacy of the end result.

3 Problematic themes related to recognition

In laying out some of the possible responses to claims for recognition, the previous section also pointed out some problematic issues that may arise. Given the size of the undertaking, and the wide range of complexities of identity politics which have indeed occupied the efforts of various scholars, the issues presented here are necessarily modest and only aimed at acknowledging the unease and lack of certainty that exists in the struggle for recognition. However, at the same time, it is important not to surrender but to keep trying to respond to human hardship, whichever form it takes.

Debates over identity politics are generally heated and offer neither single nor flawless 'solutions' or blueprints for determining the 'appropriateness' and/or necessary limitations of political or legal claims for recognition. Honneth, for example, has criticised Fraser for leaving out from her analysis many of the social struggles that occur in the shadows of the political public sphere.[109] Identity politics also include the new religious right and fundamentalisms, the resistance of the white ethnic communities against people of colour and various versions of nationalism.[110] These are equally manifestations of identity politics and focusing only on relatively attractive and peaceful movements, usually on the left, leaves out identity politics projects that pursue their goals by means of social exclusion.

---

107 *Ibid*, pp. 42–43.
108 Benhabib (2002), p. 71.
109 Honneth (2003), p. 122.
110 *Ibid*, p. 121.

Social esteem can just as well be sought in small militaristic groups, whose code of honour is dominated by the practice of violence, as it can in the public arenas of a democratic society. The sense of no longer being included within the network of social recognition is in itself an extreme ambivalent source of motivation for social protest and resistance.[111]

On the other hand, it is not only violent nationalisms and religious fundamentalisms that can be in conflict with democratic values. Peaceful identity groups may also be parochial,

> while displaying intense internal bonds, some status groups can also be highly exclusive, creating strong oppositional forces between 'self' and 'other', so characteristic of racism and other forms of discrimination.... Similarly, status groups may create oppressive internal hierarchies, including subordination of women, or be highly intolerant of those who do not conform to community norms, including gays and lesbians.[112]

These are problematic issues that make it difficult to decide which claims for recognition should be trumps and indeed which deserve the backing of the law. Competing claims for recognition based on conflicting schemas of value urge the need to respond to questions such as: which claims are genuinely emancipatory and which are not? Which recognition struggles foster justice and which do not? And which merit our support and which do not?[113] For Fraser, the answer is generally: those which pursue parity of participation but the parity standard can only be properly applied dialogically, through democratic processes of public debate.[114] In her view, participatory parity enjoins removal of economic obstacles to full social participation, thus supplying a standard for adjudicating claims for redistribution: only claims that diminish economic disparities are warranted. On the other hand it also enjoins the dismantling of institutionalised cultural obstacles, thereby supplying as well a standard for adjudicating claims for recognition: only claims that promote status equality are justified.[115]

---

111 Honneth (2007), p. 77.
112 Fredman (2007), p. 226.
113 Fraser (2003), p. 223.
114 *Ibid*, p. 230.
115 *Ibid*. Following Fraser, the parity standard needs to be applied bifocally, ensuring that reforms aimed at reducing class disparities do not end up exacerbating status disparities and vice versa. Likewise, it must be applied with an eye to cross-cutting axes of subordination, ensuring that reforms aimed at fostering, for example, gender parity do not worsen disparities along other axes, such as sexuality, religion and race.

In largely democratic societies, however, it seems clear that the law does tend to 'take a side' or that it has to have a position in the sense that it adheres to a series of values such as equality which would impede recognition claims that entail discrimination against members of other identity groups and indeed against members of one's own identity group. Therefore, not all claims for recognition can be legitimately made arguing for or appealing to the recognition of one's identity. This may dissatisfy some groups at different points in time; however, the opportunity of contestation and political deliberation on identity matters should remain open and demand the constant examination of dominant views and positions which to some degree alleviates this dissatisfaction. In Fraser's view, a theory of justice should meet two conditions: it must be sufficiently general as to avoid sectarianism, and it must be sufficiently determinate to adjudicate conflicts.[116] In practice, this has proved to be quite difficult. For example, in the context of 'multicultural' societies which are likely to include communities some of whose practices offend against the values of the majority, Parekh lists four principles generally canvassed in much of the popular and philosophical discourse which help decide whether to tolerate or not some practices such as female circumcision, polygamy and the wearing of the *hijab*. First, some writers appeal to *universal human rights* and argue that since these represent the moral minimum and are 'culturally neutral', they provide universally valid standards or evaluation. Second; for others, every society has historically acquired character or identity embodied in its *core or shared values*. Since the latter form the basis of its way of life, it has both a right and a duty to disallow practices that offend against them. Third, some writers maintain that since moral values are culturally embedded, society should disallow *only those practices that cause harm to others*, for to go further would amount to cultural imperialism. Fourth, some argue that since universally valid values are not available, since the concept of core values is problematic and since harm cannot always be defined in a culturally neutral manner, the most desirable and indeed the only possible course of action is to engage in an *open-minded and morally serious dialogue* with minority 'spokesmen' and act on the resulting consensus. Although such a consensus might involve making concessions and compromises that many of its members might feel uneasy about, it is all they have to go on in a deeply divided society.[117] This is, as will be seen, to a large extent what a remedy for ED should entail.

Given the size of the undertaking, these principles are reproduced here without further elaboration. Nevertheless, they demonstrate the variety of approaches and the intricacy of conflicting claims in contemporary societies. This is not the place to go any further but to admit that the waters

116 Fraser (2003), pp. 223–224.
117 Parekh (2006), pp. 265–266.

are muddy and at the same time to insist that, however challenging, there are harms experienced by disadvantaged groups which require consideration and imagination to develop strategies for their redress without creating or worsening other harms or disparities. In this sense, for example, the risk of 'group or culture reification' needs to be considered. This means the risk of:

> Essentialising the idea of culture as the property of an ethnic group or race ... overemphasising their boundedness and distinctiveness; it risks potentially legitimising repressive demands for communal conformity; and by treating cultures as a badge of group identity, it tends to fetishize them in ways that put them beyond the reach of critical analysis.[118]

Cultures, identity groups and indeed individuals are dynamic and changing, not discrete and static wholes. They exist in permanent dialogue with 'others' and adopt and imitate elements of each other. Members can disagree in many respects but this is something that is repressed when cultures and identity groups are essentialised and stereotyped. The relevance of this in the debate over recognition is that an unchallenged valorisation of a culture and identity as a whole and for the sake of it, without dialogue and intra-group contestation can lead to the reinforcement of oppressive conducts. This is especially true when such groups feel under attack. In times of 'cultural threat' the condemnation of certain oppressive beliefs and conducts will not be challenged by members of that same culture who, in other circumstances, would do so. Therefore, valorising cultures along a single axis drastically simplifies people's self-understandings, denying the multiplicity of their identifications. Moreover, it puts pressure on individuals to conform to a group type, discouraging dissidence.[119] Recognition should, therefore, be a process of permanent contestation which must not underestimate people's multiple identities and group's porousness.

Another important problem that cannot be disassociated from recognition is the need for parallel redistribution. This is to say that, very often, claims for recognition also entail or further require some sort of redistribution. Manifestations of disrespect can indeed have economic consequences and these should be redressed not only by granting symbolic recognition but also material resources. For example,

> the equal pay for work of equal value focuses on the ways in which market distributions can entrench misrecognition. On the other hand,

---

118 Benhabib (2002), p. 4.
119 See Fraser (2003), p. 76.

the availability of a defence of justification permits market based considerations to prevent full redress of misrecognition of women's work.[120]

Another example is that 'while the law may be able to insist on equal rights for part-time workers, status-based interventions cannot address the lack of child-care or training which leads women to predominate in low-paid part-time jobs'.[121]

Something similar happens the other way round, where redistribution without recognition keeps the 'beneficiaries' in question stigmatised and seen as in permanent 'need of help'. For example:

> a pervasive cultural devaluation of female caregiving inflects support for single mother families as getting something for nothing. In this context, welfare reform cannot succeed unless it is joined with struggles for cultural change aimed at revaluing caregiving and the feminine associations that code it.[122]

Other examples are the 'culture of poverty' where people in economic difficulties are seen to be deserving of their plight given their lack of hard work and industry rather than attributing their circumstances to the economic system that keeps them in that place. The approach should therefore be twofold – for example, the cultural devaluation of these categories, the feminine and the 'poor', needs to be redressed in both the economic and cultural spheres.[123]

VI Conclusions

Printed and audiovisual production and reproduction of images and messages that use demeaning stereotypes, ridicule, malign or disparage people on the grounds of their belonging to a disadvantaged group, are matters of injustice. They limit participatory parity, hinder the self- and social-esteem of the individuals that belong to the targeted groups and maintain status subordination.

---

120 Fredman (2007), p. 220.
121 *Ibid*, p. 221.
122 Fraser (2003), p. 65.
123 Based on a deeper understanding of substantive equality, which constitutes the conceptual framework for the inter-penetration of redistributive and recognition issues, Fredman suggests that corresponding legal measures need to be constructed to reflect these principles. There are two main ways in which this can be done, the most promising being positive duties to promote equality and justiciable socio-economic rights. See Fredman (2007), pp. 218–234; and Fredman (2008).

On this view, injustice is not only a matter of economic maldistribution but also of misrecognition and thus justice requires not only the redistribution of material resources, but also the preclusion of institutionalised norms that systematically depreciate some categories of people and the qualities frequently associated with them. One way of doing this in order to redress the injustice of cultural imagery and symbols that we have called *everyday discrimination* is to provide the legal and institutional means with which to challenge discriminatory images and messages; politicise culture; and make media available for the self definition and expression of disadvantaged groups. The next chapter takes the argument further and contends that misrecognition can also be understood legally through the concept of discrimination.

VII References

Apple, Michael (1990), *Ideology and Curriculum*, 2nd ed., London: Routledge.

Auchmuty, Rosemary (2008), 'The Married Women's Property Acts: equality was not the issue', in Hunter, Rosemary ed., *Rethinking Equality Projects in Law: Feminist Challenges*, Oxford: Hart.

Baker, John, Lynch, Kathleen, Cantillon, Sara and Walsh, Judy (2004), *Equality: From Theory to Action*, Houndmills: Palgrave Macmillan.

Benhabib, Seyla (2002), *The Claims of Culture: Equality and Diversity in the Global Era*, Princeton, NJ: Princeton University Press.

Cooper, Davina (2000), 'And you can't find me nowhere: relocating identity and structure within equality jurisprudence', *Journal of Law and Society*, vol. 27, no. 2.

Crenshaw, Kimberlé (1989), 'Demarginalizing the intersection of race and sex: a Black feminist critique of antidiscrimination doctrine, feminist theory and anti-racist politics', *University of Chicago Legal Forum*, vol. 140.

Dworkin, Ronald (1981), 'What is equality? Part II: equality of resources', *Philosophy and Public Affairs*, vol. 10.

Dworkin, Ronald (2002), *Sovereign Virtue: The Theory and Practice of Equality*, Cambridge, MA: Harvard University Press.

Fanon, Franz (1990), *The Wretched of the Earth*, Harmondsworth: Penguin Books.

Fraser, Nancy (2003), 'Social justice in the age of identity politics: redistribution, recognition, and participation', in Fraser, Nancy and Honneth, Axel. *Redistribution or Recognition? A Political-Philosophical Exchange*, London: Verso.

Fraser, Nancy (2005a), 'Reframing justice in a globalising world', *New Left Review*, vol. 36.

Fraser, Nancy (2005b), 'Mapping the feminist imagination: from redistribution to recognition to participation', *Constellations*, vol. 12, no. 3.

Fredman, Sandra (2007), 'Redistribution and recognition: reconciling inequalities', *South African Journal of Human Rights*, vol. 23.

Fredman, Sandra (2008), *Human Rights Transformed: Positive Rights and Positive Duties*, Oxford: Oxford University Press.

Fredman, Sandra (2011), *Discrimination Law*, 2nd ed., Oxford: Oxford University Press.

Frye, Marilyn (1983), *The Politics of Reality: Essays in Feminist Theory*, Trumansburg, NY: The Crossing Press.

Galston, William (1980), *Justice and the Human Good*, Chicago, IL: University of Chicago Press.

Guasp, April, Gammon, Anne and Ellison, Gavin (2013), *Homophobic Hate Crime: The Gay British Crime Survey 2013*, Stonewall and YouGov.

Hall, Julie (2015), 'Here's what's really happening when white saviours try to save Muslim women', http://everydayfeminism.com/2015/03/white-saviors-muslim-women (accessed 7 April 2015).

Honneth, Axel (2003), 'Redistribution as recognition: a response to Nancy Fraser', in Fraser, Nancy and Honneth, Axel, *Redistribution or Recognition: A Political-Philosophical Exchange*, London: Verso.

Honneth, Axel (2007), *Disrespect: The Normative Foundations of Critical Theory*, Cambridge: Polity.

Hunter, Rosemary (2008), 'Alternatives to equality', in Hunter, Rosemary ed., *Rethinking Equality Projects in Law: Feminist Challenges*, Oxford: Hart.

Koltay, András (2012), 'The right of reply in a European comparative perspective', available at SSRN: http://ssrn.com/abstract=2162935 (accessed 26 August 2015).

Kukathas, Chandran and Pettit, Philip (1990), *Rawls: A Theory of Justice and Its Critics*, Cambridge: Polity.

Kymlicka, Will (2002), *Contemporary Political Philosophy*, 2nd ed., Oxford: Oxford University Press.

Marx, Karl (1977), *Capital: A Critique of Political Economy*, vol. I, Harmondsworth: Penguin.

Mill, John Stuart (1965), 'Principles of political economy', in *Collected Works*, Toronto: University of Toronto Press.

Miller, David (1976), *Social Justice*, Oxford: Clarendon Press.

O'Fathaigh (2012), 'The recognition of a right of reply under the European Convention', *Journal of Media Law*, vol. 4, no. 2.

Parekh, Bhikhu (2006), *Rethinking Multiculturalism: Cultural Diversity and Political Theory*, Houndmills: Palgrave.

Rawls, John (1972), *A Theory of Justice*, Oxford: Oxford University Press.

Said, Edward (1985), *Orientalism*, Harmondsworth: Penguin Books.

Sen, Amartya (1995), *Inequality Reexamined*, Oxford: Oxford University Press.

Sen, Amartya (2009), *The Idea of Justice*, London: Allen Lane.

Taylor, Charles (1994), 'The politics of recognition', in Gutman, Amy, ed., *Multiculturalism: Examining the Politics of Recognition*, Princeton, NJ: Princeton University Press.

Young, Iris Marion (1990), *Justice and the Politics of Difference*, Princeton, NJ: Princeton University Press.

Young, Iris Marion (1997), 'Unruly categories: a critique of Nancy Fraser's dual systems theory', *New Left Review*, vol. I, no. 222.

Chapter 3

Cultural aspects of discrimination

I Introduction

The images and messages that constitute *everyday discrimination* (ED) are matters of misrecognition and therefore injustice. They limit participatory parity, hinder the self- and social-esteem of the individuals that belong to the targeted groups and maintain status subordination.

Recognition, like redistribution, is both a political and philosophical term. Philosophically it is a normative paradigm; politically, it refers to claims raised by political actors and social movements in the public sphere.[1] The struggle for recognition targets 'cultural injustices', which are rooted in social patterns of representation, interpretation and communication which determine relations of domination or subordination.[2] These cultural injustices – as Fraser calls them – are often legally enforced and/or put into practice by institutions, such as the family, media, police and schools. Some examples are: masculine/Eurocentric curricula, demeaning stereotypical representation in the media, lack of participation in the media, the use of male-oriented language, and various forms of exclusion from the 'public' sphere; for example, the lack of ramps in public buildings renders people with mobility difficulties invisible and excludes them from participating in public life. Recognition is thus a matter of justice and should be understood as an issue of 'social status' which urges the examination of the effects that institutionalised patterns of cultural value (the criteria through which we evaluate our own behaviours/traits and those of others) have on the relative standing of people:

> if and when such patterns constitute actors as peers, capable of participating on a par with one another in social life, then we can speak of reciprocal recognition and status equality. When in contrast, institutionalised patterns of cultural value constitute some actors as inferior,

---

1 See Fraser (2003), p. 9.
2 *Ibid*, p. 13.

excluded, wholly other or simply invisible, hence as less than full part-
ners in social interaction, then we should speak of misrecognition and
status subordination.[3]

This chapter contends that misrecognition can be understood legally
through the concept of discrimination. Even though there is no universally agreed upon meaning in law of discrimination, much of the legal narrative suggests that discrimination means unfavourable treatment of one
relative to another, rooted in and/or resulting in status subordination
where some actors are treated as inferior and/or rendered invisible by
virtue of their group membership. The evolution of anti-discrimination
law (ADL) in the UK shows that, although it has had status-based inequalities at its core (recognition), it has not, however, expressly considered
some critical cultural aspects of discrimination such as demeaning stereotypical representation in the media as harms in and of themselves which,
according to the recognition paradigm, require individual assessment and
redress. Authors like Bamforth, Malik and O'Cinneide, however, have
included and indeed analysed together hate speech, hate crimes and harassment in their *Discrimination Law: Theory and Context* book. This is relevant because these authors acknowledge the connections between these
issues (which are good examples of the cultural devaluation and status
subordination of the groups they affect) and discrimination. These concepts, like ED, address fundamentally dignitary harms and are issues of
misrecognition as understood by Fraser. And so, although they do not
conform to traditional Discrimination Law standards (these issues do not
need a comparator), they form a part of the same system. Bamforth *et al.*
argue that there are also practical reasons why these three issues overlap
and can be discussed together:

> Harassment is both recognised as a form of discrimination, and also
> one way in which hate crimes can be committed; hate speech raises
> independent issues, and at the same time sexist speech in the work-
> place can sometimes be regulated as a form of discriminatory
> harassment.[4]

Recognition is an element of justice satisfied when the patterns of cultural value express equal respect for all participants and ensure that all
have an equal opportunity for achieving social esteem. This idea is not
antithetical to the legal conceptual framework. As stated above, one
example of the way ADL can comprehend the inherent harm of status
subordination is its recognition of harassment, a clear manifestation of

---

3 See *ibid*, p. 29.
4 See Bamforth *et al* (2008), p. 449.

disrespect, often described as a violation of the dignity of the person which includes the creation of hostile or humiliating environments.

Misrecognition is generated in societies where there are relations of oppression and domination. It therefore affects the individuals that belong to groups that deviate from the 'norm' or dominant standards and, therefore, members of these groups are not attributed the status of peers. They are often denied opportunities and their needs are not recognised. On this definition, misrecognition can amount to discrimination. This is the case when the exclusion or unfavourable treatment inflicted upon a certain group is related to deprecating structural and institutional patterns of cultural value that affect such a group. For example, the gender pay gap, which is based consciously or unconsciously on stereotypical gender roles and in the devaluation of women and of traits coded as feminine. And so, even though misrecognition is not a legal term, its political and philosophical underpinnings can inspire and enrich a broader scope for ADL action and fuel its potential to target critical cultural aspects of discrimination such as ED as harms in and of themselves. Following this line of thought, this chapter argues that discrimination works at various interacting levels which support and reinforce each other. These are structural, institutional, personal and cultural. The chapter will explore them all, thereby showing that discrimination is not a spontaneous and random unfavourable allocation of goods, services and entitlements, but is maintained and made operational through a variety of processes and practices which should be assessed against their cultural context and such cultural context should itself be assessed. Indeed, the idea of ED follows from an understanding of discrimination as a multidimensional problem that cannot be disassociated from 'culture'.

The chapter is divided into three parts. Briefly and only schematically, the first part looks at the understanding of discrimination in the UK's legislation. The second part offers sociological analyses that explore discrimination as a multidimensional problem; and the third analyses some of the difficulties associated with dealing with the cultural aspects of discrimination.

II Law's understanding of discrimination

The development of ADL in Britain is summarised by Hepple in the following way:

> Over the past 45 years, struggles for equality in Britain have resulted in the gradual recognition of legal rights of a wider range of disadvantaged groups and the expansion of the law from formal to substantive equality to deal not only with individual acts of discrimination, harassment and victimisation, but also subtler forms of indirect

discrimination. It has also been recognised that equal treatment does not mean identical treatment, and that full and effective equality entails accommodating differences.[5]

Indeed, the Equality Act 2010 reflects the 'expansiveness of equality rights', the steady recognition of grounds on which discrimination takes place and the move from formal to substantive equality. For example, the Race Relations Act 1965 was based on the notion of formal equality 'likes must be treated alike'. This Act covered direct racial discrimination but only in places of public resort, such as public houses and hotels. The Race Relations Act 1968 also followed a formal equality approach but extended coverage to employment, housing, goods and services. The transition from formal equality to substantive equality began with the extension of legislation to discrimination on the grounds of sex through the Equal Pay Act 1970 and the Sex Discrimination Act 1975. The latter introduced the concept of indirect or adverse effects of discrimination and provisions permitting positive action. Another novel introduction was the creation of an Equal Opportunities Commission, in charge of strategic enforcement and assisting individuals. The then new Race Relations Act 1976 followed this model and a Commission for Racial Equality superseded the Race Relations Board and Community Relations Commission (created by the Race Relations Act 1965 and Race Relations Act 1968, respectively). Substantive equality was further developed in the Disability and Discrimination Act 1995 through the recognition that disability discrimination is asymmetrical, and measures to achieve substantive equality therefore included a duty to make reasonable adjustments for a disabled person.[6]

The Equality Act 2010 replaces previous ADL[7] and much of its reforms have been as a result of the need to implement European legal obligations. These include: Council Directive 75/117/EEC (on equal pay for men and women); Council Directive 76/207/EEC (on equal treatment for men and women in respect of employment, as amended by the European Parliament and Council Directive 2002/73/EC); Council Directive 2000/43/EC (on equal treatment between persons irrespective of racial or ethnic origin); Council Directive 2000/78/EC (establishing a general framework for equal treatment in employment and occupation, including the grounds of religion or belief, disability, age and sexual orientation); Council Directive 2004/113/EC (on equal treatment between men and women in the access to and supply of goods and services); and European Parliament and Council Directive 2006/54/EC (on equal opportunities

5 Hepple (2010), p. 21.
6 See *ibid*, pp. 11–13.
7 The Act covers Great Britain (England, Scotland and Wales) but not Northern Ireland, which has devolved powers on these matters.

and equal treatment of men and women in matters of employment and occupation, recast). Also relevant in this context is article 141 of the EC Treaty (on equal pay for men and women).[8]

The 2010 Act includes nine protected characteristics (age, disability, gender reassignment, marriage and civil partnership, pregnancy and maternity, race, religion or belief, sex and sexual orientation) and expands positive duties on public authorities to advance equality in respect of all protected characteristics. Positive duties in Britain are further discussed in this chapter (III, 2) given that they are in part a response to *discrimination at an institutional level*, and for the need to mainstream equality.

The Equality Act 2010 has 218 sections and is organised in 16 parts. This is no place to discuss its entirety but only to identify Britain's understanding of discrimination through its main concepts: direct discrimination, indirect discrimination, harassment and victimisation. Section 13 (1) provides that 'A person (A) discriminates against another (B) if, because of a protected characteristic, A treats B less favourably than A treats or would treat others.' The provision thus follows the formal or symmetrical model where likes must be treated alike thereby working as a prohibition of less favourable treatment.

Indirect discrimination, on the other hand, aims to achieve substantive equality. As defined in section 19 of the Equality Act 2010, indirect discrimination occurs where an apparently neutral provision, criterion or practice is applied by a person (A) against another (B), and puts or would put B and anyone who shares B's protected characteristic at a particular disadvantage when compared with persons who do not share that characteristic. Therefore, what matters is the adverse impact or effects on the group to which B belongs. It is nevertheless possible to justify indirect discrimination if A can show that the provision, criterion or practice was a proportionate means of achieving a legitimate aim.

Victimisation, although not considered by the Act to be a species of discrimination in the sense that there is no need for a comparator, is a paramount concept in ADL.[9] Protection from victimisation potentially encourages complaints by ensuring that complaining about discrimination or helping someone else is 'safe' and will not have detrimental repercussions. In Britain, there is victimisation if a person is subjected to a detriment because they do a protected act, such as bringing proceedings under the Act or giving evidence in good faith (s. 27).

The Equality Act 2010 also includes harassment (s. 26). There are three types considered: the first one covers unwanted conduct which is related

---

8 See Doyle *et al* (2010), p. 2.

9 Under previous legislation, a person complaining of victimisation had to establish that there was a comparator who would not have been unfavourably treated in comparable circumstances. See Hepple (2010), p. 18.

to a relevant protected characteristic and has the purpose or effect of violating the *dignity* of a person or of creating an intimidating, hostile, degrading, humiliating or offensive environment. The second type is conduct of a sexual nature or related to gender reassignment or sex, which has the same purpose or effect as the first type of harassment. The third type is treating someone less favourably because they have either rejected or submitted to conduct of a sexual nature or related to gender reassignment or sex. The protected characteristics are: age, disability, gender reassignment, race, religion or belief, sex and sexual orientation. However, the Act excludes harassment related to religion or belief, or related to sexual orientation, from its application to the provision of services, the exercise of public functions and the disposal, management and occupation of premises. This means that the prohibition of harassment related to these characteristics is confined to the workplace and that 'British law allows the verbal bullying of gays and lesbians – a particular problem in schools'.[10] The inclusion of harassment in ADL will be further discussed in Chapter 9. At this point it is only important to notice that while recognising that it is necessary to protect human dignity and to prohibit the creation of an intimidating, hostile, degrading, humiliating or offensive environment, concerns about freedom of religion and freedom of expression have prevented British ADL legislation from further developing and addressing what this book considers to be cultural aspects of discrimination. For example, according to Hepple, 'it was feared that a cartoon "offensive" to some Muslims, or a Christian preaching against homosexuality in a way "offensive" to gays and lesbians, would constitute harassment'.[11]

British legislation is no stranger to the protection of human dignity through ADL, and the case of harassment is an example. Moreover, the Equality and Human Rights Commission often uses the language of 'dignity' and, indeed, the Commission has a statutory duty under the Equality Act 2006 to encourage and support the development of a society in which: people's ability to achieve their potential is not limited by prejudice or discrimination; there is respect for and protection of each

---

10 *Ibid.* However, the Equality Duty referred to in this chapter (III, 2) can lead a school to review its anti-bullying policy to prevent homophobic conduct. See the research by Lough Dennell and Logan (2015), which found that one in four of the pupils surveyed said they were aware of peers in their school experiencing prejudice-based bullying, while just over half of pupils who had themselves experienced bullying said they had reported it to their school. The most commonly experienced forms of prejudice-based bullying include race, disability, sexual orientation and perceived economic status. Stonewall's research by Guasp *et al* (2014), found that 86 per cent of the secondary-school teachers and 45 per cent of the primary-school teachers surveyed say that pupils in their schools have experienced homophobic bullying.

11 Hepple (2010), pp. 18–19.

individual's human rights; there is *respect for the dignity* and worth of each individual; each individual has an equal opportunity to participate in society; and there is mutual respect between groups based on understanding and valuing of diversity and on shared respect for equality and human rights.[12]

The role of the Commission is in general terms to: ensure people are aware of their rights; work with employers, service providers and organisations to help them develop best practice; work with policy makers, lawyers and the Government to make sure that social policy and the law promote equality; and use its powers to enforce the laws already in place. The Commission is responsible for monitoring the effectiveness of the equality and human rights enactments and advising on the effectiveness of enactments, as well as the likely effect of a proposed change of law (Equality Act 2006, s. 11). As a UN-accredited National Human Rights Institution, the Commission is required to 'promote and ensure the harmonisation of national legislation, regulations and practices with the international human rights instruments to which the State is a party'.[13] As it can be inferred from the Commission's statutory duties, its intervention (in some fashion) with regard to ED is conceivable and we will come back to this in Chapter 7.

The UK has also been involved in cases where the protection of human dignity is related to non-discrimination. For example, in *I. v UK*, the European Court of Human Rights noted that 'the very essence of the Convention [European Convention on Human Rights] is respect for human dignity and human freedom'.[14] The case concerned the multiple violations to the right to respect for private and family life (article 8) and the right to marry and found a family (article 12) when the UK failed to provide for legal recognition of permanent change of gender. The Court considered that no concrete or substantial hardship or detriment to the public interest had been demonstrated as likely to flow from any change to the status of transsexuals and that 'society may be reasonably expected to tolerate a certain inconvenience to enable individuals to live in dignity and worth in accordance with the sexual identity chosen by them at great personal cost'.[15] With regard to article 14 (non-discrimination), the Court considered that 'the lack of legal recognition of the change of gender of a post-operative transsexual lies at the heart of the applicant's complaint

---

12 Equality Act 2006, s. 3.
13 Principles relating to the Status of National Institutions, *The Paris Principles*, adopted by General Assembly Resolution 48/134 of 20.12.1993. This includes the European Convention on Human Rights, incorporated in the Human Rights Act 1998.
14 *I v United Kingdom*, App. No. 25680/94 (Eur Ct HR 11 July 2002), 70.
15 *Ibid*, 71.

under art. 14 of the Convention'.[16] However, these issues were examined under article 8 and resulted in the finding of a violation of that provision; therefore, the Court considered that no separate issue arose under article 14 and made no separate finding. While problematic in many regards, the protection of human dignity can also be a justification for the redress of ED. This will be further discussed in Chapter 9.

Much more could be said about the complexities and gaps in British ADL; however, our purpose is simply to point out that the UK's ADL has been incremental with regard to: the characteristics it protects; its scope; and the remedies available. ADL's evolution also shows that (although problematic) there are connections between discrimination as the law 'originally' understood it and predominantly 'dignitary harms' such as harassment and indeed ED.

I A place for everyday discrimination within anti-discrimination law

The origins and evolution of ADL are unique to each jurisdiction. Although targeting similar types of harm, the grounds on which discrimination is legally acknowledged to exist, the 'areas of life' covered and the actions or omissions considered in anti-discrimination statutes widely differ among them and so do the rationales for their inclusion or exclusion.[17] Nevertheless, there are common grounds between different jurisdictions generated both at formal and informal levels. The European Union, for example, calls for concerted action and to some extent harmonises some aspects of ADL in Europe.[18] Similarly, there are 'voluntary' forms in which ADLs in different countries 'talk to each other' via judicial or academic dialogue given the various common points of reference between jurisdictions; therefore, for example, referring to Canadian or South African court decisions in the UK is not an uncommon doctrinal practice, particularly regarding certain concepts such as 'human dignity' for ADL purposes, as we will see in Chapter 9.[19] Moreover, at an ordinary people's level, feelings of unfairness and claims for the redress of injustice

---

16 *Ibid*, 88. Until recently the European Court of Human Rights has tended to shy away from the complexities of article 14, preferring instead to base its decisions on other articles of the Convention. See, in this regard, O'Cinneide (2008), pp. 81–82.

17 In this regard see, generally Bamforth (2004).

18 At the UK level, however, while there have been pressures for harmonisation, particularly as between domestic and EU law, the pattern of protection is still not uniform, and the European Convention of Human Rights continues to operate in parallel to anti-discrimination legislation. See Fredman (2011), p. 143.

19 Some of the most important ADL authors in the UK often refer to Canadian and South African case law and doctrine. See, for example, Fredman (2002; 2011); and Bamforth *et al* (2008).

are unaware of and dispassionate about the 'issues of comparability' that may arise from a comparative law perspective. Increasingly, ordinary people know how problems are dealt with in foreign jurisdictions and can legitimately claim similar protections. Although different contexts will determine different recognition/enactment processes, as long as the same experiences of oppression or discrimination exist in different places, it can be expected that similar solutions should be pursued either by those affected or by their representatives. This isn't, however, anything new – the history of the legal recognition of harassment as a form of discrimination is an example; it originated in the US and was then followed by other jurisdictions including the UK and the European Union.[20] Similarly, in some jurisdictions hate speech/harmful speech provisions are included in ADL or Equality Law statutes. This is the case, for example, in Mexico (Federal Law for the Prevention and Elimination of Discrimination 2003, amended in 2014), South Africa (Promotion of Equality and Prevention of Unfair Discrimination Act 2000); and, with variations, most of the jurisdictions within Australia (e.g. the Anti-Discrimination Act 1977 of New South Wales which is the most representative; the Discrimination Act 1991 of the Australian Capital Territory; the Discrimination Act 1998 of Tasmania;

---

20 The original impetus to regulate harassment using ADL came from feminist scholars, such as Catharine MacKinnon (1979), who argued that sexual harassment was a patriarchal practice that caused harm to working women. Seven years after MacKinnon and other feminist advocates developed their theoretical arguments, the US Supreme Court recognised that harassment could also be a form of discrimination. In *Meritor Savings Bank v Vinson* 477 US 57 (1986) it was unanimously held that where a supervisor in a workplace harasses a subordinate because of the subordinate's sex, that supervisor 'discriminates' on the basis of sex. Canadian case law (*Janzen v Platy Enterprises Ltd* (1989) 1 SCR 1284), British (*Strathclyde Regional Council v Porcelli* [1986] ICR 564) and indeed EU legislation (Directive 2006/54/EC) have followed a similar approach; and the International Labour Organisation Committee of Experts has recognised that sexual harassment is a form of discrimination under ILO Convention No. 111, which is concerned with the promotion of equality of opportunity in public and private employment. See, generally, MacKinnon and Siegel (2004).

and the Anti-Discrimination Amendment Act 2001 of Queensland).[21] Although the processes of their inclusion and the ways in which these jurisdictions describe and deal with hate speech – and indeed subtler forms of harmful speech – varies, the common ground is that these jurisdictions have made the connection between harmful speech and discrimination. This connection is not totally alien to the British context. Indeed, a discussion in the UK about the reasons why incitement to racial hatred (the oldest 'hate speech' legislation in the UK) was included in the Public Order Act instead of in an anti-discrimination or equality document wouldn't be a novelty. Indeed, the offence was first introduced in the Race

---

21 In Mexico, the Federal Law for the Prevention and Elimination of Discrimination, article 9, establishes that: promoting hatred and violence through messages and images in the mass media; and incitement to hatred, violence, rejection, mockery, vilification, persecution or exclusion, are discriminatory practices. The National Council for the Prevention and Elimination of Discrimination can investigate and adjudicate complaints about alleged discriminatory practices, including the former (articles 64–70). The Council facilitates a conciliation process and can impose a series of administrative measures and sanctions such as compulsory training courses, compensation, public reprimands, public and private apologies and the guarantee of no repetition of the act or omission considered discriminatory (articles 83 and 83 Bis). There are also, however, criminal law provisions on hate speech at a local level; for example in the Criminal Code for Mexico City, article 206. The New South Wales anti-discrimination legislation makes it unlawful for a person, by a public act, to incite hatred towards, serious contempt for or severe ridicule of, a person or group of persons on the grounds of the race, transgender identity, homosexuality, or HIV/AIDS of the person or members of the group. See New South Wales Anti-discrimination Act 1977, 20(C), 20(D), 38(R), 38(S), 38(T), 49ZS, 49ZT, 49ZTA, 49ZXA, 49ZXB and 49ZXC. Serious vilification includes threatening physical harm towards, or towards any property of, the person or group of persons, or inciting others to threaten physical harm towards, or towards any property of, the person or group of persons. A person shall not be prosecuted unless the Attorney General has consented to the prosecution. Similarly, in South Africa, hate speech is included in the Promotion of Equality and Prevention of Unfair Discrimination Act 2000. See, chapter 2 Prevention, Prohibition and Elimination of Unfair Discrimination, Hate Speech and Harassment, section 10. Prohibition of hate speech. The proviso establishes that no person may publish, propagate, advocate or communicate words based on one or more of the prohibited grounds, against any person, that could be reasonably construed to demonstrate a clear intention to – (a) be hurtful; (b) be harmful or incite harm; (c) promote or propagate hatred. The prohibited grounds are race, gender, sex, pregnancy, marital status, ethnic or social origin, colour, sexual orientation, age, disability, religion, conscience, belief, culture, language and birth; or any other ground where discrimination based on that other ground causes or perpetuates systemic disadvantage; undermines human dignity; or adversely affects the equal enjoyment of a person's rights and freedoms in a serious manner that is comparable to discrimination on a prohibited ground. See the Act's definitions in chapter 1, section 1. Definitions, (1) 'prohibited grounds'. Remedies of a civil nature can be imposed; however the court may refer cases to the Director of Public Prosecutions having jurisdiction for the institution of criminal proceedings in terms of the common law or relevant legislation. See, sections 10 (2) and 21(2)(n).

Relations Act 1965, section 6.[22] However, in 1976 this offence was relocated in the Public Order Act 1936 now Public Order Act 1986, which creates offences commonly used by the UK police to deal with public disorder and violence. According to Barendt,

> Many Members of Parliament thought (that the public order legislation, now Public Order Act 1986) was a more appropriate place for a criminal law rule than a statute concerned with improvements to race relations (Race Relations Act 1965 section 6).[23]

However, as Barendt points out, there was something bizarre about adding to public order legislation a provision, the terms of which have nothing whatsoever to do with a likely *breach of the peace*. Other commentators argue that the underlying thinking is that 'allowing speech which abuses racial or religious groups lends respectability to racist views, which in turn may cause a breakdown in public order'.[24] Malik points out that the concern with public order, rather than a concern with regard to the rights of dignities of minorities, provided the background for the early regulation of racist speech.

> This concern with public order is reflected in the language and context of the early incitement offence which, shared a lineage with the earlier common law offences of sedition and mischief which also focused on (i) intention; (ii) raising discontent amongst those to whom the speech is addressed; and (iii) promoting hostility between different classes of such subjects.[25]

In this way, we can advance that, generally speaking, hate speech provisions can be either concerned with the protection of public order or of human dignity and this determines the type of legislation where provisions are included, the kind of harm they seek to redress and the mechanisms in place to that effect. This, along with European instruments calling for the creation of non-criminal law mechanisms against incitement to hatred and discrimination, and the level of adequacy of criminal law legislation, are further explored in Chapters 5 and 6.

---

22 The Race Relations Act 1965 was a response of the Labour Government to campaigns by, among others, members of the Movement for Colonial Freedom and the Campaign Against Racial Discrimination to deal with the widespread overt discrimination against recent migrants from the Caribbean and the Indian sub-continent. The Act was a kind of *quid pro quo* for the Commonwealth Immigrants Act 1962 which had made it more difficult for black and Asian immigrants to come to the UK. Hepple (2010), pp. 11–12.
23 Barendt (2005), p. 178.
24 See Nicol (2009), p. 127.
25 Malik (2009), p. 100.

In the UK, different approaches are being taken doctrinally when addressing ADL; some authors have approached their material from the direction of Employment Law and thus ADL becomes a part of this discipline.[26] Other academics recognise the 'constitutional dimensions of ADL', which include: the influence on domestic law of European Union law and the European Convention on Human Rights; the principled justifications for the legal regulation of invidious forms of discrimination; and the clashes between different prohibited grounds of discrimination and between non-discrimination and other legally protected human rights.[27] Bamforth, for example, believes that

> an *exclusively* constitutional conception of discrimination law – that is, one which left the private employment relationship wholly out of the discussion, or viewed it entirely as an appendage of a particular constitutional provision – would fall just as short of providing a complete account as does a purely employment-focused conception.[28]

He therefore suggests that we must find a place for Discrimination Law's treatment of the employment relationship albeit within a broader constitutional framework. This is to integrate the employment aspects of the subject within a constitutional framework.

> We can see how this might be done by considering the United Kingdom's incorporation of EU law via the European Communities Act 1972, and its bringing into domestic law of much of the European Convention on Human Rights via the Human Rights Act 1998.[29]

Addressing ED through ADL would ideally rely on a version of ADL which is capable of understanding discrimination in the broader narrative of oppression/domination which in turn may have an impact on different

---

26 The classic example, as explained by Bamforth *et al* (2008) is McColgan (2005).
27 Bamforth *et al* (2008) develop these dimensions through the different themes addressed in their book.
28 Bamforth *et al* (2008), pp. 12–13.
29 *Ibid*, pp. 13–14. These developments have created new rules of statutory interpretation. Statutes must in principle be read subject to the EU law and European Convention prohibitions on discrimination. This requirement is of general application, covering employment discrimination status just as much as statutes dealing with other subject matters. Moreover, the authority of this requirement derives from statutes, the European Communities Act 1972 and the Human Rights Act 1998, which are central features of the UK's current constitutional architecture. They seek to lay down ground rules for the division of power between different layers, national, EU and Convention-related; and at a national level for the powers of the executive, the courts and the legislatures (the Westminster and devolved legislatures in the case of EU law; and the devolved legislatures in the case of the Convention).

areas of law. This is an approach that acknowledges the structural, institutional and cultural arrangements that disadvantage some people and allows the development of a range of strategies that could challenge such arrangements; and this may, of course, affect both private bodies and the state.[30]

In the UK, explains Fredman,

> Discrimination law originally bound private actors in specified fields, such as employment, education, and the provision of goods and services, and public bodies were only bound to the extent that they engaged in these activities. It is only since the turn of the century that public functions more generally have been engaged.[31]

And so, it can be said with some degree of confidence that British ADL, although gradually, does go beyond Employment Law. However, an in-depth discussion about the direction that ADL in the UK will or should take in future requires a consideration of various factors and is indeed a continuous process. Whether it is likely to continue to be more salient in the Employment Law field or whether its constitutional dimensions become more prominent is the matter of a separate study. For the purposes of the legal recognition of ED, it is only necessary to point to these issues in order to show that 'the field is under construction' and that although ADL in the UK is particularly salient in an Employment Law context, it has potential to go further and indeed it has done so, as we have seen and will continue to explore in the foregoing. These things said, however, and as things stand now, the need to legally address ED and the potential of ADL to accept such a challenge are legitimate cases to be made from various angles. A challenge which is the cornerstone of the various chapters in this book.

III Various interacting levels of discrimination

The following sections offer *sociological* analyses that explore discrimination as a multidimensional problem which is maintained at various interacting levels.[32] These are: structural, institutional, personal and cultural. The levels of discrimination suggested are not independent of one another, neither is any one of them more significant than the other three.

30 Constitutionally focused approaches of this type have already been put forward by authors like Andrew Koppelman (1996), who speaks of an 'antidiscrimination project' – that is, a project that seeks to reconstruct social reality to eliminate or marginalise the shared meanings, practices and institutions that unjustifiably single out certain groups of citizens for stigma and disadvantage.
31 Fredman (2011), pp. 109–110, 143–148.
32 See Pincus (2000), Thompson (2003), Baker *et al* (2004); and Johnson (2005).

They are all part of a system that makes discrimination possible. Culture, for example, plays a role within the other three levels and conversely the other three levels play roles within culture.

To various degrees the law has addressed these levels; however, the cultural level remains largely under-theorised. As we will see in the next four chapters, the 'suggestion' that discrimination exists at a cultural level – in gender roles, everyday interactions, media representations and educational materials – is present in legal instruments (international and European, Chapter 5), as well as in the claims of the civil society and within media self-regulatory codes (Chapters 4 and 7, respectively). Nevertheless, from a legal point of view, this level of discrimination is under-theorised and access to redress is haphazard.

Discrimination, for example, in the conditions of work or in the access to goods and services is not a 'spontaneous' wrong which randomly selects victims. Discriminatory behaviours do not operate in a vacuum. Discrimination is the product of historical events, cultural assumptions, economy, and social and political conditions. Also, even where it is not recognised in law, the exclusion and/or unfavourable treatment that discrimination entails is the result of a variety of processes and is maintained and made operational at various levels.

The levels of discrimination that will be discussed in the foregoing are a continuation of the theoretical ideas discussed in Chapter 2. They arrange and further develop, from a discrimination-focused point of view, the positions of authors such as Young and Fraser.

I Discrimination at a structural level

Discrimination operates structurally through the ways in which differential status, allocation of value and access to benefits in society are structured into our society physically, politically and legally.[33] The built environment, for example, contains structural aspects of discrimination. Many people with disabilities are simply excluded from parts of their physical environment. Buildings can be inaccessible and often transport does not cater for their needs. The absence of sanitary provisions and ramps exclude people from participating in various public spaces and renders them socially invisible. Indeed, it is partially on this basis that these issues have become an important part of architectural planning. In Britain, for example, the Equality Act 2010 includes the duty to make reasonable adjustments for disabled people. This means that it recognises that bringing about equality for disabled people may mean changing the way in which employment, for example, is structured, including the removal of physical barriers. In sum, the duty to make reasonable adjustments aims to make sure that,

33 See Johnson (2005), p. 12.

as far as it is reasonable, a disabled worker has the same access to everything that is involved in doing and keeping a job as a non-disabled person (s. 20).

Issues of representation and participation are also structural aspects of discrimination. In this sense, the selection of candidates for election in parliaments[34] and wider issues of political participation and community involvement in local issues are structural matters that impact upon the involvement or exclusion of targeted groups.[35] Lack of participation means both being subjected to decisions made by others and an inability to interact as genuine peers in society (see Chapter 2, I). Participation also involves the power to make claims against the agents of oppression, whoever they are and wherever they may be. Having this power is most significant, especially in a globalising world, because transnational corporations and generally agents outside the jurisdiction of any one State are often difficult to scrutinise and do not hear complaints made by the poor and despised.[36]

The law itself can be counted as a part of structural discrimination. Its discriminatory implications can go from the male-oriented way in which the law is written – for example, through the use of male pronouns – to the clear and straightforward denial of certain rights for certain groups. The apartheid regime in South Africa, for example, was possible precisely because it was legally prescribed and enforced.[37] Moreover, the law often 'chooses' whether or not to recognise rights and/or provide remedies for certain claims. Sexual orientation, for example, is a prohibited ground of discrimination in some jurisdictions, but not in others. Indeed, according to the *International Lesbian, Gay, Bisexual, Trans and Intersex Association (ILGA) World Survey on State-sponsored Homophobia 2014*, more than 2.7 billion people live in countries where being gay is a crime and in not a single country do gay people enjoy equal rights as heterosexuals. The report, however, also highlights the progress made by LGBT groups

34 See, for example, Equality Act 2010, s. 104, which allows registered political parties to make arrangements in relation to the selection of candidates for election where there is under-representation of people with particular protected characteristics in elected bodies such as Parliament and local government. This can include single-sex shortlists. A party cannot specifically shortlist only black or Asian candidates, but it may reserve places on relevant electoral shortlists for people with a specific protected characteristic such as race or disability. See Hepple (2010), p. 20. See also Equality and Human Rights Commission (2015), p. 10.

35 See Johnson (2015). This article explains the history of a struggle to re-open a 1914 swimming baths facility in Govanhill, a deprived area in Glasgow. It is an example of the intricacies, imbalances and contestation of local authorities' power and decision making for their negative effects in local communities.

36 See Fraser (2005), pp. 78, 81, 83.

37 Some authors, however, argue that the apartheid regime was not a regime of law. See, Dyzenhaus (2010).

regarding the recognition of new rights and protections. In this regard, the report shows that more than 1.3 billion people live in countries with some form of protection against discrimination, while 780 million live in countries with same-sex marriage or civil unions. The research reflects a year of disparate advances and regressions for the lives of LGBT people around the world. Uganda, for example, has increased prosecutions of people accused of being in gay relationships, while Russia's LGBT propaganda law 2013 drew worldwide ire during the Sochi Winter Olympics.[38]

When the same identity trait suffers disadvantage in one place but not in another, the injustice becomes clearer. The disparate advances and regressions are a reminder of the given group's vulnerability. The hostilities and attacks on LGBT people wherever they occur send the same hateful message to everyone of us wherever we might be.[39] However, at the same time, the advances shown in the report also demonstrate the existence of international support networks that will maintain the struggle against LGBT discrimination. A similarly intricate injustice occurs regarding hate speech and discriminatory expression; they are recognised in some jurisdictions but not in others and the level of protection varies even though the harm to the self- and social-esteem of the targets occurs regardless of frontiers (Chapter 6).

2 Discrimination at an institutional level

One early definition of discrimination at the institutional level is:

> The collective failure of an organisation to provide an appropriate and professional service to people because of their colour, culture or ethnic origin. It can be seen or detected in processes, attitudes, and behaviour which amount to discrimination through unwitting prejudice, ignorance, thoughtlessness and racist stereotyping which disadvantage minority ethnic people.[40]

This interpretation of institutional discrimination could in fact be extended to gender, sexual orientation and other pervasive grounds of discrimination in contemporary societies. Derived from this acknowledgement of

---

38 See Itaborahi and Zhu (2014). The Russian federal 'LGBT propaganda law' has the purpose of protecting children from information advocating for a denial of traditional family values.

39 The British organisation Stonewall, whose work will be referred to in Chapter 4, has made it one of its key priorities for 2014/2015 to share their learning from the past 25 years of campaigning with lesbian, gay and bisexual people in other countries so that they too can advance equality and prevent further attacks on their rights.

40 Home Office (1999). The definition derived from the 'Report of the Macpherson Inquiry'. See Chapter 4, II, 4.

discrimination at an institutional level, in some countries such as Britain and Northern Ireland positive duties have been imposed on public institutions.[41] Positive duties (now Equality Duty in Britain) are in part the product of an acknowledgement that discrimination exists at many levels and of the fact that discrimination has not ceased to exist even though it is formally proscribed. This has therefore led law makers to develop new 'strategies'. The duties in this sense are a major challenge to the way in which discrimination had been addressed. Now, instead of focusing on the negative requirement for individuals to refrain from discriminating, the law has imposed positive duties to promote equality. These duties are proactive rather than reactive, aiming to introduce equality measures rather than solely responding to complaints by individual victims. Most importantly, the duties do not necessarily require the existence of fault or original responsibility on the part of the institution. On the contrary, the duties are imposed on such institutions in a position to promote equality.[42]

As explained by the UK Government Equalities Office, the Public Sector Equality Duty (Equality Act 2010) applies to public authorities carrying out public functions (schedule 19). The requirements of the duty are essentially to meet the needs of those who work for them and use their services. The duty requires public authorities to have regard for the need to tackle discrimination and promote equal opportunities. When designing and delivering their services, they should consider how they can make them fair for everyone. It will also ensure that decision making is based on real-life experience and evidence of need, rather than arbitrary assumptions and stereotypes.[43]

The Equality Duty consists of a general duty and specific duties set out in secondary legislation to accompany the Equality Act 2010. The general duty has three main aims which require those subject to the Equality Duty, in the exercise of their functions, to have due regard to the need to: eliminate unlawful discrimination, harassment and victimisation and other

---

41 See Fredman (2001), pp. 234–239. In the UK positive duties were originally found in the Race Relations (Amendment) Act 2000 c. 34, section 71; the Disability Discrimination Act 2005 c. 13, section 49A; and the Equality Act 2006 c. 3, section 76A. The new Equality Duty (in force from 5 April 2011) replaces the previous race, disability and gender equality duties and now covers age, disability, gender, gender reassignment, pregnancy and maternity, race, religion or belief and sexual orientation. See Equality Act 2010, 149–157.

42 See *ibid*, pp. 234–235. See also Fredman (2007), pp. 232, 234. Fredman explains that proactive models 'mainstream' equality, aiming to influence policy formation and actions, instead of simply reacting to *ad hoc* claims brought by individuals. Proactive duties are then a hybrid of policy and rights-based approaches. These models, however, carry risks; mainstreaming can degenerate into tokenism where public commitment is given in principle but where little is achieved in practice. Models based on a more specific statutory duty have more chances of success.

43 See Government Equalities Office (2011), p. 15.

conduct prohibited by the Equality Act 2010; advance equality of opportunity between people who share a protected characteristic and those who do not; and foster good relations between people who share a protected characteristic and those who do not.

The Act explains that *having due regard* for advancing equality involves: removing or minimising disadvantages suffered by people due to their protected characteristics; taking steps to meet the needs of people from protected groups where these are different from the needs of other people; and encouraging people from protected groups to participate in public life or in other activities where their participation is disproportionally low (s. 149 (3)).[44]

According to the Act, meeting different needs involves taking steps to take account of disabled people's disabilities. It describes fostering good relations as *tackling prejudice and promoting understanding* between people from different groups and it states that compliance with the duty may involve treating some people more favourably than others (s. 149 (4), (5) and (6), respectively). Tackling prejudice and promoting understanding are related to the aims and remedies pursued through the legal recognition of ED; which indeed can constitute one way to 'foster good relations'. Since this duty can support a claim for the intervention of the Equality and Human Rights Commission in the redress of ED and since the Commission is itself a listed public authority, we will discuss its potential role in Chapter 7.

3 Discrimination at a personal level

The personal level of discrimination refers to individual acts of abuse, unfavourable treatment, exclusion, harassment (including verbal abuse or insult) and physical assault. Hate crimes are probably the clearest example of an individual's expression of discriminatory beliefs. Not all of these behaviours are or need to be included as forms of discrimination in law. However, they *are* intrinsically related and often support each other. Although being discrete harms, they are all manifestations of the subordination of certain identities.

Whatever psychological dimensions there may be in individual actions, however, personal aspects of the major forms of discrimination cannot be fully understood outside their structural, institutional and cultural settings. Indeed, the personal level of discrimination is possibly the most vivid

---

44 The ultimate decision as to how to promote equality is in the hands of the authority. The authority must 'pay due regard' to the need to promote equality of opportunity, but it is not expected to take particular steps in that direction nor to achieve results. Ideally, according to Fredman, the 'due regard' standard should introduce equality considerations into the decision-making process at an early stage, mainstreaming equality into the culture of decision making itself. See Fredman (2011), pp. 307–309.

example of the interdependence and indivisibility of all the levels of discrimination (structural, institutional and cultural). For example, harms inflicted by an individual and for which he is individually punished, such as violence against women, rape and harassment, fit within patterns of behaviour of a culturally male-dominated society. In the same sense, but at the institutional level, the 'tradition' or 'common sense', often found in the police and even in courts, of blaming women for things that happen to us when we do not behave as we 'should' is both an aspect and a consequence of such a male-dominated society; and at a structural level, it should be pointed out that legislation has not until relatively recent times begun to consider domestic violence and rape within marriage as offences. These practices were highly tolerated and even 'culturally' justified.[45] An individual act, then, can represent discrimination at all levels and all levels should therefore be tackled. The law tends to punish an individual for an act of discrimination but the other levels that support the inflicted harm should also be addressed; for example, through positive duties in order to tackle discrimination at an institutional level and also by identifying and tackling the cultural assumptions and 'common sense' (discussed next) that support individual acts of discrimination.

4 Discrimination at a cultural level

The cultural level of discrimination refers to shared dominant assumptions about 'normality' which result in the exclusion and/or unfavourable treatment of certain groups. Its most pervasive fashion is what some commentators have called 'cultural imperialism'. This suggests that it is 'to experience how the dominant meanings of a society render the particular perspective of one's own group invisible at the same time as they stereotype one's group and mark it out as the Other'.[46]

The norm in cultural imperialism is the universalisation of the dominant group's experience and culture. To be effective, cultural imperialism depends on its possession of the means of interpretation and communication, including setting down legislation. This implies that cultural products will reflect the dominant group's interpretation of events in the society, their experience, values, goals and achievements. The consequence is that

---

45 According to the Office for National Statistics, females who had reported being victims of the most serious sexual offences (rape and sexual assault) in the last year (2012) were asked, regarding the most recent incident, whether or not they had reported the incident to the police. Only 15 per cent of victims of such offences said they had done so. Frequently cited reasons for not reporting the crime were that it was 'embarrassing', they 'didn't think the police could do much to help', that the incident was 'too trivial' or 'not worth reporting', or that they saw it as a 'private/family matter and not police business'. See Ministry of Justice, Home Office (2013), p. 6.

46 Young (1990), p. 59.

the experience and views of non-dominant groups can be rendered invisible and, given the normality of its own cultural expressions and identity, the dominant group constructs the difference which some groups exhibit as lack and negation. These groups become therefore marked as the Other.[47]

Cultural aspects of discrimination are often characterised as 'common sense'. Typically in the case of race, these involve assumptions about the 'normality' of white western culture and the perception of other cultures as exotic, alien or bizarre. One glaring example is in the use of language itself in order to set groups apart from each other. It is common to refer to 'ethnic minorities' on a regular basis in order to describe people who are not seen as white British, although there is no reference to 'ethnic majorities' as the corollary in respect of white British. In many areas of urban Britain today it makes even less sense because the so-called 'ethnic minorities' are very much in the majority. In the case of gender, common sense involves assumptions about the normality of male aggressiveness and leadership. Other examples are to be found in stereotyping, humour and the so-called pop-science and pseudo-science.[48]

Discrimination at the cultural level depends on commonly available ideas, which in the main remain unquestioned. They include the symbols, images, meanings, habitual comportments, stories, language and so on through which people express their experience and communicate with each other.[49] Whether one is talking of the subordination of women, the stratification of the labour force or the practice of confining and incarcerating the poor and mentally ill in workhouses, prisons or mental hospitals, one of the reasons why these relations of exclusion or subordination became embedded in social practice is because of the acceptance of ideologies regarding the subordination, control and ordering of particular classes of persons.[50]

Culture is relational: 'the symbolic meanings that people attach to other kinds of people and to actions, gestures, or institutions often significantly affect the social standing of persons and their opportunities'.[51] Advertising, the media and language all carry and reproduce critical cultural messages, not least through the battery of insults available for keeping various groups 'in their place'. The media's role in defining and reproducing cultural messages is particularly important. At the expense of

---

47 *Ibid.*
48 See Johnson (2005), p. 13. In October 2007 James Watson, a Nobel prize winner, claimed that Africans were less intelligent than westerners and that the idea that equal 'powers of reason' were shared across racial groups was a delusion. See Milmo (2007). Natural inequality has often been challenged – see, for example, Rose (2001).
49 See Young (1990), p. 23.
50 Baker *et al* (2004), p. 215.
51 Young (1990), p. 23.

their social acceptance and standing, the television industry can profit (without significant challenge) by making use of accepted and existing negative stereotypes, disproportionally depicting, for example, black people as 'baddies', Arabic people as terrorists and women as objects of sexual use.

The remedy for this injustice in cultural imagery and symbols is not a 'nice', unreal or uncritical representation but a fair one free from stereotypes. The aim is not, for example, to depict black people in what are predominantly positions occupied by white people. Rather, it is to have authentic life stories and experiences told that are not sensational, random or demeaning. The limited coverage of 'minorities' on mainstream television increases the power of stereotypes since chances to confront them with images that are real and diverse are limited. It is therefore essential to bring the media to evaluation and to build channels for accountability and contestation. Moreover, there seems to be a lack of consistency in societies that have enacted ADL. For example, in the case of gender it is claimed on the one hand that women and men are equally competent and should be considered on their merits for professional jobs. However, on the other hand, these same societies often create and mass-produce for general consumption women as 'objects' for decoration, sexual exploitation and abuse; and women continue to be mostly evaluated in respect of their beauty and youth.[52]

As previously seen at the personal level of discrimination, oppressive beliefs, deeply embedded in culture, are often used as 'justifications' for some and often the most extreme forms of violence. As Rashida Manjoo has put it,

> Rather than a new form of violence, gender-related killings are the extreme manifestation of existing forms of violence against women. Such killings are not isolated incidents that arise suddenly and unexpectedly, but represent the ultimate act of violence, which is experienced in a continuum of violence. Women subjected to continuous

---

52 See *ibid*, pp. 135–136. With regard to the intersection of age and sex discrimination this is nowhere more apparent than in the appointment of men and women as media presenters, newscasters and reporters. See, for example, Martinson (2014), about the case of the journalist Olenka Frenkiel. The article points out, among other issues, that both privately and publicly, BBC executives recognise that there is a problem with the number of older women on screen. Out of all the over-fifties appearing on screen, 82 per cent are men according to the most recent research published last year. Overall, across all major broadcasters, women over 50 make up just 5 per cent of on-screen presenters of all ages and both sexes. Frenkiel's complaint comes three years after Miriam O'Reilly won an ageism case against the BBC. In 2012 the then director general, Mark Thompson, told the *Daily Mail* that the O'Reilly case would mark a turning point for the BBC.

violence and living under conditions of gender-based discrimination and threat are always on 'death row, always in fear of execution'.[53]

Many groups live in fear of random attacks on their person and property. Harassment, intimidation or ridicule for the purpose of degrading, humiliating or stigmatising group members are also forms of violence rooted in discriminatory cultural beliefs.[54] The number and pervasiveness of incidents make such violence a social problem and a matter of discrimination since they affect not just random individuals but members of certain groups, like women, black people, gay and lesbian people, among others.[55] Living under such a threat of attack on oneself or family or friends deprives the oppressed of their freedom and dignity, and needlessly expends their energy.[56]

Cultural discrimination as outlined above refers to a multiplicity of overlapping, socially constructed *ideas and meanings* that have historical, political and economic backgrounds and which are sustained and renewed in 'everyday life', including its structural and institutional contexts. They can be represented through the spoken and written language, images, gestures, even silence in everyday social life and within institutions. These ideas and meanings can incorporate demeaning humour and negative stereotypes. More specifically, they have the power to degrade, subordinate and bring harm to targeted groups. They are manufactured and reproduced in a variety of ways but a most powerful force is the mass media. The power it has to transmit messages is what makes it a focal point of analysis of both discriminatory and anti-discriminatory practices. Although unsystematically, various international instruments related to the pursuit of equality and against discrimination have incorporated the need to challenge various practices that can be deemed 'cultural aspects of discrimination', such as media representations and discriminatory educational materials (Chapter 5). This incorporation is an example that makes clear that, to be justified and maintained, individual, institutional and structural aspects of discrimination also depend on culture and cultural representation and therefore, the cultural level of discrimination should also be tackled.

53 Report of the Special Rapporteur on violence against women, its causes and consequences, Rashida Manjoo, UN GA Human Rights Council 20th Session, 23 May 2012, A/HRC/20/16. An arguably better term for 'gender related killings' is *femicide*, a term introduced in the last century in order to recognise the impact of inequality and discrimination (including everyday forms of sexism, such as sexist language, advertising and humour) identified internationally as a root cause of violence against women. See also the work done in the UK by Womensaid and its Femicide Census, launched in February 2015: www.womensaid.org.uk/page.asp?section=00010001001400130010&sectionTitle=Femicide+Census (accessed 13 March 2015).
54 See Young (1990), p. 60.
55 See Saraga (1998).
56 See Young (1990), p. 62.

IV Some difficulties in addressing cultural aspects of discrimination

Cultural aspects of discrimination such as stereotypes in the media, ideas about a group's inferiority, subordination, humiliation, lack of respect, etc., are for the most part an unchallenged part of everyday life. They are pervasive, widespread and deeply embedded in society to the degree that their targets can internalise their subordination and even collude with and justify their own oppression. This is often done as a means of survival in a hostile cultural or political environment. Excavating and hence exposing them is clearly a very difficult task, even if the legal/political will to do so were there. However, when individuals who share the same feelings of exclusion and subordination share their experiences, what originally could have been perceived as a personal problem turns into a group or social issue. This process of *consciousness raising* is what makes it possible to articulate and challenge oppressive attitudes and behaviours. The Feminist and the Black Civil Rights movements in the US are good examples of this process of converting everyday assumptions into matters of political contestation. The ultimate aim of these processes is what Young termed 'cultural revolution'.[57] These issues will be explored in order to present first the type of difficulties that may arise when addressing cultural aspects of discrimination, and thereafter some promising ways to confront them.

1 Discrimination can be unwitting

At the legal level, discrimination does not have to be intended (e.g. Equality Act 2010, s. 19 indirect discrimination). It is the effect of the act that is important. The idea of unintentional discrimination lies at the heart of its manifestation at the *cultural level*, too:

> the vast and deep injustices some groups suffer as a consequence of often unconscious assumptions and reactions of well-meaning people in ordinary interactions, media and cultural stereotypes, and structural features of bureaucratic hierarchies and market mechanisms, in short, the normal procedures of everyday life.... This is about people just doing their jobs or living their lives, not understanding themselves as agents of oppression.[58]

Critical examples of the unconsciousness of discrimination at the cultural level can be found in the processes of colonisation of Latin America

---

57 See *ibid*, p. 153.
58 *Ibid*, pp. 41–42. This is what Young describes as oppression in a structural sense. The unconsciousness of oppression is similar to that of discrimination in the sense outlined in this analysis. Very often they both are the result of 'the normal processes of everyday life'.

and Africa and in the slave trade and its attendant 'triangular trade'. These are seen by many as the key drivers of residual elements of contemporary racism passed down through generations and accepted as 'common sense'. Early so-called explorers from continental Europe and Great Britain who 'discovered' Africa and 'African' people were able to justify their subsequent cruel treatment of them on economic grounds because of what they perceived as their uncivilised and underdeveloped ways of life and a need to civilise them through Christianity. A whole people thus came to be known as 'the white man's burden' and the notion of their so-called inferiority became embedded in the cultural life of Great Britain and continental Europe.[59] This was driven not only by politicians but by the 'cultural' manufacturing of the major institutions; the arts, education, the military, business and trade, banking and much more besides who played their part in convincing a population that slavery was justified. Such ideas and values rapidly became embedded in the family, educational and cultural mores of the time. Their residual and imperialistic elements are rooted in this history, passed down through generations and include personal behaviour, values and attitudes. To this extent they remain 'normal', unconscious and often unwitting.[60]

Unconscious habits, expressions, and the dissemination of stereotypes in cultural products, including through the media, inflict a harm even when this is not intended. Ignoring these unwitting acts and behaviours fails to capture much of the injustice of discrimination and of the social environment that serves as its fuel. The lack of intent to create a harm makes it difficult to understand the indignation of the targets and/or their right to complain. Indeed, it is not uncommon to blame the victim for being 'over-sensitive' when she is outraged by, for example, a patronising treatment or for failing to see the funny side of a sexist joke, advert or TV show.

Intentional acts are generally more morally praiseworthy or culpable than unintentional ones.[61] However, 'if unconscious reactions, habits, and stereotypes reproduce the oppression of some groups, then they should be judged unjust, and therefore should be changed'[62] because they inflict (even if unintended) harm on others. Indeed, it is the lack of understanding of the injustice created by these sort of behaviours that needs to be assessed and should be the object of the redress. In other words, and to a

59 The phrase 'the white man's burden' originally emanated from the poem by Rudyard Kipling (1899) for Queen Victoria.
60 See Yeboah (1988), pp. 73–102.
61 As we will see in Chapter 6, the issue of intentionality has often been paramount in criminal laws addressing hate speech; and indeed, images and messages can on occasion be used as 'weapons' with the intention to hurt, exclude and even exterminate. See Goldhagen (1996).
62 Young (1990), p. 150.

large extent, the comprehension of the injustice that results from unintended reactions, habits, and stereotypes that reproduce the oppression of
some groups, is the aim that should be pursued by any remedy for this
level of discrimination. And the reasons why stereotyping and discriminatory expressions are unjust should be made public so everyone takes part
in this process of politicising culture. To ask agents to *take responsibility* for
their actions is not the same thing as assigning moral, or as it often stands
now, even legal culpability to them. Young puts this in the following way:

> To *blame* an agent means to make that agent liable to punishment....
> Calling on agents to *take responsibility* for their actions, habits, feelings,
> attitudes, images and associations, on the other hand, is forward
> looking; it asks the person 'from here on out' to submit such uncon-
> scious behaviour to reflection, to work to change habits and
> attitudes.[63]

The often-unintentional character of discrimination at a cultural level
is, therefore, not something that should justify excusing it but rather something which demands different and specific strategies for its redress. A first
step in this direction is to raise consciousness about unwitting acts of discrimination at the cultural level and the harm they create. It will then be
up to the law to take this on board.

In conformity with its propensity to tie fault to intention, legal judgment too often identifies liability with blame for a damage which must be
'made whole'. Social change to break the cycle of exclusion and disadvantage that women, people of colour, disabled people, gay men and
lesbians, old people and others suffer will not be aided by the law unless
courts are willing to require forward-looking remedies of institutions
whose unconscious and unintended actions contribute to that
disadvantage.[64]

To some extent law – for example, in the UK – has done this in its
recognition of indirect discrimination and through the establishment of
the Equality Duty. However, recognition of discrimination at the cultural
level and the procurement of remedies should also be established in order
to redress harms such as ED because the cultural level of discrimination,
as discussed here, is not only an aspect of other forms of discrimination
but also creates discrete harms that require individual assessment and
redress.

63 *Ibid*, p. 151. Italics are the author's.
64 *Ibid*.

2 Internalisation of subordination

It is problematic to address discriminatory cultural practices when targets themselves may have internalised subordination, do not complain and may even support them.[65] Being socialised in an oppressive environment that stereotypes and denigrates one's dignity ensures that we understand, come to 'know' and even accept how we are defined, and renders us less likely to complain about it.

Very often target group members consciously or unconsciously support their own mistreatment. This can be either to avoid further troubles like victimisation and backlash, or to maintain a certain status or benefit. An example of this could be a black employee enduring racist jokes told by a boss or a colleague. This kind of collusion is often perceived as necessary since the targets are in a socially weaker position. Unconscious collusion is more insidious. It makes the targets contribute to their own dehumanisation. For example, when a woman blames herself for the actions of her rapist or batterer, or when she believes that sexual harassment is a condition of work.[66]

On the other hand, it is not only the targets who internalise their position. Often those with the greatest advantages assume their superiority and take it for granted: wealthy people and professionals might assume that they have to be treated with a respect not necessarily owed to other groups; physically able people hardly ever notice the non-existence of mobility facilities; and so forth. There is an absence of feeling or even awareness that one has to prove oneself, or that one's status, talent and qualifications would be questioned in any situation on the basis of social identity. Likewise, part of this phenomenon is that in order to succeed in an oppressive environment, members of devalued status groups often adopt the dominant group's standards and values without challenge; for example, when women behave 'like men' in order to succeed in male-dominated environments.

The normalisation of oppression in everyday life is achieved when we internalise attitudes and roles that support and reinforce systems of domination without question or challenge and the *status quo* becomes perceived as normal, natural and correct. Given this scenario, it is possible to suggest

65 See Fanon (1986). Even though Fanon's contributions to ideas about internalised subordination refer to a specific colonial context, they are still influential today. Using psychoanalytical theory to explain the feelings of dependency and inadequacy that black people experience in a white world, he speaks of the divided self-perception of the black subject who has lost his native cultural originality and embraces the culture of the mother country. As a result of the inferiority complex engendered in the mind of the black subject, he will try to appropriate and imitate the cultural code of the coloniser. The behaviour, Fanon argues, is even more evident in upwardly mobile and educated black people who can afford to acquire trappings of white culture.

66 See Adams *et al* (1997), p. 21. See also Faludi (1993).

that the internalisation of subordination is not only an obstacle to the redress of discrimination at the cultural level, but also a clear symptom of structurally and institutionally deep-seated discriminatory patterns and practices. It also affects how the law can be used to redress discrimination. The law usually requires a specific complainant and people are not usually expected to act on behalf of others. Moreover, dignitary harms, and generally harms against disadvantaged groups (such as domestic violence, harassment and rape) tend to be under-reported.[67] There is an element of shame and indeed of guilt from the side of the victim who might have internalised her subordination, be embarrassed and does not want to create a fuss or bring more attention to her mistreatment. In the case of ED, many people may indeed want to actively support its production and reproduction, because for them it might be funny, cathartic or an assertion of their superiority and thus they may contend that challenging ED is just political correctness gone mad.[68] Moreover, discriminatory images and messages may create in some an ambivalent sense of relief of not being one of those whose status is demeaned or who have become scapegoats for the things that 'have gone wrong' in society. Some people in this situation may therefore prefer to wear a 'badge' of neutrality and 'keep their heads below the parapet', as it were. These positions are neither unexpected nor do they constitute insurmountable obstacles; in retrospect, the history of 'equality rights' has been indeed a struggle against powerful majorities; and as Abel has put it 'what is denigrated as political correctness today may be taken for granted tomorrow'.[69] These issues are further explored in Chapters 7 and 8.

3 Cultural change

Even though it is clear that cultural change is necessary in order to eradicate discrimination, the strategies for such change are not so obvious; however, some success can be contingent upon processes of *consciousness raising* and the *politicisation of culture*. Cultural change can occur when 'despised' groups seize the means of cultural expression and use them to

67 See, for example, footnote 45.
68 The meaning of the expression 'political correctness' has varied through the decades. Nowadays it is a term used and criticised by both 'the political left and the right'. The left tends to criticise it as a self-evaluation, in order to describe either an over-commitment to various left-wing political causes, or a tendency by some of those dedicated to these causes to be more concerned with rhetoric and vocabulary than with substance. On the other hand, the right tends to pick up the term mockingly to refer to the positions of left-wing politics in general and has used it to *undermine initiatives for equality*. See, on the use and history of the term 'political correctness': Dunant (1995), Aufderheide (1992), Cummings (2001), Kurzweil and Phillips (1994), Williams (1995) and Thomas *et al* (2004).
69 Abel (1998), p. 277. See also, Williams (1995).

redefine a positive image of themselves.[70] Various acts of discrimination against women, attitudes, symbols, images and so on were not overtly challenged until the Feminist movements of the 1970s. Women began sharing their experiences in a process of consciousness raising and realised that what was originally experienced as a private, personal problem had in fact political dimensions.

Consciousness raising is a process by which identity groups share their experiences of frustration, unhappiness and anxiety, and find common patterns of oppression. The Black Liberation Movement of the late 1960s undertook similar discussions in order to make it clear that the depression and self-deprecation of oppressed groups was a function of social forces and not their own identity per se.[71] Consciousness-raising groups provide a process for discovering how members of subordinated groups can collude in maintaining an unequal system, identify the psychological as well as social factors that contribute to internalising oppressive beliefs, and explore how to raise consciousness to resist and challenge such systems both inside our own consciousness and externally in the world.[72] At the same time, once the aspects of social life that were perceived as 'natural' are recognised as changeable, the oppressed groups are in a position to politicise culture by identifying and articulating the social conditions that construct it and thus confront the cultural imperialism that denigrates their specific group experience. The Feminist slogan 'the personal is political'

> signalled that no aspect of everyday life would be exempt from reflection and potential criticism – language, jokes, styles of advertising, dating practices, dress, norms of childrearing, and countless other supposedly mundane and trivial elements of behaviour and comportment.[73]

The slogan implies the politicisation of culture by individuals that share similar experiences and therefore recognise that their problems are not personal problems but group problems rooted in the devaluation of their identity group. Cultural change is possible only to the degree that individuals and institutions become aware of and change their habits so as to challenge these devaluations throughout their various behaviours and functions.

The intention of politicising culture is ultimately to produce a *cultural revolution*. This involves challenging both the association of some groups

---

70 See Young (1990), p. 11.
71 *Ibid*, p. 153.
72 See Adams *et al* (1997), p. 8.
73 Young (1990), p. 87.

with inferiority and the politicisation of these group definitions. Despised and oppressed groups challenge cultural imperialism when they question the dominant norms of virtue, beauty, and rationality, putting forward their own positive definition of themselves as a group and thereby pluralising norms.[74] This entails an acknowledgement that the dominant norms have excluded the experiences of oppressed groups and that these norms need to be re-evaluated, a process which will need to include the removal of their assumed neutrality 'badge'.

The law cannot force a process of consciousness raising, but what it can do is respond to the claims of those who have identified and questioned various cultural assumptions and institutional practices that have a negative role in their lives and ask for change. While the law can play only a small part in cultural change as we have seen, that part lays the groundwork, is fundamental/structural and can include recognising harms done through discrimination at the cultural level, such as ED, expanding its repertoire of remedies and providing for a broader range of potential claimants (see Chapters 7–9).

V Conclusions

Misrecognition can be understood legally through the concept of discrimination. Even though misrecognition is not a legal term, its political and philosophical underpinnings can inspire and enrich a broader scope for ADL action and fuel its potential to target cultural aspects of discrimination, such as ED, as harms in and of themselves. British ADL has potential to recognise ED; it has been expanding through the decades, responding to newly recognised protected characteristics and has developed new and appropriate remedies for different types of discrimination in areas of life beyond employment. The UK's ADL recognises dignitary harms such as harassment and can therefore understand what is at stake regarding ED. Moreover, as we shall see in the next four chapters, ADL's recognition of ED can be justified from various angles: groups from the organised civil society, the international community and European instances have all identified in various ways the misrecognition inflicted through ED and have required its redress. ADL could therefore be one possibility to challenge this discriminatory practice alongside media regulatory bodies (Chapter 7).

---

74 *Ibid*, p. 153.

VI References

Abel, Richard L. (1998), *Speaking Respect: Respecting Speech*, Chicago, IL: University of Chicago Press.

Adams, Maurianne, Bell, Lee Anne and Griffin, Pat (1997), *Teaching for Diversity and Social Justice*, London: Routledge.

Aufderheide, P., ed. (1992), *Beyond PC: Toward a Politics of Understanding*, St Paul, MN: Graywolf Press.

Baker, John, Lynch, Kathleen, Cantillon, Sara and Walsh, Judy (2004), *Equality: From Theory to Action*, Houndmills: Palgrave Macmillan.

Bamforth, Nicholas (2004), 'Conceptions of anti-discrimination law', *Oxford Journal of Legal Studies*, vol. 24, no. 4.

Bamforth, Nicholas, Malik, Maleiha, O'Cinneide, C. and Bindman, Geoffrey (2008), *Discrimination Law: Theory and Context*, London: Thomson, Sweet & Maxwell.

Barendt, Eric (2005), *Freedom of Speech*, 2nd ed., Oxford: Oxford University Press.

Cummings, Michael (2001), *Beyond Political Correctness: Social Transformation in the United States*, Boulder, CO: Rienner.

Doyle, Brian, Casserley, Catherine, Cheetham, Simon, Gay, Vivienne and Hyams, Oliver (2010), *Equality and Discrimination: The New Law*, Bristol: Jordans.

Dunant, Sarah, ed. (1995), *The War of the Words: The Political Correctness Debate*, London: Virago.

Dyzenhaus, David (2010), *Hard Cases in Wicked Legal Systems: Pathologies of Legality*, Oxford: Oxford University Press.

Equality and Human Rights Commission (2015), *Equality and Human Rights Law during an Election Period: Guidance for Local Authorities, Candidates and Political Parties*.

Faludi, Susan (1993), *Backlash: The Undeclared War Against Women*, London: Vintage.

Fanon, Franz (1986), *Black Skin: White Masks*, New York: Pluto Press.

Fraser, Nancy (2003), 'Social justice in the age of identity politics: redistribution, recognition, and participation', in Fraser, Nancy and Honneth, Axel, *Redistribution or Recognition? A Political-Philosophical Exchange*, London: Verso.

Fraser, Nancy (2005), 'Reframing justice in a globalising world', *New Left Review*, vol. 36.

Fredman, Sandra (2001), 'Equality: a new generation?' in *Equality Law: Reflections from South Africa and Elsewhere*, South Africa: Claremont.

Fredman, Sandra (2002), *Discrimination Law*, Oxford: Oxford University Press.

Fredman, Sandra (2007), 'Redistribution and recognition: reconciling inequalities', *South African Journal of Human Rights*, vol. 23.

Fredman, Sandra (2011), *Discrimination Law*, 2nd ed., Oxford: Oxford University Press.

Goldhagen, Daniel Jonah (1996), *Hitler's Willing Executioners: Ordinary Germans and the Holocaust*, London: Vintage.

Government Equalities Office (2011), *Equality Act 2010: Public Sector Equality Duty. What Do I Need to Know? A Quick Start Guide for Public Sector Organisations*.

Guasp, April, Ellison, Gavin and Satara, Tasha (2014), *The Teachers' Report: Homophobic Bullying in Britain's Schools*, Stonewall.

Hepple, Bob (2010), 'The new single Equality Act in Britain', *The Equal Rights Review*, vol. 5.

Home Office (1999), 'Report of the Macpherson Inquiry' Cm. 4262-I, 24 February.

Itaborahi, Lucas Paoli and Zhu, Jingshu (2014), *State Sponsored Homophobia 2014: A World Survey of Laws – Criminalisation, Protection and Recognition of Same-sex Love*, International Lesbian, Gay, Bisexual, Trans and Intersex Association.

Johnson, Andrew (2005), *Social Justice in Professional Roles*, Strathclyde University, Faculty of Education.

Johnson, Andrew (2015), 'Far more than a swimming pool', in De Main, Helen, ed., *United we will Swim: 100 Years of Govanhill Baths*, Luath Press Ltd.

Koppelman, Andrew (1996), *Antidiscrimination Law and Social Equality*, New Haven, CT: Yale University Press.

Kurzweil, Edith and Phillips, William (1994), *Our Country, Our Culture: The Politics of Political Correctness*, Boston, MA: Partisan Review Press Book.

Lough Dennell, Brandi-Lee and Logan, Caitlin (2015), *Prejudice-based Bullying in Scottish Schools: A Research Report*, Equality and Human Rights Commission.

McColgan, Aileen (2005), *Discrimination Law: Text, Cases and Materials*, 2nd ed., Oxford: Hart.

MacKinnon, Catharine (1979), *Sexual Harassment of Working Women*, New Haven, CT: Yale University Press.

MacKinnon, Catharine and Siegel, Riva B., eds, (2004), *Directions in Sexual Harassment Law*, New Haven, CT: Yale University Press.

Malik, Maleiha (2009), 'Extreme speech and liberalism', in Hare, Ivan and Weinstein, James, eds, *Extreme Speech and Democracy*, Oxford: Oxford University Press.

Martinson, Jane (2014), 'Journalist Olenka Frenkiel says BBC sexism and ageism still an issue', *Guardian*, 7 November, available at www.theguardian.com/media/2014/nov/07/bbc-journalist-olenka-frenkiel-reject-gagging-clause (accessed 13 April 2015).

Milmo, Cahal (2007) 'Fury at DNA pioneer's theory: Africans are less intelligent than Westerners', *Independent*, 17 October, available at www.independent.co.uk/news/science/fury-at-dna-pioneers-theory-africans-are-less-intelligent-than-westerners-394898.html (accessed 19 August 2015).

Ministry of Justice, Home Office (2013), *An Overview of Sexual Offending in England and Wales*, Official Statistics Bulletin, 10 January.

Nicol, Andrew, Sharland, Andrew and Millar, Gavin (2009), *Media Law and Human Rights*, 2nd ed., Oxford: Oxford University Press.

O'Cinneide, Colm (2008), 'The right to equality: a substantive legal norm or vacuus rhetoric?', *UCL Human Rights Review*, vol. 1, no. 1.

Pincus, Fred L. (2000), 'Discrimination comes in many forms: individual, institutional and structural' in Adams, Maurianne, Blumenfeld, Warren, Castenada, C., Hackman, H., Peters, M. and Zuniga, X., eds, *Readings for Diversity and Social Justice*, London: Routledge.

Rose, Hilary and Rose, Steven (2001), *Alas Poor Darwin: Arguments Against Evolutionary Psychology*, London: Verso.

Saraga, Esther, ed. (1998), *Embodying the Social: Constructions of Difference*, London: Routledge.

Thomas, Linda, Singh, Ishtla and Peccei, Jean (2004), *Language, Society and Power*, London: Routledge.

Thompson, Neil (2003), *Promoting Equality: Challenging Discrimination and Oppression*, 2nd ed., Houndmills: Palgrave Macmillan.

Yeboah, Samuel Kennedy (1988), *The Ideology of Racism*, London: Hansib.

Young, I.M. (1990), *Justice and the Politics of Difference*, Princeton, NJ: Princeton University Press.

Demeaning stereotypical representation in the media

A pervasive case of *everyday discrimination*

I Introduction

Following Fraser's multidimensional approach to justice, *everyday discrimination* (ED) is a matter of misrecognition and thus injustice (Chapter 2). It is also a form of discrimination when discrimination is understood as a problem that exists and is made operational at various interacting levels, including the cultural (Chapter 3). One of its cultural manifestations is media's manufacture and reproduction of stereotypes.

The first part of this chapter will offer an analysis of the significance of stereotypes in maintaining, producing and indeed manufacturing discrimination. Even though stereotypes circulate and are even embedded in society in a variety of ways – such as in everyday interactions (including electronic communications and social media), jokes, sporting and recreational activities, assumptions within the family, educational materials, and employment requirements, procedures and practices – their exponential production and reproduction in the mass media (television, radio, press, advertising and the internet) is a most significant force in sustaining them and thus makes them ideologically available to justify and fuel the exclusion and unfavourable treatment of targeted groups. Indeed, as we have seen, the printed and audiovisual production and reproduction of images and messages that use demeaning stereotypes form integral parts of the definition of ED. Following this line of thought, the second part of the chapter focuses on the significance of 'media stereotyping and representation' in discrimination; and the third part takes the argument further and explores the claims, experience and proposals made by the organised civil society in this regard.

II Stereotypes and discrimination

Originally, the word stereotype 'derives from an aspect of the printing process in which a mould is made so as to duplicate patterns or pictures

on to the page'.[1] The political journalist Lippmann first saw the appropriateness of the term to describe how people use cognitive moulds in order
to reproduce images of people or events in their minds, the 'pictures in
our heads' as he called them.[2] In this light, stereotyping appears as a value-
neutral and harmless process that in fact helps people to manage huge
amounts of information. For example:

> We understand the world by referring individual objects, people or
> events in our heads to the general classificatory schemes into which –
> according to our culture – they fit. Thus we decode a flat object on
> legs on which we place things as a 'table'. We may never have seen
> that kind of 'table' before, but we have a general concept or category
> of 'table' in our heads, into which we fit the particular objects we per-
> ceive or encounter. In other words, we understand 'the particular' in
> terms of its 'type'.[3]

Categories do help individuals to construct meaning, but stereotyping
people means objectifying them. Simplifying, essentialising and generalis-
ing about people is a different matter and indeed deeply problematic,
especially when this happens in a context of uneven power relationships
between groups. For example, when groups perceived as alien are evaluated by another group or culture through rigid and ethnocentric standards, the result is often the marginalisation, exclusion and even
demonisation of those who do not 'fit' and are perceived as the 'Other'.
In the same sense, according to Lippmann, the idea that stereotypes are
harmless tools for dealing with people is problematic given that stereotypes are not neutral, but often the projection upon the world of our own
sense of value. Behind their defence 'we can continue to feel ourselves
safe in the position we occupy'.[4] These problematic considerations about
the use of stereotypes in referring to people can be better understood
through the sociological approach. Such an approach does not dismiss the
cognitive roots of stereotypes but develops a social understanding of their
use and implications.

According to the sociological approach, stereotypes are not mere generalisations that help people manage information, but are *products of
culture* acquired through socialisation processes. From this perspective,
stereotypes are manufactured by culture and have values attached. This
approach draws our attention to a social rather than an individual and isolated process. Stereotypes in the sociological model are the measure of

---

1 Brown (1995), p. 82.
2 See Lippmann (1922), p. 4.
3 Hall (1997), p. 257.
4 Lippmann (1922), p. 96; see also Dyer (2002), p. 11.

what is and what is not considered good and acceptable. They can set the rules that determine which groups are to be valued and which are not, which groups we fear, and which will be subordinated and so forth. This is so because stereotypes are

> embedded in the culture in which we are raised and live. They are conveyed and reproduced in all the usual socio-cultural ways through socialisation in the family and at school, through repeated exposure to images in books, television and newspapers, etc.[5]

For example, we learn our gender roles effortlessly; they are reinforced in most social ambits and products. They often derive from an unquestioned 'common sense' and are manifested in images and actions that, for the most part, are uncontested. Thus, our gender roles become plainly self-evident truths.

The analysis that follows is based on various studies and some empirical research produced in different disciplines such as anthropology, sociology, psychology and cultural studies. It is an attempt to provide grounding and some meaning to the use and implications of stereotypes. The ideas explored will assist in understanding why stereotypes are an issue of misrecognition and discrimination.

1 Stereotypes sustain misrecognition and discrimination

Stereotypes can serve an ideological function. Ideology is a complex concept and can be understood in different ways. In one view, it denotes a set of beliefs that are produced and reproduced to legitimise a particular *status quo*. Ideology, then, has to do with legitimising the power of a dominant social group or class, as the way in which meaning or signification serves to sustain relations of domination through a series of actions or omissions that will tend to promote certain values by excluding those which may contradict the ruling ones.[6] Althusser, on the other hand, points to a concept where 'ideology represents the way I live my relations to society as a whole, which cannot be a question of truth or falsehood.'[7] In this sense, ideology is not an enforced framework of beliefs, but the way in which we all participate in power relationships and produce our own

---

5 Brown (1995), p. 83.
6 Those actions or omissions, as Eagleton explains, can include: promoting beliefs and values congenial to it; naturalising and universalising such beliefs so as to render them self-evident and apparently inevitable; denigrating ideas which might challenge them; excluding rival forms of thought, perhaps by some unspoken but systematic logic; and obscuring social reality in ways convenient to itself (including masking or suppressing social conflicts). See Eagleton (1991), pp. 5–6.
7 *Ibid*, p. 18.

harm or benefit. Ideology, however, can also make reference to a set of values and beliefs that may contest the current dominant ideology and will try, perhaps through the same strategies, to achieve some limited power or even attempts to overturn the existing power. This is to say that ideology is, or could be, contested through another ideology that, in turn, will need to justify not a *status quo*, but a will or a hope, by denouncing the contradictions, distortions and inconsistencies of the ruling ideology. In this sense, Gramsci's understanding of ideology is useful when, while recognising the embeddedness of ideology in *praxis*, it also regards it both as the means by which the powerful establish their hegemony and as an instrument of social transformation and counter-hegemony.[8] This has arguably been the case of movements such as the Feminist, Marxist, anti-racist, gay and lesbian liberation, human rights, disability rights, anti-poverty and global solidarity movements.[9]

Stereotypes as ideological tools are caught up in this myriad of possible genesis and functions and the foregoing explains how this may happen. These things said however, what matters in the context of ED is that demeaning stereotypes are constantly reproduced, they have the power to further disadvantage and sustain the status subordination of the groups they target, and there is not a significant opportunity for them to be challenged.

As ideological tools, stereotypes reinforce a particular view of the world and serve to reinforce and justify a certain *status quo*. A stereotype needs to convince both its agent and its target that individuals share characteristics based on their membership of particular groups. While stereotypes can serve both to disrupt and justify the *status quo*, in an unequal world in which even broadly democratic societies are hugely stratified according to wealth, power and privilege, attribution (via stereotypes) to any group of a particular characteristic has an ideological function. In societies in which structural racism, sexism or homophobia are pervasive, attributed characteristics cannot be value-free. So while some groups are routinely depicted as clearly inferior, such as those routinely depicted as 'lazy' or 'stupid', even where denigrations are not explicit in this way, such as the depiction of women as 'natural carers', there are value assumptions attached. In both situations, stereotypes have the effect of justifying and reinforcing their subordinated situation and at the same time normalising the social system that may have created that deprivation in the first place. Moreover, such depictions endorse the dominant group's right to its privileged position.[10] In other words, stereotypes, even if not overtly, have the capacity to demonstrate why some people are in power and why certain groups are

---

8 Baker *et al* (2004), p. 212. The reference to Gramsci is from Gramsci (1971).
9 *Ibid*, pp. 195–196.
10 Brown (1995), pp. 85–86; see also Eagleton (1991).

not. Similarly, stereotypes may also justify the need to keep things the way they are for safety, cultural, economic, military or other reasons.

That said, stereotypes need to be repeated in order to gain acceptance. The repetition of the same stereotype of a group (in films, for example) renders it part of the landscape. It then becomes deeply embedded in the culture to the extent that we come to expect it, and if it is not there, it causes surprise.[11] For example, humour studies have demonstrated that the use of stereotypes in racist, sexist, homophobic and other demeaning 'jokes' is fundamental in the sense that without them jokes would make no sense. Humour is usually perceived as harmless; however, it reinforces and helps to justify and normalise discrimination against various groups:

> repeating stereotypes is crucial to the jokes, or they would not work at all. Humour depends largely on stereotyping to work. It must convince people that certain people with certain traits are, look, think and must be treated in a certain way.[12]

On the other hand, stereotypes are not static; stereotyping fluctuates depending on the social and power relationships in a society. According to Ramírez and Peterson, depending on the power relationship between groups, one of three different stereotyping scenarios can arise: cooperative, stratified or oppositional.[13] In the first case, the 'out-group' assimilates into the mainstream, becoming virtually indistinguishable from it. That is the case, for example, of the Irish community in the US. They have evolved from being a thoroughly denigrated immigrant group to becoming so mainstreamed that there have been two presidents of Irish descent. When such 'social equilibrium' is reached, the stereotypes diminish or evaporate in an assimilation process. However, there are factors that make that 'assimilation process' more difficult. For example, consider the case of marginalised groups who, unlike the Irish, do not have fair skin, do not share the dominant group's Christianity and do not speak English.[14] Under the stratified scenario, groups share unequal power.

> The dominant group is likely to create stereotypes of the subdominant, clustering around two sets of characteristics: harmless (with outgroup members portrayed as childlike, irrational, and emotional) when they pose no threat, or dangerous (treacherous, deceitful, cunning) when they do.[15]

11 See Ramírez (2002), pp. 18–19.
12 Ainsworth (1997).
13 See Ramírez (2002), pp. 25–26; and Peterson (1982), pp. 163–168.
14 See Ramírez (2002), pp. 26–27.
15 *Ibid*, p. 27.

The third scenario is the oppositional, where fear and hatred can erupt into violence. This happens when dominant groups feel they are losing their privilege. This is often the case when groups think they are competing for the same resources. The dominant group's description of the subordinated becomes even more derogatory, leading them to describe the other as 'fanatical', 'extremist' and 'aggressive'. The change of terminology is a convenient way for members of the in-group to rationalise their own violent or ungenerous impulses.[16] Moreover, a particular context or event can increase not only the quantity but also the extent of harm and negative implications of stereotyping in people's lives. For example, in recent years there has been a three-way intertwined rise in anti-Muslim, anti-immigrant and anti-benefit sentiments generated or renewed in the contemporary contexts of the War on Terror (since 2001), the legal and 'illegal' movement of people between frontiers and the Global Financial Crisis that peaked in 2008. There is a plethora of examples of Islamophobic images, messages and attitudes running parallel to an incendiary rhetoric about people on benefits, including an almost cathartic assignation of blame in which 'job-stealing-immigrants' and working-class people are the scapegoats of a falling economy. Arguably the stereotypes generated in these contexts, such as the 'Muslim terrorist', the 'benefit scrounger' and the 'slobbish single mother', serve as a means to explain an adverse political and economic climate which cannot, however, be attributed to ordinary people who do not have the power to make political or economic decisions of any significant scale.[17]

Stereotyping often assumes that a dominant group targets a subordinated group. However, stereotypes can also go the other way round; it is unequal power relationships that make the difference and determine the negative effect of demeaning descriptions. The disenfranchised may elaborate a demeaning stereotype for their oppressor, but their description will create no significant harm to his economy or status. Moreover, the mass media produces, reproduces and communicates dominant attitudes to the widest audience; therefore, the stereotypes that are more available are those that target the disenfranchised groups. 'He who has the bigger stick has the better chance of imposing his definitions of reality'.[18]

---

16 *Ibid.*
17 For an analysis of the evidence of increased prejudice and hostility towards Muslims since 11 September 2001, see Abrams and Houston (2006). See also the analysis of the anti-Muslim politics of the BNP in Goodall (2007), p. 94. Examples of the generation of demeaning stereotypes that affect working-class people are discussed in Jones (2011), who explores how the working class has gone from 'salt of the earth' to 'scum of the earth'. Jones points to a complex reality: the increasing poverty and desperation of people left abandoned by the aspirational, society-fragmenting policies of both Tories and New Labour.
18 Dyer (2002), p. 12; see also Ramírez (2002), p. 21.

Even though stereotypes do help to sustain a system where discrimination takes place, privileging some while demeaning others, it needs to be noted that stereotyping mostly occurs unwittingly, subtly and at a subliminal level. However, despite this being the case, what matters is that misrecognising groups through stereotypes constitutes a form of injustice that needs to be redressed.

2 Stereotypes and reality

Stereotypes may have a basis in fact; there might be some correspondence between lived experience and stereotypes. However, any real-life correspondence between a group member's behaviour and a quality said to be characteristic of the entire group is only an isolated part of a much larger story. Indeed, 'there were and are Mexican bandits, lazy African Americans, and Italian American gangsters; but banditry, laziness, and criminality are not culture specific, nor do those qualities represent the group's complete experience'.[19] In the same sense, women, in fact, do most of the housework but it does not follow that housekeeping is all women are able or want to do. Very often stereotypes tenuously derive from *only* one chosen aspect of social reality but they are not a description of such a reality. The actual characteristics of a group are complex and undetermined, its members have multiple identifications and no culture or identity exists in a vacuum. Nevertheless, 'a group's culturally distinctive behavior patterns or the particular socio-economic circumstances in which it finds itself could provide the seed bed in which certain stereotypical perceptions about it could readily flourish'.[20] This is to say that stereotypes are often both reproductions and creations. They tell people what they are supposed to be or do and, at the same time, condition their existence to fitting into the stereotype applied to them.

One of the consequences of actually believing and using stereotypes to construct meaning is that stereotypes cause their possessor to view future evidence in terms of the available categories, and to act accordingly. Stereotypes in this view can become programmes for action and may induce or justify acts that can go from simple disliking to committing acts that would be unthinkable against members of one's own group. Moreover, stereotypes also affect the image and attitudes that targeted groups adopt for themselves, provided that everyone knows the same stereotypes and are called to follow the same beliefs.[21] For example:

19 Ramírez (2002), p. 16; see also Dyer (2002), pp. 12–13.
20 Brown (1995), p. 84.
21 See Ramírez (2002), pp. 19–21; and Brown (1995), p. 106.

one series of experiments may indicate how early those attitudes are formed. In order to determine young children's racial attitudes, researchers presented youngsters with a black doll and a white doll and asked questions about which were 'nice' and which were 'bad'. Most of the young white children picked the white doll as looking nice and the black doll as looking bad.... Black children presented with the dolls also labelled the black doll as not nice but bad, though not to the degree that the white children did.[22]

Research of this kind also reveals another important aspect of stereotyping, namely the 'internalisation of subordination' (Chapter 3, IV, 2). This is to say, when the targets of stereotyping actually believe their inferiority and justify their own oppression. Moreover, since stereotypes are associations of a social category with certain characteristics, they may have an impact on social judgements. Therefore, it could be expected that someone who possesses a stereotype about a certain group will not keep her/his beliefs aside when encountering an individual from that group. On the contrary, the stereotype emerges and the stereotypical characteristics are often consciously or unconsciously attributed. That said, it is possible to anticipate further consequences. Members of stereotyped groups are evaluated consistently against their stereotype and, therefore, the individual from the targeted group will be on an uneven playing field when, for example, competing for goods and services. Members from stereotyped groups can be judged to be a more or less suitable employee, tenant, student or whatever.[23] Finally, it is clear that the former is possible because stereotypes invoke consensus, otherwise they would not be effective. Stereotypes proclaim 'this is what everyone – you, me and us – think members of such-and-such a social group are like, as if these concepts of these social groups were spontaneously arrived at by all members of society independently and in isolation'.[24] Stereotypes are thus taken as if they express general agreement about certain groups' characteristics. However, it is hardly ever questioned where the stereotypes come from; most astonishing is that, for the most part, it is from stereotypes that we get our ideas about social groups.

3 Stereotypes are ill-founded generalisations

Stereotypes are simplistic generalisations. They apply a reductive, all-or-nothing logic through which people belonging to a certain group ought

---

22 Ramírez (2002), p. 20. This makes reference to the famous doll experiments which studied children's attitudes towards race, conducted in the US by Clark and Clark (1947). More empirical studies are in Brown (1995), pp. 81–116.
23 See Brown (1995), p. 90.
24 Dyer (2002), p. 14.

to, by that sole reason, have a certain trait or traits.[25] Studies about stereotypes have concluded that the degree of rigidity and shrillness of a stereotype indicates the degree to which it is an enforced representation that
points to a reality whose invisibility and/or fluidity threatens the received
definitions of society promoted by those with the 'biggest sticks'.[26] The
rigidity of stereotypes is thus an implicit though sometimes explicit
method of enforcing them; and the more derogatory and prevalent they
are, the more significant and shielded is the reality they are trying to
mask/justify. For example, the stereotype of the 'Chav' – the demeaning
caricature of the British working class – has made working-class people
objects of fear and ridicule.[27] The stereotype of the 'tracksuit-wearing
drunken layabouts' includes demeaning attribution of accents, mannerisms, behaviours and tastes such as having tattoos, and the use of casual
sports clothing. The caricature has a series of dehumanising functions; it
makes it safe to insult them; it makes it more difficult to empathise with
them; and it makes it easier to blame them for 'their' own economic crisis.
As explained by Jones, after the 2010 general election, a Government led
by Conservative millionaires took office with an aggressive programme of
cuts (which were also proposed in its 2015 General Election Manifesto),
unparalleled since the early 1920s; and while the global economic crisis
that peaked in 2008 may have been triggered by the greed and ineptitude
of the affluent banking elite, it has been mostly working-class people who
are expected to pay the price – this is to say, to take the blame. This has
created a hostile environment where resistance to attempts to trim down
the welfare state has turned the Government against its users.[28] Jones
offers a good example of the rigidity and shrillness of stereotypes that
work to mask an uncomfortable reality. As he explains it, to justify the
slashing of welfare benefits, Jeremy Hunt – a senior Conservative minister
with an estimated wealth of £4.1 million – argued that:

> long-term claimants had to 'take responsibility' for the number of chil-
> dren that they had, and that the state would no longer fund large
> workless families. In reality, just 3.4 per cent of families in long-term
> receipt of benefits have four children or more. But Hunt was tapping
> into the age-old prejudice that the people at the bottom were breed-
> ing out of control, as well as conjuring up the tabloid caricature of the
> slobbish single mother who milks the benefits system by having lots of

25 See Ramírez (2002), pp. 15–16; and Brown (1995), pp. 84–85.
26 See Dyer (2002), pp. 16–17.
27 *Chavs* is a term that originates from the Romany word for child, *chavi*. Following Jones
    (2011), p. 2, from *Little Britain*'s Vicky Pollard to the demonisation of Jade Goody, media
    and politicians alike dismiss as feckless, criminalised and ignorant a vast, underprivileged
    swathe of society that has become stereotyped by one hate-filled word: *chavs.*
28 See Jones (2011), p. 11.

children. The purpose was clear: to help justify a wider attack on some of the most vulnerable working-class people in the country.[29]

Stereotyping is selective. It selects only some traits among the many available that shape individuals. 'Stereotypes flatten, homogenise, and generalise individuals within a group, emphasising sameness and ignoring individual agency and variety.'[30] This is particularly relevant in two respects: stereotypes describe groups and affect the individuals that belong to the stereotyped group. They give little or no chance at all for the consideration of individuality; and second, stereotypes tend to reduce people to one characteristic and diminish their potential for proving different abilities and strengths in other areas. For example, the stereotype of black people being good athletes. This stereotype not only generalises but also ignores and dismisses black people's ability to undertake other activities like intellectual work.[31] Lack of information or prejudiced information about the out-group ignores contradictory information and therefore is a very poor predictor. In this sense, it is critical to note that stereotypes are powerful, especially when applied to minorities or under-represented groups in society. Being fewer in number or less visible in mainstream institutions or positions of power strengthens the stereotype because there is little chance to actually get to know and understand individual members of the stereotyped group. Even in these cases, the individuals are often perceived as exceptions to the 'rule'.

4 Stereotypes in action

The foregoing offers some examples of the modes in which stereotypes obstruct their targets' participation as peers in society. It thus exemplifies the ways in which the existence, maintenance and reproduction of stereotypes in the ways outlined above can be a central dynamic in discrimination.

29 *Ibid*, p. 11.
30 Ramírez (2002), p. 16.
31 Hoberman (1997) argues that the athleticising of black identity encourages a disdain for academic achievement. He wrote about American society's fixation on black athletic achievement. In his view, this obsession, shared by both blacks and whites in the media, in corporate America, and by athletes themselves, has come to play a disastrous role in African-American life and a troubling role in the country's race relations. The sports fixation originates in the painful century-long exclusion of blacks from every other path to high achievement. Rich, flamboyant superstars lend credence to age-old prejudices, recycled 'scientific' theories disparaging black intelligence, and stereotypes of black violence. These arguments, while made in 1997, remain relevant today, despite and probably renewed by the emergence of a 'mixed race' president. See, for example, Carrington (2010), who addresses the intersection of race, sport and politics in twentieth-century Britain and the US.

An example of the link between stereotyping and discrimination – in this case institutional racism – can be found in the Macpherson Inquiry which followed the public shock resulting from the murder of a black teenager, Stephen Lawrence, in the UK and the failure of the Metropolitan Police, who, by drawing on their stereotyped image of black teenagers, did not investigate properly. The notes that Dr Oakley submitted to the inquiry are particularly helpful in illustrating this issue. He pointed out that:

> Police work, unlike most other professional activities, has the capacity to bring officers into contact with a skewed cross-section of society, with the well-recognised potential for producing negative stereotypes of particular groups. Such stereotypes become common currency of the police occupational culture. If the predominantly white staff of the police organisation have their experience of visible minorities largely restricted to interactions with such groups, then negative racial stereotypes will tend to develop accordingly.[32]

Oakley moved to conclude that institutional racism ought to be challenged; otherwise, minorities would be receiving less favourable treatment than the majority. While police officers may act on stereotypes in an unconscious or unwitting way, disadvantage is nevertheless created and, if anything, such unconsciousness is part of the problem, not a justification.[33] Unfavourable treatment is institutionalised because it is part of the culture of the professional role and is reinforced symbiotically by racism against black people elsewhere, say in the media, in housing, in education and so on. The stereotypes and jokes the police may create within their professional culture form part of a systematic exclusion and misrecognition in all inevitably intertwined areas of social life. Indeed, institutional discrimination also can be found in the use of stereotypical assumptions and ethnocentrism in recruitment processes generally. Very often this works in an unconscious way. Having the same cultural background as the interviewer can certainly be an advantage since both interviewer and

32 Home Office (1999), 6.31.
33 Twelve years later, the Neyroud Review of Police Leadership and Training Home Office, 5 April 2011, found that a 'White Male Culture' still dominates the police. In 2014, a black female firearms officer, Carol Howard, one of only two black women out of 700 officers in the diplomatic protection group, brought a claim of discrimination at the Central London Employment Tribunal. PC Carol Howard told the Employment Tribunal that in the wake of the police shooting of Mark Duggan in 2011 she felt she was used to improve the image of the Metropolitan Police. In PC's Howard view, the Metropolitan Police had failed to learn the lessons of the Macpherson Report. The Employment Tribunal ruled that the police had 'singled out and targeted' her for almost a year and the actions of acting Inspector Dave Kelly were deemed 'vindictive and spiteful'. See Williams (2014).

interviewee share the same verbal and non-verbal communicative behaviour and there is less room for misinterpretation. Ethnocentrism is largely what lies at the heart of many stereotypes. It involves a process in which members of the dominant culture believe they are all different, but non-members of their race or culture are all the same. As a result:

> It seems likely that there may be a greater predisposition on the part of white managers to regard white job candidates as individuals, as opposed to their black counterparts, who may be more likely to be treated as representatives of a stereotyped category.[34]

This is to say that certain identities are discriminated against only on the basis of a certain degree of likelihood that the worst predictions of their group's stereotype may be fulfilled.[35] However, the problem of unconsciousness remains. Recruiters are often unaware that their stereotypical notions of acceptability are related to their repertoire of ethnic stereotypes. They may decide the fate of candidates using ambiguous criteria in processes that are hard to challenge without a deep cultural change in recruitment processes.

Stereotypes about women's roles are often seen as just 'common sense' and thus affect women in employment.[36] Gender roles are pervasively reinforced culturally through education, television, advertising, magazines, etc. And so, for example, 'domestic responsibilities are viewed positively for men because they are believed to indicate stability and motivation, but negatively for women since they suggest divided loyalties between home and work'.[37] It is not yet part of the employment culture to recognise women as individuals who will not necessarily either want or accept most responsibility for household and children; and, by the same token,

---

34 Connolly (2004), p. 17.
35 See, for example, *Alexander v Home Office* [1988] 2 All ER 118 CA. In this case 'a prisoner complained that he was refused (more desirable work) in the kitchen. This was because he displayed the usual traits associated with people of his ethnic background being arrogant, suspicious of staff, anti-authority, devious and possessing a very large chip on his shoulder ... [which seemed] ... common in most coloured inmates.' See Connolly (2004), p. 171. For a deeper analysis of ethnocentrism and stereotypes in recruitment processes, see Jenkins (1986), pp. 74–78, 92–97.
36 See, for example, *Hurley v Mustoe* [1981] IRLR 208, EAT, where the applicant was rejected for a waitressing job because she had four young children. The employer had a policy not to employ women with young children because in his experience they were unreliable; *Horsey v Dyfed CC* [1982] IRLR 395, EAT. This case involves the assumption that wives follow their husbands and abandon their jobs; *Schmidt v Austicks Bookshops Ltd* [1977] IRLR 360, EAT. This case has to do with dress codes and their reinforcement of the stereotypes of male and female characteristics. Men, being usually serious, responsible and mature, whereas women needing to appear decorative handmaidens.
37 Collinson *et al* (1990), p. 61.

'housework' is not yet recognised as a valuable social and economic contribution for which both women and men are equally responsible and are equally well equipped. It is not yet part of the cultural imagery to see men and women committed in equal measure to a family and with concomitant responsibilities. Very often, employers' motivation in preferring men is to save money by avoiding the costs that hiring a woman may involve (e.g. absences due to pregnancy and maternity). However, gender equality is a political decision; a matter of justice that requires governments to take positive action and allocate resources to protect women and men's opportunities when they have a family. It is also of paramount importance to begin a shift in attitudes towards work which includes challenging the existence of men and women's stereotypical patterns of life and the economic value attached to them.

III The significance of media stereotyping and demeaning representation in discrimination

As we have seen, stereotypes and the misrecognition they entail towards certain groups is often a central dynamic in discrimination. Challenging discrimination based on stereotypes is a complex project and tribunals have a role to play,[38] but challenging stereotypes crucially needs to include assessment and contestation of media representations (in television, radio, press, advertising and the internet). While demeaning stereotypes are produced and reproduced in everyday interactions, including social media, and they should be challenged, the mass media is special. It informs to a large extent many of the most important issues we talk about in our social networking communications and picks up and publicises effectively some of the points we raise in electronic communications, including our blogs.

---

38 For example, from *R (on the application of European Roma Rights Centre) v Immigration Officer at Prague Airport* [2005] IRLR 115 HL – a case where the Roma were being treated more sceptically than the non-Roma – we learn that the object of the legislation is to ensure that each person is treated as an individual and not assumed to be like other members of the group, whether or not most members of the group do have such characteristics. A person may be acting on beliefs or assumptions about members of the sex or racial group involved which are often true and which, if true, would provide a good reason for the less favourable treatment in question, but what may be true of a group may not be true of a significant number of individuals within that group. *Bradford Hospitals NHS Trust v Al-Shahib* [2003] IRLR 4 EAT. The EAT overruled a tribunal's decision that an applicant of Iraqi origin was less favourably treated on the ground of race when his employers withdrew his membership of their gym after he had broken certain rules. The EAT said that while it may sometimes be legitimate for a tribunal to take into account differences in behaviour which reflect racial and cultural differences, it is wrong for a tribunal to make findings based on the existence of such differences unless there is some evidential basis for them, such as expert evidence. For a tribunal simply to assume that a particular ethnic group has a specific characteristic is fundamentally wrong, even if the assumption is made for benign purposes.

This, again, because it has the power, including online, to exponentially determine what constitutes an issue (and this power itself can and should be diversified).

General-interest intermediaries, as Sunstein calls them, such as those who operate newspapers, magazines and broadcasting stations (mass media), have, largely by happenstance, done much of the historical work of streets and parks – 'the public-forum' in the early twentieth century. Therefore, albeit potentially, the mass media has a democratic function in the sense that it can provide information we wouldn't necessarily have looked for ourselves or selected in advance and thus it can help us encounter alternative issues and stances towards such issues outside our intimate relations, preferred topics and traditional views.[39] This is particularly important in contemporary societies, where the wide availability of information through the internet can create 'information cocoons' and the isolation of individuals in 'their own worlds'.[40] As Sunstein has put it,

> in a democracy, people do not live in echo chambers or information cocoons. They see and hear a wide range of topics and ideas. They do so even if they did not, and would not, choose to see and to hear those topics and those ideas in advance.[41]

He goes on, quoting Justice Brandeis' idea about an 'inert people' being the greatest threat to freedom: 'To avoid inertness, a democratic public must certainly be free from censorship. But the system of free expression must do far more than avoid censorship; it must ensure that people are exposed to competing perspectives.'[42]

Exposing people to competing ideas lies at the heart of the politicisation of culture and the contestation of discriminatory messages and images that we advocate in order to redress ED. Once a message or an image loses its power to hurt because it has been critically exposed and rebutted, it is likely to fall outside use and this is something that can be better achieved by challenging the mass media in a similar way in which we challenge or should challenge discriminatory views and attitudes in everyday life. However, even though the internet offers the opportunity to confront the

39 See Sunstein (2007), p. 217. Whether these general-interest intermediaries actually promote such exposure to a variety of views is arguable and indeed is the theme addressed in this book, but the point is that they could play a most important role in favour of democracy and for the contestation of ED.

40 The concern about like-minded people speaking or listening mostly to one another has been fuelled in part by the rise of terrorism. But the dangers of echo chambers go beyond terrorism; they entail the risk of people sorting themselves into enclaves in which their own views and commitments are constantly reaffirmed. See *ibid*, p. xii.

41 *Ibid*, p. xi.

42 *Ibid*.

views disseminated through the mass media (via Facebook or Twitter) and can help create networks among like-minded people who will contest dominant oppressive ideas, it also engenders the risk of individuals listening only to like-minded individuals and indeed to produce extremism. We therefore need to both challenge mass media when it is being used to discriminate (and/or itself becoming an echo chamber of the views of the powerful); and turn it into a proper 'public-forum' which harbours a wide range of subjects and speakers and where there are institutional channels to complain and launch objections. This is the creation of a 'culture of free expression'.[43] It is therefore paramount to diversify the mass media and make it a medium through which to communicate and challenge as many views as possible and, crucially, to present the experience of underrepresented groups and their own definitions of themselves.

At another level, addressing the mass media in particular is important because the media's production and reproduction of demeaning stereotypes not only informs various forms of discrimination, as we have seen, but also because their very expression is itself a discriminatory practice. Moreover, challenging ED in the mass media represents challenges that are different from those of private interactions or of social networking sites. We cannot launch an immediate reply to a comment, a message or an image broadcasted on television, radio or massively disseminated in advertising. There are also significant power imbalances when it comes to ordinary citizens, media proprietors and advertisers – this is further discussed in Chapter 7.

The significance of mass media stereotyping and demeaning representation in discrimination has been exposed and challenged by those affected (section IV), and indeed also by the international community and domestic jurisdictions (Chapters 5–7). Moreover, various authors have commented on demeaning stereotypical representation in the media as an aspect of injustice and discrimination. For Young, as we have seen (Chapter 2), media stereotyping is injustice, not of material distribution, but of cultural imagery and symbols.[44] Its significance rests on the indivisible relationships such images and messages have with the social standing of persons and their opportunities. Indeed, there is a normative contradiction between proclaiming equality in formal rules and institutions while, at the same time, protecting the mass-production and distribution of materials that abuse and degrade economically and culturally dominated groups in society, thus creating new and distinct forms of group-specific disadvantage while sustaining and justifying existing ones. Fraser has made similar remarks. She treats demeaning stereotypical depiction in the media as a form of misrecognition, more specifically as a form of *disrespect*

---

43 Sunstein (2007), p. 222.
44 *Ibid*, p.23.

which means to be routinely maligned or disparaged in stereotypical public cultural representations.[45] Demeaning stereotypical representation in the media is hence a form of status subordination. For example, in the case of homophobia, status subordination encompasses demeaning stereotypical representation, working along with shaming and assault, exclusion from the rights and privileges of marriage and parenthood, curbs on rights of expression and association, harassment and disparagement in everyday life and denial of the full rights and equal protection of citizenship.[46] As can be noted, demeaning stereotypical representation in the media is only one among many other aspects of injustice; and one among other legally and non-legally recognised forms of discrimination that manufacture and maintain status subordination.

Similarly, MacKinnon and Hall have argued about the role of the media and culture in the construction and perpetuation of discrimination. MacKinnon, for example, has written extensively about pornography as a discriminatory practice. She argues that pornography is a form of abuse, enacting and promoting the power of one social group over another – subordinating women and children and promoting sexual harassment, child abuse, battering and rape.[47] Hall, on the other hand, was a prominent figure in cultural studies. He wrote about mass media prejudice when covering black communities in the UK (West Indians, Asians and Africans) and the exclusion of black and minority ethnic journalists. Hall was clear in pointing out that negative racial images cannot be resolved by using a few more black faces on the screen, or by an extra documentary or two on immigrant problems. Neither could the causes be traced simply to casual discrimination on racial matters within the broadcasting organisations. Hall saw the roots of the problem set deep within the broadcasting structures themselves[48] – for example, in their policies of recruitment, promotion, decision-making processes and responding to sponsors' demands. As a result, 'good' liberal broadcasters, as well as 'bad' racialist ones, are both constrained by these structures.[49] Hall was also emphatic about the crucial role of the mass media in defining the problems and issues of public concern. They, he argued, are the main channels of public discourse in our segregated society; they transmit stereotypes of one group to other groups; they attach feelings and emotions to problems and they set the terms by which problems are defined as 'central' or 'marginal':[50]

---

45 See Fraser (2003), p. 13.
46 *Ibid*, p. 18.
47 See MacKinnon (1994).
48 See, Hall (1971). Similar arguments are raised in Hall (1997).
49 *Ibid*.
50 *Ibid*.

Blacks participate, then, in broadcasts defined by the media as 'black problems': and they do so within constraints, given in the very professional definition of what constitutes 'good television', by the producers themselves. It is very rare indeed to see a programme where blacks themselves have defined the problem as they see it. Now it matters a great deal whether studio discussions are based on the premise that black people constitute a problem for Mr. Enoch Powell, or that Enoch Powell constitutes a problem for black people.[51]

Hall spoke directly about key targets of black concern: the drama and entertainment programmes that reinforce stereotypes. These – he explained – exert a much stronger impact on the formation of popular attitudes than current affairs programmes.[52] His views, expressed in 1971, remain relevant today and are replicated by others, as we shall see. Moreover, the participation of black, Asian and minority ethnic groups (BAME) in the creative media industries is declining. According to the latest *Creative Skillset 2012 Employment Census*, total employment in the creative media industries grew by more than 4,000 between 2009 and 2012. However, despite this increase, representation of BAME people fell. It declined from 7.4 per cent of the total workforce in 2006 to 6.7 per cent in 2009 and was just 5.4 per cent in 2012.[53] At 8.9 per cent London had the highest representation; however, given the high representation in the wider London economy (28.8 per cent) it was in fact the least representative region.[54]

These figures indicate an under-representation in employment which, as Hall contended, is more than a numerical problem; it is both cause and by-product of the media structures themselves. Employing more BAME people is a necessary step, but it is equally important to identify and change the processes, procedures and culture within the industry which has prevented BAME people from participating in the first place. This should be followed by and/or parallel to a scrutiny of the points of

51 *Ibid.* Enoch Powell was a Conservative Party member between 1950 and 1974. He was controversial through most of his career, especially for his views on immigration and national identity and for his opposition to Commonwealth immigration and the Race Relations Act 1968, which he found offensive and immoral. His 'Rivers of Blood' speech (1968) warned of dire social consequences of the Act and immigration where the existing (white) indigenous population would be 'dominated and overawed' by the new immigrants. The media coverage and notoriety of the speech many felt led to the surprise General Election victory of the Conservatives in 1970.

52 See Hall (1971).

53 Brooks *et al* (2012), p. 4. Creative Skillset is the licensed Sector Skills Council for Entertainment Media, Fashion and Textiles, Publishing and Advertising, Marketing and Communications. The Census provides insight into the changing composition of the industries' employment patterns and geography over time.

54 *Ibid*, p. 19.

view and experiences that have been ignored or misrepresented in media products; including the selection of matters of concern and the stances presented on such matters. These issues are further discussed in Chapter 8. At this point, the relevant facts are, on the one hand, that the census reveals alarming figures which reinforce the need to imagine ways in which the media might be transformed; and on the other, that such transformation should acknowledge and evaluate the intertwined relationship between media's constitution and its products so that fairer representation can be achieved.

Misrecognition via demeaning stereotypical depiction in the media has been targeted by political scientists, philosophers and social movements seeking participatory parity. Although inadequately, media self-regulatory bodies in the UK are dealing with these issues and have produced codes and guidelines for avoiding demeaning stereotypical representation. This is discussed in Chapter 7. What, on the other hand, seems to be little explored and therefore this book seeks to address are: the legal dimension of this particular issue of misrecognition, and the possibilities for bringing it as a form of discrimination explicitly to the legal agenda (Chapters 8 and 9).

As we saw in Chapters 2 and 3, and following authors such as Fanon, it can be argued that the damage to self-esteem and the lack of social-esteem lies at the root of major forms of discrimination and, moreover, they serve as their driver and fuel. In *The Wretched of the Earth*, Fanon argued that the colonisers' major weapon was the imposition of their negative image of the colonised on the subjugated people, who, in order to be free, must first of all purge themselves of such deprecating self-images:

> When we consider the efforts made to carry out the cultural estrange-ment so characteristic of the colonial epoch, we realise that nothing has been left to chance and that the total result looked for by colonial domination was indeed to convince the natives that colonialism came to lighten their darkness. The effect consciously sought by colonialism was to drive into the natives' heads the idea that if the settlers were to leave, they would at once fall back into barbarism, degradation and bestiality.[55]

Therefore, it is not surprising that the struggle against a deprecated self-image has been crucial to various social movements seeking emancipation from domination, which is both economic and ideological. Another example where the deprecation of identities constitutes and sponsors major forms of discrimination leading even to genocide can be found in Goldhagen's study of German attitudes toward the Jews. He used the

55 Fanon (1990), p. 169.

socialisation model to explain how Germans learned to despise Jews. The explanation of the roots of the Holocaust is suggested via 'cognitive models', that is to say prevalent beliefs and values, which were:

> derivative of and borne by the societal conversation, linguistically and symbolically. When beliefs and images are uncontested or are even just dominant within a given society, individuals typically come to accept them as self-evident truths.... An individual learns the cognitive models of his culture, like grammar, surely and effortlessly.[56]

The studies by Fanon and Goldhagen suggest that demeaning stereotypes and the deprecation of certain groups are transmitted in a variety of ways, all of which ought to be challenged. The media is one such way given that on a daily basis and from childhood, thousands of media images surround us. The mass media are in many cases our first and only contact with places or people outside our family and local community associations. Images and the values attached to them can be found on billboards, TV, radio, magazines and their advertisements, video games, the internet, public areas and public transport. Powerfully, the media establishes ways of seeing things, dressing, interacting and even thinking. Its omnipresence, attractiveness and magnetism, especially in passive consumption societies, make the media something like a guide to how we should view each other, our gender roles and what we define as 'normal' or correct in terms of social behaviour. The media not only reflects the way things 'naturally' are, it selects which things it 'reflects', shapes our reality and guides our behaviours and attitudes. Consciously or unconsciously, for information or for profit, the media has the power to guide collective fears and desires. This is achieved in a variety of ways including the use, manufacture and, crucially, the reproduction of stereotypes. Individuals do have the ability to discern for themselves but as social beings we construct knowledge out of available information. Whether or not the media follows a particular agenda or whether or not the media's bias is conscious or unconscious is arguable and actually not very significant, for the fact remains: the media has the power to foster and maintain the status

56 Goldhagen (1996), p. 46.

subordination (misrecognition) of disadvantaged groups in society.[57] There are, of course, committed and responsible journalists and producers who do not profit, for example, from racism or sexism. However, tabloids, comedy shows and advertising agencies frequently rely on demeaning stereotypes to be funny and attractive or to sell what they want to sell. To be funny adverts are often racist; to be attractive, adverts need naked or semi-naked women in arousing positions (Chapter 7). The result is that women and black people – among other disrespected groups

57 The power of the media to sustain discrimination and oppression has been analysed in a variety of ways. For Althusser (2001), p. 104, communications, press, radio and television, etc., along with other institutions such as religion, education, family, law, the political system, trade unions and culture (literature, sports, arts) constitute the 'ideological state apparatuses' whose function is the reproduction of the relations of production. This means that the institutions listed above contribute to the same result: keeping things the way they are – for example, our gender roles, the subordination of women, the disrespect of black identities and so on. Under Althusser's analysis, each ideological state apparatus contributes to this result in the way proper to it. For example, 'the communications apparatus by cramming every "citizen" with daily doses of nationalism, chauvinism, liberalism, moralism, etc., by means of the press, the radio and television. The same goes to the cultural apparatus (the role of sport in chauvinism is of the first importance), etc.' Whether or not the maintenance of relations of oppression and domination works in the interest of the State as such is arguable. Increasingly, it is not only governments who control our fears and desires for particular purposes but the multinational corporations, and diverse agencies seeking economic, political and ideological power. More examples of the analysis of the power of the media to sustain discrimination can be found in Cosby (1994). She refers to violence in television and films but also to stereotyping and its negative effects on its targets. Her study concludes that negative television imageries of African-Americans instruct African-Americans to hate themselves and instruct other ethnic people to dislike African-Americans. Other studies, such as that of Bradley Greenberg (1972), p. 46, offer similar examples. His research on the impact of television's portrayal of blacks on white viewers reveals that white children are more likely than black children to learn about the other race from television. Forty per cent of the white children attributed their knowledge about how blacks look, talk and dress to television. Those white children who had the least opportunity to interact with blacks were most likely to believe that television portrayals of blacks were realistic. Similar results arose in Poindexter and Stroman (1981); Stroman (1991); Huston et al (1992); and Wimmer (1986), p. 406. The latter in particular argues that the media possess the power to change perceptions, and if properly encouraged may change perceptions of racial prejudices and discrimination. He also warns that if broadcast media are not encouraged to address minority issues and continually misrepresent minorities, social distances that perpetuate societal stratification could be exacerbated. Similarly, Kretzmer (1987), p. 453, noted that the prevalence of racism or racial prejudice is likely to encourage racial discrimination. Conversely, allowing racial discrimination is likely to encourage the spread of racism and racial prejudice. A broad analysis of the influence of the media in US society and the various studies undertaken in this regard can be seen in Worthy (1995) and Baker and Dessart (1998). With regard to Latinos' representation in particular, see Roman (2000). More specifically about stereotyping, see Ronner (1997). She emphasises that discrimination and stereotyping often go hand in hand. See also Parenti (1986), who, like Chomsky (2002), contends that the news media distort public perceptions of race, class and gender.

– remain, for the most part, in a subordinated position in both the main-stream/dominant cultural imagery and the economic sphere.

IV Claims, points of view and proposals from the organised civil society

As we have seen, the significance of media stereotyping and demeaning representation in discrimination has been discussed in academia for a number of years. It has also been considered, to various degrees, in inter-national human rights documents (Chapter 5) and media regulatory bodies (Chapter 7). This section addresses the point of view of the targets and their initiatives.

As discussed in Chapter 2, participation is a dimension of justice which includes the power to make claims against the agents of oppression. This section therefore stresses the need for full consideration and actions to address the claims raised by groups that have been discriminated against in various forms, including through stereotypes and demeaning repres-entation in the media. Their participation with specific regard to challeng-ing ED will be further explored in Chapters 7 and 8.

Chapter 3 identified, at a theoretical level, processes which are helpful in challenging the cultural aspects of discrimination such as consciousness raising and the politicisation of culture. It was established that cultural change occurs when 'despised' groups seize the means of cultural expres-sion and use them to redefine a positive image of themselves. This section takes the argument further and introduces, as examples, the claims, research and proposals made by some organisations which have, in various ways, undergone these processes and have therefore, identified and articu-lated the social conditions that construct their disadvantage/oppression at various levels, including the cultural.[58]

While acknowledging that being at the forefront of campaigning can sometimes bring internal and external dissent, the opinion, concerns and research undertaken by the organised civil society cannot be ignored in a democratic society.[59] Putting them at the centre of the debate informs and legitimises the actions that need to be taken in order to recognise and redress the harms they have identified. At the same time, this approach can encourage a culture of participation and inspire other members of society to get organised and express their views in a persuasive manner. Moreover, as will be seen in Chapter 6, the need to mobilise the civil

58 The following sections refer to the work and points of view of individually named organi-sations. They, of course, do not represent the view of an entire identity group.

59 Identity groups may be parochial and highly exclusive. They can also create oppressive internal hierarchies, including the subordination of women and the disparagement of homosexuality. These problematic themes in identity politics were discussed in Chapter 2, V, 3.

society in order to combat speech injuries has been included in recommendations such as Council of Europe Recommendation No. R (97) 20.[60] While this Recommendation refers to hate speech, the same call appears apposite for demeaning stereotypical representation in the media because while the law can play only a small part in cultural change, as we have seen, that part lays the groundwork, is fundamental/structural and can include recognising harms done through discrimination at the cultural level, such as ED, expanding its repertoire of remedies and providing for a broader range of potential claimants.

There are a variety of organisations working against discrimination, often focusing on specific grounds such as race, religion or sexual orientation. Some of them have been created in order to challenge a specific problem; for example, Ligali began its growth in early 2000 with the aim of challenging the negative representation of the African British community across all forms of media.[61] Their original motivation was based on the fact that members of their community, spanning ages, occupations, gender and specific cultural backgrounds, regularly expressed profound and frustrated opinions about the detrimental and offensive way in which African people were represented in the media. After a year in existence, however, Ligali became a magnet for more general community concerns. They realised that the causes of some of the problems faced by the African community in Britain were often *multi-faceted* and the subsequent solutions also needed to be holistic if real and effective change for the better was to be achieved. As such, their work has extended beyond African misrepresentation in the media and now also focuses on independent cultural media production and holistic education.

Unlike Ligali, groups such as Stonewall were not initially created in order to challenge demeaning representation in the media.[62] Stonewall was founded in 1989 by a small group of women and men who had been active in the struggle against Section 28 of the Local Government Act 1988. Section 28 was a controversial amendment to the UK's Local Government Act 1986, introduced by the Conservative Party and enacted in 1988.[63] The amendment stated that a local authority 'shall not intentionally promote homosexuality or publish material with the intention of

60 The measures indicated in the fifth indent of the Appendix to this Recommendation are aimed at mobilising civil society and the victims of hate speech to help combat this phenomenon.
61 Ligali is a non-profit voluntary pan-African human rights organisation. They work for the socio-political and spiritual empowerment of African people whose heritage is directly from Africa or indirectly via African diasporic communities, such as those in the Caribbean and South America. See www.ligali.org (accessed 1 March 2015).
62 See www.stonewall.org.uk (accessed 1 March 2015).
63 The amendment was repealed in 2000 in Scotland, and in 2003 in the rest of the UK by Section 122 of the Local Government Act 2003.

promoting homosexuality' or 'promote the teaching in any maintained school of the acceptability of homosexuality as a pretended family relationship'.

Stonewall's aim at the outset was to create a professional lobbying group that would prevent attacks on lesbians, gay men and bisexuals (LGB people) from ever occurring again. Stonewall has subsequently put the case for equality on the mainstream political agenda by winning support within the main political parties. It has actively campaigned for equalisation of the age of consent, lifting the ban on LGB people serving in the military, securing legislation allowing same-sex couples to adopt, securing civil partnerships and then equal marriage, tackling homophobia and homophobic bullying in schools, and recently ensuring that the Equality Act 2010 protected LGB people in terms of goods and services. It has also conducted research and produced reports in areas such as employment, health, families, hate crime, housing, immigration and asylum, social exclusion, the Public Sector Equality Duty, sport, later life, biphobia, disability, gender, faith and media. Indeed, one of Stonewall's key priorities is to promote fair coverage of LGB people in the print and broadcast media – so that gay people are visible, portrayed realistically and discussed sensitively. As can be noted once again, demeaning stereotypical representation in the media is but one of many issues that disadvantages certain groups, but it is however connected to all of them.

Stonewall has pointed out that for many gay people the media provides their first images of gay sexuality – it can provide positive role models, and can help them realise they are not alone. However, the media can also be damaging to gay people and to society at large when it reinforces stereotypes and perpetuates homophobic views. In this regard, Stonewall has carried out a number of research projects. For example, in *The Teachers' Report 2009*, a survey of 2,000 staff working in schools, it was found that two-thirds of secondary-school and three in four primary-school teachers believe homophobic language in broadcast media affects the frequency of homophobic language and homophobic bullying in schools.[64] Things have not changed; the latest *Teachers' Report* (2014) shows that 69 per cent of primary-school teachers and 75 per cent of secondary-school teachers believe homophobic language used by celebrities or in the media affects the frequency of homophobic language and bullying in schools.[65]

In 2007, research into British attitudes towards lesbian and gay people in the UK found that almost one-fifth of people thought TV is responsible for anti-gay prejudice and 38 per cent felt that TV and other media such as radio have a duty to reduce anti-gay prejudice. Nearly three-quarters of people felt that the media frequently uses gay people as the subject of

64 See Guasp (2009), p. 15.
65 See Guasp *et al* (2014), pp. 10, 28.

jokes. Eighty-three per cent also believed that the media relies heavily on cliché stereotypes of gay people.[66] A later report in 2013 reveals that these feelings have not changed, which reinforces the need to bring the media to evaluation and to demand fair representation. The report *Gay in Britain 2013*, on lesbian, gay and bisexual people's experiences and expectations of discrimination revealed that the broadcast media's portrayal of LGB people continues to be judged both sparse and unrealistic by a significant number of gay people: 57 per cent say there is 'too little' portrayal of LGB people on television; and 49 per cent think current portrayal of LGB people in UK television is unrealistic.[67]

The recommendations that followed this research are relevant for the redress of ED and indeed they are apposite not only regarding sexual orientation but also for other pervasive grounds of ED, as we will see. These recommendations include that broadcasters and producers should make sure that their output includes realistic and non-clichéd portrayal of LGB people, in both factual and dramatic programming. This inclusion should be creative and involve characters where their sexual orientation is incidental to the subject or the storyline; Ofcom and broadcasters should train their staff to handle complaints about homophobia on screen appropriately and should consult with LGB people to better understand their concerns; the Creative Diversity Network should promote and encourage realistic portrayal by sharing and celebrating good practice; and 'talent executives' and other recruiters into the media industry should take specific action to address the shortage of openly lesbian and bisexual presenters.[68]

More specifically in the context of media representation, in 2005 Stonewall conducted research into how the BBC represents lesbian, gay and bisexual people. They monitored 168 hours of peak-time TV on BBC One and BBC Two. During that time, lesbian and gay people and their lives were realistically portrayed for just six minutes. Moreover, it was found that gay life is most likely to appear in entertainment television, and is rarely featured in factual programmes, like documentaries and the news. Likewise, it was noted that BBC programmes frequently use gay sexuality to make jokes or as an insult, and rely heavily on stereotypes.[69]

In 2010, similar research was carried out regarding LGB people's representation in Youth television. Key findings from the sample of 126 hours demonstrate that 49 per cent of all portrayal was stereotypical. Gay

---

66 See Cowan (2007), p. 13.
67 See Guasp (2013), p. 3.
68 See *ibid*, p. 22. The Creative Diversity Network is a forum made up of the biggest names in the broadcast industry, including BAFTA, BBC, Channel 4, Creative Skillset, PACT, ITN, Media Trust, S4C, Sky and Turner Broadcasting. Its mission is to take joint responsibility for action on diversity.
69 See Cowan and Valentine (2006), p. 6.

people were depicted as figures of fun, predatory or promiscuous; 31 per cent of all portrayal was realistic but negative, gay people were upset or distressed, most often about their sexual orientation; passing references depicted gay people largely for comic effect, to tease or insult; only seven minutes featured scenes where homophobia was challenged; and only 37 seconds of 126 hours and 42 minutes of output portrayed a scene where sexuality was an explicit focus in a positive and realistic context.[70] The recommendations that followed this research resonate with previous recommendations and many of them can be extended to challenge ED on other grounds besides sexual orientation. For example, some of the recommendations of this study include guidelines that should be developed between broadcasters and Ofcom to ensure more positive portrayals of gay characters; young people don't want to see gay participants (in game, chat and reality shows) recruited if their sexual orientation is being used simply for entertainment value; and programme makers should be given guidance on how to avoid casual or inadvertent homophobia and also on how to challenge homophobia appropriately where it arises.[71]

Stonewall's findings about the opinion of gay and straight people from across the UK reveal that it is necessary to have more documentaries to help everyone understand lesbian and gay lives and not just ones focusing on negative issues; more positive role models for young gay people; more realistic and non-sensationalised/clichéd gay characters in soaps and drama; and a more diverse range of lesbian and gay identities beyond the urban stereotypes.[72] Besides the many recommendations Stonewall has made to the media, it has set up a 'media monitor' to improve the reporting of lesbian, gay and bisexual media issues by helping people to tell the media what they think. However, the outcome of the complaints from the public is determined by the media industry (Chapter 7). Ligali also monitors mainstream media. Their actions include monitoring, investigating and publicly challenging any media institutions that publish, broadcast, perform or distribute material that is 'defamatory', anti-African, sexist and offensive to African people in Britain and throughout the world. The organisation aims to eradicate negative ethnic and cultural stereotypes and images across the media and challenge historically ingrained perceptions that stigmatise and caricature African people. Part of this monitoring also involves challenging media and institutional use of offensive, degrading and repressive terminology that seeks to dehumanise African people and disconnect them from their culture and history. With regard to the issues of visibility and stereotypical representation, the organisation

70 Guasp (2010), pp. 3, 14.
71 *Ibid*, pp. 16–17.
72 Cowan and Valentine (2006), p. 7.

encourages the media institutions to incorporate a sufficient quantity of quality African British programming into their schedules, particularly that which does not conform to a stereotypical and offensive remit.

Another example of research carried out by the organised civil society with regard to media representation is the work of the Islamic Human Rights Commission.[73] In 2007 it produced a study entitled *The British Media and Muslim Representation: The Ideology of Demonisation*. This research identifies the language and discourse relating to Islam and Muslims prevalent in television, news programmes, literature (both classic and popular) and mainstream cinema films. The study addresses the following questions: how has the western media generally covered Islam and Muslims? What are the prevailing discourses about Islam and Muslims that can be identified in selected forms of media? What are the concerns about media reporting and why does representation matter? And, what action can Muslims expect the government to take to remedy unfairness?[74] Their concern about 'representation in the media' has to do with the consideration that media representation of 'minorities' and 'minority group' issues – or indeed the lack of representation – is a key factor in determining how 'majority' audiences think about 'minorities' in their societies. According to the study: 'Whilst on the one hand media creates the "invisibility of minorities" by marginalising their voices, on the other, actual portrayals more often than not fall into restricted and negatively stereotyped contexts.'[75]

Making use of both theoretical analyses on representation and empirical studies undertaken by the Commission itself, the research points out – and coincides with Ligali's and Stonewall's view – that the issue of misrepresentation is not disconnected from discrimination and injustice in other contexts since the media discourse is often the main source of people's knowledge, attitudes and prejudices. Moreover, it adds that when discourse is about 'minority groups' and the audience has limited contact with these groups, the role of the media as the sole provider of information becomes even more critical.[76]

The research concludes that, from a human rights perspective, 'demonised representation' is one of the deepest and most effective anti-human rights practices, as it has the potential not just to 'libel' or demonise a particular person, but can demonise all members of the represented community, e.g. all Muslims or all British Muslims. The potential for societal

73 The Islamic Human Rights Commission was set up in 1997. It is an independent, not-for-profit campaign, research and advocacy organisation based in London, UK. It has consultative status with the UN Economic and Social Council. See www.ihrc.org (accessed 2 March 2015).
74 See Ameli *et al* (2007), p. 9.
75 *Ibid*, p. 8.
76 *Ibid*.

discord as a result is clear and, as the research shows, is in part understood to be having serious repercussions for the everyday lives of 'minorities', particularly Muslim 'minorities' in the UK.[77] Government and other relevant institutions can implement the recommendations contained in the research. They are divided into three strands of action: tackling structural/institutionalised Islamophobia; dealing with problematic content; and facilitating understanding of Muslim standpoint(s) within the media. With regard to representation,

> Notable complaints include the perpetual portrayal of Muslims in dramas as problematic, terrorists, violent, misogynistic etc, and necessarily so as defined by their religion. By perpetuating such stereotypes, the cycle of vilification remains unbroken. As drama often follows news, many long running series are currently weaving terrorist criminality involving Muslims into their plots. Other recurring storylines involve forced marriage. There are few if any notable fictional characters who are incidentally (religiously) Muslim or whose religiosity is a positive factor in a storyline.[78]

The recommendations of the Commission are thus to monitor the representation of Muslims. This task is initially in the hands of the broadcasters. However, according to the Commission, government needs to be involved in order to avoid a superficial self-analysis by media producers.[79] Likewise, the Commission recommends effective consultation; both the Government and the media are called on to consult with scholars who are qualified to give rulings and statements on Muslim issues, and to state which scholars they have consulted. Other organisations, such as 'Media Diversified', coincide with this point and have indeed created a *Media Diversified Experts Directory*. This is a resource for media outlets of all sizes across all mediums. It is a searchable and managed database of experts and professionals from a variety of fields, all of whom have experience in media settings. The directory connects broadcast, print and radio producers with commentators who have expertise on a wide range of topics and come from diverse backgrounds.[80] This initiative was created in the context of the latest Creative Skillset census, referred to earlier (III), and

---

77 See *ibid*, p. 98.
78 *Ibid*, p. 100.
79 *Ibid*.
80 Live since July 2013, Media Diversified is a non-profit organisation which seeks to cultivate and promote skilled 'writers of colour' by providing advice and contacts and by promoting content online through its own platform. See http://directory.mediadiversified. org (accessed 2 March 2015).

which showed a decline in the percentage of BAME working in the media industry; from 7.4 per cent in 2006 to 5.4 per cent in 2012.[81]

Effective consultation, according to the Islamic Human Rights Commission, enables those with questions about the validity of portrayals or discussion about Muslims to provide effective critiques. The research insists that Muslims welcome debate and discussion about their beliefs and values – what they complain about is that they are unable to articulate their viewpoints and reciprocate critique on a level playing field. In addition, it is claimed that consultation with Muslims should not simply be about 'Muslim issues'. Muslims are also citizens and if they or any other group are not represented and/or have no voice, media producers need to question this absence and its implications for the credibility of the media.[82] Paying attention to context, including the existence of diverse opinions within Islam, is also considered important in determining whether there is unfair representation and thus forms part of the recommendations. The Commission seeks contextualisation about both controversial and uncontroversial aspects of Islam. In their research they point out that even basic aspects of Islam are portrayed in negative and uncontextualised ways. Thus, for example, practices such as 'arranged' marriages are portrayed as 'forced' marriages rather than marriages by introduction and are assumed to be the norm.[83]

With specific regard to representation (the way in which Muslims are portrayed), the Commission's recommendations are aimed at tackling overt vilification and demonisation of Muslims. In their view, effective recourse must be made available to those offended to: (1) complain about offending work, and (2) to achieve some form of recompense, either by way of apology, correction or right of reply.[84] In the opinion of the Commission, self-regulation needs to be coupled with effective forms of accountability which ultimately only government can set.[85] Current watchdogs, as perceived by the respondents in the Commission's research, afford little scope for people to complain about generalised prejudice in the media. Respondents stated time and again that they had given up complaining about misrepresentation as nothing was done. In order to respond to this, a central recommendation is to enact legislation that would create watchdogs with teeth, which in turn would prevent irresponsible production.[86]

Ligali's dissatisfaction with the way in which mainstream media operates and about its products is also clear. They have indeed opted for the

81 Brooks *et al* (2012), p. 4.
82 Ameli *et al* (2007), p. 103.
83 *Ibid*, p. 102.
84 *Ibid*, pp. 100–101.
85 *Ibid*, p. 102.
86 *Ibid*, p. 101.

creation of an 'African media', which includes creating cultural media resources of diverse educational, historical, social, artistic and current African interests presented and produced by African people with the primary aim of empowering and informing. This is to be achieved by establishing and/or supporting independent African British national TV and radio stations, together with production companies that adhere to a principle of social, community and political responsibility. While it is important that disadvantaged groups design their own way forward and work together as a group for their own self-fulfilment without 'outsider' interference, the case of the media is special, as we have seen. Mass media should not be a means for the exclusive dissemination of dominant values; it should be a public forum, open, plural and, most important of all, subject to contestation (Chapters 7 and 8).

These are only some organisations, which indeed are quite complex, and a deeper analysis of their ideology and structure would be desirable. However, they have only been presented here as examples because the claims, points of view and proposals of the targets of ED should be central guidelines for any actions taken towards its redress. Importantly, too, they embody and confirm the validity of stereotyping theory already discussed. Moreover, these organisations show striking parallels. On the one hand, regarding their identification of the role of demeaning representation in the bigger picture of discrimination; and, on the other, regarding their dissatisfaction and limited power, as things stand now, to effectively challenge mainstream media despite the force and persuasiveness of their arguments.

V Conclusions

Demeaning stereotypical representation in the media is one of the most pervasive forms that ED takes. Stereotypes are very often – consciously or unconsciously – the drivers of discrimination. They frequently determine the treatment the targeted groups receive and can indeed hinder their participation as peers in society.

In the experience of the organised civil society that challenges discrimination, demeaning stereotypical representation in the media is but one of many interrelated discriminatory practices that disadvantage the target groups. Organisations contesting discrimination have undertaken a variety of projects aimed at challenging group-specific disadvantages, including challenging the media for its production and reproduction of demeaning stereotypes. The problem in this regard is that the media is more powerful than they are and often has the last word (Chapter 7).

Now that we have explained that ED is a matter of injustice (misrecognition) and a form of discrimination at a cultural level, the next three chapters will provide examples of ways in which law at both international and local levels has understood and addressed the kind of harm ED creates.

VI References

Abrams, Dominic and Houston, Diane M. (2006), 'Equality, diversity and prejudice in Britain'. Report for the Cabinet Office Equalities Review 2006, Centre for the Study of Group Processes, University of Kent.

Ainsworth, Stuart (1997), 'Banning Manning vs. whitewashing racism'. Paper delivered at the 1997 International Society of Humor Studies Annual Conference, Oklahoma City, USA.

Althusser, Louis (2001), *Lenin and Philosophy and Other Essays*, New York: Monthly Review Press.

Ameli, Saied, Marandi, Syed Mohammed, Ahmed, Sameera, Kara, Seyfeddin and Merali, Arzu (2007), *The British Media and Muslim Representation: The Ideology of Demonisation*, British Muslims Expectations of the Government, Islamic Human Rights Commission.

Baker, William and Dessart, George (1998), *Down the Tube: an Inside Account of the Failure of American Television*, New York: Basic Books.

Baker, John, Lynch, Kathleen, Cantillon, Sara and Walsh, Judy (2004), *Equality: From Theory to Action*, Houndmills: Palgrave Macmillan.

Brooks, David, Campbell, Mike, Connolly, Milo; Heyer, Neil and Flintham, Neil (2012), *Creative Skillset Employment Census of the Creative Media Industries*, Creative Skillset.

Brown, Rupert (1995), *Prejudice: It's Social Psychology*, Oxford: Blackwell.

Carrington, Ben (2010), *Race, Sport and Politics: The Sporting Black Diaspora*, London: Sage.

Chomsky, Noam (2002), *Media Control: The Spectacular Achievements of Propaganda*, 2nd ed., New York: Seven Stories Press.

Clark, Kenneth and Clark, Mamie (1947), 'Racial identification and preference in negro children', in Maccoby, Elenor ed., *Readings in Social Psychology*, New York: Henry Holt.

Collinson, David, Knights, David and Collinson, Margaret (1990), *Managing to Discriminate*, London: Routledge.

Connolly, Michael (2004), *Townshend-Smith on Discrimination Law: Text, Cases and Materials*, London: Cavendish.

Cosby, Camille (1994), *Television's Imageable Influences*, Lanham, MD: University Press of America.

Cowan, Katherine (2007), *Living Together: British Attitudes to Lesbian and Gay People*, Stonewall.

Cowan, Katherine and Valentine, Gill (2006), *Tuned Out: The BBC's Portrayal of Lesbian and Gay People*, Stonewall.

Dyer, Richard (2002), *The Matter of Images: Essays on Representation*, 2nd ed., London: Routledge.

Eagleton, Terry (1991), *Ideology: An Introduction*, London: Verso.

Fanon, Franz (1990), *The Wretched of the Earth*, Harmondsworth: Penguin Books.

Fraser, Nancy (2003), 'Social justice in the age of identity politics: redistribution, recognition, and participation', in Fraser, Nancy and Honneth, Axel, *Redistribution or Recognition? A Political-Philosophical Exchange*, London: Verso.

Goldhagen, Daniel Jonah (1996), *Hitler's Willing Executioners: Ordinary Germans and the Holocaust*, London: Vintage Books.

Goodall, Kay (2007), 'Incitement to religious hatred: all talk and no substance'. *Modern Law Review*, vol. 70, no. 1.

Gramsci, Antonio (1971), *Selections from the Prison Notebooks of Antonio Gramsci*, ed. and tr. Quintin Hoare and Geoffry Nowell-Smith, London: Lawrence and Wishart.

Greenberg, Bradley (1972), 'Children's reaction to TV blacks', *Journalism Q* vol. 7, no. 101.

Guasp, April (2009), *The Teachers' Report: Homophobic Bullying in Britain's Schools*, Stonewall.

Guasp, April (2010), *Unseen on Screen: LGB People in Youth TV*, Stonewall.

Guasp, April (2013), *Gay in Britain: Lesbian, Gay and Bisexual People's Experiences and Expectations of Discrimination*, Stonewall.

Guasp, April, Ellison, Gavin and Satara, Tasha (2014), *The Teachers' Report: Homophobic Bullying in Britain's Schools*, Stonewall.

Hall, Stuart (1971), 'Black men, white media', BBC Television debate on racial images, as quoted in *The Chronicle*, independent internet magazine focusing on the black African Caribbean experience in Britain and the African diaspora, available at www.thechronicle.demon.co.uk (accessed 19 August 2008).

Hall, Stuart, ed. (1997), *Representation, Cultural Representation and Signifying Practices*, Milton Keynes: Open University Press.

Hoberman, John (1997), *Darwin's Athletes: How Sport has Damaged Black America and Preserved the Myth of Race*, Boston, MA: Houghton Mifflin.

Home Office (1999), 'Report of the Macpherson Inquiry' Cm. 4262-I, February 24.

Huston, Aletha (1992), *Big World, Small Screen*, Lincoln, NB: University of Nebraska Press.

Jenkins, Richard (1986), *Racism and Recruitment: Managers, Organisations and Equal Opportunity in the Labour Market*, Cambridge: Cambridge University Press.

Jones, Owen (2011), *Chavs: The Demonization of the Working Class*, London: Verso.

Kretzmer, David (1987), 'Freedom of speech and racism', *Cardozo Law Review*, vol. 8, no. 445.

Lippmann, Walter (1922), *Public Opinion*, New York: Harcourt Brace.

MacKinnon, Catharine (1994), *Only Words*, London: Harper Collins.

Parenti, Michael (1986), *Inventing Reality: The Politics of News Media*, New York: St. Martin's Press.

Peterson, Anaya Royce (1982), *Ethnic Identity: Strategies of Diversity*, Bloomington, IN: Indiana University Press.

Poindexter, Paula and Stroman, Carolyn (1981), 'Blacks and television: a review of the research literature', *Journal of Broadcasting*, vol. 103.

Ramírez Berg, Charles (2002), *Latino Images in Film: Stereotypes, Subversion and Resistance*, Austin, TX: University of Texas Press.

Roman, Ediberto (2000), 'Who exactly is living la vida loca? The legal and political consequences of Latino-Latina ethnic and racial stereotypes in film and other media', *Journal of Gender, Race and* Justice, vol. 4, no. 37.

Ronner, Amy (1997), 'The Cassandra curse: the stereotype of the female liar resurfaces in Jones v. Clinton', *University of California, Davis Law Review*, vol. 31, no. 123.

Stroman, Carolyn (1991), 'Television's role in the socialization of African American children and adolescents', *Journal of Negro Education*, vol. 60.

Sunstein, Cass (2007), *Republic.com 2.0*, Princeton, NJ: Princeton University Press.

Williams, Rachel (2014), 'Police officer Carol Howard v the Met: "I was absolutely humiliated"', *Guardian*, 9 September, available at www.theguardian.com/uk-news/2014/sep/09/carol-howard-black-female-police-officer-discrimination-met-tribual-victory (accessed 20 August 2015).

Wimmer, Kurt (1986), 'Deregulation and the market failure in minority programming', *Hastings Communications and Entertainment Law Journal*, vol. 8, no. 329.

Worthy, Patricia (1995), 'Diversity and minority stereotyping in the television media: the unsettled First Amendment issue', *Hastings Communications and Entertainment Law Journal*, vol. 18, no. 509.

Young, Iris Marion (1990), *Justice and the Politics of Difference*, Princeton, NJ: Princeton University Press.

Chapter 5

International and regional underpinnings for the redress of *everyday discrimination*

I Introduction

The images and messages that have been identified as *everyday discrimination* (ED) are an integral part of discrimination at the cultural level. This includes a multiplicity of overlapping, socially constructed ideas, meanings, behaviours and practices that can be represented through the spoken and written language, images, gestures and even silence in everyday social life, as well as within institutions, and they can incorporate demeaning humour and stereotypes. These ideas, meanings, behaviours and practices are manufactured and reproduced in a variety of ways, including through the mass media, which is particularly important given its power without significant challenge to transmit images and messages that demean and degrade entire categories of disadvantaged people.

The international community, through the United Nations (UN) and regional systems such as the European Council and the European Union, have acknowledged the role of culture in discrimination and, indeed, the role of speech and the media in maintaining and reinforcing discrimination. Concern over hate speech is particularly well documented (Chapter 6). However, the international community has also shown concern about more generalised ways in which hostility and disrespect towards certain groups are manifested through speech; nevertheless, the language used to refer to these more subtle forms is not straightforward and there is no recognised/singular concept to define them. Sometimes, as we shall see, international instruments refer to the media's role in perpetuating those stereotypes that constrain women's opportunities and are gender discriminatory, to forms of unfair portrayal, to the media's contribution to the spread of xenophobic and racist sentiments, and to the need for tolerance and respect for the equal dignity of all human beings.

Exploring some of the UN and regional instruments that have addressed both the role of culture in discrimination generally and the role of the media in discrimination in particular, this chapter will demonstrate that ED is a worldwide concern that dates back at least to the 1970s and that issues raised since then remain relevant today.

II United Nations

The UN has shown concern about the harm inflicted on women both through a lack of participation in the media industry and through demeaning and stereotypical representation in media products. *The Platform for Action of the Beijing Conference on Women 1995*[1] is the most explicit instrument addressing discrimination against women in the media. Based on the Conference's diagnosis, the Platform for Action denounces the fact that the lack of balanced pictures of women's diverse lives and contributions to society together with violent and degrading or pornographic media products are negatively affecting women and their participation in society.

Within the Platform there are two strategic objectives which it can be said are related to 'discrimination in the media', both with regard to discrimination in participation and discrimination through portrayal. The Strategic Objective (J.1) is to increase the participation and access of women to expression and decision-making in and through the media and new technologies of communication; and the Strategic Objective (J.2) is to promote a balanced and non-stereotyped portrayal of women in the media. The Platform for Action clearly acknowledges that women's participation in the media is essential to combat gender discrimination. Women's participation is not only necessary in quantity in order to tackle under-representation in the industry's workforce and positions of power and decision-making; participation is also important when considering the kind of roles women play in media products. Additionally, the Platform stresses the need to actively involve women in the development of the codes and guidelines that will promote a balanced and non-stereotyped portrayal of women (at 241 (d)). Moreover, in order to monitor these commitments the actions foreseen by the Platform include the need to establish media watch groups that can monitor and consult with the media in order to ensure that women's needs and concerns are properly reflected (at 242 (a)).

With regard to women's portrayal in particular, the Platform lists a series of actions that should be taken. In general terms these are aimed at promoting research and strategies for information and education, not only for the public at large via campaigns to raise awareness, but also at the institutional level by encouraging gender-sensitive training for media professionals, including media owners and managers. More specifically in this regard, there is a call to develop approaches and train experts who can apply gender

---

1 UN, *Beijing Declaration and Platform for Action*, adopted at the Fourth World Conference on Women, 27 October 1995. The UK was represented at this Conference.

analysis to media programmes (at 245 (e)). In order to achieve a fairer portrayal that simultaneously challenges current sex-role stereotypes, the Platform includes provisions regarding the promotion of the equal sharing of family responsibilities and the dissemination of information aimed at eliminating spousal and child abuse and all forms of violence against women, including domestic violence (at 245 (a)). At the same time, it highlights the need to produce media materials about women leaders, *inter alia*, as leaders who bring to their position of leadership many different life experiences and multiple roles. More specifically a provision in this regard is to encourage the media to refrain from presenting women as inferior beings and exploiting them as sexual objects and commodities, rather than presenting them as creative human beings, key actors and contributors to and beneficiaries of the process of development (at 243 (d)).

The Platform stresses the necessity of promoting the concept that sexist stereotypes displayed in the media are 'gender discriminatory', degrading in nature and offensive (at 243 (e)). It also makes clear that local legislation is needed, especially in the case of pornography and the projection of violence against women and children in the media (at 243 (f)). Specifically, there is a call to governments and other relevant actors to promote an active and visible policy of mainstreaming a gender perspective in policies and programmes (at 238).

The Platform's provisions also concern advertising organisations since the Conference concluded that there is a worldwide trend towards consumerism that has created a climate in which advertisements and commercial messages often portray women primarily as consumers and target girls and women of all ages inappropriately (at 236). Moreover, as the diagnosis produced by the Conference concluded, the lack of gender sensitivity in the media can be found generally, in public, local, national and international media organisations; and therefore, the Platform called on governments to encourage, consistent with freedom of expression, the positive involvement of the media in development and social issues (at 239 (h)).

The position of women varies extensively locally, nationally and internationally, particularly when examining the media as an institution and its employment of women. Therefore, what for some women today is an already accomplished goal, for other women there is still a long way to go to achieve. Moreover, while the Conference dates back to 1995, 20 years later many of the issues raised, particularly about women's representation, remain visibly relevant today in mainstream media, including the internet. According to the *Geneva NGO Forum Beijing+20*, gender discrimination and stereotyping remain an issue which nowadays is exacerbated by new technologies and social media.[2] Hence it is the case that the guidelines

---

2 See UN Economic Commission for Europe, *Geneva NGO Forum Beijing+20, Regional Review Outcome Document Declaration and Recommendations*, 3–5 November 2014, p. 12.

and provisions included in the Platform are still valuable reflections worth remembering, updating and echoing.

Making changes in education in order to challenge discrimination at a cultural level, including discriminatory messages and stereotypes, is one of the oldest and recurrent proposals within UN instruments. In this regard, the *Convention on the Elimination of all Forms of Discrimination Against Women* (CEDAW), pointed out in 1979 that it was necessary to revise textbooks, school programmes and teaching methods with a view to eliminating stereotyped concepts.[3] This Convention is often described as an international bill of rights for women. It defines what constitutes discrimination against women and sets up an agenda for national action to end such discrimination. The Convention aims at *enlarging our understanding of human rights*, as it formally recognises the influence of *culture and tradition* in restricting women's enjoyment of their fundamental rights. In fact, noting the relationship between culture and the constraints on women's social, political and economic lives, the preamble of the Convention stresses that 'a change in the traditional role of men as well as the role of women in society and in the family is needed to achieve full equality of men and women'. This means that States parties are therefore obliged to work towards the modification of social and cultural patterns of individual conduct in order to eliminate 'prejudices and customary and all other practices which are based on the idea of the inferiority or the superiority of either of the sexes or on stereotyped roles for men and women' (article 5).

The role of culture and tradition in maintaining discrimination can be seen in stereotypes, customs, norms and mores which give rise to the multitude of legal, social, political and economic constraints on the advancement of women. That said, these stereotypes, customs, norms and mores are not only promoted by tradition, religion or practices justified through religious beliefs, but also by the mass media through its constant demeaning representations and degrading pornography, which in Western democratic societies are often celebrated, promoted and protected as free speech. The UN analysis of 'Harmful Traditional Practices' 20 years ago expressed the need to challenge the practices that reinforce the economic and political subordination of women, perpetuate their inferior status and inhibit structural and attitudinal changes to eliminate

---

3 UN General Assembly, *Convention on the Elimination of all Forms of Discrimination Against Women*, 18 December 1979, UN Treaty Series, vol. 1249, article 10(c). The UK (with reservations regarding articles 1, 2, 9, 11, 13, 15 and 16) is a State Party to this Convention. The implementation of CEDAW is monitored by the UN Committee on the Elimination of Discrimination Against Women. State parties must submit a report to the Committee every four years, setting out how they are implementing the Convention. See, for example, the Submission on the Seventh Periodic Report of the United Kingdom, Equality and Human Rights Commission (2013).

gender inequality.[4] Cultural practices that are harmful to women in the west, such as certain 'beauty' practices including cosmetic surgery and the sexual objectification of women in popular culture and advertising, were not included.[5] There seems to have been a western bias in the selection of practices that fitted the UN category.[6] Indeed, the only western practice included in the UN analysis was violence against women. The other practices considered – not often associated with western values or traditions – were female genital mutilation, forced feeding of women, early marriage, son preference and its implications for the status of the girl child, female infanticide, dowry price, virginity tests and foot binding. Although in some ways considered harmful, western practices such as the promotion of a particular body image, the use of women as sexual objects for entertainment and advertising, and generally the social valuing of women's appearance and youth over their intelligence, capacities and contributions to society have not been understood in the international arena as 'harmful traditional practices'. This omission was unfortunate. It replicated the dominant culture's view that only the practices of 'others' are 'cultural' while 'ours' are natural and 'normal' and it fails to call on western State parties to examine their own engrained cultural practices that harm women and their health.

These things said, however, the concluding observations that followed the last examination of the UK's progress in advancing CEDAW's commitments in 2013 revealed that women's sexual stereotyping in the media is considered an issue that affects women, particularly in matters of power, decision-making and voice. The CEDAW Committee signalled its concern about the high degree of stereotyping and use of sexual images of women by the media and in advertising, an issue highlighted in the Leveson Inquiry.[7] However, the Committee also noted the efforts made in the UK to raise awareness of body confidence issues. CEDAW recommendations are therefore to:

> Continue to work with the media and advertising industries to stop them representing women and girls in a stereotypical way and to put into effect the recommendations of the Leveson Inquiry, including

4 See UN Office of the High Commissioner for Human Rights, Fact Sheet No. 23, *Harmful Traditional Practices Affecting the Health of Women and Children*, August 1995.

5 See Zanardo (2010).

6 See Jeffreys (2005). Jeffreys argues that western beauty practices such as make-up, dress codes, cosmetic surgery (self-mutilation by proxy) and labiaplasty do fit the criteria of harmful cultural practices. They are a form of oppression and should be included within UN understandings of harmful cultural practices.

7 The Leveson Inquiry on the culture, practice and ethics of the press will be addressed in Chapter 7.

having a regulator to stop the media reporting in a discriminatory way.[8]

The work in relation to 'body confidence issues' that CEDAW noted is the *UK Government Body Confidence Campaign* that recognises that both sexes are burdened by popular culture, which often results in low body confidence and low self-esteem. There is a particular impact on women and girls, with many females appearing heavily 'photoshopped' with 'perfectly thin' figures. Actions taken so far include the creation of an industry award to reward the inclusion of body diversity in magazines and the development of a teaching pack for primary schools to help understand the doctoring of body image in the media and ensure that children are educated on this issue.[9]

Another example of international concern about stereotyping in the media is in the *Durban Declaration and Programme of Action, 2001*.[10] One of the most important contributions of this Declaration is its acknowledgement of the importance of taking into account the context where stereotyping takes place. The report expresses this as follows:

> We are conscious that humanity's history is replete with terrible wrongs inflicted through lack of respect for the equality of human beings and note with alarm the increase of such practices in various parts of the world, and we urge people, particularly in conflict situations, to desist from racist incitement, derogatory language and negative stereotyping.
>
> (General Issue 62)

Context is paramount in determining whether there is discrimination and it is often a conflict situation that triggers discrimination and stereotyping. Specifically with regard to the media, the Declaration noted that

> certain media, by promoting false images and negative stereotypes of vulnerable individuals or groups of individuals, particularly of migrants and refugees, have contributed to the spread of xenophobic and racist sentiments among the public and in some cases have encouraged violence by racist individuals and groups.
>
> (General Issue 89)

8 Equality and Human Rights Commission (2014). See, in particular, 'Eliminating sexual stereotyping in the media', pp. 54–55.
9 See Government Equalities Office (2013).
10 UN, *Durban Declaration and Programme of Action,* adopted at the World Conference Against Racism, Racial Discrimination, Xenophobia and Related Intolerance, 8 September 2001. The UK was represented at this Conference.

In order to redress the harm inflicted through stereotypes, the Programme of Action calls on governments to intensify their efforts in the field of education and to encourage the media to avoid stereotyping based on racism, racial discrimination, xenophobia and related intolerance (Issue 146). Specifically, it urges States to include human rights education, in order to promote an understanding and awareness of the causes, consequences and evils of racism, racial discrimination, xenophobia and related intolerance. It encourages educational authorities and the private sector to develop educational materials, including textbooks and dictionaries, aimed at combating these phenomena. In this context, it calls upon States to give importance to textbook and curriculum review and amendment, so as to eliminate any elements that might promote racism, racial discrimination, xenophobia and related intolerance or reinforce negative stereotypes, and to include material that refutes such stereotypes (Issue 127).

The issues raised and the calls on governments included in this *Declaration and Programme of Action* remain, if not more so, highly relevant today and indeed, the concerns about migrants' representation and reporting in the media have intensified, particularly after the World Economic Crisis that started in 2007, which has often found a scapegoat in migration (Chapter 4, II), and the mass migration to Europe from Syria and other war-torn African and Middle Eastern countries in 2015. Nevertheless, further follow-up events to this Declaration proved problematic. Arguing issues related to the potential of the Conference to curb freedom of expression and promote anti-Semitism, many western states boycotted the *Durban Review Conference of 2009*, held in Geneva on 20–24 April 2009, where indeed the Iranian President Mahmoud Ahmedinejad gave an inflammatory speech condemning Israel as racist and questioning the Holocaust.[11] Subsequently, the General Assembly High-level Meeting of 22 September 2011 to commemorate the *10th Anniversary of the Durban Declaration and Programme of Action* was also boycotted by many western states, including this time the UK.[12] Given the political complexities of this decision, and the various issues around the Durban follow-up events which deserve an in-depth examination, I have only focused on some of the points related to the role of the media and culture in discrimination. These were issues raised in the Declaration of 2001 (adopted by consensus) and they remain relevant today for the lives of people currently affected by racism, xenophobia and related forms of intolerance.

11 Various representatives at the 2009 Conference walked out during Ahmedinejad's speech. See Pogrund (2009).
12 See Bayefsky (2011).

Tensions in the international community regarding freedom of expression and religious intolerance and discrimination intensified after the 9/11 terrorist attacks on the US. However, they existed before. Indeed, the UN passed for a number of years, since 1999, a series of controversial Resolutions tabled by the Organisation of the Islamic Conference aimed at 'combating defamation of religions'. These Resolutions included concern about religious stereotyping and negative representation in the media on the one hand, and concern about manifestations of intolerance and discrimination in matters of religion and belief on the other. The last Resolution addressing these issues using the language of 'defamation' passed in 2010 (UN Human Rights Council, Resolution 13/16, 'Combating defamation of religions', A/HRC/RES/13/16, 15.4.2010). It exposed the need to take measures to eliminate the increasing acts of racism and xenophobia (at 13), and concern about the introduction and enforcement of laws and administrative measures that specifically discriminate against and target persons with certain ethnic and religious backgrounds, particularly Muslim minorities following the events of 11 September 2001 (at 5).

With specific regard to the media, the Resolution of 2010 deplored the use of the print, audio-visual and electronic media, including the internet, and any other means to incite acts of violence, xenophobia or related intolerance and discrimination towards any religion, as well as the targeting of religious symbols, places and venerated persons (at 10). The call was for governments to provide within their respective legal and constitutional systems adequate protection against acts of hatred, discrimination, intimidation and coercion 'resulting from defamation of religions', and incitement to religious hatred in general, and to take all possible measures to promote tolerance and respect for all religions and beliefs (at 14).

These Resolutions were severely criticised, the argument being that the concept of 'defamation of religions' runs against international law and free speech. Moreover, it was feared that they had the potential to promote and strengthen already existing blasphemy laws.[13] Other critics, while acknowledging existing instances of hostility and discrimination based on religion or belief, opposed the protection of religions as such

---

13 See, for example, article 19 (2010); Groves (2008); and Langer (2014).

and argue instead for the protection of believers.[14] This line of argument was successful and in 2011 the Human Rights Council shifted from protecting beliefs to protection of believers in its Resolution 16/18 on 'Combating intolerance, negative stereotyping and stigmatisation of, and discrimination, incitement to violence and violence against, persons based on religion or belief'.[15] Similarly, the same year, the Human Rights Committee, released General Comment No. 34, 'Article 19: Freedoms of opinion and expression'. According to its paragraph 48,

> Prohibitions of displays of lack of respect for a religion or other belief system, including blasphemy laws are incompatible with the Covenant, except in the specific circumstances envisaged in article 20, paragraph 2 of the Covenant. Such prohibitions must also comply with the strict requirements of article 19, paragraph 3, as well as such articles as 2, 5, 17, 18 and 26. Thus, for instance, it would be impermissible for any such laws to discriminate in favour of or against one or certain religions or belief systems, or their adherents over another, or religious believers over non-believers. Nor would it be permissible for such prohibitions to be used to prevent or punish criticism of religious leaders or commentary on religious doctrine and tenets of faith.[16]

In this context it is worth remembering that the common law offences of blasphemy and blasphemous libel in England and Wales – which only

14 See, for example, UN General Assembly, *Report of the United Nations High Commissioner for Human Rights and Follow-up to the World Conference on Human Rights*, Addendum. Expert seminar on the links between articles 19 and 20 of the International Covenant on Civil and Political Rights: 'Freedom of expression and advocacy of religious hatred that constitutes incitement to discrimination, hostility or violence' (Geneva, 2–3 October 2008), A/HRC/10/31/Add.3 of 16 January 2009. The objective of the Expert seminar was twofold: to address the underlying human rights concerns behind the concept of 'defamation of religions', presenting an approach based on human rights law; and to ensure a sound legal interpretation of articles 19 and 20 of the Covenant. See also the points of view raised in Council of Europe, 'European Commission for democracy through law (Venice Commission). Report on the relationship between freedom of expression and freedom of religion: the issue of regulation and prosecution of blasphemy, religious insult and incitement to religious hatred', adopted by the Venice Commission at its 76th Plenary Session (17–18 October 2008), CDL-AD(2008)026, 23 October 2008. Similarly, the Parliamentary Assembly of the Council of Europe has issued two documents in this topic. See, Recommendation 1805(2007) on 'Blasphemy, religious insults and hate speech against persons on grounds of their religion', 16 September 2008; and Resolution 1510(2006) on 'Freedom of expression and respect for religious beliefs', 28 June 2006.
15 See, UN General Assembly, Human Rights Council Resolution, A/HRC/RES/16/18, 12 April 2011, This is the landmark resolution which replaced calls to combat 'defamation of religions' with commitments to address religious intolerance through the promotion of freedom of expression, freedom of religion or belief and non-discrimination.
16 UN ICCPR Human Rights Committee, General Comment No. 34, 'Article 19: freedoms of opinion and expression', CCPR/C/GC/34, 12 September 2011.

protected the Christian faith – were only abolished relatively recently by the Criminal Justice and Immigration Act 2008, ch. 5, s. 79.[17] The latest Resolution on 'Combating intolerance, negative stereotyping and stigmatisation of, and discrimination, incitement to violence and violence against, persons based on religion or belief' was adopted by consensus in 2013.[18] In a similar way to its predecessors, this Resolution expresses deep concern at 'the continued serious instances of derogatory stereotyping, negative profiling and stigmatisation of persons based on their religion or belief, as well as programmes and agendas pursued by extremist organisations and groups, in particular when condoned by Governments' (at 1). Many of its recommendations are in line with the remedies pursued in this book in order to confront the images and messages of ED and indeed they also coincide with the measures provided for by other UN instruments seeking to redress cultural aspects of discrimination as we have seen. For example, the Resolution considers education, awareness-building and dialogue as useful mechanisms for combating denigration, negative religious stereotyping and existing misconceptions (at 4, 6 and 8 (g)). The Resolution recognises that 'the open public debate of ideas, as well as interfaith and intercultural dialogue, at the local, national and international levels can be among the best protections against religious intolerance and can play a positive role in strengthening democracy and combating religious hatred' (at 6). This is in tune with the ideas that have been put forward so far in this book. The issue is, however, how to make possible such open dialogue and how to make it fair. As we have anticipated, the targets of discriminatory images and messages should be able to complain on a level playing field and bring their 'counter-arguments' to the public forum so there can be a proper dialogue, but this needs to be legally permitted and institutionally supported, as we shall see in Chapters 7–9.

Some well-known cartoons that have been published by western media in Denmark, *Jyllands-Posten*, and France, *Charlie Hebdo*, depicting Muslims and the Prophet Muhammad in a variety of roles within the 'terrorist/barbaric gaze' have harmed the everyday lives of many individuals and some of the responses against the cartoonists have been simply evil criminal acts.[19] Opinions about the issue are polarised – for and against the production of cartoons of this type – with all sorts of nuances in between which

---

17 The last successful prosecution defined blasphemy as 'any contemptuous, reviling, scurrilous or ludicrous matter relating to God, Jesus Christ or the Bible, or the formularies of the Church of England as by law established'. *Whitehouse v Gay News Ltd and Lemon* [1979] AC 617, at 665.

18 UN General Assembly, Human Rights Council Resolution 22/L.40, A/HRC/22/L.40, 18 March 2013.

19 See, for example, *Kasem Said Ahmad and Asmaa Abdol-Hamid v Denmark*, Communication no. 1487/2006, UN Doc. CCPR/C/92/D/1487/2006, 18 April 2008. See also Alfandari *et al* (2011) and Tariq Ghazi (2006).

should not be disregarded. The novelist and journalist Will Self has pointed out a possible test we could apply to identify whether something is merely offensive, egregiously offensive or in fact political satire if 'by satire is meant the deployment of humour, ridicule, sarcasm and irony in order to achieve moral reform'.[20] Self's test derives from Finley Peter Dunne's idea of what newspapers do, which includes 'afflict the comfortable and comfort the afflicted'.[21] This is what satire should do, but the trouble is, according to Self, that 'with a lot of so-called satire directed against religiously-motivated extremists, it is not clear who it is afflicting, or who it is comforting'.[22] Self questions whether the cartoonists at *Charlie Hebdo* were really satirists and in this question he also considers the fact that the memorial issue of Charlie Hebdo had a print run of 1,000,000 copies, financed by the French Government – the institution satirists should never cease attacking.[23] Consistent with the participatory parity thread embedded in this book, we also need to ask, who constructs the images and messages? Who is in the images? Whose views are represented? Whose views are repressed? What/whose images have we not seen? And in all cases, why? The determination of who in fact is afflicted is problematic and cannot possibly be determined in the abstract; it is context, culture and historically specific, but the questions here proposed can be a start. It is not possible to engage at this point in what should be a lengthy and rigorous case study. However, it is a good opportunity to reiterate the principles that have been identified so far in this book such as the core idea that without an effective opportunity to respond *with speech*, images and messages with power to 'afflict the afflicted' would in fact be sustaining existing relations of oppression and domination. Unchallenged potentially discriminatory images and messages can assert and maintain status subordination; they can constitute obstacles to participatory parity and therefore can be unjust. The following chapters will provide more arguments in this line of thought aiming ultimately at contributing to the achievement of a culture of fair freedom of expression *for all*, which should include a legally backed and effective opportunity to contest mainstream dominant views (including those potentially discriminatory) by mainstream dominant channels. This in the end has the potential to promote a fairer and richer political debate, thereby reinforcing free speech values.

20 See Self (2015a).
21 Dunne was a Chicago-based humorist born in 1867. He was aware of the power of institutions, including his own, and put his description of journalism into the mouth of a fictional Irish bartender, Mr Dooley. See Self (2015b).
22 See Self (2015a).
23 *Ibid.*

III Council of Europe

In 1984 the Council of Europe adopted Recommendation No. R (84) 17 on 'Equality between women and men in the media' (25 September 1984). The Recommendation recognised that the media plays an important part in forming social attitudes and values and offers immense potential as an instrument for social change. It therefore recommended that the governments of the Member States contribute to the promotion of equality between women and men in the electronic and printed media by taking appropriate steps with a view to implementing a series of measures. These measures referred in general terms to both women's participation in the media industry, particularly in media supervision and management bodies (at 6, 8 and 9), and to women's representation (at 3 and 11). In this latter regard, the Recommendation called on governments to stimulate evaluation through national research on the impact and influence of entertainment programmes where sex stereotyping and prejudices are manifest. The issue not explored in 1984 but which should necessarily follow such research is what to do to redress the harm once its significance has been articulated. A later Parliamentary Assembly Resolution 1751(2010) (25 June 2010) on 'Combating sexist stereotypes in the media' revisited the issue and is particularly enlightening about both the nature of the problem and actions that are needed for its redress. The Resolution summarises many of the issues that have been explored so far and, indeed, points out that 'sexist stereotypes are a means of discrimination' (at 3). According to this Resolution.

> The sexist stereotypes conveyed vary from humour and clichés in the traditional media to incitement to gender-based hatred and violence in the Internet. Sexist stereotypes are too frequently trivialised and tolerated under the banner of freedom of expression. Furthermore, these stereotypes are often subtly conveyed by the media which reproduce the attitudes and opinions seen as the norm in societies where gender equality is far from reality. Accordingly, all too often, court action cannot be taken against sexist stereotypes nor can they be penalised by regulatory or self-regulatory authorities except in cases of the most serious violations of human dignity.
>
> (At 2)

The calls made in this Resolution replicate many of the demands made by the organised civil society on other grounds of discrimination, such as race, religion or belief and sexual orientation (Chapter 4, IV) and echo measures such as education and training, which are invariably invoked in order to address discrimination at a cultural level. In this case, in order to learn how to recognise, be aware of and overcome stereotypes, the Resolution refers to the need for education to be involved (at 5). The

Parliamentary Assembly also makes a series of calls which are particularly relevant for the redress of what we have called ED. For example, it calls on Member States to 'promote the introduction and/or effective functioning of regulatory or self-regulatory media authorities to guarantee respect for human dignity; to contribute to the fight against discrimination including gender-based discrimination; and to promote not only diversity but also equality between women and men' (at 6.3). It reiterates the need for codes of good practice to proscribe sexist practices and images (at 6.4); the introduction of quotas or other positive measures to improve the representation of women in public media (at 6.5); and the need to put in place structures to monitor and/or strengthen self-regulatory mechanisms for reporting on stereotyped portrayals, drawing, where they prove effective, on the mechanisms for denouncing sexist advertising (at 6.6).

Besides this Resolution, the Parliamentary Assembly issued Recommendation 1931(2010) on 'Combating sexist stereotypes in the media' (25 June 2010) which invited the Committee of Ministers to draw up in conjunction with the relevant steering committees, a European code of good practice for Member States that would combat sexist stereotypes in the media, and a handbook for media strategies that would combat gender stereotypes drawing on existing best practices.[24] In 2013 a new Recommendation in the area of gender equality and media was adopted, Council of Europe Recommendation CM/Rec(2013)1 on 'Gender equality and media' (10 July 2013). This Recommendation follows the line of the documents it precedes. It points out similar problems and offers similar solutions. This reveals that the problem of stereotyping and sexism in the media has not ceased to exist and that the Member States have not properly addressed their calls.[25]

The Council of Europe has been prolific in its production of Resolutions and Recommendations that make reference to the role of stereotypes and the media in gender discrimination. In addition there are initiatives referring to the role of the media in discrimination on other grounds. In this regard, in 1997 the Committee of Ministers of the Council of Europe adopted Recommendation No. R (97) 21 on 'The media and the promotion of a culture of tolerance' (30 October 1997). The Recommendation is based on the appreciation that the media can make a

---

24 See Gender Equality Commission (2014) and Gender Equality Commission (2015). See also the Council of Europe Gender Equality Strategy 2014–2017, in particular the strategic objective 1, 'Combating gender stereotypes and sexism'.

25 Other documents from the Council of Europe related to this topic are: Recommendation No. R (90) 4 on 'The elimination of sexism from language', 21 February 1990; Recommendation CM/Rec(2007)13 on 'Gender mainstreaming in education', 10 October 2007; Resolution 1557(2007), and Recommendation 1799(2007), both from 26 June 2007 and on 'The image of women in advertising'; and Recommendation 1555(2002) on 'The image of women in the media', 24 April 2002.

positive contribution to the fight against intolerance, especially where it fosters a culture of understanding between different ethnic, cultural and religious groups in society. The Recommendation is, as its name suggests, focused on the promotion of a culture of tolerance through the media. Therefore, its suggestions affect mainly media professionals, including media proprietors, managers, editors, writers, programme makers, journalists and advertisers. The measures suggested are to be implemented by schools for journalism, regulatory and self-regulatory bodies as well as media organisations in the context of the exercise of the media profession. The means of action are set out in the Appendix to the Recommendation and include education. In this regard, the recommendation is for schools of journalism and media training institutes to introduce specialist courses in their core curricula with a view to developing a sense of professionalism which is attentive to both the involvement of the media in multi-ethnic and multicultural societies and to the contribution which the media can make to a better understanding between different ethnic, cultural and religious communities (at 1). With regard to broadcasting and advertising, the Appendix mentions examples of good practices and invites media regulatory bodies to address the problems of discrimination and intolerance within their codes of conduct (at 4). More specifically, it lists a series of issues on which the media enterprises should reflect, such as reporting factually and accurately on acts of racism and intolerance; reporting in a sensitive manner on situations of tension between communities; avoiding derogatory stereotypical depiction of members of cultural, ethnic or religious communities in publications and programme services; treating individual behaviour without linking it to a person's membership of such communities when it is irrelevant; depicting cultural, ethnic and religious communities in a balanced and objective manner and in a way which also reflects their own perspectives and outlook; alerting public opinion to the evils of intolerance; deepening public understanding and appreciation of difference; challenging the assumptions underlying intolerant remarks made by speakers in the course of interviews, reports, discussion programmes; and considering the influence of the source of information on reporting and the 'diversity of the workforce' in the media enterprises, including the extent to which it corresponds to the multi-ethnic, multicultural character of its readers, listeners or viewers (at 2).[26] In this latter regard it is worth recalling the decline in the

26 Other documents of the Council of Europe addressing this topic are: Lange (2009); European Commission against Racism and Intolerance, General Policy Recommendation no. 6 on 'Combating the dissemination of racist, xenophobic and anti-Semitic material via the Internet', 15 December 2000; Commissioner for Human Rights, Issue discussion paper, 'Ethical journalism and human rights', CommDH(2011)40, 8 November 2011; and Recommendation 1768(2006) on 'The image of asylum seekers, migrants and refugees in the media', 5 October 2006.

participation of black, Asian and minority ethnic people (BAME) in the creative media industries in Britain identified by the latest *Creative Skillset 2012 Employment Census* referred to in the previous chapter. The participation of BAME people in the creative media industries declined from 7.4 per cent of the total workforce in 2006 to 5.4 per cent in 2012.[27] This shows that the challenge of 'lack of diversity of the workforce in media enterprises' identified in 1997 has not been overcome.

The Recommendation is only persuasive within a context of the sensitive area of media freedom and because there is no contending freedom or right when it comes to striking a balance between free speech and 'the promotion of a culture of tolerance'. The latter is more often than not just a matter of good practice that only virtuous media outlets would respect should they choose to do so.

In 2009 the Council of Europe issued Recommendation CM/Rec(2009)5 on 'Measures to protect children against harmful content and behaviour and to promote their active participation in the new information and communications environment' (8 July 2009).[28] This document establishes that it is a priority for the Council of Europe to protect freedom of expression and human dignity in the information and communications environment by ensuring a coherent level of protection for minors against harmful content and developing children's media literacy skills (at 1). The reasons why adults are not protected against such harms or are not seen to need media literacy skills are arguable and have not been explored. The issues that the Recommendation targets clearly do not only affect children, but the public in general. For example, the Recommendation mentions the risk of harm that may arise from content and behaviour, such as online pornography, the degrading and stereotyped portrayal of women, the portrayal and glorification of violence and self-harm, 'demeaning, discriminatory or racist expressions' or apologia for such conduct, bullying, stalking and other forms of harassment (at 2). The degrading and stereotyped portrayal of women, for example, does not only affect children but also has an impact on anyone who watches it. Crucially, it affects women and our participation as peers in society. It is an affirmation of our status subordination and permitting misogynistic content is an example of a pattern of cultural value of women and what is coded as feminine (Chapter 2). This affects women's self and social esteem, which necessarily affects our opportunities within and conditions of employment. Therefore, the need for media literacy skills is not

---

27 Brooks *et al* (2012), p. 4.
28 Other documents from the Council of Europe relevant in the area of media, children and discrimination are: Recommendation No. R (92) 19 on 'Videogames with a racist content', 19 October 1992; and Recommendation 1882(2009) on 'The promotion of internet and online media services appropriate for minors', 28 September 2009.

confined to children; and crucially, harmful content should not be simply shrouded but challenged.

The actions that the Council recommends include: (1) encouraging the development and use of safe spaces (walled gardens), as well as other tools facilitating access to websites and internet content appropriate for children; (2) promoting the further development and voluntary use of labels and trustmarks allowing parents and children to easily distinguish non-harmful content from content carrying a risk of harm; (3) promoting the development of skills among children, parents and educators to understand better and deal with content and behaviour that carries a risk of harm; and (4) bringing the recommendation and its appended guidelines to the attention of all relevant private and public stakeholders (at 6).

With regard to hateful and discriminatory expression disseminated through the internet, the Council of Europe issued the *Additional Protocol to the Convention on Cybercrime, concerning the criminalisation of acts of a racist and xenophobic nature committed through computer systems* (28 January 2003) (the UK has not yet signed this Protocol). Within this Protocol, the measures to be taken at a national level include that each Party shall adopt such legislative and other measures as may be necessary to establish as criminal offences under its domestic law, when committed intentionally and without right, distributing, or otherwise making available, racist and xenophobic material to the public through a computer system (article 3 (1)).[29] The Protocol distinguishes between 'hateful and discriminatory' expression. For example, a Party may reserve the right not to attach criminal liability to a conduct where the material advocates, promotes or incites discrimination that is not associated with hatred or violence, provided that other effective remedies are available (article 3(2)). Although the disassociation from hatred and violence is arguable, this could be considered background support for the legal recognition and redress of ED through the internet. The Protocol loses its strength, though, when it authorises a Party to dismiss 'cases of discrimination' for which, due to established principles in its national legal system concerning freedom of expression, it cannot provide for effective remedies (article 3 (3)). This is evidence of the impossibility of striking a balance between free speech and non-discrimination when there is no statutorily recognised protection against discriminatory speech (that is not hate speech). Freedom of expression 'savings' also demonstrate lack of imagination and the existence of some sort of 'legal paralysis' driven by a fear of endangering core liberal values.

---

29 The Protocol also considers two other behaviours in computer systems that are motivated by racism or xenophobia. These are: threatening with the commission of a serious criminal offence and insulting publicly. Similar to the criminalisation of the distribution of racist and xenophobic materials, the offence needs to be intentional and without right. See articles 4 and 5, respectively.

This so-called paralysis makes it difficult to even enquire or make the case for the need for alternatives to censorship. As the next chapters will argue, new and more appropriate legal remedies should be developed in order to deal with speech harms without curbing free speech values.

In 2011 the Committee of Ministers adopted Recommendation CM/ Rec(2011)7 on 'A new notion of media' (21 September 2011). This Recommendation is in some way a corollary of the Council's work engaging with new media issues. It addresses the following themes: the purpose of the media, media and democracy, media standards and regulation, developments in the media ecosystem and a new notion of media. The Recommendation reminds us that the media is 'a tool for freedom of expression in the public sphere, enabling people to exercise their right to seek and receive information' (at 1). But the 'media ecosystem', that is 'all the actors and factors whose interactions allows the media to function and to fulfil their role in society' (at 5) has changed; 'developments in information and communication technologies and their application to mass communication have led to significant changes in the media ecosystem' (at 5); and thus, the Committee of Ministers adopts a new broad notion of media which 'encompasses all actors involved in the production and dissemination, to potentially large numbers of people of content for example, information, analysis, comment, opinion, education, culture, art and entertainment in text, audio, visual, audiovisual or other form, and applications which are designed to facilitate interactive mass communication (for example social networks) or other content-based, large-scale interactive experiences (for example online games), while retaining (in all the cases) editorial control or oversights of the contents' (at 7). And all actors, whether new or traditional, should be offered a policy framework which guarantees an appropriate level of protection and provides a clear indication of their duties and responsibilities in line with the Council's standards (at 7).

Supplementing the Recommendation is an Appendix entitled 'Criteria for identifying media and guidance for a graduated and differentiated response'. It comprises two substantive parts including an extensive list of relevant Council of Europe standards. Relevant for the redress of ED is that once again, an instrument from the Council of Europe refers to the role of culture and media in discrimination as it has been discussed in this chapter. Within the substantive part on 'Standards applied to media in the new ecosystem', the Recommendation refers to 'Media's Responsibilities', which includes 'respect for dignity and privacy'. According to the Recommendation (at 84), 'Media should exercise special care not to contribute to stereotypes about members of particular ethnic or religious groups and to sexist stereotypes'. It then continues to say that 'Representatives of all groups should be offered the opportunity to contribute to content, express their views and explain their understanding of facts' and that 'media should consider adopting a proactive approach in this respect'. Making it institutionally possible to complain and have a right of reply in order to contest the demeaning stereotypes criticised in this document could in fact be a way of being proactive and giving representatives of all groups the opportunity to contribute to content. Similarly useful in this regard is another standard set out in the Appendix, which is 'Media pluralism and diversity of content'; as the Recommendation puts it, 'pluralism will not be automatically guaranteed by the existence of a large number of means of mass communication accessible to people ... the ability to shape or influence public opinion or people's choices may lie with one or only a few actors' (at 79).[30] So, the Recommendation reiterates the need to monitor trends and concentration in order to introduce regulations if required with a view to guarantee transparency of media ownership (at 80). The Recommendation also predicates some success in the theme of pluralism by investing in public service media. In its view, if adequately equipped and funded (including fostering its ability to resort to relevant tools – for example, to facilitate interaction and engagement) public service media could counterbalance the misuse of the power of the media in situations of strong media concentration (at 81 and 82). This may contribute to the creation of a proper public forum as we described in Chapter 4, III. Moreover, as the Recommendation points out, 'the new ecosystem offers an unprecedented opportunity to incorporate diversity into media governance, in particular as regards gender balanced participation in the production, editorial and distribution process (at 83). However, as we have previously pointed out (Chapter 4, IV), such 'diversity into media governance' is necessary not only in media operated by disadvantaged groups themselves, but, crucially, within mainstream media institutions which have the most power. In this way we could have a better chance of ensuring a balanced representation and coverage by media and to combat stereotypes.

IV European Union

The European Union through the European Parliament and the Council has also shown concern about the significance of the media in discrimination; for example, in its Recommendation (2006/952/EC) on the 'Protection of minors and human dignity and on the right of reply in relation to the competitiveness of the European audiovisual and on-line information services industry'.[31] The Recommendation builds upon an earlier

---

30 For discussions on 'media pluralism', see Gardam and Levy (2008).
31 OJ L 378/72 of 27 December 2006.

Recommendation of 1998, which remains in force.[32] However, the Recommendation of 2006 extends the scope to include media literacy, the cooperation and sharing of experience and good practices between regulatory, self-regulatory and co-regulatory bodies, action against discrimination in all media, and the right of reply concerning online media.

The Recommendation recalls the Charter of Fundamental Rights of the European Union, in particular article 1, which refers to the inviolability, respect and protection of human dignity. Indeed, the Recommendation establishes that the European Union should gear its political action to preventing any form of violation of the principle of respect for human dignity. It calls on the Community to protect consumers from 'incitement to discrimination' based on sex, racial or ethnic origin, religion or belief, disability, age or sexual orientation and of combating such discrimination and continues to explain that: such action should strike a balance between the protection of individual rights on the one hand and freedom of expression on the other (at 5). The question that remains unanswered is precisely which are those individual rights – in the context of discrimination – against which free speech should be balanced. The Recommendation does acknowledge that this is a grey area since it also establishes that it is the responsibility of Member States to define the notion of incitement to hatred or discrimination in accordance with their national legislation and moral values (at 5). Arguably, this definition would articulate the precise right that would be balanced against free speech and indicate the kind of remedy appropriate should there be a violation. It would certainly seem that the idea of ED floats in the imagery not only of the civil society that has complained about it (Chapter 4, IV) but clearly also in the international community and in Europe. However, legally speaking this harm has not yet been fully acknowledged or even understood and neither has it been uniformly defined. What has been developed more clearly is the idea of 'hate speech'. However, as it will be explored in the next chapter, hate speech legislation does not capture the harm of ED, nor does it contemplate appropriate remedies for the sort of harm ED creates.

As its name indicates, the Recommendation of 2006 invites Member States to consider introducing measures regarding the right of reply or equivalent remedies in relation to online media; and Annex 1, 'Indicative guidelines for the implementation, at national level, of measures in domestic law or practice so as to ensure the right of reply or equivalent remedies in relation to on-line media', further explains what this means within the Recommendation. In so doing it also reveals further problems

---

32 Council Recommendation (98/560/EC) on 'The development of the competitiveness of the European audiovisual and information services industry by promoting national frameworks aimed at achieving a comparable and effective level of protection of minors and human dignity', OJ 7 270 of 7 October 1998.

that would need to be considered should the right of reply be implemented with regard to ED. For example, who would be entitled to the
right of reply? According to the Annex, 'any natural or legal person,
regardless of nationality, whose legitimate interest, in particular but not
limited to reputation and good name, have been affected by an assertion
of facts in a publication or transmission'. How to judge a 'legitimate
interest' in the context of ED and whether only the 'assertion of facts' can
be contested would then be the issues. As has been stated from the outset,
it is necessary to imagine appropriate remedies for ED and the right of
reply is only a basis but it needs to be adjusted. The right of reply may be
particularly appropriate in the online environment given that 'it allows for
an instant response to contested information and it is technically easy to
attach the replies from the person affected'. However, what matters for
the redress of ED is the principle. This is, 'the opportunity to contest', as
established in the Annex, should be 'within a reasonable time after the
request has been substantiated and in a manner appropriate to the publication or transmission to which the request refers'; and counting with procedures 'whereby disputes so as to the exercise of the right of reply or the
equivalent remedies could be subject to review by courts or similar independent bodies'. Moreover, as the Annex points out, 'the right of reply is
without prejudice to other remedies available to persons whose "right to
dignity", honour, reputation or privacy have been breached by the media'.

With regard to women's portrayal, the Recommendation of 2006 recalls
the Council Resolution (95/C 296/06) on 'The image of women and men
portrayed in advertising and the media'[33] and invites the Member States
and the Commission to take adequate measures to promote a diversified
and realistic picture of the skills and potential of women and men in
society. That said, what is most striking is that:

> when tabling its proposal for a Council Directive implementing the
> principle of equal treatment between men and women in the access to
> and supply of goods and services, the Commission noted that the por-
> trayal of the sexes in the media and in advertising raises important
> questions about the protection of the dignity of men and women, but
> concluded that, in the light of other fundamental rights, including the
> freedom and pluralism of the media, it would not be appropriate to
> address these questions in that proposal but that it should take stock
> of these questions.[34]

33 OJ C 296 of 10 November 1995.
34 Recommendation (2006/952/EC) on 'The protection of minors and human dignity and
    on the right of reply in relation to the competitiveness of the European audiovisual and
    online information services industry', OJ L 378/72 of 27 December 2006, at 17.

The Council Resolution on 'The image of women and men portrayed in advertising and the media' confirmed (at 2) that 'sexual stereotyping in advertising and the media is one of the factors in inequality which influence attitudes towards equality between women and men' and that 'this highlights the importance of promoting equality in all areas of social life'. As it has been noted from the outset, discriminatory images and messages do not only influence discriminatory attitudes but are discriminatory attitudes in themselves. However, the points raised in the Resolution of 1995 and recalled in the Recommendation of 2006 reveal that an analysis of the inequality between women and men regarding their access to supply of goods and services leads necessarily to areas that the law has not yet fully explored but which are nevertheless spaces that sustain discrimination (Chapter 3). The language of the Recommendation of 2006 is very careful; however, it does reveal that the role of the media in discrimination is evident when looking at the bigger picture and that culture, media depictions and discrimination are intrinsically related. That said, the balance continues to be a hard one to strike because while the freedom of the media is backed by the protection of free speech, the protection of human dignity (as it refers to demeaning portrayal) is often not clearly backed by a legally recognised right or freedom. Therefore, it is not surprising that discriminatory portrayal is only 'taken stock of'. Indeed, the Recommendation of 2006 clearly establishes that 'nothing in [the] recommendation prevents Member States from applying their constitutional provisions and other legislation and legal practices regarding freedom of expression' (at 20). Therefore, the Recommendation is limited to calling on Member States to encourage the media industry, without infringing freedom of expression or of the press; and to the audiovisual and online information services industry and other parties concerned to consider effective means of avoiding and combating discrimination based on sex, racial or ethnic origin, religion or belief, disability, age or sexual orientation in audiovisual and online information services and of promoting a diversified and realistic picture of the skills and potential of men and women in society (at 3).

The European Union has therefore shown its concern with the role of the media in discrimination, particularly regarding what it has called 'the protection of minors and of human dignity' as we have seen. Nevertheless, there is also a more specific indication of concern about discrimination and representation in advertising. This is found in the Audiovisual Media Services Directive (AVMSD),[35] where it is established that Member States

35 Directive 2010/13/EU of the European Parliament and of the Council on 'The coordination of certain provisions laid down by law, legislation or administrative action in Member States concerning the provision of audiovisual media services', OJ L 95/1 of 15 April 2010.

shall ensure that audiovisual commercial communications provided by media service producers under their jurisdiction comply with a series of requirements, including that audiovisual commercial communications shall not, among other things, prejudice respect for human dignity; and include or promote any discrimination based on sex, racial or ethnic origin, nationality, religion or belief, disability, age or sexual orientation (art. 9). With regard to the protection of minors, this Directive reiterates the views expressed in the Recommendation of 2006 previously explored, and establishes that in order to protect minors against the negative effects of pornographic or violent programmes, such programmes, when broadcast, must be preceded by an acoustic warning or identified by the presence of a visual symbol throughout the broadcast (art. 27). This Directive is also relevant with regard to the 'right of reply' and is expressed in similar terms as the Recommendation of 2006. However, this Directive establishes that 'a right of reply or equivalent remedy shall exist in relation to all broadcasters under the jurisdiction of a Member State (art. 28 (2)). The AVMS Directive is the latest regulatory framework of the audiovisual media services in the European Union. It is also relevant with regard to 'hate speech'. Indeed, the AVMS Directive governs EU-wide coordination of national legislation in the area of 'incitement to hatred' and for this reason it will be further explored in the next chapter.

V Conclusions

The international and regional instruments discussed in this chapter acknowledge that discrimination and culture, including education, educational materials, methods and curricula, norms, traditions, derogatory language, media depictions and the use of stereotypes in advertising, are intrinsically related. Although the grounds of discrimination they cover, their geographical application and their binding effect varies, the instruments included in this chapter echo similar harms and propose similar remedies. The instruments acknowledge that speech can be harmful in subtle forms that often escape hate speech regulations. However they also unanimously fear responses against such subtle forms which would infringe freedom of expression. These instruments reveal, on the one hand, that ED floats in their imagery as an existing harm but, on the other, that such a harm is not clearly understood as justiciable nor as backed by a specific right or remedy and thus, can hardly be balanced with free speech. Similarly, the idea that incitement to hatred and discrimination are violations of human dignity is frequently invoked, particularly in the European context. However, it is not clear how exactly this violation could be legally challenged.

The instruments discussed cover a timescale of over 30 years. They have raised similar issues over the decades but there is evidence of very little or no success at all in the problems they identified. ED is therefore an old problem that cuts across nations and which requires taking seriously the issues that have been identified and to develop new approaches to understand and explain the harm so that effective remedies can in turn be provided.

VI References

Alfandari, Julia, Baker, Jo and Atteya, Regula Amnah (2011), 'Defamation of religions: international developments and challenges on the ground', SOAS International Human Rights Clinic Project, SOAS School of Law Research Paper No. 09/2011.

Article 19 (2010), 'UN Human Rights Council: Article 19 calls on HRC members to vote against proposed resolution on "Combating Defamation of Religions"', statement of 22 March.

Bayefsky, Anne (2011), 'The UK expected to join ten other countries in boycotting UN's anti-Semitic "Durban III" Event', *Fox News*, 14 September, available at www.foxnews.com/opinion/2011/09/14/uk-joins-ten-other-countries-in-boycotting-uns-anti-semitic-durban-iii-event.html (accessed 16 April 2015).

Brooks, David, Campbell, Mike, Connolly, Milo; Heyer, Neil and Flintham, Neil (2012), *Creative Skillset Employment Census of the Creative Media Industries*, Creative Skillset.

Equality and Human Rights Commission (2013), *Submission on the Seventh Periodic Report of the United Kingdom to the United Nations Committee on the Elimination of all Forms of Discrimination Against Women*.

Equality and Human Rights Commission (2014), *Concluding Observations of the Committee on the Elimination of Discrimination Against Women: Understanding What Governments Need to do to Advance Women's rights in Great Britain*.

Gardam, Tim and Levy, David A.L. (2008), *The Price of Plurality: Choice, Diversity and Broadcasting in the Digital Age*, Reuters Institute for the Study of Journalism.

Gender Equality Commission (2014), *Gender Equality and Media at National Level: Compilation of Good Practices from Member States*, Council of Europe.

Gender Equality Commission (2015), *Handbook on the Implementation of Recommendation CM/Rec(2013)1 of the Committee of Ministers of the Council of Europe on 'Gender Equality and the Media'*, Council of Europe.

Government Equalities Office (2013), *Body Confidence Campaign: Progress Report*, Policy Paper, 28 May.

Groves, Steven (2008), 'Why the U.S. should oppose "Defamation of Religions" Resolutions at the United Nations', Heritage Foundation, Backgrounder, No. 2206, available at www.heritage.org/research/reports/2008/11/why-the-us-should-oppose-defamation-of-religions-resolutions-at-the-united-nations (accessed 23 August 2015).

Jeffreys, Sheila (2005), *Beauty and Misogyny: Harmful Cultural Practices in the West*, London: Routledge.

Lange, Yasha, ed. (2009), *Living Together: A Handbook on Council of Europe Standards on Media's Contribution to Social Cohesion, Intercultural Dialogue, Understanding, Tolerance and Democratic Participation*, Council of Europe.

Langer, Lorenz (2014). *Religious Offence and Human Rights: the Implications of Defamation of Religions*, Cambridge: Cambridge University Press.

Pogrund, Benjamin (2009), 'Durban II, another opportunity missed', *Guardian*, 24 April, available at www.theguardian.com/commentisfree/2009/apr/24/durban-racism-conference-ahmadinejad (accessed 16 April 2015).

Self, Will (2015a), 'The Charlie Hebdo attack and the awkward truths about our fetish for free speech', VICE Media LLC, 9 January, available at www.vice.com/en_uk/read/will-self-charlie-hebdo-attack-the-west-satire-france-terror-105 (accessed 16 April 2015).

Self, Will (2015b), 'A point of view: what's the point of satire?', *BBC News Magazine*, 13 February 2015, available at www.bbc.co.uk/news/magazine-31442441 (accessed 20 April 2015).

Tariq Ghazi, Muhammad (2006), *The Cartoons Cry*, Bloomington, IN: Author House.

Zanardo, Lorella (2010), *Il Corpo Delle Donne*, Milan: Feltrinelli.

Chapter 6

Everyday discrimination and hate speech

I Introduction

The concept of *everyday discrimination* (ED) is aimed at capturing harmful expressions that hate speech legislation has not and should not cover at a criminal law level. Hate speech is the term most commonly used in order to make reference to speech that is threatening, abusive or insulting and intended to stir up hatred against people on grounds which are specified in the relevant legislation. Although every jurisdiction that has enacted hate speech laws has done so in different terms, the former are some common denominators that help us differentiate hate speech from discriminatory mainstream discourse. This is to say differentiation from the prejudice and stereotyping that are normalised and presented as the ordinary truth about the world in which we live – the images and messages identified in this book as ED. One example may help clarify this distinction: a hate speech expression is 'Death to the Jews!' This is blatant hate speech, it calls for murder. An ED message would be something like 'The Jews are usurious people with whom one should be very careful.' This sort of statement would hardly fit any legal hate speech description. It might be a statement in an advert or in a newspaper or could even be found as a 'joke'. However it can stereotype, ridicule, malign, disparage and harm the self- and social-esteem of the group. Statements like this do not grant the status of peers to their targets. They signal them as dangerous, different 'from us' and, when unchallenged, these statements jeopardise participatory parity.

Whether in general hate speech is more damaging than ED is arguable, however, the fact is that hate speech is more often recognised and resisted than ED. The international community and many local jurisdictions have recognised the harm of hate speech and have put limits on freedom of expression by penalising the most extreme manifestations of hatred, often when they are intended, are threatening and/or call for violence. However, generalised prejudice and stereotyping that could be equally damaging to the self- and social-esteem of the target groups have not been granted the same legal recognition and neither have appropriate remedies been developed. Given the similarities and connections between hate speech and ED, this chapter will explore hate speech at a doctrinal, international and local level in order to identify weaknesses and ultimately correct some of its flaws through the creation of a new concept (in Chapter 8) which is aimed at capturing and redressing the injustice and discrimination found in many everyday images and messages.

This chapter is not a comparative study; instead, it tries to make a conceptual study through the analysis of some arguments of principle and some legal initiatives at an international, regional and local level with particular emphasis on British legislation. Crucially, although recognising and endorsing the need for freedom of expression considerations, the analysis of hate speech in this study stresses and calls for a more clear recognition of the predicament in which this sort of speech leaves its targets and the society as a whole. It is not about a speech that 'X or Y hates'; or as Waldron has put it, the harm of hate speech is not to the 'liberal feelings' it is not about them:

> [T]he issue is not just *our* learning to tolerate thought that *we* hate – we the First Amendment lawyers, for example. The harm that expressions of racial hatred do is harm in the first instance to the groups who are denounced or bestialized in pamphlets, billboards, talk radio, and blogs. It is not harm ... to the white liberals who find the racist invective distasteful. Maybe we should admire some [ACLU] lawyer who says he hates what the racist says but defends to the death his right to say it, but ... [t]he [real] question is about the direct targets of abuse.[1]

II Some arguments of principle

The images and messages of ED are both harmful in themselves and are also indicators and often the beginning of further discriminatory attitudes and behaviours. In 1954 Allport proposed a five-point scale in order to describe the ways in which prejudice operates. The scale is not mathematically constructed, but it shows the array of behaviours and actions that may issue from prejudiced attitudes and beliefs. At the top of the scale is what Allport named 'antilocution'. This refers to people talking to each other about their prejudices with like-minded friends, and occasionally with strangers. Antilocution can have various levels of intensity; for example, hostility can be shown through name-calling and epithets, which generally

---

1 Waldron (2012), pp. 9–10. Waldron is quoting his review in Waldron (2008), for the book by Anthony Lewis (2007), *Freedom for the thought we hate: a biography of the first amendment*, Basic Books; ACLU stands for American Civil Liberties Union).

are born out of long-standing and historical hostility but it can also include threatening, abusive and insulting expressions which, as will be shown, are often considered 'hate speech'. Moreover, 'as antilocution reaches higher levels of hostility, the chances are considerable that it will be positively related to open and active discrimination, possibly to violence'.[2]

The second point of the scale is 'avoidance'. In this case, according to Allport, the prejudice is more intense, it leads the individual to avoid members of the disliked group. The bearer of prejudice does not directly inflict harm upon the group she or he dislikes. This point of the scale is only about withdrawal. The third point of the scale is 'discrimination', meaning the making of detrimental distinctions of an active sort. This involves the exclusion of the targeted groups from certain types of employment, from residential housing, political rights, educational or recreational opportunities, churches, hospitals or from social privileges. This may be enforced legally or by common custom. The fourth point of the scale refers to 'physical attack'. Prejudice at this point erupts into violence against either a group of people or against the property of such a group. Finally, the fifth point of the scale is 'extermination'. This refers to lynching, pogroms, massacres, etc. The clearest example is Hitler's programme of genocide marking the ultimate degree of violent expression of prejudice.[3]

Of course, engaging in 'mild' antilocution, does not necessarily mean that the prejudiced person will move to a higher level on the scale. However, unchallenged activity on one level starts creating the necessary conditions for transition to a further level. Indeed, as will be shown in this chapter, the idea of 'incitement to hatred and discrimination' in legislation follows to some degree the view that certain kinds of expression incite and/or stir up hatred and discrimination. However, the problem of antilocution, be it in the form of discriminatory or indeed hate speech, is not just its connection to or triggering of further behaviours. Discriminatory speech inflicts a harm in and of itself. In this sense, it is not 'just speech' but a form of discrimination that demeans reputation, a practice of 'cultural segregation'; a kind of 'punch' to the self- and social-esteem of the target groups. It promotes their disadvantage; it is a verbal form that inequality takes; and a link in systemic discrimination that keeps target groups in subordinated positions. Therefore the harm of discriminatory speech is not only what it *says* but what it *does*. In this way it is similar to MacKinnon's analysis of pornography. According to her:

> Together with all its material supports, authoritatively saying someone is inferior is largely how structures of status and differential treatment

2 Allport (1979), pp. 50–51.
3 *Ibid*, pp. 14–15.

are demarcated and actualised. Words and images are how people are placed in hierarchies, how social stratification is made to seem inevitable and right, how feelings of inferiority and superiority are engendered, and how indifference to violence against those on the bottom is rationalised and normalised. Social supremacy is made, inside and between people, through making meanings. To unmake it, these meanings and their technologies have to be unmade.[4]

Thus, following MacKinnon, social inequality is substantially created and enforced, that is, *done* through words and images. They constitute a sign of segregation accomplished through meaningful symbols and communicative acts in which saying it is doing it.[5]

Discrimination does not divide into acts on one side and speech on the other. The words and images are either direct incidents of such acts, such as making pornography or requiring Jews to wear yellow stars, or are connected to them, whether immediately, linearly, and directly, or in more complicated and extended ways.[6]

Despite the existence of subtle and insidious forms of discriminatory expression (ED), legislation has generally tended to outlaw seemingly 'more serious' harms often referred to as 'hate speech' in criminal law acts and codes.[7] According to Barendt,

legislation should be drafted carefully to ensure that only speech which is really [sic] wounding to the dignity of the targeted groups is caught by the criminal law. It is the responsibility of the courts to ensure that this boundary is not crossed to permit the proscription of speech which is merely offensive either to minority groups or to the majority.[8]

Criminal law provisions are the result of lengthy, complex and heated debates where arguments and counter-arguments about the adequacy or inadequacy of speech regulation have been put forward. Even when some kind of harm done through hate speech is recognised – be it to public order or to the dignity of the person – it remains difficult to decide where

---

4 MacKinnon (1994), p. 21.
5 *Ibid*, pp. 9–10.
6 *Ibid*, p. 21.
7 Including hate speech in criminal law statutes means that it will be the State against the perpetrator of hate speech and the objective of the sanctions is generally retribution through, for example fines or imprisonment.
8 Barendt (2005), p. 175.

to draw a line between hate speech and protected expression. Indeed, as Barendt points out:

> Racist speech, or hate speech against any group, is a form of political speech. The arguments used to justify its proscription can also be adopted to justify banning any speech encouraging the formation of beliefs and attitudes the government dislikes. However despicable its content, racist speech should be tolerated, as otherwise it will prove impossible to resist moves to outlaw other types of less objectionable material.[9]

This is so on the view that democracy demands the free flow of ideas and no government should in principle have the power to decide what can and cannot be said. Moreover, individuals are free agents and we should all be free to decide what kind of information and ideas we wish to seek, receive and impart, including making them available to the widest audience. In other words,

> If it is to respect the moral autonomy of individuals, the state may not prevent their access to speech on the grounds that it may persuade them to adopt particular beliefs or to act on those beliefs. That includes incitements to disobey the law or resist the government.[10]

Freedom of expression therefore assumes that listeners will generally be able to make rational assessments of the claims made to them and the Government should not be the arbiter of this; on the contrary, the Government should be an object of scrutiny in this context. Fear of prosecution can have a chilling effect which will inhibit the exposure of ideas that may fall in the prohibited categories, therefore jeopardising both democracy and individual agency.

Other arguments of principle against hate speech regulation are based on the idea that silencing ideas no matter how despicable they may be only conceals them for a short period of time and makes them clandestine, but it neither eliminates nor challenges them. Furthermore, as Barendt opines, 'it is sometimes dangerous to drive unpleasant ideas underground, for they may surface later in a more dangerous form'.[11] Moreover, the prohibition of the expression of certain ideas can indeed make the speaker or publisher a martyr to the cause of freedom of expression and give hate speech wider currency than it would otherwise enjoy.[12]

9 *Ibid*, p. 172.
10 *Ibid*, p. 170.
11 *Ibid*, p. 9.
12 *Ibid*, p. 176.

Therefore, from a freedom of expression perspective, the best response to hate speech is not proscription but to meet bad speech with more speech.[13] This kind of response is convincing but only to the degree that 'more speech' is in fact possible. It is true that democracy requires the free flow of ideas; however, it is also true that society does not necessarily receive all of the ideas associated with a certain issue but only those ideas that are able to be put forward, usually as a result of power, status and economic resources.

According to Barendt, the argument that hate speech infringes freedom of expression by silencing, or by disparaging, the speech of the targeted group does not make clear how hate speech silences its victims. He argues that such speech may make them less inclined to speak or render their speech less effective, but does not inhibit their legal freedom to communicate their views. However, banning hate speech does infringe the right of the speaker.[14] A problem with this argument is that it seems to find it acceptable that some people's right to free speech is in fact poorer than others', and this is problematic. On the other hand, the argument assumes that the means to express or launch a reply to hate speech are in place by the mere existence of a right to freedom of expression. However, and often, this is not the case. The targets of hate speech are usually in a position of status subordination, socially and economically disadvantaged. Therefore, while it is true that the right to free speech exists for all in the abstract, the presumption of equality for all in the 'market place of ideas' fails to capture the reality that the opportunity to respond to hate speech requires effective access to material and procedural resources. Where there is an imbalance in the access to these resources, there is no effective contestation and hate speech lays unchallenged.

Proscription of hate speech is therefore not unreservedly convincing but neither is the unreserved protection of freedom of expression. The moral autonomy of individuals is not respected if they cannot effectively make informed choices by having access to as many arguments as possible around relevant issues and receiving information that may contradict and expose prejudices. None of the arguments expressed above necessarily suggest that hate speech legislation is utterly inefficient: it has a most important role to play in making clear that expression matters when it comes to social relations; that there is a harm to individuals and to society as a whole in the dissemination of threatening, abusive and prejudiced sentiments; and that those who wilfully intend to cause harm are crossing the boundaries of freedom of expression and should therefore be made criminally accountable. Although the aims and terms of hate speech legislation in different jurisdictions vary considerably, this sort of legislation

13 *Ibid*, p.172.
14 *Ibid*, p. 174.

generally makes an important political point about the value of all members of society and the condemnation of expression that harms the self, social esteem and psychological integrity of hate speech targets. Hate speech legislation, therefore, is both important to recognise and protect the dignity of its targets and to penalise intentional behaviours, but it is necessary to use tightly drawn laws to penalise criminally the wounding expressions of hate and to look for alternative mechanisms for expressions that do not fall into necessarily tight criminal hate speech categories but that nevertheless cause harm.

III Hate speech in UN Conventions

The Universal Declaration of Human Rights of 1948 (UDHR) provides in article 19 that 'everyone has the right to freedom of opinion and expression'. The UDHR is not an enforceable international treaty, but an assertion of fundamental rights principles. The original intention of the UN was that binding international human rights instruments would follow the UDHR with reasonable speed. However, it was not until 1966 that the International Covenant on Civil and Political Rights (ICCPR), which is relevant with regard to freedom of expression and hate speech, was adopted by the UN. Under article 2 of the ICCPR, each State party undertakes, among other things, to respect and ensure the rights contained within it to those in its territory and subject to its jurisdiction and to ensure that any person whose rights or freedoms are violated shall have an effective remedy.

The relevant provisions with regard to freedom of expression and hate speech are in articles 19 and 20. Article 19 provides that:

1   Everyone shall have the right to hold opinions without interference
2   Everyone shall have the right to freedom of expression; this right shall include freedom to seek, receive and impart information and ideas of all kinds, regardless of frontiers, either orally, in writing or in print, in the form of art, or through any other media of his choice
3   The exercise of the rights provided for in paragraph 2 of this article carries with it special duties and responsibilities. It may therefore be subject to certain restrictions, but those shall only be such as are provided by law and are necessary:

   a   For respect of the rights and reputations of others;
   b   For the protection of national security or public order, or of public health or morals.

Article 20:

1   Any propaganda for war shall be prohibited by law

2   Any advocacy of national, racial, or religious hatred that constitutes incitement to discrimination, hostility or violence shall be prohibited by law.

The Human Rights Committee (HRC), as the organ in charge of supervising and enforcing the ICCPR, takes the view that there is no inconsistency between the provision in article 19 and article 20 and that the requirements of article 20 are fully compatible with the right to freedom of expression contained in article 19.[15] The UK, however, entered a reservation to article 20 which, in the interest of freedom of speech, provides that it regards its existing legislation as adequate to address concerns of public order and reserves the right not to introduce further legislation.[16]

The International Convention on the Elimination of All Forms of Racial Discrimination 1965 (ICERD) is also a UN Convention relevant with regard to freedom of expression and hate speech, but unlike ICCPR, this is focused on racial discrimination, which means: any distinction, exclusion, restriction or preference based on race, colour, descent or national or ethnic origin which has the purpose or effect of nullifying or impairing the recognition, enjoyment or exercise, on equal footing, of human rights and fundamental freedoms in the political, economic, social, cultural and any other field of public life (article 1.1). ICERD established a Committee on the Elimination of Racial Discrimination (CERD) which receives periodic reports from the State parties and makes recommendations and suggestions upon them to the UN General Assembly (articles 8 and 9). The relevant articles with regard to hate speech and freedom of expression are articles 4 and 5, respectively.

Article 4
States parties condemn all propaganda and all organisations which are based on ideas or theories of superiority of one race or group of persons of one colour or ethnic origin, or which attempt to justify or promote racial hatred and discrimination in any form, and undertake to adopt immediate and positive measures designed to eradicate all incitement to, or acts of, such discrimination and, to this end, with due regard to the principles embodied in the UDHR and the rights expressly set forth in article 5 of this Convention, inter alia:

---

15 See Hare (2009), p. 64; General Comment No. 10: Freedom of Expression (article 19), 29 June 1983; and General Comment No. 34: Freedoms of opinion and Expression (article 19), 12 September 2011.
16 See Feldman (1995), p. 70. The text of States' reservations can be consulted on the UN website, Treaty Collection, Status of Treaties.

(a) Shall declare an offence punishable by law all dissemination of ideas based on racial superiority or hatred, incitement to racial discrimination, as well as all acts of violence or incitement to such acts against any race or group of persons of another colour or ethnic origin, and also the provision of any assistance to racist activities, including the financing thereof;

(b) Shall declare illegal and prohibit organisations, and also organised and all other propaganda activities, which promote and incite racial discrimination, and shall recognise participation in such organisations or activities as an offence punishable by law;

(c) Shall not permit public authorities or public institutions, national or local, to promote or incite racial discrimination.

Article 5
In compliance with the fundamental obligations laid down in article 2 of this Convention, State parties undertake to prohibit and to eliminate racial discrimination in all its forms and to guarantee the right of everyone, without distinction as to race, colour, or national or ethnic origin, to equality before the law, notably in the enjoyment of the following rights ... (viii) The right to freedom of opinion and expression.

Article 4 is narrower than article 20 of the ICCPR since, by definition, it only applies to racial hate speech. However article 4 goes beyond the obligations imposed by the ICCPR given that: it requires criminal sanctions rather than mere legal prohibition; extends to the dissemination of ideas based on racial superiority as well as incitement to discrimination or hatred; and requires the prohibition of organisations which promote or incite racial discrimination.

According to the CERD, article 4 is consistent with the protection of freedom of speech and has urged state parties to adopt legislation to comply with the full obligations contained in article 4 (General Recommendation No. 15: Organised violence based on ethnic origin (article 4), 23 March 1993, para. 4). In fact, the CERD has criticised the UK Government for its reservation to the Convention and expressed the view that it is not compatible with article 4(b).[17] The reservation reads as follows:

The United Kingdom wishes to state its understanding of certain articles in the Convention. It interprets article 4 as requiring a party to

17 See Report of the Committee on the Elimination of Racial Discrimination, A/55/18; CERD/C/SR.1430, 21 August 2000; General Recommendation No. 1: States parties' obligations (article 4), 25 February 1972; and General Recommendation No. 7: Legislation to eradicate racial discrimination (article 4), 23 August 1985; and Hare (2009), p. 72.

the Convention to adopt further legislative measures in the fields covered by sub-paragraphs (a), (b) and (c) of that article only in so far as it may consider with due regard to the principles embodied in the Universal Declaration of Human Rights and the rights expressly set forth in article 5 of the Convention (in particular to the right to freedom of opinion and expression and the right to freedom of peaceful assembly and association) that some legislative addition to or variation of existing law and practice in those fields is necessary for the attainment of the end specified in the earlier part of article 4.[18]

The CERD has expressed its concern regarding this restrictive interpretation of article 4 and maintained that such interpretation is in conflict with the State party's obligation under article 4 (b) of the Convention since all provisions of article 4 are of a mandatory character.[19] The UK has therefore made important reservations but, as we will see, it has also enacted relevant legislation in recent years.

Both Conventions from the UN utilise the language of 'incitement' and both the CERD and the HRC have a collection of cases in which they have implicitly addressed the issue of 'incitement to discrimination, hostility or violence' embodied in either cartoons, messages, images, pamphlets and the like.[20] Despite the array of cases in which speech is seen to incite discrimination, they show no clear understanding of the term and neither is there a set of guidelines to identify incitement. Whether cartoons, messages and images can amount to incitement to discrimination is most often inferred from the context.

Incitement is a term borrowed from the vocabulary of criminal law. For example, in the UK there was a common law inchoate crime of incitement 'where D urged or persuaded others to perpetrate crimes. This offence was committed at the point when D had successfully communicated with

---

18 In practice, this means the UK does not outlaw organisations that express views that may be regarded as racist. See also CERD concluding observations 2003. Available at www. unhchr.ch/tbs/doc.nsf/(Symbol)/CERD.C.63.CO.11.En?Opendocument (accessed 4 May 2015); as well as the 2008 Universal Periodic Review Conclusions, available at http://lib.ohchr.org/HRBodies/UPR/Documents/Session1/GB/A_HRC_8_25_Add1_ United-Kingdom.pdf, which called on the UK to reconsider its interpretation of Article 4. See Equality and Human Rights Commission (2011), p. 5.

19 Report of the Committee on the Elimination of Racial Discrimination, A/55/18, at para. 356.

20 Cases before the CERD include 030/2003, *The Jewish community of Oslo, the Jewish community of Trondheim, Rolf Kirchner, Julius Paltiel, the Norwegian Antiracist Centre, and Nadeem Butt v Norway*; 027/2002 *Kamal Quereshi v Denmark*; 022/2002 *POEM and FASM v Denmark*; and 004/1991 *L.K. v the Netherlands*. Cases before the HRC include 953/2000 *Ernst Zündel v Canada*; 736/1997 *Malcolm Ross v Canada*; 550/1993 *Robert Faurisson v France* and 104/1981 J.R.T. and the *W.G. party v Canada*.

P.'[21] With regard to speech, 'inciting speech is speech that leads, at least potentially, to bad results, and laws that attempt to curb such speech seek to prevent or minimize these bad results'.[22] Incitement to discrimination, hostility, violence or hate through speech coincides, in part, with ED as described in this study. The problem with referring to this discriminatory practice as 'incitement', however, is its consequence-focused approach in which what matters is not what the speech *does* in itself but its potential to trigger something else and the chances of that happening. The freestanding act of harming through speech is hence disregarded. The consequence-focused approach of 'incitement' is also problematic since isolating factors and the determination of their contribution to particular effects is not feasible. This is not to deny that speech may well contribute to bad results and behaviours, but to insist that discriminatory speech is harmful in itself. Since the UK and indeed many other jurisdictions use the language of incitement and/or other consequence-focused terms such as 'stirring up hatred', the issue will be revisited in the next sections.

IV A kaleidoscope of hate speech legislation

Hate speech laws exist in a number of jurisdictions, which means, at the very least, there is shared concern about the use of speech in the interest of oppression. However, every jurisdiction is unique in the way in which it has framed the harm; in the frequency of its convictions; in the way it interprets its provisions under specific circumstances; and in the way it balances hate speech provisions with the protection of freedom of expression. Moreover – although in similar historical contexts or indeed after the same historical events – the specific reasons why any singular jurisdiction has enacted legislation of this sort varies in each case. It could be because a jurisdiction follows its international commitments, because it responds to local pressure, a mix of both, etc. These things said, however, the fact that hate speech legislation exists in a particular jurisdiction does not mean it is solid and/or finds overall unconditional local support. Similarly, the fact that some jurisdictions, most notably the US, do not have hate speech legislation, should not be taken as a sign about a whole country's rejection of this type of laws.

> Not everyone in America is happy with the constitutional untouchability of racist leaflets in Chicago, Nazi banners and uniforms in Skokie

---

21 Simester *et al* (2010), p. 286. The common law offence of incitement was abolished by the Serious Crime Act 2007, which created new inchoate offences of assisting and encouraging a crime. It does not follow, however, that crimes of incitement no longer exist in English law, since a number of statutory offences use the language of inciting crimes. See p. 287.

22 Gavison (1995), p. 49.

(Illinois), and the burning of crosses in Virginia; not everyone thinks that lawmakers must be compelled to stand back and let this material deface their society.[23]

There is therefore myriad positions about hate speech legislation internationally, within a single jurisdiction and maybe even under the same roof. I will therefore discuss some conceptualisations of hate speech in a very general sense aiming only at gaining some theoretical understanding. The discussion in this section is made on the basis that ideas about the adequacy or inadequacy of hate speech legislation inspire, they travel, are shared and discussed by groups and individuals regionally and internationally regardless of the political will of a government or of the political party in power to participate or not in international conventions or agreements, or to improve or repeal this sort of legislation. In this sense, the myriad positions about hate speech laws also reveals a significant issue, not only about hate speech laws but also about many equality-related rights generally. These are rights gained against powerful majorities and in this sense they may be considered counter-hegemonic. But they are fragile and are significantly shaped and protected to a more or less favourable extent depending on who is in power and on the economic and political climate. Similarly, the existence and the need for hate speech laws only makes sense when it is set against a context of historical and contemporary power imbalances, including the residual elements of imperialism, colonialism, and their attendant race discrimination. Only when acknowledging this background do hate speech laws make sense. For example, being verbally abused, insulted or threatened because of one's race, religion or sexual orientation would matter very little to someone (X) – and indeed it is unlikely to happen – in a context where, for example, when X opens most books, X reads his story, told by his peers. When X goes to school, people with whom he shares religious values and customs teach and assess him. X is most likely to have a job interview and be employed by his peers. Then, back home, X watches the news and it is presented from his perspective; this is to say, in ways in which importance is given mostly to the ways in which events affect him. In sum, despite the existence of comments and ideas about privilege that X may or may not find unjustified or uncomfortable; and indeed, despite the existence of laws aimed at challenging discrimination, everything generally favours his identity (consciously or

---

23 Waldron (2012), p. 12. Opposition to these laws is by no means unanimous or monolithic. Legal academics and law makers are divided on the matter. 'There were state, municipal, and village ordinances enacted and waiting to be struck down in *Virginia v. Black*, 538 U.S. 343 (2003) in *R.A.V. v. City of St. Paul*, 505 U.S. 377 (1992) and in *Collin and the National Socialist Party v. Smith (Village President of Skokie)*, 578 F.2d 1197 (1978) and there was a state law enacted in Illinois, waiting to be upheld by the Supreme Court in *Beauharnais v. Illinois*, 343 U.S. 250 (1952)'.

unconsciously). X has no reason to fear any identity-based ill treatment because his sexual orientation, his religion and his racial attributes are in the main respected, positively valued and dominant at a structural, cultural and institutional level (Chapter 3).

Hate speech laws are therefore located in an ideologically, historically, and constitutionally kaleidoscopic setting. Generally speaking, however, it can be said that they tend to protect public order and/or human dignity. Some countries include hate speech provisions in criminal law codes or statutes and some others in different sorts of civil law legislation, including anti-discrimination legislation, authorising, however, action at a criminal law level under certain circumstances, as we noted in Chapter 3, II, 1; that is the case, for example, in Mexico, New South Wales and South Africa.[24] New Zealand is another example. In this country there is a distinction between racial disharmony as a form of discrimination and inciting racial disharmony, which is closer to the idea of hate speech. They are both located in the Human Rights Act 1993. 'Racial disharmony' is in part 2, Unlawful discrimination, under the headline, Other forms of discrimination, section 61(1):

> It shall be unlawful for any person – (a) To publish or distribute written matter which is threatening, abusive or insulting, or to broadcast by means of radio or television words which are threatening, abusive or insulting; or (b) To use in any public place as defined in section 2(1) of the Summary Offences Act 1981, or within the hearing of persons in any such public place, or at any meeting to which the public are invited or have access, words which are threatening, abusive or insulting; or (c) To use in any place words which are threatening, abusive, or insulting if the person using the words knew or ought to have known that the words were reasonably likely to be published in a newspaper, magazine or periodical or broadcast by means of radio or television, – being matter or words likely to excite hostility against or bring into contempt any group of persons in or who may be coming to New Zealand on the ground of the colour, race, or ethnic or national origins of that group of persons.

Inciting racial disharmony is located in part 6, section 131 (1):

> Every person commits an offence and is liable to conviction to imprisonment for a term not exceeding 3 months or to a fine not exceeding $7,000 who, *with the intent* to excite hostility or ill-will against, or bring to contempt or ridicule, any group of persons in New Zealand on the ground of the colour, race, or ethnic or national origins of that group

24 See Chapter 3, footnote 21.

of persons, – (a) publishes or distributes written matter which is threatening, abusive or insulting, or broadcasts by means of radio or television words which are threatening, abusive or insulting or (b) uses in any public place, or within the hearing of persons in any such public place, or at any meeting to which the public are invited or have access, words which are threatening, abusive or insulting – being matter or words likely to excite hostility or ill-will against, or bring into contempt or ridicule, any such group of persons in New Zealand on the ground of the colour, race, or ethnic or national origins of that group of persons.

Then, section 132 warns, in a similar way as happens in South Africa and New South Wales, that 'No prosecution for an offence against section 131 shall be instituted without the consent of the Attorney General.' New Zealand shares with the UK's Public Order Act 1986 the use of the words 'threatening, abusive or insulting' in order to describe unlawful expressions. Other jurisdictions use the language of defamation, applied to groups; and others refer to incitement to hatred on certain grounds. These grounds also vary depending on the jurisdiction; however, they tend to be disadvantaged groups; in this way acknowledging the power imbalances referred to earlier on. With regard to the use of the language of 'defamation', an example is in the German Criminal Code, section 130:

> Whoever, in a manner that is capable of disturbing the public peace: 1. Incites hatred against a national, racial, religious group or a group defined by their ethnic origins, against segments of the population or individuals because of their belonging to one of the aforementioned groups or segments of the population or calls for violent or arbitrary measures against them; or 2. Assaults the human dignity of others by insulting, maliciously maligning an aforementioned group, or *defaming* segments of the population, shall be liable to imprisonment from three months to five years.

The Danish Criminal Code, section 266b (1) uses a different type of language; it refers to a group of people being threatened, scorned or degraded:

> Any person who, publicly or with the intention of wider dissemination, makes a statement or imparts other information by which a group of people are threatened, scorned or degraded on account of their race, colour, national or ethnic origin, religion, or sexual inclination, shall be liable to a fine or to imprisonment for any term not exceeding two years.

In Canada, the Criminal Code 1985, section 319 (1) and (2) refers to public incitement to hatred and wilful promotion of hatred, respectively:

(1) Every one who, by communicating statements in any public place, incites hatred against any identifiable group where such incitement is likely to lead to a breach of the peace is guilty of (a) an indictable offence and is liable to imprisonment for a term not exceeding two years; or (b) an offence punishable on summary conviction.

(2) Every one who, by communicating statements, other than in private conversation, wilfully promotes hatred against any identifiable group is guilty of (a) an indictable offence and is liable to imprisonment for a term not exceeding two years; or (b) an offence punishable on summary conviction.

Hate speech legislation therefore has conceptualised the harm in various ways and has established different thresholds for prosecution. Moreover, hate speech legislation has tended to be incremental regarding the grounds protected, but its enactment and permanence is highly dependent on particular political contexts, as we will see in the case of the UK.[25] From a doctrinal point of view, we can appreciate an interaction and relation between concepts such as defamation, public order and dignity in hate speech provisions. According to Waldron, laws regarding group defamation are set up to

vindicate public order, not just by preempting violence, but by upholding against attack a shared sense of the basic elements of each person's status, dignity, and reputation as a citizen or members of society in good standing – particularly against attacks predicated upon the characteristics of some particular social group.[26]

The concept of defamation is complex and was not originally created to protect disadvantaged groups; however, we understand the way in which it has been moulded to accommodate protection for

the basics of each person's reputation against attempts (for example) to target all the members of a vulnerable racial or religious group with some imputation of terrible criminality – an imputation which, if

25 After the attacks on the offices of the weekly *Charlie Hebdo* that published cartoons deemed by many as Islamophobic, and the attack on a kosher supermarket leaving 17 people dead in January 2015, the French President Françoise Holland vowed to make the fight against racism one of his main personal causes. Plans include moving 'hate speech', already a criminal offence, to France's General Penal Code. See Chrisafis (2015).

26 Waldron (2012), p. 47.

sustained in a broad front, would make it seem inappropriate to continue according the elementary but important status of citizenship to the members of the group in question.[27]

These things said, however, as established earlier, what hate speech laws protect and what they do not cover is country-specific and requires individual analysis. Nevertheless, this should not paralyse enquiring about better ways of understanding the harm at a theoretical level and to put these ideas forward. Waldron's concept of 'assurance' as the value that hate speech laws should protect is a good example of this. For him, 'assurance' means that in a well-ordered society,

> Everyone can enjoy a certain assurance as they go about their business. They know that when they leave home in the morning, they can count on not being discriminated against or humiliated or terrorized. They can feel secure in the rights that justice defines; they can face social interactions without the elemental risks that such interaction would involve if one could not count on others to act justly, there is security, too, for each person's proper pride and dignity against the soul-shrivelling humiliation that a discriminatory rebuff can give rise to.[28]

His views are not very different from what we have argued since the beginning of this book. For Waldron, the issue is

> the harm done to individuals and groups through the disfiguring of our social environment by visible, public, and semipermanent announcements to the effect that in the opinion of one group in the community, perhaps the majority, members of another group are not worthy of equal citizenship.[29]

In this book I have argued that these are matters of misrecognition and therefore injustice. Defamatory, threatening, abusive, insulting remarks; and the scorn and ridicule to which hate speech provisions refer, harm the human dignity of its targets because they are assaults against their status and thus their self- and social-esteem are compromised thereby

---

27 *Ibid.* According to Parekh (2006), p. 314, 'communal libel' is a form of social and political exclusion, a declaration of hostility against a section of one's fellow citizens, and strikes at the very root of communal life. See also Polelle (2003). However, the concept of defamation applied to groups has been problematic. See Chapter 5, II; and Strossen (1992), p. 302.
28 Waldron (2012), pp. 83–84.
29 *Ibid*, p. 39. On this view, *everyday discrimination* could be understood as 'the cumulative effect on the visible environment of numerous individual defacements', pp. 89–90.

negating participatory parity. The concept of human dignity is problematic, as we shall see in Chapter 9; however, it is a value constantly invoked as something important for everyone without distinction and so, ultimately, it urges or should urge its proponents (be it judges, legislators or commentators) to clarify what they mean and what they believe matters for everyone and should therefore be respected/protected. On Waldron's view dignity is a matter of status, 'it indicates the importance of paying attention to the way in which a person's status as a member of society in good standing is affirmed and sustained'.[30] He contends that

> protecting people from assaults on their dignity indirectly protects their feelings, but it does so only because it protects them from a social reality – a radical denigration of status and an undermining of assurance –, which as it happens, naturally impacts upon their feelings.[31]

This raises the important issue that although feelings matter – offence matters – what hate speech laws are or should be directed against is the creation of an environment 'a social reality' which negates participatory parity. It is not about Y 'taking' offence but about the speaker littering the environment, 'undermining assurance' and thereby affecting Y. Ultimately it is a matter of justice. This is to say, a model of justice which alongside redistribution requires recognition (contesting status denigration) in order to achieve participatory parity.

V Legal responses to hate speech in the UK

In the UK there are various provisions addressing forms of hate speech. Legislation has been incremental and piecemeal regarding the grounds protected and the provisions have been located within the Public Order Act 1986, therefore, hate speech is framed as a public order offence. At a regional level, the UK is a member of the Council of Europe and is subject to the jurisdiction of the European Court of Human Rights. Moreover, the UK is also a member of the European Union and thus also has concomitant obligations deriving from the Union. Some of the relevant European Recommendations with regard to the role of culture in discrimination were considered in the previous chapter. This section is focused on hate speech.

---

30 *Ibid*, pp. 141–142.
31 *Ibid*, p. 108.

To date there are three areas covered in the UK: race, religion, and sexual orientation.[32] The oldest legislation is that which covers incitement to racial hatred. It was first introduced in the Race Relations Act 1965, section 6 'against a background of increased post-war immigration from the Commonwealth, and the prospect of the rise of a far-right political movement and later Powellism'.[33] The provision in this Act made it an offence to publish written matter or make a speech in public which was threatening, abusive or insulting, and likely to stir up racial hatred, if the defendant actually intended to cause such hatred. In 1976 this offence was relocated to the Public Order Act 1936 and the requirement of intention to cause racial hatred abandoned; it was enough if, having regard to all the circumstances, hatred was likely to be stirred up against any racial group.[34]

Currently, part 3 of the Public Order Act 1986, sections 17–29 refers to racial hatred, which means 'hatred against a group of persons defined by reference to colour, race, nationality (including citizenship) or ethnic or national origins' (s. 17).[35] The acts now *intended or likely to stir up racial hatred* are: the use of words or behaviour or display of written material; publishing or distributing written material; public performance of play; distributing, showing or playing a recording; broadcasting or including a programme in a cable programme service; and possession of racially

32 The racial hatred offences in sections 18–23 of the Public Order Act 1986 apply in England and Wales and Scotland. The offences of stirring up hatred on the grounds of religion and sexual orientation in sections 29B to 29F of the Public Order Act 1986 apply to England and Wales only. In Scotland, racist acts and remarks are usually prosecuted under the Criminal Law: (Consolidation) (Scotland) Act 1995 or as an aggravated offence under the Crime and Disorder Act 1998 with other hate crimes: Religious Prejudice under section 74 Criminal Justice (Scotland) Act 2003, Sexual Orientation and Transgender Identity under section 2 Offences (Aggravation by Prejudice) (Scotland) Act 2009, Disability under section 1 Offences (Aggravation by Prejudice) (Scotland) Act 2009. Hate crimes related to other characteristics are also prosecuted as aggravated offences attached to a substantive charge. Other laws prohibit offensive behaviour which is likely to incite public disorder at, or travelling to and from, football matches. These laws protect a range of protected groups including religious groups, social or cultural groups with religious affiliation, ethnic or national groups, or groups defined by sexual orientation, transgender identity or disability (Section 1 Offensive behaviour at football matches and threatening communications (Scotland) Act 2012) and are regularly used in practice to combat sectarianism. For example, a 'Football Banning Order' may be imposed preventing the accused from attending any football matches throughout the UK or abroad for up to ten years. Scottish law also protects the right to express views opposing the marriage of same-sex couples (Section 16 of the Marriage and Civil Partnership (Scotland) Act 2014 and the Prosecution Guidance in relation to Same-Sex Marriage). See Equality and Human Rights Commission (2015), pp. 11–15.

33 Malik (2009), p. 99. See the political views of Enoch Powell in Chapter 4, footnote 51.

34 See Race Relations Act 1976, s. 70.

35 Offences under part 3 of the Public Order Act 1986 carry a maximum sentence of seven years imprisonment, a fine or both. See, section 27.

inflammatory material (ss. 18–23). These offences involve expressions which are threatening, abusive or insulting and intended or likely, having regard to all the circumstances, to stir up racial hatred.

The Racial and Religious Hatred Act 2006 created a new part 3A in the 1986 Act (ss. 29A–29N). This came into force on 1 October 2007 after some years of legislative debate concerning, among other issues, protection of Muslims from attacks which were a backlash against Islamic extremism.[36] Religious hatred is defined in section 29A as 'hatred against a group of persons defined by reference to religious belief or lack of religious belief'. The structure of part 3A generally corresponds to part 3. Nevertheless, there are at least three significant differences. One is that the act or material concerned must be threatening, unlike the racial hatred provisions where the material can be threatening, abusive or insulting. A second difference is that the act must be intended and not merely likely to stir up religious hatred having regard to all the circumstances. The third difference is the addition of a 'freedom of expression protection' saving in section 29J which has no equivalent in part 3 and establishes that:

> Nothing in this Part shall be read or given effect in a way which prohibits or restricts discussion, criticism or expressions of antipathy, dislike, ridicule, insult or abuse of particular religions or the beliefs or practices of their adherents, or proselytising or urging adherents of a different religion or belief system to cease practising their religion or belief system.[37]

With regard to 'hate speech' on the grounds of sexual orientation, the Criminal Justice and Immigration Act 2008 (c.4), section 74 and schedule 16 amended sections 29A to 29N and inserted sections 29AB and 29JA to part 3A of the Public Order Act 1986, making it an offence to stir up hatred on the grounds of sexual orientation. These provisions came into force on 23 March 2010. The new section 29AB defines hatred on the grounds of sexual orientation as 'hatred against a group of persons defined by reference to sexual orientation (whether towards persons of the same sex, the opposite sex or both)'. The foreseen acts intended to stir up hatred on the grounds of sexual orientation correspond to the acts considered for racial hatred and hatred against persons on religious grounds. However, like their religious counterparts, they need to be intended and threatening and not merely abusive or insulting as is the case for racial hatred. Section 29JA, the same as its religious hatred

---

36 See Nicol *et al* (2009), p. 126; and Malik (2009), p. 96.
37 British laws prohibiting blasphemy (against the Christian faith) were repealed by the Criminal Justice and Immigration Act 2008, ch. 5, s. 79.

counterpart (s. 29J), includes a saving 'protection of freedom of expression' which reads as follows:

> In this Part, for the avoidance of doubt, the discussion or criticism of sexual conduct or practices or the urging of persons to refrain from or modify such conduct or practices shall not be taken of itself to be threatening or intended to stir up hatred.

The Marriage (Same Sex) Couples Act 2013 amended this section, including a 'new saving'. The provision reproduced above became subsection (1) of section 29JA and the following subsection (2) was inserted:

> In this part, for the avoidance of doubt, any discussion or criticism of marriage which concerns the sex of the parties to marriage should not be taken of itself to be threatening or intended to stir up hatred.

These savings, the same as their religious counterpart (s. 29J), serve a function; they protect freedom of expression. However, they do not protect the targets from any bullying, harassment and/or the ED that may occur through such protected behaviours. For example, the bullying of people to modify their sexual orientation because it is 'wrong' to be gay. Therefore, it is also for these reasons that we need to develop alternative mechanisms with which to challenge the behaviours that do not meet criminal law standards. The regulation of freedom of expression and its limits in the UK is, of course, to a large extent informed by the Convention for the Protection of Human Rights and Fundamental Freedoms, commonly known as the European Convention on Human Rights and Fundamental Freedoms (ECHR). In fact, the long title to the UK Human Rights Act 1998 declares its purpose to 'give further effect to rights and freedoms guaranteed under the European Convention on Human Rights'.[38] The ECHR, in force since 1953, originated in a context of the results of two world wars in the first half of the twentieth century and the slide into totalitarianism in Germany, Italy and Spain in the 1930s. Therefore, the ECHR is in part a response to the rise of fascism in Europe and to the language of hatred of regimes such as the Nazis in Germany. This is the background that informed the risk of speech used not only for freedom and the discovery of truth but also in the interest of oppression.[39]

---

38 The Human Rights Act 1998 puts an obligation on courts to interpret legislation 'so far as it is possible to do so' compatibly with the Convention; and an obligation on all public authorities to act in conformity with the Convention.

39 See Hare (2009), p. 76.

The articles of the ECHR relevant for the discussion of freedom of expression and hate speech are 10, 14 and 17. Article 10 of the ECHR provides:

1. Everyone has the right to freedom of expression. This right shall include freedom to hold opinions and to receive and impart information and ideas without interference by public authority and regardless of frontiers. This article shall not prevent States from requiring the licensing of broadcasting, television or cinema enterprises.
2. The exercise of these freedoms, since it carries with it duties and responsibilities, may be subject to such formalities, conditions, restrictions or penalties as are prescribed by law and are necessary in a democratic society, in the interests of national security, territorial integrity or public safety, for the prevention of disorder or crime, for the protection of health or morals, for the protection of the reputation or rights of others, for preventing the disclosure of information received in confidence, or for maintaining the authority and impartiality of the judiciary.

Article 14 provides a subsidiary right to be free from discrimination by stating:

> The enjoyment of the rights and freedoms set forth in this Convention shall be secured without discrimination on any ground such as sex, race, colour, language, religion, political or other opinion, national or social origin, association with a national minority, property, birth or other status.

This enables a complaint of unequal treatment to be made in conjunction with one or more of the substantive rights under the Convention or Protocols. In addition to the limitations on the right of freedom of expression in article 10 (2), which include the protection of the rights of others, article 17 provides that:

> Nothing in this Convention may be interpreted as implying for any State, group or person any right to engage in any activity or perform any act aimed at the destruction of any of the rights and freedoms set forth herein or at their limitation to a greater extent than is provided for in the Convention.

The European Commission of Human Rights and the European Court of Human Rights have frequently drawn upon articles 10 (2), 14 and 17 to resist attempts by propagandists to allege violations of article 10.[40]

40 See Nicol *et al* (2009), p. 128.

In *Norwood v UK*, the applicant had placed a BNP poster in his window with a photograph of the Twin Towers on fire and the words 'Islam out of Britain – Protect the British People'. He was convicted of a racially aggravated offence under the Public Order Act 1986. The Court held that article 17 operates to remove the protection of article 10 for this act of expression, stating that such a 'general, vehement attack against a religious group, linking the group as a whole with a grave act of terrorism, is incompatible with the values proclaimed and guaranteed by the Convention, notably tolerance, social peace and non-discrimination'.[41]

According to the European Court of Human Rights:

> Freedom of expression constitutes one of the essential foundations of [a democratic] society, one of the basic conditions for its progress and for the development of every man [sic]. Subject to paragraph 2 of Article 10 [of the ECHR], it is applicable not only to 'information' or 'ideas' that are favourably received or regarded as inoffensive or as a matter of indifference, but also to those that offend, shock or disturb the State or any sector of the population. Such are the demands of that pluralism, tolerance and broadmindedness without which there is no 'democratic society'. This means, amongst other things, that every 'formality', 'condition', 'restriction' or 'penalty' imposed in this sphere must be proportionate to the legitimate aim pursued.[42]

Moreover, in *Erbakan v Turkey*, the Court established that:

> [T]olerance and respect for the equal dignity of all human beings constitute the foundations of a democratic, pluralistic society. That being so, as a matter of principle it may be considered necessary in certain democratic societies to sanction or even prevent all forms of expression which spread, incite, promote or justify hatred based on intolerance…, provided that any 'formalities', 'conditions', 'restrictions' or 'penalties' imposed are proportionate to the legitimate aim pursued.[43]

These landmark judgments authorise jurisdictions to introduce hate speech legislation. However they also show that although there is no freestanding 'right to offend', offensive remarks are protected in the interest of democracy and that restrictions or penalties must be proportionate to the legitimate aim pursued. This makes sense for democracy. However, it

---

41 *Norwood v UK* (App No 23131/03), 16 November 2003. The British National Party is a far right political party in the UK.
42 *Handyside v the United Kingdom* judgment of 7 December 1976, 49.
43 *Erbakan v Turkey* judgment of 6 July 2006, 56.

is only fair when we can all effectively make use of our freedom of expression in order to communicate our views and respond to ideas that 'offend, shock or disturb'. Crucially, some of these 'ideas' may fit the description of ED and so they should be named for what they are and not merely lurk behind their medium/vehicle – freedom of expression. In this regard it can be said that the harm the expression of discriminatory images and messages causes to the self- and social-esteem of its targets is to a large extent actualised and is aggravated by the fact that frequently such an attack is not even at the very least recognised, it has no name, is often trivialised and there is no institutional support to contest it even when there are clear power imbalances.

On the other hand, as we have seen, hate speech is more widely recognised. Another example of this is the Council of Europe Recommendation No. R (97) 20 of 30 October 1997. This Recommendation condemns all forms of expression which incite racial hatred, xenophobia, anti-Semitism and all forms of intolerance, since they undermine democratic security, cultural cohesion and pluralism. It also notes that such forms of expression may have a greater and more damaging impact when disseminated through the media, but is also aware of the need to fully respect its editorial independence and autonomy.

The Appendix to this Recommendation understands hate speech as

> covering all forms of expression which spread, incite, promote or justify racial hatred, xenophobia, anti-Semitism or other forms of hatred based on intolerance, including: intolerance expressed by aggressive nationalism and ethnocentrism, discrimination and hostility against minorities, migrants and people from immigrant origin.

The Appendix outlines seven principles that governments of Member States should follow when reviewing their domestic legislation and practice. These principles include *the need to have civil and administrative law provisions alongside criminal provisions.* Specifically, principle 2, which recommends that governments of the Member States should establish or maintain a sound legal framework consisting of civil, criminal and administrative law provisions on hate speech which enable administrative and judicial authorities to reconcile in each case respect for freedom of expression with respect for human dignity and the protection of the reputation or the rights of others. Principle 2, fifth indent, suggests that governments of Member States examine ways to enhance the possibilities to combat hate speech through civil law – for example, by allowing interested non-governmental organisations to bring civil law actions, providing for compensation for victims of hate speech and providing for the possibility of court orders allowing victims a *right of reply* or ordering retraction. As established in the Explanatory Memorandum, paragraph 34, the measures indicated in the fifth indent are aimed at mobilising civil society and the victims of hate speech to help combat this phenomenon. These measures suggest a number of legal tools to enhance the possibilities available under civil law, given that criminal law may not always be suited to deal with particular instances of hate speech, and civil law generally offers greater flexibility in this regard. The Explanatory Memorandum, however, does not explicitly refer to subtle forms of hate speech (ED) that the criminal law is unable to accommodate; the concern of the Council of Europe is with regard to the need to have alternative mechanisms available in order to protect human dignity without infringing freedom of expression.

The European Union has also manifested its position against hate speech. Indeed, as we noted in Chapter 5, the Audiovisual Media Services Directive[44] does not only establish legal, regulatory and administrative provisions related to the provision and distribution of audiovisual media services (radio broadcasting, television and cinema), it also governs EU-wide coordination of national legislation in the area of 'incitement to hatred'. It establishes in article 6 that:

> Member states shall ensure by appropriate means that audiovisual media services provided by media services providers under their jurisdiction do not contain any *incitement* to hatred based on race, sex, religion or nationality.[45]

According to the European Commission, this is an issue, for example, with 'channels that endorse violence against individuals or groups as the solution to social or political conflicts'.[46] EU countries, however, have limited power to act against hate speech channels from outside the EU, such as outside satellite channels that can be picked up in parts of the EU. The Commission therefore regularly raises the issue of hate speech broadcasters in its political dialogue with the countries concerned, particularly those where the broadcasters are based. Nevertheless, EU countries can restrict broadcast of unsuitable content (article 2 (4)–(6)). This means restricting the re-transmission of unsuitable on-demand audiovisual content – e.g. neo-Nazi propaganda that may not be banned in its country of origin.

---

44 Directive 2010/13/EU of the European Parliament and of the Council, OJ L 95/1 of 15 April 2010.

45 Italics are the author's. Media service provider is the natural or legal person who has editorial responsibility for the choice of the audiovisual content of the audiovisual media service and determines the manner in which it is organised. Other initiatives in Europe regarding hate speech in the internet were discussed in Chapter 5, III and IV.

46 EU Audiovisual and Media Policies, available at http://ec.europa.eu/archives/information_society/avpolicy/reg/tvwf/incit/index_en.htm (accessed 5 March 2015).

VI Weaknesses of hate speech laws in the UK

Even though the rationale and the debates around hate speech legislation in the UK have considered 'the hurt racist speech causes members of minority groups' and arguments about psychological injury, harm to self-esteem and the targets' right to equality have been put forward doctrinally,[47] hate speech provisions are located in the Public Order Act 1986, which creates offences commonly used by the UK police to deal with public disorder and violence.[48]

UK legislation has been incremental with regard to the grounds protected. There are mixed opinions in this regard. The grounds protected are some of those which have faced systematic disadvantage by discrimination and are therefore entitled to the assistance of the law. However, it is also true that protection has been granted to groups for which there is an elite political opinion swinging in their favour, often as a result of a dramatic event; but also for those groups that rely on effective campaigning like the persuasive efforts of Stonewall to criminalise hatred on the grounds of sexual orientation.[49] Therefore, the UK's 'hatred' laws have been enacted at 'adequate' political times when there is evidence, successfully presented, about hatred and/or discrimination against those particular groups. Nevertheless, the grounds protected are not the only ones that systematically experience discrimination and therefore hate speech laws seem incomplete. For example, pornography is arguably a form of hate speech that is threatening, abusive and insulting to women. However, the harm it causes has not been considered in legislation as a form of hate speech against women.[50] Given this background, commentators have argued that 'it may be better that there be no hate speech bans, which are

47 See, for example Home Office, *Review of Public Order Act 1936 and Related Legislation* (Cmnd 7891, 1980), para. 107; and Barendt (2005), p. 171. 'Along with the civil law of race discrimination these provisions [hate speech provisions] recognise that there are fundamental rights of others, not to be abused and discriminated against, which must be protected from the evils of racist sentiment'. Nicol *et al* (2009), p. 127.
48 See Chapter 3, II, 1.
49 Goodall (2009), pp. 212–214.
50 Pornography, according to Cram (2006), p. 141, 'causes injury to those women involved in the commercial production of pornography; causes injury to those victims of sex crimes where the perpetrator has been motivated by access to violent sexually explicit materials and contributes to the social conditioning that tolerates discrimination against women and makes it, if anything, less likely that their contributions to public debate and community life will be taken seriously.' In the UK, the Criminal Justice and Immigration Act 2008 criminalises the possession of extreme pornography, namely, images of bestiality, necrophilia, and life-threatening or serious violence. The 1959 Obscene Publications Act, until the enactment of the 2008 Act, was the primary statutory mechanism for regulating adult pornography.

a threat to freedom of expression than the legitimacy of human rights law be undermined by fragmentary developments'.[51]

These fragmentary developments have also increased the threshold; for example, for religious and sexual orientation hatred, the threshold is higher than that for racial hatred. These both require proof of both threat and specific intent as opposed to racial hatred legislation, which considers acts intended or 'likely, having regard to all the circumstances, to stir up hatred'; and where the matters do not need to be only threatening but also can be abusive or insulting. The higher threshold in the new provisions means, according to Goodall – referring to sexual orientation – that the provision:

> would be almost unenforceable unless the accused confesses. Equally, how easy will it be to prove, in the face of a not-guilty plea, that words were not just insulting or abusive, but were actually intended to be threatening and furthermore were intended to stir up others to hatred of gay men and lesbians as a group?[52]

The high thresholds are important in the view of some analysts since there are freedom-of-speech concerns that justify either no legislation or very narrowly drafted legislation.[53] Such narrowness in existing legislation also includes restriction of the foreseeable behaviours. For example, as Barendt warns,

> It is doubtful whether the law covers the publication in a scientific journal of an article suggesting that one racial group is inherently inferior in intelligence to another. An article of this character is certainly unpleasant and offensive, but it is unlikely that a court would find it amounts to abusive or insulting speech.[54]

Moreover, there are various expressions that, despite being harmful, are nevertheless protected given the potential harm that their proscription would entail for freedom of expression. Indeed, the protections of freedom of expression in sections 29J and 29JA of the Public Order Act 1986 authorise a series of behaviours that could constitute ED as described

---

51 Goodall (2009), p. 216; see also Heinze (2006), p. 543; for whom western European hate speech bans are inherently discriminatory, and should be abolished.
52 Goodall (2009), p. 222.
53 Hare (2006), p. 538.
54 Barendt (2005), p. 178.

in this book.[55] This is not to suggest that these behaviours should be included in criminal law statutes but that alternative mechanisms are necessary for behaviours that are necessarily beyond the limits of criminal law. As Malik points out in the context of religious hatred:

> The debate about criminalising incitement to religious hatred has been a costly distraction from a much needed discussion about how to address the very real harm caused by hate speech. Within this debate, it is essential to identify the precise source of risk of harm. The most powerful source of hate speech against vulnerable minorities such as Muslims is, mainstream public discourse. This type of speech and representation cannot be addressed through incitement to hatred provisions.[56]

Malik identifies the need for responsible speech on the part of politicians and the media. With regard to the latter, she considers that while there is harm in extreme forms of speech, such as those addressed by hate speech laws,

> it is also the case that there is prejudice and stereotyping in the mainstream media which, in many cases, will have a more widespread influence. Prejudice and stereotypes in the mainstream media may in fact be more pernicious because these views and representations are normalised and presented as the ordinary truth about the world in which we live.[57]

Malik joins the argument about the need for alternative mechanisms. She refers to a range of non-legal responses to hate speech; for example, forms of cultural policy which would build capacity within minority communities to participate in public debates. Malik considers this as a response compatible with the liberal free speech principle

> because although a liberal state cannot easily interfere with free speech, it can prioritize a concern with the autonomy and wellbeing

---

55 Section 29JA was 'neither originally included in the provisions proposed by the government nor thought necessary by the Parliament Joint Committee on Human Rights. It was inserted by the House of Lords at the eleventh hour. They had done the same thing two years before when they forced through an amendment to religious hatred provisions to include a similar provision.' Goodall (2009), p. 214. See also *Fifth Report,* January 2008, HMSO, para. 1.64: the Committee stated that the provisions as introduced provided in their view 'an appropriate degree of protection for human rights'; and HL Debs, *passim,* 7 May 2008, on the amendments regarding incitement to religious hatred in the original Bill creating part 3A.

56 Malik (2009), p. 105.

57 *Ibid,* p. 106.

of individuals who are victims of hate speech, and use investment and cultural policy to develop their capacity to respond to speech.[58]

A further issue with regard to the criminalisation of hate speech is the necessary element of intent. Many manifestations of prejudice, hostility, abuse and insult may be hard to prove to be intentional and may in fact be unwitting; however, they are damaging nevertheless and thus, action even if not at the criminal level is necessary. Moreover, as Goodall suggests, part 3 of the Public Order Act 1986 *is not* exactly a ban on hate speech, rather, a ban on speech that seeks to incite others to hate, which is a significantly narrow category given that it requires proof of specific intent to stir up others, which places a substantial burden on the prosecution.[59]

Requiring that hate speech or publications stir up hatred is deeply problematic. This requirement neglects the harm that hateful expression inflicts in and of itself. In other words, it neglects the predicament in which it puts its targets; and as Barendt points out,

> It would be difficult to prosecute successfully the dissemination of hate speech only to members of that group; a restricted publication would be unlikely to stir up hatred against them, although it might cause them considerable psychological distress. In contrast, distribution of hate material among members of an extremist political party would certainly meet the requirement that publication stirs up hatred, although the distress caused to members of the target group would then be indirect.[60]

This suggests that the offences would be too narrowly drafted if their objective were to protect targeted groups against emotional wounds and infringement of their dignity. If this were the case, 'it might be better if the law simply penalised the publication of hate speech, whether or not it was likely to cause an eruption of hatred against a particular group'.[61]

In conclusion, even though criminal law is often too narrow in dealing with expressions of hatred, it is nevertheless necessary to draw tight lines when it comes to criminal prosecutions. Hate speech laws are important, not only because they may in many circumstances be used to fight hate speech, but also because they have a symbolic and legal value; they send the message that hate speech is not protected speech but an offence. However, they may be better used if efforts were concentrated on strong cases where prosecution is likely to result in a conviction.

58 *Ibid.*
59 Goodall (2009), p. 224.
60 Barendt (2005), p. 179.
61 *Ibid.*

> In the area of hate speech, there is a real danger that suspects will present themselves to the pubic as 'martyrs' or 'victims' or, in the event of acquittal, that they present the outcome of the case as a victory for their views.[62]

It might be better therefore to have alternative mechanisms that will tackle the acts and grounds not foreseen in criminal law and channel, when necessary, extreme cases to criminal law. In the UK subtler forms of hate speech in the media are mostly addressed by media self-regulatory mechanisms and these will be explored in the next chapter.

VII Hate speech on the internet

The use of speech in the interest of oppression, this is to say, in order to manufacture and enable different forms of status subordination, segregation and exploitation has been performed with whichever medium has been available at different points in time: pamphlets, shouting in streets, then the use of the telephone, television, radio, etc.

> Long before the Internet entered our homes racist groups made use of other communication tools including the telephone networks as far back as the 1970s. For example, the Western Guard Party, a white supremacist neo-Nazi group based in Toronto, Canada, had a telephone answering machine which was used to propagate hatred.[63]

The wish to disseminate messages to the largest number of people possible is therefore nothing new, and the internet can offer just that and even better than ever before. Different types of media, for example, television, radio, press and advertising, represent different challenges to regulation and the internet is no exception, and quite possibly it is the most challenging medium to regulate to date.

The peculiarities of the internet include that there is no single entity or government in charge of its regulation; and given its 'global' nature, it calls for coordination.[64] The governments need to act together for the creation of laws and for maintaining the policing of the State and for co-coordinating and aligning national policy with initiatives and policies at both supranational and international levels of 'internet governance'. Regulation is particularly difficult when it comes to 'content'. The

62 Appendix to Recommendation No. R (97) 20, on 'Hate speech', Explanatory Memorandum, para. 37.
63 Akdeniz (2009), p. 8.
64 Only the 'name spaces' in the internet; the internet protocol address space and the domain name system (DNS) are directed by a maintenance organisation, the Internet Corporation for Assigned Names and Numbers (ICANN).

existence of different political, moral, cultural, historical and constitutional values between different States shrinks the chances of coming to agreements and of balancing freedom of expression with other contending rights. Indeed,

> It has become clear during the policy discussions of the last ten years that, in particular, the USA opposes any regulatory effort to combat racist publications on the internet on freedom of expression grounds based upon the values attached to the First Amendment of the USA Constitution.[65]

There are, however, other organisations and States that appreciate the need for international agreements. An example of this is the Council of Europe's Additional Protocol to the Convention on Cybercrime, concerning the criminalisation of acts of a racist and xenophobic nature committed through computer systems, Strasbourg 2003. This initiative was discussed in Chapter 5, III, where it was also noted that the UK has not yet signed this Protocol. As we know, States are free to join or not these sorts of Protocols and can make reservations to international agreements in order to reserve for themselves the right to introduce legislation only when they deem such new laws necessary. Nevertheless, while it is undeniable that there are cultural, historical, political and legal differences between jurisdictions, it is equally undeniable that the same harm – the harm of hate speech to identifiable identity groups – exists regardless of frontiers and indeed may 'feel the same' regardless of the geographical location. Asserting and promoting the subordination of women – for example, through the dissemination of a message or image that glorifies gang rape – harms women in the US as much as it does women in Mexico, Australia, the UK or South Africa, regardless of the many differences among these jurisdictions; if anything, as a matter of solidarity, but also because women are still vulnerable in most jurisdictions. The same can be said about other identity groups that may stand in a vulnerable position, be it at a cultural, economic or political level. Therefore, the predicament of the targets of hate speech should be more clearly recognised and considered when speaking about the obstacles that the differences among jurisdictions represent for concerted regulation. I have commented on this before in the context of homophobia (Chapter 3, III, 1), where it was noted that the hostilities and attacks on LGBT people wherever they occur send the same hateful message to everyone of us wherever we might be and serve as an indicator of the vulnerability of homosexual people. Moreover, as we shall see, the role of the organised civil society in the regulation of the internet is, and it could be anticipated that it will continue to

65 Akdeniz (2009), p. 19.

be, of paramount importance. Identity groups (regardless of frontiers and even precisely because of unfair frontier-based disparities – this is to say, regardless of different jurisdictions' values and even precisely because of some jurisdictions' values) can contribute to the creation of internet 'content' policies and 'terms of service' or 'community standards' that will help identify instances of hate speech and make well substantiated complaints. There are, however, problematic issues related to claims based on 'identity'. This was discussed in Chapter 2, V, 3. Nevertheless, the point remains; the views and the predicament of identity groups as a result of hate speech online should be at the centre of any discussion about content regulation.

The growing problem of hate speech on the internet has therefore prompted responses from a variety of agents, including governments, supranational and international organisations, as well as the organised civil society. However, given the internet's decentralised and borderless nature, the challenges it represents for regulation remain and the question as to who is going to set the standards for the internet governance remain unanswered. There are, however, constant initiatives, changes and developments from different stakeholders. Looking back at some initiatives and pointing to some current developments can therefore help us get an idea of the size and complexity of internet regulation. Indeed, as it has already been suggested, it is more common to speak about the internet's governance instead of regulation. This is because the role of the nation-state is not exclusive and more varied forms of regulation come into play. A working definition of internet governance is 'the development and application by governments, the private sector and civil society, in their respective roles, of shared principles, norms, rules, decision-making procedures, and programs that shape the evolution and use of the Internet'.[66] This definition emanated from an initiative from the UN General Assembly Resolution 56/183 of 21 December 2001, which endorsed the holding of the World Summit on the Information Society (WSIS) in two phases. The first phase in Geneva, December 2003 took place with the objective to develop and foster a clear statement of political will and take concrete steps to establish the foundations for an information society for all, reflecting all the different interests at stake. The second phase took place in Tunis, November 2005; its objective was to put Geneva's Plan of Action into motion as well as to find solutions and reach agreements in the fields of internet governance, financing mechanisms, and follow-up and implementation of the Geneva and Tunis documents.

Among the most important insights derived from the Tunis phase two is the recognition of the necessity for a multi-stakeholder platform for an

---

66 Tunis Agenda for the Information Society, WSIS-05/TUNIS/DOC/6(Rev.1)-E, of 18 November 2005, 34.

effective governance of the internet. The WSIS Tunis Agenda for the Information Society affirmed that the management of the internet encompasses both technical and public policy issues:

> [it] should involve all stakeholders and relevant intergovernmental and international organisations. In this respect, it is recognised that:
>
> a.   Policy authority for Internet-related public policy issues is the sovereign right of States. They have rights and responsibilities for international Internet-related public policy issues.
> b.   The private sector has had, and should continue to have, an important role in the development of the Internet, both in the technical and economic fields.
> c.   Civil society has also played an important role on Internet matters, especially at community level, and should continue to play such a role.
> d.   Intergovernmental organizations have had, and should continue to have, a facilitating role in the co-ordination of Internet-related public policy issues.
> e.   International organizations have also had and should continue to have an important role in the development of Internet-related technical standards and relevant policies.[67]

Building on paragraphs 109 and 110 of the Tunis Agenda, the WSIS forum is organised each year and has since 2003 served as a platform for coordination of multi-stakeholder activities, information exchange, creation of knowledge and sharing of best practice. As things stand now and given the particular nature of the internet, multi-stakeholders cooperation seems so far a promising approach.[68]

The prominence given to the State is nevertheless clear; however, there are alternatives and additional measures to State legislation, particularly with regard to the regulation of content. These are in general terms self- and co-regulatory initiatives.[69] For example, companies that offer Web 2.0

---

67 *Ibid*, 35.
68 See the World Summit on the Information Society website at www.itu.int/wsis/index.html (accessed 22 March 2015).
69 Some documents which have encouraged self-regulation and co-regulatory initiatives regarding internet content are: the Declaration on Freedom of Communication on the Internet adopted by the Committee of Ministers of the Council of Europe on 28 May 2003; the Council of Europe Recommendation Rec (2001) 8, of 5 September 2001 on self-regulation concerning cyber-content; and the European Union's Action Plan on promoting safer use of the internet, Decision No. 854/2005/EC of the European Parliament and of the Council establishing a Multiannual Community Programme on promoting safer use of the internet and new online technologies, PE-CONS 3688/1/04Rev1, Strasbourg, 11 May 2005.

services such as Google, YouTube, Facebook, Blogger and others have adopted policies and community standards indicating the kind of content that is not permitted and can therefore be reported and ultimately removed.[70] However, as will be seen in the next chapter, self-regulation is often not enough and does not sufficiently protect targeted groups. Although harmful content can be reported, companies like Facebook and YouTube set their own guidelines and decide by themselves whether or not a particular content is harmful and they do not necessarily understand the harm of hate speech nor their responsibility in its propagation. Users may well have the right to report; '[h]owever, such reports often are ignored and the content proliferates faster than conscientious users can report it'.[71]

There are a number of mechanisms that have been used around the globe in order to contest hate speech on the internet. They are all controversial, under construction and entail a number of technical and legal conundrums.[72] Some of these mechanisms are: (a) blocking orders. These are court orders requiring internet service providers (ISPs) to block access to people, within their jurisdiction, to particular websites. They are controversial and of limited effect, if anything, because harmful content can reappear with a different name or in a jurisdiction where such content is

70 Web 2.0 is a term which refers to new technologies designed to be used on the world wide web with the intention of enhancing information sharing and collaboration among users rather than simply retrieving information, with interactivity taking centre stage. See Akdeniz (2009), p. 14.

71 *Ibid*, p. 112. Remarks made by Christopher Wolf, Chair, Anti-Defamation League Internet Task Force to the Commission on Security and Cooperation in Europe (US Helsinki Commission): Briefing on Hate in the Information Age, Washington DC, 15 May 2008, at http://archive.adl.org/nr/exeres/6c6e9436-cb7a-44e0-8704-e669729e8a6c,8c8c250f-da79-405f-b716-d4409cab5396,frameless.html (accessed 21 May 2015).

72 These mechanisms are aimed at 'controlling' what ISPs do. An ISP is an organisation that provides services for accessing broadband, using or participating in the internet (e.g. the ordinary person's everyday use of the internet through mailbox for which the ISP could be Yahoo! Mail, Gmail, AOL, etc.). The mechanisms that are outlined in this section can be said to interfere with 'net neutrality'. This is, with the guarantee that no content or application could be discriminated against by a network owner. This was guaranteed by the way in which the internet was first built. This is to say that the technology of the internet didn't have the capacity to discriminate because this was not in its code. Nowadays, 'net neutrality' is a regulatory commitment which is still being debated. Nevertheless, any idea of neutrality where there are power imbalances in society at large is arguable. There can be no neutrality when only some people can effectively put content forward, attract advertisers' revenue, and when their ideas or 'content' is in mainstream culture and is dominant anyway. The principles of net neutrality are, however, very significant regarding technical and commercial aspects of the internet. For example, those related to treating all data on the internet equally by not charging differently by user, content, site, etc. For example, charging Yahoo to deliver its search results faster and more reliably than Google's. For 'net neutrality' discussions, see Wu (2003), pp. 141–176 and, generally, Lawrence Lessig's works, available at www.lessig.org/?s=Net+neutrality (accessed 28 May 2015).

allowed.[73] (b) notice-based liability for ISPs and takedown procedures. This was primarily developed to combat child pornography and entails notices to ISPs to take down content over which in general terms they have knowledge and control. These are particularly used in Europe.[74] (c) Internet hotlines for reporting illegal content. For example, the work done by the International Network Against Cyber Hate, which acts as an umbrella organisation for hotlines specialised in racist content. It was founded in 2002 aiming at combating discrimination on the internet [sic]. It is a foundation under Dutch Law based in Amsterdam but it can receive complaints from all over the world where the exact location of the discriminatory expression is provided (URL, newsgroup or other locations).[75] These types of hotline police and assess content and, if found illegal or against the ISP's own terms of service or community standards, they seek to have the hate sites or expressions removed from the servers. Their work has been particularly successful fighting anti-Semitism and it would be desirable to have equally strong hotlines to challenge hate on other grounds. (d) Rating and filtering systems. These are tools that 'enable users to make their own decisions on how to deal with unwanted and harmful content'.[76] They can include rating systems and electronic labels in web documents to vet their content before a computer displays them. A major problem with these mechanisms is that although they make it possible to hide things from our children and indeed to prevent ourselves from seeing expressions of hatred, the harm in the propagation of hate messages that manufacture the status subordination, exclusion and exploitation of some people, including perhaps our own identity group, is still out there. Moreover, what in fact is vetoed or filtered is up to the companies that design and develop the software and it may over- or under-include different types of material. (e) Information, education and awareness campaigns. The internet is a medium and therefore it can also be used to raise awareness, to find like-minded people who share experiences of oppression and are

73 In early 1996, Deutsche Telekom blocked users of its subsidiary T-Online computer network from accessing internet sites used to spread anti-Semitic propaganda. Deutsche Telekom was responding to demands by Mannheim prosecutors who were investigating Ernst Zundel and his Toronto-based Zundelsite. This initial attempt to block access to Zundel's website resulted in the controversial material being copied and mirrored all over the internet. Discussion and details for this case are in Akdeniz (2009) pp. 67–69, 116.

74 See Directive 2000/31/EC of the European Parliament and of the Council of 8 June 2000 on certain legal aspects of information society services, in particular electronic commerce, in the internal market ('Directive on Electronic Commerce').

75 Uniform resource locator (URL) is the global address of documents and other resources on the world wide web. It provides a mechanism for retrieving them.

76 Decision No. 854/2005/EC of the European Parliament and of the Council of 11 May 2005 establishing a Multiannual Community Programme on promoting safer use of the internet and new online technologies, Annex I, Action 2: Tackling unwanted harmful content.

therefore capable of articulating the harm, give it a name, offer a strong counter-speech in response to hate speech and make successful complaints. A problem that remains is nevertheless one about power imbalances and access to resources. It is for this reason that legal and institutional backing is always necessary when it comes to disadvantaged groups. Given that fighting hate speech is a legitimate claim and given that its targets are in a position of disadvantage, the State should incentivise, promote and facilitate their access to a medium and the procedural and material means to in effect contest bad speech with more speech. Without a counter-speech that is actually 'heard' there is no real communication and hate speech becomes something similar to the children's game in which one rings a doorbell and then everyone runs away, facing no consequences whatsoever and gladly being aware of that.

As we have mentioned earlier, the civil society (including international NGOs) has a very important role to play in the regulation of the internet. Indeed, a good example of this is the week-long campaign by Women Action and the Media (WAM!), the Everyday Sexism project and the activist Soraya Chemaly to remove supposedly humorous content endorsing rape and domestic violence via Facebook.[77] Examples included a photograph of the singer Rihanna's bloodied and beaten face, captioned with 'Chris Brown's Greatest Hits', a reference to the assault by her ex-boyfriend; a photograph of a woman in a pool of blood had the caption 'I like for her brains'; and another photograph, of a man holding a rag over a woman's mouth, was captioned 'Does this smell like chloroform to you?'[78]

The campaigners were successful in persuading advertisers to withdraw their adverts from Facebook. This was possible due to the more than 57,000 tweets; the over 4,900 emails sent highlighting the issue under the hashtag #FBrape; protests of more than 100 advocacy groups; and the support of over 60 feminist groups signing an open letter calling on Facebook to:

1. Recognize speech that trivializes or glorifies violence against girls and women as hate speech and make a commitment that you will not tolerate this content.
2. Effectively train moderators to recognize and remove gender-based hate speech.

---

77 WAM! is a non-profit organisation dedicated to building a robust, effective and inclusive movement for gender justice in the media. See www.womenactionmedia.org (accessed 22 May 2015). The Everyday Sexism project exist to catalogue instances of sexism experienced by women on a day-to-day basis. See http://everydaysexism.com (accessed 22 May 2015).
78 Rory (2013).

3. Effectively train moderators to understand how online harassment differently affects women and men, in part due to the real-world pandemic of violence against women.[79]

In response Facebook did bring the argument for freedom of expression and explained the fact that they include a diverse community of more than a billion people.[80] However, the pressure from the community and the loss of revenue from advertisers (at least 15 companies removed their adverts, including Nissan UK, Nationwide UK, J Street and WestHost) proved successful and Facebook took on board the petitions made in the letter. Facebook's Terms of Service, section 3, Safety, include a numeral 7 where they establish that 'You will not post content that: is hate speech, threatening, or pornographic; incites violence; or contains nudity or graphic or gratuitous violence'.[81] Now, according to their Community Standards, 'Facebook removes hate speech, which includes content that directly attacks people based on their race, ethnicity, national origin, religious affiliation, sexual orientation, sex, gender, or gender identity, or serious disabilities or diseases.'[82] Facebook warns, however, that they

> do allow humor, satire, or social commentary related to these topics, and [they] believe that when people use their authentic identity, they are more responsible when they share this kind of commentary. For that reason, [they] ask that Page owners associate their name and Facebook Profile with any content that is insensitive, even if that content does not violate our policies.[83]

Facebook, however, can be subject to the laws of particular territories and governments can ask them to remove certain content that violates local laws. Nevertheless, as happens with most internet content, if it does not violate their Community Standards but the content is illegal under local law, then they may make it unavailable *only* in the relevant country or territory.[84] Once again we can appreciate that local governments and State regulation are important, and although with limitations are fundamental

79 Nelson (2013). Letter of 21 May 2013, available at www.womenactionmedia.org/face-bookaction/open-letter-to-facebook (accessed 22 May 2015).
80 See Facebook's response of 28 May 2013, 'Controversial, harmful and hateful speech on Facebook', by Marne Levine, VP of Global Public Policy, available at www.facebook.com/notes/facebook-safety/controversial-harmful-and-hateful-speech-on-facebook/5744306559 11054 (accessed 26 June 2015).
81 Facebook Terms of Service, available at www.facebook.com/legal/terms, date of last revision 30 January 2015 (accessed 22 May 2015).
82 Facebook Community Standards, available at www.facebook.com/communitystandards (accessed 18 May 2015).
83 *Ibid.*
84 *Ibid.*

in order to make a difference. In this regard, to mention just one example, the police in England, Wales and Northern Ireland run a hate crime (including internet hate speech) legal advice and reporting website named 'True Vision'. The website explains that, as we have seen, it is an offence to stir up hatred on the grounds of race, religion and sexual orientation. Regarding the internet, it explains that:

> The content of a website can also be illegal when it threatens or harasses a person or a group of people. If this is posted because of hostility based on race, religion, sexual orientation, disability or transgender identity then we [the police] consider it to be a hate crime. Illegal material could be in words, pictures, videos, and even music and could include; messages calling for racial or religious violence, web pages with pictures, videos or descriptions that glorify violence against anyone due to their race, religion, disability, sexual orientation or because they are transgender, and chat forums where people ask other people to commit hate crimes.[85]

The police are thus making and explaining the connection that may exist between hate speech and hate crimes assisted by the internet. The police explain that it is the responsibility of the Director of Public Prosecutions to decide who should be prosecuted.[86] As we have noted, internet content, although it might be viewed virtually anywhere, is not subject to every country's laws and, for example, in the UK an offence is committed only where the person who posts or controls the material is in this country. Thus, for example, if someone inside the UK posts on a US site then that can be illegal in the UK even when such content might not be illegal in the US. In other words, 'the person posting is always responsible for their content and web hosts could be if they, for instance, encourage or knowingly allow it to remain'.[87]

The police in England and Wales offer people who believe they have encountered hate online that might be illegal three options. (1) Report it to the web administrator, for example to Facebook or YouTube, using the 'report' option. Other websites have a 'contact us' page where it should be possible to contact the website's owner. (2) Report it to the hosting company. This is, if a website itself is hateful or supports violence, then it should be

---

85 True Vision, illegal hate content, www.report-it.org.uk/reporting_internet_hate_crime (accessed 25 May 2015).
86 In order to ensure consistency amongst prosecutors, the Director of Public Prosecutions has produced 'Guidelines on prosecuting cases involving communications sent via social media', available at www.cps.gov.uk/legal/a_to_c/communications_sent_via_social_media/index.html (accessed 25 May 2015).
87 True Vision, websites from outside the UK, www.report-it.org.uk/reporting_internet_hate_crime (accessed 25 May 2015).

reported to its 'host', which is to say the company that provides the place where the website sits.[88] (3) Report illegal internet material to the police. The first two options largely depend on the Terms of Service of the companies involved where they establish the kind of content that is permitted. The third option instead is for content that expressly matches the description of illegal content in the UK if such content originates in the UK.[89]

Hate speech on the internet is therefore a matter of content that cannot be regulated by a single government or agency. There are constantly new developments, forums and initiatives; and indeed, we as consumers are in a process of learning both how to use this technology and the ways in which it can negatively affect us. If legislating and prosecuting for hate speech on the internet is difficult, more difficulties can be expected for the recognition and contestation of ED in this medium. However, the principles that we have established so far, which we will continue to elaborate upon in the next chapters, will be useful in order to recognise the harm caused (in whatever medium it appears), name it and raise awareness, which in themselves can start redressing the sense of helplessness that this sort of misrecognition generates.

VIII Conclusions

There is an internationally shared concern about the use of speech in the interest of oppression; although in different ways, many jurisdictions around the world have enacted hate speech legislation. They tend to focus on extreme forms; often intended behaviour and threatening speech that calls for violence. Hate speech laws are nevertheless controversial and difficult to enforce because they involve considerations of a moral, ideological, political and legal nature. However, their mere existence has a symbolic value and they should be used to prosecute the most blatant cases of hate speech. This, however, leaves untouched the prejudice and stereotypes of mainstream public discourse (ED) even though they might be equally damaging and more pernicious. Although not uniformly recognising these expressions as forms of discrimination, there are initiatives, particularly in the self-regulatory codes for radio, press, television and advertising, aiming at preventing them; this is what the next chapter will address in the British context.

---

88 It is possible to find out which company hosts a website by entering their web address on the 'Who is hosting this?' website, available at www.whoishostingthis.com (accessed 25 May 2015).

89 Illegal content can be reported at www.report-it.org.uk/your_police_force (accessed 25 May 2015). The police further explain that crimes on the internet are located where the person is when they post the material, but this location is often not known, even if we know who is suspected of posting it. The Home Office rules say that if the location is not known then it is the responsibility of the force where the complainant lives to commence enquiries.

IX References

Akdeniz, Yaman (2009), *Racism on the Internet*, Council of Europe.

Allport, Gordon W. (1979), *The Nature of Prejudice*, New York: Perseus.

Barendt, Eric (2005), *Freedom of Speech*, 2nd ed., Oxford: Oxford University Press.

Chrisafis, Angelique (2015), 'France launches major anti-racism and hate speech campaign', *Guardian*, 17 April, available at www.theguardian.com/world/2015/apr/17/france-launches-major-anti-racism-and-hate-speech-campaign (accessed 15 May 2015).

Cram, Ian (2006), *Contested Words: Legal Restrictions on Freedom of Speech in Liberal Democracies*, Aldershot: Ashgate.

Equality and Human Rights Commission (2011), *From Local Voices to Global Audience: Engaging with the International Convention for the Elimination of All Forms of Racial Discrimination*.

Equality and Human Rights Commission (2015), *Legal Framework on Freedom of Expression*.

Feldman, David (1995), 'Freedom of expression', in Harris, D. and Joseph, S., eds, *The International Covenant on Civil and Political Rights and United Kingdom Law*, Oxford: Clarendon.

Gavison, Ruth (1995), 'Incitement and the limits of Law', in Post, Robert, ed., *Censorship and Silencing: Practices of Cultural Regulation*, Getty Research Institute Publications and Exhibitions Program.

Goodall, Kay (2009), 'Challenging hate speech: incitement to hatred on grounds of sexual orientation in England, Wales and northern Ireland', *The International Journal of Human Rights*, vol. 13, nos. 2–3.

Hare, Ivan (2006), 'Crosses, crescents and sacred cows: criminalising incitement to religious hatred', *Public Law*, vol. 3.

Hare, Ivan (2009), 'Extreme speech under international and regional human rights standards', in Hare, Ivan and Weinstein, James, eds, *Extreme Speech and Democracy*, Oxford: Oxford University Press.

Heinze, Eric (2006), 'Viewpoint absolutism and hate speech', *Modern Law Review*, vol. 69, no. 4.

Home Office (1999), 'Report of the Macpherson Inquiry' Cm. 4262-I, 24 February.

MacKinnon, Catharine (1994), *Only Words*, London: HarperCollins.

Malik, Maleiha (2009), 'Extreme speech and liberalism', in Hare, Ivan and Weinstein, James, eds, *Extreme Speech and Democracy*, Oxford: Oxford University Press.

Nelson, Sara C. (2013), '#FBrape: Will Facebook heed open letter protesting "Endorsement of rape & domestic violence"?', *Huffington Post UK*, 28 May, available at www.huffingtonpost.co.uk/2013/05/28/fbrape-will-facebook-heed-open-letter-protesting-endorsement-rape-domestic-violence_n_3346520.html?utm_hp_ref=uk (accessed 22 May 2015).

Nicol, Andrew, Sharland, Andrew and Millar, Gavin (2009), *Media Law and Human Rights*, 2nd ed., Oxford: Oxford University Press.

Parekh, Bhikhu (2006), *Rethinking Multiculturalism: Cultural Diversity and Political Theory*, Houndmills: Palgrave.

Polelle, Michael (2003), 'Racial and ethnic group defamation: a speech-friendly proposal', *Boston College Third World Law Journal*, vol. 23, no. 213.

Rory, Carroll (2013), 'Facebook gives way to campaign against hate speech on its pages', *Guardian*, 29 May, available at www.theguardian.com/technology/2013/may/29/facebook-campaign-violence-against-women?CMP=EMCNEWEML 661912 (accessed 22 May 2015).

Simester, A.P., Spencer, J.R., Sullivan, G.R. and Virgo, G.J. (2010), *Simester and Sullivan's Criminal Law: Theory and Doctrine*, 4th ed., Oxford: Hart.

Strossen, Nadine (1992), 'Balancing the rights to freedom of expression and equality: a civil liberties approach to hate speech in campus', in Coliver, Sandra, ed., *Striking a Balance: Hate Speech, Freedom of Expression and Non-discrimination*, London: Article XIX.

Waldron, Jeremy (2008), 'Free speech and the menace of hysteria', *New York Review of Books*, vol. 55, available at www.nybooks.com/articles/21452 (accessed 1 September 2015).

Waldron, Jeremy (2012), *The Harm in Hate Speech*, Cambridge, MA: Harvard University Press.

Wu, Tim (2003), 'Network neutrality, broadband discrimination', *Journal on Telecommunications and High Tech Law*, vol. 2.

Chapter 7

The regulation of *everyday discrimination* in the media

1 Introduction

In this book, *everyday discrimination* (ED) means the printed and audiovisual production and reproduction of images and messages that use demeaning stereotypes, ridicule, malign or disparage people on the grounds of their belonging to a disadvantaged group, be it with such grounds in conscious thought, perception, knowledge or consequence. While discriminatory images and messages can exist in the workplace, at school, in the provision of services and generally in everyday interactions,[1] the regulatory aspects that are addressed in this chapter refer to ED in the media – television and radio including content on demand, the press and advertising in all of these and on the internet.

Although there are some commonalities, particularly at the European level, the media is regulated in a variety of ways around the world and each jurisdiction is unique. The regulators can be governmental agencies, committees and professional associations (the media industry). There is usually a mix of two or more of these depending on the jurisdiction. The arguments of principle discussed in Chapter 6 with regard to freedom of speech, and in particular its limits regarding hate speech legislation, also apply to the media; indeed, hate speech laws in the UK as well as regional instruments relevant to this jurisdiction addressing freedom of expression and its limits often expressly include hate speech transmitted through printed and electronic media. Therefore, the media is not free to spread hate speech although it can report on hate speech (Chapter 8). Now, as discussed in Chapter 5, the international community through the UN and regional systems such as the Council of Europe and the European Union has – to various degrees – acknowledged that speech can be harmful in subtle forms that escape hate speech regulation, but it has also shown concern about further regulation that may infringe freedom of

---

1 Discriminatory images and messages in contexts other than the media may constitute harassment, either under the Equality Act 2010, or if directed at an individual under the Protection from Harassment Act 1997.

expression. As established from the outset and throughout this book (in particular Chapters 2 and 8), the redress of ED advocated in this book does not seek or demand censorship; it argues instead in favour of meeting bad speech with more speech, which ultimately reinforces free speech values and underpinnings such as democracy and pluralism, which the media should respect and procure.

Speaking of media freedom as such is nevertheless problematic and raises various questions. For example, who has the right to press and media freedom? Is it the proprietors, editors or journalists? Or is it the consumers whose right it is to receive information? Also, is the media exercising free speech that produces debate or is the information provided just another commodity? None of these questions has a simple answer.[2] For some authors, the media is no more than a tool for freedom of expression. It is an instrumental rather than a primary or fundamental human right and, therefore, 'special privileges and immunities should only be recognised insofar as they promote the values of freedom of speech, in particular the public interest in pluralism in its sources of information'.[3] The media's exercise of free speech is therefore different from an individual's and, as explored in Chapter 4 (IV), the media's power is greater than that of individuals, given its resources and wide audience. But a free media is essential for democracy, it can be a most useful check on government and has the potential to function as a 'public watchdog' in imparting information and ideas of public interest. This brings with it certain responsibilities aimed at securing pluralism, understood as 'the diversity of sources of information and the range of opinion available to the public';[4] for example, through the recognition of a right to reply which, although controversial, does not disproportionately infringe media freedom. In the words of Barendt, 'Editorial freedom, like the press freedom of which it is an aspect, is subordinate to freedom of speech, which is arguably better served by recognition of the right of reply with which the editors right conflicts.'[5]

Given this background, governments are frequently limited to the establishment of general rules for the media; for example, about content that can be harmful (as expressly set out in relevant legislation) and about the conditions for licensing. Media content that falls outside express freedom of speech limits is most frequently 'self-regulated'. Self-regulation is in general terms aimed at establishing competition strategies, fulfilling governmental obligations, giving response to the pressures from the organised civil society and audiences and interpreting legislation. Likewise, the

2 See Barendt (2005), pp. 441–444.
3 *Ibid*, p. 422.
4 *Ibid*, p. 444.
5 *Ibid*, p. 427. See also Chapter 2, footnotes 103–105.

media industry is frequently in dialogue with the Government in order to achieve common goals, often referred to as co-regulation.

The organised civil society and advertisers can indirectly regulate the media. Civil society organisations are often integrated without interest in financial gain by people involved in specific issues; for example, combating racial or religious discrimination (Chapter 4, IV). They – on their own – lack any real power to influence media decisions about content; however, they can raise awareness, create pressure and, on some occasions, support complaints against specific media products. Such support frequently carries arguments which may have an influence on media policies. On the other hand, although not formally recognised, advertisers and/or sponsors *do* have an influence on media content. Most media outlets, be they private or public, largely depend on advertising revenue and sponsors to subsist, and advertisers can regulate the media in a rather peculiar way. They can implicitly or explicitly make content demands of the media, backing these with a threat to stop sponsorship if their demands are not met.

The 'media' can include magazines, films, theatre productions and virtually any means of bringing to the public images or messages for entertainment or information. While the theoretical analysis presented in the previous chapters of this study can apply to any of these media, the regulatory aspects discussed in this chapter are limited to television, radio, press and advertising (including their internet remit) in the UK. Even though this jurisdiction does not formally recognise discriminatory speech as a form of discrimination, the type of harm to which ED refers has, to some extent, been addressed in this country. The discussion that follows is therefore limited to discriminatory content as understood by media regulatory bodies in the UK. Their codes, guidelines and some adjudications are discussed in order to present the way in which ED has been addressed, identify problems, and suggest alternative ways to better respond to the claims of those afflicted. The ultimate aim is to derive some general principles that, once adjusted to the specific regulatory frameworks and contexts of individual jurisdictions, may help them to better redress this type of harm and guarantee more effectively free speech for all.

II Regulation of discriminatory media content in the UK

Discriminatory media content in the UK is addressed in a variety of ways. There are regulatory bodies for radio and television, advertising and the press. Each of these has a standards code and sometimes guidelines that are intended to prevent discriminatory content (although not always framed as discriminatory) and they all keep a record of the complaints they have dealt with. This is not particular to the UK; indeed, since 1997 the European Council had invited media regulatory bodies to address the problems of discrimination and intolerance within their codes of conduct.[6]

Media regulatory bodies in the UK can monitor possible breaches of their codes; nevertheless they tend to be reactive after receiving complaints from the public. That said, the organised civil society is on many occasions dissatisfied as little seems to be done, especially about generalised prejudice and issues that the media considers too petty to deserve consideration and because it is ultimately up to the media industry to decide how to adjudicate. Then, the politicisation of culture is to some degree jeopardised by the frustration generated by the media having the last word (Chapter 4, IV).

I The regulation of radio and television

Ofcom (Office of Communications) is the regulatory authority for the UK's communications industries, with responsibilities across television and radio sectors, fixed-line telecoms, mobiles, postal services and the airwaves over which wireless devices operate. Ofcom is accountable to the UK Parliament and funded by fees from industry for regulating broadcasting and communications networks, as well as grant-in-aid from the Government. It operates under a number of Acts of Parliament, in particular the Communications Act 2003. The Act establishes that Ofcom's principal duty is to further the interest of citizens and of consumers, where appropriate by promoting competition (c 21, part 1, section 3 (1)). In this regard Ofcom has, among others, the legal duty to ensure that people who watch television and listen to the radio are protected from *harmful and offensive* material (c 21, part 1, section 3 (2)). As required under the Communications Act 2003, Ofcom has drawn up a 'Code' covering standards in programmes, sponsorship, product placement in television programmes, fairness and privacy. Ofcom has revised its Broadcasting Code at irregular intervals (2005, 2008, 2009, 2010, 2011) and the most recent version took effect in 2013, covering all programmes broadcast on or after 21 March 2013.

The Ofcom Broadcasting Code also gives effect to a number of requirements relating to television in the Audiovisual Media Services Directive[7] and has been drafted in the light of the Human Rights Act 1998 and the European Convention on Human Rights. In particular, in the light of the right to freedom of expression, as expressed in article 10 of the Convention, encompassing the audience's right to receive creative material,

---

6 See Appendix to Recommendation No. R (97) 21, on 'The media and the promotion of a culture of tolerance', 4.
7 Directive 2010/13/EU of the European Parliament and of the Council, OJ L 95/1 of 15 April 2010.

information and ideas without interference but subject to restrictions prescribed by law and necessary in a democratic society. This article goes together with article 8, regarding the right to a person's private and family life, home and correspondence; article 9, the right to freedom of thought, conscience and religion; and article 14, the right to enjoyment of human rights without discrimination on grounds such as sex, race and religion.[8]

In sum, the Code sets standards for television and radio shows, and broadcasters have to follow these rules. Besides harm and offence, the rules cover other areas such as impartiality and accuracy, sponsorship and commercial references as well as fairness and privacy. The section of the Code that in a way addresses content similar to that identified with the concept of ED is section 2, Harm and Offence, whose principle it is to ensure that generally accepted standards are applied to the content of television and radio services so as to provide adequate protection for members of the public from the inclusion in such services of harmful and/or offensive material. Section 2 lists a series of rules, one of which is relevant with regard to discriminatory content. This is 2.3:

> In applying generally accepted standards broadcasters must ensure that material which may cause offence is justified by the context. Such material may include, but is not limited to, offensive language, violence, sex, sexual violence, humiliation, distress, violation of human dignity, discriminatory treatment or language (for example on the grounds of age, disability, gender, race, religion, beliefs and sexual orientation). Appropriate information should also be broadcast where it would assist in avoiding or minimising offence.[9]

Ofcom has produced a series of guidelines and research for each section of the Code. Within the guidelines for section 2, Harm and Offence, there are two items directly related to the issue of ED in television and radio. Regarding 'offensive language', the guidelines tell broadcasters that:

---

8 The Ofcom Broadcasting Code (incorporating the Cross-promotion Code) 21 March 2013, p. 2.
9 Context includes (but is not limited to): the editorial content of the programme, programmes or series; the service on which the material is broadcast; the time of broadcast; what other programmes are scheduled before and after the programme or programmes concerned; the degree of harm or offence likely to be caused by the inclusion of any particular sort of material in programmes generally or programmes of a particular description; the likely size and composition of the potential audience and likely expectation of the audience; the extent to which the nature of the content can be brought to the attention of the potential audience, for example by giving information; and the effect of the material on viewers or listeners who may come across it unawares.

Racist terms and material should be avoided unless their inclusion can be justified by the editorial of the programme. Broadcasters should take particular care in their portrayal of culturally diverse matter and should avoid stereotyping unless editorially justified. When considering such matters broadcasters should take into account the possible effects programmes may have on particular sections of the community.[10]

Following this guideline, we can appreciate that racist language and material may in fact be included in programmes if their inclusion can be justified. However, it wouldn't be senseless to anticipate that broadcasters and the audience may have different interpretations and disagree on whether racist terms or materials are justified in particular instances. Therefore, it is important to raise awareness about ED and about the existence of a Broadcasting Code and guidelines so that broadcast instances of ED may be contested effectively, putting forward the arguments that explain why it is deemed – in a particular situation – that the use of racist language or materials is discriminatory. The fact that the Code and the guidelines recognise the potential for harm is important; but a well-informed civil society that is capable of articulating the harm and explaining the reasons why a certain content is unfair and in breach of the Code is also necessary. In turn, the latter can be a mechanism for the politicisation of culture, which allows maligned groups to express themselves and contest demeaning language and representations. Another area where the guidelines show instances of harm but which depend on a 'well-armed' population to contest them is under the headline 'Discriminatory treatment or language (for example, matters relating to age, disability, gender, race, religion and sexual orientation).' The guidelines explain that there is a relationship between representation, meaning the presence and inclusion of a diverse range of people on screen; and portrayal, meaning the roles involved and the way in which minority groups are presented in programmes.[11] Indeed, Ofcom's research has found that:

> Viewers and listeners appreciate programmes that are representative of the diverse society in which they live. If there is an under-representation, the use of stereotypes and caricatures or the discussion of difficult or controversial issues involving that community may be seen as offensive in that it is viewed as creating a false impression of that minority.[12]

10 Ofcom Guidance Notes, Section 2: Harm and Offence, Issue Ten: 23 July 2012, pp. 2–3.
11 *Ibid*, p. 3.
12 See Ofcom Guidance Notes, Section 2: Harm and Offence, Issue Nine: 16 December 2009, p. 3.

The relationship between misrepresentation and under-representation is a recurrent issue. The under-representation of disadvantaged groups adds to the harm of sporadic representations being stereotypical and demeaning. This is in fact a most important aspect of ED that will be further discussed in Chapter 8. The guidelines generally do not fully acknowledge any harm; they are limited to informing broadcasters of the feelings of the viewers, and/or of the way in which things 'may be seen'. These things said, however, detailing what the harm of demeaning representation consists of may not be Ofcom's most appropriate role. As we will explore in III, 1, this type of work – the recognition of the harm created through ED, and guidance on elements for its identification – may be better placed in an institution with relevant expertise and which has responsibility for the elimination of discrimination and the promotion of equality and human rights.

The authority responsible for regulating on-demand programmes on behalf of Ofcom is ATVOD (Authority for Television on Demand). On-demand services are therefore not subject to Ofcom's Broadcasting Code. However, they must abide by a set of minimum standards under European law which are set out in ATVOD's Rules and Guidance.[13] In this regard, the relevant rule is number 10: Harmful material: material likely to incite hatred, which indicates that: 'An on-demand programme service must not contain any material likely to incite hatred based on race, sex, religion or nationality.'[14] The guidance of this rule is generally in line with the British hate speech legislation explored in Chapter 6. It explains that:

> 'Hatred' is a strong word. It is neither the purpose nor the intention of section 368 E (1) of the Act [Communications Act 2003] to restrict legitimate freedom of speech by prohibiting or restricting discussion, criticism or expressions of antipathy, dislike, ridicule, insult or abuse for groups covered by this requirement. For example it is permissible to express criticism, dislike or ridicule of a religious belief system or its practices or urge its adherents to cease practicing or to express *views which are sexist, insulting or offensive but which stop short of being likely to incite hatred.*[15]

It is worth noting the inclusion of 'sex' as a ground protected from hate speech, although it is not considered within the hate speech provisions of the Public Order Act 1986. Hate speech on the grounds of sex is also

---

13 We can only complain about a programme on a regulated video-on-demand service; full list available at www.atvod.co.uk/regulated-services/directory-of-notif.ed-services (accessed 10 June 2015).

14 ATVOD Rules and Guidance. Statutory Rules and Non-Binding Guidance for Providers of On-Demand Programme Services (ODPS). Edition 3.0, 5 May 2015, p. 11.

15 *Ibid.* Italics are the author's.

considered in Facebook's Community Standards (Chapter 6, VII). These inclusions mean that the harm of hate speech on the grounds of sex is recognised by some media and that pressure exists for its recognition where it is not. It is also important to notice that the guidance follows the terms used in the 'freedom of expression saving provisions' (ss. 29J and 29JA) of the Public Order Act 1986 and, therefore, allows an array of expressions that may coincide with discriminatory speech as understood through the concept of ED. However, as noted from the outset, the recognition of ED is not aimed at censorship but at the politicisation of culture so that expressions that misrepresent, stereotype, ridicule, denigrate and segregate members of our community will not remain out of scrutiny. The dangers of leaving these sorts of images and messages 'untouched' are too great – these discriminatory images and messages can become accepted definitions and set unfavourable standards of treatment. Ultimately the images and messages of ED are matters of misrecognition and therefore are unjust (Chapter 2).

Although Ofcom does not have the power to approve programmes before they are broadcast, it may launch investigations on its own initiative as well as investigate complaints made by any person or body who considers that a broadcaster has failed to comply with the standards reflected in the Broadcasting Code.[16] Complaints can be registered online and Ofcom publishes its decisions on broadcasting standard cases in its *Broadcast Bulletin*. It is nevertheless disappointing that although Ofcom will acknowledge every complaint it receives, it will not normally correspond any further with individual complainants. Ofcom assesses the gravity of a complaint, whether it raises substantive issues under the Code and whether there may have been a breach of a particular provision and which actions to take further.[17] This reinforces the need for a strong and organised civil society that can make complaints that will be taken seriously.

If something in a specific radio or television programme that has been broadcast 'concerns' the consumer, she can use the online form provided. This form can be used whether the programme was on a BBC TV channel or radio station. Ofcom's complaints website explains that if the programme was on BBC iPlayer or S4C's Clic, the complaint should be to the BBC or to the S4C Authority in the first instance. Nevertheless, if their response is not satisfactory, the consumer can complain to Ofcom by completing an online form. If the programme was on another on-demand TV

---

16 See Ofcom Procedures for investigating breaches of content standards for television and radio, 1 June 2011, 1.7.
17 *Ibid*, 1.17–1.20.

or radio service, the authority responsible is, as mentioned earlier, the ATVOD.[18]

Ofcom's online complaint form includes four steps. First, in order to handle the complaint, to provide the consumer with information and to take appropriate action, Ofcom requires the consumer to provide personal details (name, address and e-mail). The consumer can oppose these details being passed on to the broadcaster. However, Ofcom warns that it may not be able to deal with the complaint if they cannot disclose these details. Second, the consumer has to provide the time, date, channel and name of the programme that raises the complaint. In third place, the form requires the consumer to give the complaint a subject. The fourth and final step is to give a description of the issue in no more than 1500 characters.[19]

The procedure for dealing with complaints is explained in the 'Procedures for investigating breaches of content standards for television and radio', which took effect from 1 June 2011. Ofcom's guidelines and procedures are, however, subject to amendment and change at any time; therefore, consumers need to 'keep up to date' by themselves. Ofcom has a statutory duty under the Communications Act 2003, section 325 to establish procedures for the handling and resolution of complaints about the observance of standards set under section 319 and broadcasters are required by the terms of their licences to observe those standards in the provision of their services. Moreover, section 325(1) of the Act requires broadcasters themselves, in addition to Ofcom, to establish their own procedures for the handling and resolution of complaints.[20]

Although Ofcom can make exceptions, there is a time-limit in making a complaint, which is within 20 working days of the broadcast of the relevant programme or the occurrence of the matter under complaint.[21] This again is an example of the need to further assist complainants, possibly through the Equality and Human Rights Commission (EHRC), but certainly, as things stand now, access to redress is haphazard and any success in complaining requires a society capable of reacting effectively in such timescale and under the conditions established by Ofcom.

Based on an initial assessment and review of the relevant broadcast, Ofcom will consider whether there may have been a breach of particular

18 See ATVOD's complaints procedures for determining breaches of ATVOD rules relating to VOD services, in force from January 2014, available at www.atvod.co.uk/complaints (accessed 8 July 2015).
19 The online complaint form is available at https://stakeholders.ofcom.org.uk/tell-us/webflow/broadcast-complaints (accessed 10 June 2015).
20 See Ofcom Procedures for investigating breaches of content standards for television and radio, 1 June 2011, 1.4.
21 *Ibid*, 1.13–1.16.

provisions of the Broadcasting Code which Ofcom considers requires a response from the broadcaster. If not, Ofcom will decide not to investigate further and will publish its decision in its *Broadcast Bulletin*.[22] The procedures do not mention nor do they require that complaints should be assessed by a particular person or group of people with some level of expertise. In cases of discriminatory content this should be a necessary requirement since prejudice and discriminatory beliefs and attitudes are often so normalised that an ordinary member of Ofcom's staff is not necessarily in a position to effectively understand or assess such a complaint. Where nevertheless Ofcom considers that a broadcaster may have failed to comply with particular provisions of the Code, Ofcom will write to the relevant broadcaster summarising the material parts of the complaint, setting out the particular provisions of the Code which it considers are relevant and applicable, and inviting the broadcaster to make representations in response.[23]

Ofcom does accept 'representations from third parties'. However, these are related to persons/bodies who may be directly affected by the outcome of Ofcom's investigation and determination of a complaint and who may have interests independent of the relevant broadcaster of that programme; for example, presenters, producers and/or independent programme makers. Ofcom will take those representations (which may differ from those of the broadcaster) into account and include those persons/bodies in its decision-making process under these procedures.[24] The organised civil society working against discrimination in its various forms could greatly benefit from something similar to this admission of third parties representations. For example, when a case is under investigation, different groups of the organised civil society could communicate their views in respect of a particular case where a breach to the code is alleged; in this way a better balance could be achieved.

On receipt of the broadcaster's representations, Ofcom will prepare a preliminary view on the substance of the complaint. This will contain a summary of the complaint(s); a summary of the material parts of the programme/broadcast to which the complaint(s) relates; the particular provisions of the Broadcasting Code which Ofcom considers are relevant and applicable to the complaint(s); and Ofcom's preliminary assessment of whether any breaches of those provisions have occurred and the reasons for that assessment.[25] On receipt of the preliminary view, the broadcaster and any relevant third party may make further representations.[26] This begs

---

22 *Ibid*, 1.20.
23 *Ibid*, 1.22.
24 *Ibid*, p. 7.
25 *Ibid*, 1.25.
26 *Ibid*, 1.27.

the question as to why the complainant is not given any chance to further explain the reasons for his or her complaint in the light of Ofcom's preliminary view. Moreover this also adds to the need to accept third-party representations from the organised civil society working against discrimination.

Once Ofcom has considered the broadcaster's representations on its preliminary view, it will reach its final decision and inform the broadcaster, which will be given the opportunity to correct factual inaccuracies only.[27] The decision is finally published in Ofcom's *Broadcast Bulletin* on its website. Ofcom might judge that an issue is in breach, resolved or not in breach of their rules and the decisions are held on the broadcasters' compliance records. If a broadcaster breaks the rules repeatedly, or in a way that Ofcom considers to be serious, then Ofcom can impose sanctions such as a substantial fine, shortening or even taking away the channel or station's licence to broadcast. Ofcom's range of sanctions include: a decision to issue a direction not to repeat a programme or advertisement; issue a direction to broadcast a correction or a statement of Ofcom's findings which may be required to be in such form, and to be included in programmes at such times, as Ofcom may determine; impose a financial penalty; shorten or suspend a licence (not applicable to the BBC, S4C or Channel 4).[28]

Sanctions such as issuing a direction not to repeat a programme or to broadcast a correction or a statement are not antithetical to the remedies pursued in order to redress ED. These are the type of remedies that can help politicise culture by working as a response to discriminatory images and messages. They could offer the opportunity to show and publicise counter-arguments that will expose instances of prejudice and unfairness.

2 The regulation of the press

The regulation of the press in the UK has been under particular scrutiny for the past four years and it is up to the present day relatively uncertain and under construction. To date, IPSO, the Independent Press Standards Organisation, is the independent regulator for the newspaper and magazine industry. It was launched on 8 September 2014 and replaces the PCC (Press Complaints Commission), which was severely criticised during the

---

27 *Ibid*, 1.29.
28 See Ofcom's Procedures for the consideration of statutory sanctions in breaches of broadcast licenses, 19 July 2013, 1.11.

Leveson Inquiry and in its Report.[29] This was a two-part Inquiry investigating the role of the press and police in the wake of the phone-hacking scandal of the now defunct *News of the World* tabloid. The Inquiry was set up by Prime Minister David Cameron, and Lord Justice Leveson was appointed chairman.

Part 1 of the Inquiry examined the culture, practices and ethics of the press and, in particular, the relationship of the press with the public, police and politicians. Part 2 of the Inquiry cannot commence until the current police investigations and any subsequent criminal proceedings have been completed. The hearings for part 1 opened on 14 November 2011 with the following words by Justice Leveson:

> The press provides an essential check on all aspects of public life. That is why any failure within the media affects all of us. At the heart of this Inquiry, therefore, may be one simple question: who guards the guardians?[30]

During eight months of hearings, a range of witnesses were called to give evidence under oath at the Royal Courts of Justice in London. Witnesses included alleged victims of press intrusion (from celebrities to ordinary people hit by tragedy), journalists, newspaper executives and proprietors, police, communications advisers and politicians. The Report on Part 1 of the Inquiry was published on 29 November 2012 and includes, among others, the following recommendations: newspapers should continue to be self-regulated, and the Government should have no power over what they publish; there had to be a new press standards body created by the industry, with a new code of conduct; that body should be *backed by legislation*,

---

29 See, Leveson LJ (2012), *Executive summary*, paras 41–46. Criticisms included that the PCC was not actually a regulator at all. In reality, it was a complaints-handling body. It lacked independence, the Editors' Code Committee which set the rules was wholly made up of serving editors and was separate from the PCC. Its members were appointed by the Press Standards Board of Finance, itself entirely made up of senior industry figures, which also controlled the PCC's finances and appointment of the PCC chair. There was no universal coverage because membership was voluntary and there was a concentration of power in relatively few hands. Its powers were inadequate, especially regarding the right to conduct an effective investigation. The PCC was at the mercy of what it was told by those against whom the complaint was made. Further, even when complaints were upheld, the remedies at its disposal were woefully inadequate and enforceable only by persuasion. In practice, the PCC proved itself to be aligned with the interests of the press. When it did investigate major issues it sought to head off or minimise criticisms of the press. The PCC did not monitor press compliance with the Code and the statistics it published lacked transparency and, in the end, high-profile complainants almost invariably turned to the courts instead of using the PCC.

30 See the Background to the Inquiry at the National Archives, available at http://webarchive.nationalarchives.gov.uk/20140122145147/http://www.levesoninquiry.org.uk (accessed 19 June 2015).

which would create a means to ensure the regulation was independent and effective; and the arrangement would provide the public with confidence that their complaints would be dealt with seriously, and ensure the press were protected from interference.[31] Leveson specifically proposed a system under which the independence and effectiveness of a self-regulator set up by the press could be assured through a process of independent audit or 'recognition'.[32]

Prime Minister David Cameron reportedly promised to implement the recommendations, provided they were not 'bonkers'. However, soon after the Report was published, he said he was not convinced legislation underpinning self-regulation was right.[33] It is worth remembering now that this Inquiry was specifically into the press, not into the media more generally, and that as we have seen, broadcasters are regulated by Ofcom, which is backed by law. Cameron rejected the idea of legislation to underpin the new system of regulation of the press and, instead, the 'compromise solution' was a Royal Charter on self-regulation of the press. The main political parties agreed its terms on 18 March 2013 and the Charter was approved by the Privy Council on 30 October 2013.[34]

Although considered arcane by many, a Royal Charter allowed the Conservative/Liberal Democrat Coalition Government to avoid a statutory underpinning for the new self-regulation of the press and for the setting up of its independent audit. A Royal Charter is an ancient and uniquely British instrument for creating corporations (including the BBC). It is a way 'of turning a collection of individuals into a single legal entity.... Over 1000 such Charters have been granted since the Middle Ages, the oldest being those granted to the Universities of Cambridge (1231) and Oxford (1248).'[35] This is not what Leveson proposed but it is the way in which his proposals would be implemented, and to date it is an early stage to judge the efficacy of both: the proposals themselves and the mechanisms for their implementation. The process to amend the Royal Charter on self-regulation of the press is established in its article 9, and unlike an Act of Parliament, the Charter cannot be amended by politicians; instead, the Charter can only be added to, supplemented, varied or omitted if the proposed change is ratified by a unanimous resolution of all members of the board of the 'Recognition Panel' (this is the self-regulator's independent audit); and a draft of the amendment is approved by a resolution of both Houses of Parliament with at least two-thirds of members voting in support.

31 See Leveson LJ (2012), *Summary of recommendations*, paras 1–33.
32 *Ibid*, paras 27–33.
33 See Mason (2012); and Halliday and Wintour (2012).
34 See Tomlinson (2014), p. 5.
35 *Ibid*, p. 16.

The system of self-regulation established by the Charter implements two key innovations proposed by Leveson: first, the mechanism for 'recognition' or audit of the self-regulator(s) set up by the press themselves; and second, a series of incentives to membership of the self-regulatory bodies enshrined in law.[36] The second innovation brings together the need for incentives together with the imperative of providing an improved route to justice for individuals. Leveson proposed an arbitration service for civil legal claims against publishers and participation in the arbitration system would be a condition of membership of the new self-regulatory body. The arbitration system should have the following characteristics: be staffed by retired judges or senior lawyers with specialist knowledge of media law; arbitrations would operate in an inquisitorial model, and the process would be free for complainants to use; frivolous or vexatious claims would be struck out at an early stage; and, crucially, if a publisher does not subscribe to the new self-regulator and, as a result, does not offer free arbitration to claimants, then the courts could deprive the publisher of its costs in any reasonably arguable legal claim against it even if the publisher is successful in that litigation.[37]

As noted earlier, one of the key innovations proposed by Leveson is the establishment of an audit for the self-regulator set up by the press. He originally proposed that Ofcom, as the existing communications regulator, took up such a role. However, he recognised that 'this would be controversial (because the Chairman and the Chief Executive of Ofcom are appointed by Government ministers)'.[38] On 3 November 2014, the PRP (Press Recognition Panel) was created in order to fulfil the role of the self-regulator(s) audit. It is an independent body which in general terms considers whether the press regulators meet the recognition criteria recommended by the Leveson Report and now part of the Royal Charter.[39] The requirements for recognition include the need for the self-regulator to have: an independent board; a standards code (which must take into account the importance of freedom of speech, the public interest and the protection of sources and must cover standards of conduct, respect for privacy and accuracy); a whistleblowing hotline for journalists; an adequate and speedy complaints handling mechanism; a simple and credible

---

36 *Ibid*, p. 5.
37 *Ibid*, p. 13. See also, Leveson LJ (2012), *Summary of recommendations*, para. 22; and *Executive summary*, para. 67.
38 Tomlinson (2014), p. 10.
39 The Recognition Panel itself has to be independently appointed, and the members of the board must have senior-level experiences in a public, private or voluntary sector organisation (editors, former editors and current publishers are excluded, as are current members of the national and devolved legislature and all Government ministers). See Leveson LJ (2012), *Summary of recommendations*, paras 1–5. See also the incipient job of the PRP in its website, http://pressrecognitionpanel.org.uk/60/ (accessed 25 June 2015).

investigations power with the power to impose appropriate and proportionate sanctions, including financial sanctions limited to 1 per cent of
turnover, with a maximum of £1 million; the power to require the publication of corrections or apologies and, if necessary, their size and prominence; and, an arbitral process for civil legal claims against members of a
recognised regulator that is free for complainants to use and is overall
inexpensive.[40]

Although it is not an outcome to be advocated and in the end it would
represent a failure on the part of the industry, following Leveson's recommendations there could be more than one regulator, should more than
one seek recognition and meet the criteria. However, 'a new system of
regulation should not be considered effective if it does not cover all significant new publishers'.[41] Unfortunately the situations outlined above could
serve to describe the current context. Although IPSO is in fact the regulator of over 1,400 print titles and over 1,000 online titles, publishers such
as the *Guardian*, the *Independent* and the *Financial Times* have yet to sign
up. Moreover, IPSO has been criticised for not following Leveson's recommendations and it is considered that it would be likely to fail the recognition criteria.[42] However, IPSO has made it clear that it will not seek
recognition. The PRP therefore has currently no one to audit; at least by
the end of 2015, because IPSO has a rival, the Independent Monitor for
the Press (Impress), which is due to seek recognition later in 2015.[43]

There is therefore a landscape of uncertainty, which incidentally reveals
the intricacies and the many interests around the regulation of the press.
The interests of the press are clearly protected and celebrities usually find
a way to defend themselves by virtue of their economic resources, power
or influence. However, ordinary people remain vulnerable to press abuses
and of course this is also the case with the images and messages of ED disseminated through the press. Given the uncertainties of the current situation, we shall only look at IPSO's Editors' Code of Practice (which is
almost exactly the same as that of the obsolete PCC) and contrast it with
some of Leveson's recommendations regarding discriminatory content.

IPSO, like Ofcom, handles complaints about breaches to the Editors'
Code of Practice and, similarly, it is in a position to impose sanctions
which are also similar to the remedies pursued in this book in order to
redress ED. Remedies as set up in the complaints procedure, paragraph 5,
include 'the publication of its upheld adjudication and/or correction ...

---

40 *Ibid*, paras 1–24.
41 *Ibid*, para. 23.
42 IPSO has been criticised by organisations such as the Media Standards Trust (2013). The
    Trust's assessment shows that, of the 38 Leveson recommendations applicable to a new
    self-regulatory body, IPSO satisfies 12 and fails 20.
43 Details of the Impress Project can be found on its website, available at http://impress-
    project.org (accessed 24 June 2015). See also Sweney (2015).

[and] the nature, extent and placement of corrections and adjudications will be determined by the Complaints Committee'.[44] IPSO's sanctions, however, do not include apologies, which are a most important part in the redress of ED and were in fact recommended by Leveson, for individuals and for groups:

> In relation to complaints, the Board should have the power to direct appropriate remedial action for breach of standards and the publication of corrections and apologies. Although remedies are essentially about correcting the record of individuals, the power to require a correction and an apology must apply equally in relation to individual standards breaches (which the Board has accepted) and to groups of people (or matters of fact) where there is no single identifiable individual who has been affected.[45]

IPSO's Code reproduces exactly the provision included in the extinct PCC Code regarding discriminatory content; this is clause 12, which reads as follows:

Discrimination
i) The press must avoid prejudicial or pejorative reference to an individual's race, colour, religion, gender, sexual orientation or to any physical or mental illness or disability.
ii) Details of an individual's race, colour, religion, sexual orientation, physical or mental illness or disability must be avoided unless genuinely relevant to the story.[46]

It is significant that this Code, like its predecessor, acknowledges that prejudicial or pejorative reference to people on the grounds of race, colour, etc., is 'discrimination'. However, it is important to notice that the Code fails to understand the group-based implications of any kind of discrimination. Discrimination can and does affect individuals, but it only does so because the individual belongs to a certain group and therefore the harm is to the entire group.

During the time of the PCC, the 'Advice Section' of the Code included explanatory notes for the 'victims of discrimination' [sic]. This section acknowledged that even when an article that presumably discriminated

---

44 See IPSO's Complaints procedure, para. 5. Remedies, available at www.ipso.co.uk/IPSO/procedure.html (accessed 24 June 2015). See also the Independent Press Standards Organisation CIC Regulations 2013, regulations no. 63–65.
45 Leveson LJ (2012), *Summary of recommendations*, para. 15.
46 See PCC Editors' Code of Practice, available at www.pcc.org.uk/cop/practice.html (accessed 25 June 2015). See also IPSO Editors' Code of Practice, available at www.ipso.co.uk/IPSO/cop.html (accessed 25 June 2015).

did not mention an individual in particular, it could nevertheless be subject to complaint. However, the advice provided was to complain, making reference to a breach of other clauses of the Code, such as clause 1, on accuracy (which in IPSO's Editors' Code remain the same as in its predecessor).[47] Even though to some degree this was helpful in any attempt to challenge discriminatory content in the press, not acknowledging the group-based implications of discrimination is incorrect. In fact, it was possible to verify this in the PCC's website section on FAQs (frequently asked questions). The question was frequently asked as to why clause 12 did not apply to groups of people. The PCC's response was that 'The Code was specifically designed to protect individuals, and any equivalent protection for groups of people would place serious restrictions on freedom of expression. Clause 12 (Discrimination) is designed to prevent named individuals from being subjected to discriminatory reference.'[48] This problematic point was also picked up by Leveson, '[B]odies representing the interests of groups or minorities cannot complain to the PCC about discriminatory or inaccurate coverage. These are points which have been repeatedly identified as a weakness in the self-regulatory system.'[49] Leveson therefore recommended that:

> The Board should have the power to hear complaints about breach of the standards code by those who subscribe. The Board should have the power (but not necessarily in all cases depending on the circumstances the duty) to hear complaints *whoever they come from*, whether personally and directly affected by the alleged breach, or a *representative group affected* by the alleged breach, or a *third party seeking to ensure accuracy* of published information. In the case of third party complaints the views of the party most closely involved should be taken into account.[50]

Moreover, Leveson's recommendations explicitly noted the issue of discriminatory reporting and recommended that:

> [C]onsideration should also be given to Code amendments which, while fully protecting freedom of speech and the freedom of the press, would equip that body [the self-regulatory body] with the power to

---

47 See PCC Code Advice for Complainants, available at www.pcc.org.uk/code/advice_for_complainants.html?article=Mzg2NA== (accessed 19 June 2015).

48 Although the Press Complaints Commission closed on 8 September 2014, the PCC's site will continue to be maintained 'for a period' (not specified) in order to provide a record of the organisation's work. See, PCC FAQs, www.pcc.org.uk/faqs.html#faq2_5 (accessed 19 June 2015).

49 Media Standards Trust (2013), p. 17.

50 See Leveson LJ (2012), *Summary of recommendations*, para. 11. Italics are the author's.

intervene in cases of allegedly discriminatory reporting, and in so doing reflect the spirit of equalities legislation.[51]

These recommendations have not been fully followed by IPSO and, as the Media Standards Trust assessment of IPSO has noted,

> there is no explicit provision in the IPSO scheme to direct how code amendments are made.... Such an amendment to the code would be at the total discretion of the Editors' Code of Practice Committee, rather than the regulator ... [and] there is no reference to discriminatory reporting or equalities legislation in the IPSO documents.[52]

It is therefore disappointing that neither the concerns of the public already identified by the PCC and then exposed by Leveson made any difference in either the development of IPSO's Editor's Code nor in its complaints procedure. Moreover, according to the Media Standards Trust,

> In the IPSO regulations, obstacles are deliberately put in the way of complainants that are contrary to Leveson's recommendations and would prevent almost all complaints from representative groups.... A representative group complaint has to be a 'significant' Code breach, and there has to be a 'substantial' public interest in taking the complaint [IPSO CIC Regulations 2013, regulation no. 8]. This is such a high bar that very few complaints from these groups are ever likely to make it through.... [Moreover] there is no definition given of what 'significant' means. Nor is it made clear how a judgement may be made of the significance of an inaccuracy before the complaint has been considered [and so one can expect that no remedies are likely to be accorded to groups in cases of ED].[53]

As noted earlier, not all publications are regulated by IPSO and therefore complaints can only be brought about publications that abide by the Editors' Code of Practice. A list of these can be found on IPSO's website. These things said, however, Leveson recommended that

> all those who subscribe [publishers subscribing to the press regulator] have an adequate and speedy complaint mechanism; it [the press regulator] should encourage those who wish to complain to do so through that mechanism and should not receive complaints directly

51 *Ibid*, para. 38.
52 Media Standards Trust (2013), p. 37.
53 *Ibid*, pp. 17–18. See also IPSO guidance on making a complaint at www.ipso.co.uk/IPSO/makingacomplaint.html (accessed 24 June 2015).

unless or until the internal complaints system has been engaged without the complaint being solved in a appropriate time.[54]

Therefore, responsible publishers should in any case have their own code and complaints procedure. If these were effective, and appropriate respect and consideration were accorded to groups in cases of alleged ED, it is likely that consumers themselves would be supporting self-regulation without the need for legislation to 'tighten things up'. For example, Facebook's inclusion of hate speech on the grounds of sex in its Community Standards (Chapter 6, VII) was the result of the pressure from the organised civil society together with the threat of loss of revenue from advertisers.[55] Although not free from problematic aspects, these two conditions proved to be more powerful mechanisms for effective content regulation than any particular government's intervention. Facebook's example also verifies the need for more support and recognition of the role that the organised civil society can play in content regulation; including in the drafting of the editors' codes, which in fact was also one of Leveson's recommendations.[56] These things said, however, State legislation in Facebook's case was also crucial even if at a 'ground-laying level' because in the end, the inspiration and arguments for having hate speech on the grounds of sex within the Community Standards was assisted by the existence, in many jurisdictions, of hate speech laws protecting other characteristics.

The problems (discussed in Chapter 4, IV) identified by the civil society in relation to the lack of understanding and consideration for the harm created against groups who are routinely maligned and disparaged in stereotypical representations, and about the inadequate handling of complaints regarding discriminatory representation in the media, have not been overcome/addressed despite the efforts of both the organised civil society and Leveson's recommendations. Complaint procedures continue to be unfavourable to groups; they almost exclusively represent the interests of the publishers and there is no expertise or sensibility to deal with complaints about ED. Only as an example, as described by the Media Standards Trust, 'the investigations process is not simple and credible as Leveson said it should be. It allows for up to six interventions by the publisher. In contrast, there is no opportunity for the victim to

---

54 Leveson LJ (2012), *Summary of recommendations*, para. 10.
55 See the statement of 28 May 2013 by the organisation Women Action and the Media (WAM!) about their campaign together with the Everyday Sexism Project to 'Take action to end gender-based hate speech on Facebook', available at www.womenactionmedia. org/fbagreement (accessed 26 June 2015).
56 Leveson LJ (2012), *Summary of recommendations*, para. 36. A regulatory body should consider engaging in an early thorough review of the code (on which the public should be engaged and consulted) with the aim of developing a clear statement of the standards expected of editors and journalists.

intervene.'[57] The likelihood is therefore that complaints about discrimination will be poorly handled, if at all, and that people will continue to give up complaining unless they can find support elsewhere.

3 The regulation of advertising

The Advertising Standards Authority (ASA) is the UK's independent regulator of advertising across all media. It acts on complaints made about ads, applies the Advertising Codes written by the Committees of Advertising Practice and keeps a record of its adjudications. The UK advertising regulatory system is a mixture of self-regulation for non-broadcast advertising and co-regulation for broadcasting advertising; for TV and radio advertising, the ASA regulates under a contract from Ofcom. With regard to advertisements accompanying VOD (video-on-demand), the ASA entered from December 2009 into a co-regulatory partnership with Ofcom. Given that with the rise of VOD consumers are able to watch programmes at a time of their own choosing, it was necessary that these new services be subject to the same standards as 'linear programming' on TV. This implies that the consumers may complain about an ad accompanying VOD content which is, for example, allegedly inappropriately targeted around a suitable programme.

The growth of internet content and internet usage includes the production and viewing of advertising and therefore, from September 2010, the Committee of Advertising Practice (CAP), the body responsible for writing the CAP Code, announced the extension of the ASA's online remit to cover advertisers' own marketing communications on their own websites and in other non-paid-for space under their control, such as networking sites like Facebook and Twitter.[58]

The system is paid for by the industry, which also writes the rules, and those rules are enforced by the ASA. The ASA is funded by advertisers through an arm's length arrangement in which the fees are collected by the Advertising Standards Board of Finance (Asbof) and the Broadcast Advertising Standards Board of Finance (Basbof). The funding consists of a 0.1 per cent levy on the cost of buying advertising space and a 0.2 per cent levy on some direct mail. The ASA also receives income from charging for some seminars and premium industry advice services. The separate funding mechanism is aimed at ensuring the ASA does not know which advertisers choose to fund the system or the amount they contribute. The levy is the only part of the system that is voluntary. This means

57 Media Standards Trust (2013), p. 4. See also Independent Press Standards Organisation CIC Regulations 2013, regulations no. 40–62.
58 See the evolution of advertising regulation in the UK, available at www.asa.org.uk/About-ASA/Our-history.aspx (accessed 29 June 2015).

that advertisers can choose to pay the levy, but they cannot choose to comply with the Advertising Codes or the ASA's rulings.

The advertising industry takes responsibility for writing the advertising standards codes and enforcing the ASA's rulings through the CAP, which represents the main industry bodies representing advertisers, agencies and media owners.[59] With regard to enforcement, the ASA affirms that the majority of UK advertising is within the codes and that when it upholds complaints, most advertisers agree to change or remove the challenged advertisement. Media owners also agree not to run advertisements that breach the codes. However, for those who persistently flout the rules, the ASA can rely on the backing of the Office of Fair Trading and Ofcom – for example, by referring a broadcaster to Ofcom if a licensee is not abiding by the rules.

The UK advertising industry therefore sets its own standards and is governed by codes of practice that are intended to protect consumers and to create a level playing field for advertisers. These codes are the responsibility of two industry committees, the Committee of Advertising Practice (CAP), and the Broadcast Committee of Advertising Practice (BCAP). These Codes are then administered by the ASA. The CAP Code sets the standards for non-broadcast advertising (e.g. print, online), sales promotion and direct marketing (e.g. telesales and email). The section of this Code which is relevant for the contestation of ED in advertising is section 4, Harm and Offence. Its principle is that 'Marketers should take account of the prevailing standards in society and the context in which marketing communications is likely to appear to minimise the risk of causing harm or serious or widespread offence.'[60] The section then lists a series of rules, one of which addresses in some way concerns about ED:

> 4.1. Marketing communications must not contain anything that is likely to cause serious or widespread offence. Particular care must be taken to avoid causing *offence on the grounds of race, religion, gender, sexual orientation, disability or age.* Compliance will be judged on the context, medium, audience, product and prevailing standards.
>
> Marketing communications may be distasteful without necessarily breaching this rule. Marketers are urged to consider public sensitivities before using potentially offensive material.

59 See www.cap.org.uk/About-CAP/Who-we-are/Our-committees.aspx#.VZJqYBwui4A (accessed 30 June 2015).

60 UK Code of Non-broadcast Advertising, Sales Promotion and Direct Marketing (CAP Code), 12th edition, 1 September 2010.

The fact that a particular product is offensive to some people is not grounds for finding marketing communication in breach of the code.[61]

This rule corresponds to the twelfth edition of the CAP Code which came into force on 1 September 2010. An earlier, 2003, version of this Code considered content of the type described above as a matter of 'Decency (avoiding serious or widespread offence)' and the rule was almost the same as the current one.[62] However, as we have argued in this book, discriminatory speech is not merely a matter of offence. Speaking offence carries the risk of blaming the victim for being too sensitive or for 'taking' offence when offence might not have been intended. We have argued instead for speaking about injustice and discrimination (at a cultural level) and for the contestation of images and messages that demean, stereotype and ridicule, thereby impeding participatory parity. These ideas in fact are not too far away from the ways in which the advertising industry has – through its research and experience – been 'pushed' to understand the harm. Although it has not yet articulated the harm accurately, there is evidence to show that the Committee has realised that demeaning and stereotypical images and messages in advertising can be discriminatory; or at the very least, that there is a relationship between demeaning stereotypical representation and discrimination. For example, before September 2010 there were two Codes for broadcast adverts: one for radio and a different one for television. The Radio Advertising Standards Code was in place since November 2004 and was the responsibility of the BCAP. It set out the rules that govern advertisements on any radio station licensed by Ofcom. The relevant rules – regarding ED – within this Code were as follows:

> 2.9 Good Taste, Decency and Offence To Public Feeling
> a) offensive and profane language must be avoided;
> b) salacious, violent or indecent themes, or sexual innuendo or *stereotyping likely to cause serious or general offence*, should be avoided;
> c) references to minority groups should not be *stereotypical*, malicious, unkind or hurtful;
> d) references to religious or political beliefs should not be offensive, deprecating or hurtful, and the use of religious themes and treatments by non-religious groups should be treated with extreme care;
> e) those who have physical, sensory, intellectual or mental health disabilities should not be *demeaned or ridiculed*;

61 *Ibid.* Italics are the author's.
62 British Code of Advertising, Sales Promotion and Direct Marketing, 4 March 2003. This Code included (at 5.1) sex instead of gender and it did not include age.

f) the handling of films, plays, music tracks or websites with sala-
cious, violent or sexual themes and/or titles requires careful consideration. Audio clips should portray the product's true nature
and clips containing bad language, sexual innuendo and/or gratuitous violence should normally be avoided;

g) humour should not be used to circumvent the intention of Code
Rules.[63]

This provision did not use the language of discrimination; instead, it
referred to the potential of stereotyping to cause serious or general
offence and, specifically, it referred to references to minority groups,
which should not be 'stereotypical', malicious, unkind or hurtful. Stereotypes, as we explained in Chapter 4, are on many occasions the drivers of
discrimination and for this reason they are relevant regarding ED. Other
sections of the Code, however, did make specific reference to sexual and
racial discrimination.

2.12 Sexual discrimination
It is illegal (with a few exceptions) for an advertisement to discriminate against women or men in opportunities for employment, education and training and the provision of accommodation, goods,
facilities and services.[64]

The Code did not consider demeaning representation of women as discrimination. It only referred to discrimination against women and men in
the access to goods and services. With regard to racial discrimination, it
took a wider approach.

2.13 Racial Discrimination
a) It is illegal (with a few exceptions) for an advertisement to discriminate on grounds of race;

b) Advertisements must not include any material which *might reasonably be construed by ethnic minorities to be hurtful or tasteless.*[65]

Even though sexual and racial discrimination were included in this
Code, the way in which this was done did not reflect a specific concern
with representation. Instead, the reason why sections 2.12 and 2.13 were
included was because of the prohibitions set out in the Sex Discrimination
Act 1975 (s. 38) and Race Relations Act 1976 (s. 29) in relation to the

---

63 The Broadcast Committee of Advertising Practice (BCAP) Radio Advertising Standards
Code, November 2004. Italics are the author's.
64 *Ibid.*
65 *Ibid.* Italics are the author's.

advertising of jobs and/or to the advertising of an intention to engage in behaviours considered discrimination. Indeed, the Code did not explain to which exceptions it referred. It advised that this information should be sought from the Equal Opportunities Commission and the Commission for Racial Equality (Now both incorporated within the EHRC).

With regard to television, prior to September 2010 the BCAP Television Advertising Code set out the rules that governed advertisements on any television channel licensed by Ofcom.[66] The rules were framed to ensure that advertisements were legal, decent, honest and truthful, and did not mislead or cause harm or serious or widespread offence. Since November 2004 the Code had been the responsibility of the BCAP, under contract from Ofcom. The Code was an updated edition of the 2002 Independent Television Commission (ITC) Advertising Standards Code.[67] The relevant section of the 2004 BCAP Code for the purposes of this analysis was Section 6: Harm and Offence:

> 6.1. Offence
> Advertisements must not cause serious or widespread offence against generally accepted moral, social or cultural standards, or offend against public feeling.
>
> 6.6. Harmful or negative *stereotypes*
> Advertisements must not prejudice respect for *human dignity* or humiliate, stigmatise or *undermine the standing* of identifiable groups of people.[68]

The explanatory notes for this section mentioned various important aspects, such as the use of humour and its potential for offence or distress; the need to avoid anything which could encourage or condone the idea that some serious negative characteristics were associated with a particular group; the need for sensibility about the use of certain groups that are generally recognised to encounter prejudice; particular care with children since stereotyping of both children and adults can encourage bullying; and the need to seek appropriate guidance to counter prejudice.[69]

The ASA has recommended that appropriate guidance should be sought in order to avoid stereotyping and indeed although it only accounts for a small part of the ASA's work, complaints about offence are often the most high-profile. Offence, according to the ASA's online database,

---

66 The Broadcast Committee of Advertising Practice (BCAP) Television Advertising Code, November 2004.
67 The ITC ceased to exist from 18 December 2003, and its duties were assumed by Ofcom.
68 The Broadcast Committee of Advertising Practice (BCAP) Television Advertising Code, November 2004. Italics are the author's.
69 See also Ipsos MORI (2012).

includes use of stereotypes, racism, sexism and offence on the grounds of age, sexual orientation and sex.[70] The most recent BCAP Code for broadcast advertising came into force on 1 September 2010 and replaces the previous radio and television advertising standards codes. This Code abandons reference to harmful or negative stereotypes and instead starts using the language of discrimination. Its section 4, Harm and Offence, includes the following provisions:

> 4.2. Advertisements must not cause serious or widespread offence against *generally accepted* moral, social or cultural standards.

> 4.8. Advertisements must not condone or encourage *harmful discriminatory behaviour or treatment*. Advertisements must not prejudice respect for *human dignity*.[71]

Provision 4.8 is less explicit than 6.6 in the old TV Standards Advertising Code; at least in that it does not mention the harm of stereotyping or concern about their potential for undermining the standing of identifiable groups of people; and to cause serious or general offence as did section 2.9 of the old Radio Advertising Standards Code. However, provision 4.8 uses the language of discrimination and dignity which allows the assumption that the harm of ED (demeaning stereotypical representation) may 'float' in the drafters' imagery as a form of discrimination or as a form of 'harmful discriminatory behaviour or treatment'. This is, if the new provision 4.8 is interpreted taking into account the sense/spirit of the provisions it replaces.

In fact, the inclusion of provisions on 'harm and offence' has been, to some extent, the product of research which has showed the kind of issues that disadvantaged groups themselves have identified in advertising (including issues about those so-called 'generally accepted standards' which may on occasions mask harmful generalised prejudices).

Section 6 of the old 2004 Television Advertising Code was the product of research undertaken by the ITC (Independent Television Commission). The ITC, however, made clear that it had no wish to attempt 'social engineering', no matter how praiseworthy the objective; however, it was concerned with the protection of 'vulnerable' audiences, and so with any advertising which could lead to distress, insult or actual harm to

---

70 See the CAP Advice Online database which is regularly updated, available at www.cap.org.uk/Advice-Training-on-the-rules/Advice-Online-Database.aspx?s=stereotypes (accessed 30 June 2015).

71 The UK Code of Broadcast Advertising (BCAP), 1st edition, 1 September 2010. Italics are the author's.

individuals or particular groups in society.[72] Its study 'Boxed in: offence from negative stereotyping in TV advertising'[73] examined attitudes among both the public at large and members of groups which are likely to be stereotyped. The study was mainly designed to reveal attitudes about advertising given the significant number of complaints about various kinds of stereotyping in television advertising.[74] The rise of complaints about stereotyping – it was thought – may have been a reflection of both societal changes, such as the new emphasis being placed on diversity and inclusion, and people's awareness.[75]

The report showed that ethnic minorities, those of Asian, African, Caribbean and Chinese origin, felt they were not sufficiently represented in television advertising; so negative stereotypes were likely to have a greater impact.[76] Moreover, parents and older children, who participated in the research, were concerned about stereotypes in advertisements that might lead to or condone bullying.[77] Many adult respondents in the ITC study believed the effects of advertising, like other influences in society, could be subtle and cumulative. They considered there could be a slow-drip, build-up effect in relation to stereotyping. Respondents felt this contribution should be taken into account when judgements were made about an advertisement's acceptability or likelihood to offend. Advertisements were seen by some as being guilty of creating or reinforcing negative stereotypes at a subtle or even subliminal level. But it was recognised that any effects over time would be very difficult to determine because there were so many other contributing factors. Respondents felt regulators and broadcasters should, therefore, make 'judgement calls' on individual advertisements.[78]

Some advertisements were regarded as contentious, with particular groups or individuals immediately finding them offensive. Others were recognised as having offensive potential only after reflective debate (when members of the focus groups raised issues).[79] Racism and racist attitudes were recognised as widely present in society and as an issue that received significant media coverage. Advertising was regarded by many as a medium through which racism could be either reinforced or challenged, for example by the presence or absence of ethnic minority participants, and

---

72 Sancho and Wilson (2001) p. 7. Regulators, however, are since April 2011 subject to the Public Sector Equality Duty which includes tackling prejudice and promoting understanding. See III in this chapter.
73 *Ibid.*
74 *Ibid.*
75 *Ibid.*
76 See Sancho and Wilson (2001), p. 4.
77 *Ibid.*
78 See Sancho and Wilson (2001), pp. 10–11.
79 *Ibid*, pp. 9, 18, 19.

by the ways in which they were portrayed on screen. For some groups (including ethnic minorities, some parents, those who were overweight and individuals with a strong social conscience) negative stereotyping in television advertising was a contentious issue and more likely to be raised spontaneously. People from ethnic minorities, in particular, were sensitive to issues to do with inclusion and diversity. They felt strongly that advertising as a whole does not reflect or recognise the cultural diversity of the UK. As a result, they were more likely to find negative portrayals offensive.[80] The ITC study therefore is a good example of special research that could be used in a productive way. For example, in handling cases brought to the attention of the ASA and crucially in the elaboration and interpretation of the advertising codes. The harm of stereotypes should therefore not be forgotten, but captured by the new provision framed in the language of 'harmful discriminatory behaviour or treatment'.

The concepts used in the articulation of 'harmful and offensive' content in the Codes described above reveals, at the very least, that the harm created by demeaning and stereotypical representation is to some extent related to discrimination. However, the position from explicitly opposing to the use of harmful stereotypes was replaced for a more general exclusion of 'discriminatory behaviour or treatment', and the CAP has not issued specific guidelines to interpret this provision.[81] However, it has said that:

> Marketers may use stereotypes in advertising but should be careful not to cause serious or widespread offence. The complaints received by ASA often relate to race, gender, age, sexual orientation and occupational stereotypes. Generally speaking, the ASA regards the use of light-hearted stereotypes as acceptable but marketers should be careful that they are not seen as offensive, demeaning or the subject of ridicule. That judgement is obviously subjective and the ASA and CAP will judge each ad on its merits.[82]

Therefore it is difficult to avoid the assumption that in the end the industry will have the last word about the extent to which a stereotype is 'light-hearted' or offensive. However, the industry needs to be reminded of its own research and of the views expressed by the target groups. Indeed, the ASA's most recent research on 'Public perceptions of harm

---

80 *Ibid*, p. 24.
81 See CAP Advertising Guidance (previously Help Notes) online, available at www.cap. uk/Advice-Training-on-the-rules/Help-Notes.aspx (accessed 3 June 2015).
82 See the Advice Online Database given by the CAP Executive. This, however, is not legal advice and does not bind the CAP, CAP advisory panels or the ASA; available at www.cap. org.uk/Advice-Training-on-the-rules/Advice-Online-Database/Offence-Use-of-Stereo-types.aspx#.VZZjURwugpc (accessed 3 June 2015).

and offence in the UK advertising' makes clear that participants in the research consider discrimination against specific types of people as a type of content that is 'always unacceptable' and should therefore be banned or carefully restricted.[83] Participants in this research also made clear that stereotyping in advertising continues to be an issue; it was considered among the main examples of potential types of offence in advertising. Particularly problematic in the view of the participants was women's stereotyping and the damage stereotypes can cause to the perception of minority groups.[84] These views largely coincide with those of the organised civil society working against discrimination (Chapter 4) and with statements made in various of the international instruments we explored in Chapter 5.

The use of concepts such as stereotyping, discrimination and harm to human dignity is therefore recurrent in the regulation of content of the type ED involves. Indeed, it is recurrent in most of the standards Codes we have explored in this chapter; therefore, it would be dismissive to consider this persistence a mere coincidence. The narrative of ED in this book is built on the relationships between these concepts and a general idea of justice which includes the need to redress harms to the self- and social-esteem of maligned groups created through demeaning and stereotypical representation. In fact, as evidenced in Chapter 4, demeaning stereotypical representation in the media is a most pervasive case of ED; and moreover, as we have seen, the target groups have organised themselves and expressed their concern and outrage about the media's stereotypical representations and about their connection to other forms of discrimination. In the light of the antecedents and research around the advertising standards codes, ED would seem a step closer to being acknowledged as a discriminatory practice where stereotyping plays a central dynamic.

In contrast with the self-regulation of the press, it is possible for the ASA – and indeed it is a common practice – to help the industry get their ads 'right' before they are published. This is, in general terms, by providing guidance, pre-publication advice and training. Indeed, before an ad is published or aired, the Advertising Codes require that all claims must be substantiated. The vast majority of broadcast ads are pre-cleared. Under their licences, broadcasters must take reasonable steps to ensure the ads they broadcast are compliant with the UK Code of Broadcast Advertising. There are in fact two pre-clearance centres, one for television and one for radio; and non-broadcast ads can benefit from the advice and guidelines available through CAP Advice and Training, including free bespoke pre-publication advice from the Copy Advice Team (which

---

83 Ipsos MORI (2012), p. 15.
84 *Ibid*, pp. 18, 24, 28, 29, 55. Interestingly, with regard to the use of sexual imagery to sell, some participants 'seemed to accept it as just part of life'.

includes establishing any potential issues before advertisers spend time and resources taking their campaign forward); and online resources that advertisers, agencies and media can use to check the latest positions on different advertising issues.[85] These things said, similar to what happens with radio and television programming and with the press, consumers may nevertheless complain about content they consider misleading, harmful or offensive. The procedure can be found in the ASA's website and is in general similar to the complaints procedures for radio, television and the press. Consumers can make a complaint, and an investigation will follow should the regulator consider there to have been a breach of the relevant Code.[86]

With regard to sanctions, if the ASA has judged that an ad is in breach of the Codes, then the ad must be withdrawn or amended.[87] This sort of remedy can be fine-tuned to redress ED. The mere withdrawal of an ad, for example, is not enough. Withdrawal should be accompanied by a statement about the reasons why it was removed; or in its case, why an advert had to be amended. It is precisely these reasons that need to be publicised in some way so that culture can be politicised and redefinitions of despised groups effectively put forward. Agreement about contentious issues may not be reached in many cases; and despised groups may not instantly gain sympathy about the issues that affect them; but the information will be available – speech will take place. One way to do this is through captions in adverts, but in any case the principle is to bring ideas to the public so that they can start thinking more critically and be better informed. This can help redress the harm created by ED because very often ED is the result of unconscious habits and lack of information that may contradict prejudices.

The ASA is emphatic in pointing out that they 'do not play a numbers game' when it comes to complaints. They affirm that their concern is whether the Codes have been breached.[88] However, they have kept a record of historically significant ads given the number of complaints received and, indeed, only the most complained-about ads make it to the annual reports of the ASA. However, the numbers do matter because they

---

85 See the ASA's information about its regulation, available at www.asa.org.uk/About-ASA/About-regulation.aspx (accessed 30 June 2015).

86 See the ASA's complaints procedure available at www.asa.org.uk/Consumers/How-to-complain.aspx (accessed 30 June 2015).

87 The range of sanctions for non-broadcast advertising can be found in the UK Code of Non-broadcast Advertising, Sales Promotion and Direct Marketing (CAP Code), 12th Edition, 1 September 2010, pp. 108–111; and for broadcast advertising in the UK Code of Broadcast Advertising (BCAP Code), 1st edition, 1 September 2010, 13 and 14, p. 137.

88 See the ASA's information about its regulation, available at www.asa.org.uk/About-ASA/About-regulation.aspx (accessed 30 June 2015).

represent pressure.[89] Nevertheless, it is true that a well-substantiated complaint that clearly expresses why a provision in the Code has been breached should *ideally* be enough, more so if it is backed by well-informed and articulate civil society organisations. However, as we explored in Chapter 4, the dissatisfaction of the consumers with the complaint mechanisms and the difficulties in challenging generalised prejudice and mainstream discriminatory images and messages have on many occasions dissuaded people from complaining. There have been, however, some who have complained about adverts which are considered racist, sexist, etc., and there is a record of this on the ASA's website.[90] Only as an example, we shall look at a case which involves a range of the principles and issues we have discussed so far, which, even though the case took place in 2007, remains relevant today. The case concerns four TV ads and a cinema ad for Trident chewing gum (Cadbury) that were the object of more than 519 complaints.[91]

In the first ad, a black man appeared speaking in rhyme with a strong Caribbean accent. He was shown on stage, in what appeared to be a comedy club, complaining about the blandness of chewing gum. A member of the audience gave him some Trident chewing gum. He appeared so enthusiastic about the taste of it, that he ran out of the club in an excited manner and said he 'must tell the whole world'. He was finally shown on a boat sailing past the Houses of Parliament shouting 'Mastication for the Nation' through a megaphone (the cinema ad was identical to this).

The second TV ad showed the same black man running along a busy street and shouting about Trident gum in an excited manner. He then burst into a laundrette and told the people there about Trident gum. A woman offered him some Trident Splash gum that appeared to make him

89 For example, in 2014, Paddy Power's 'IT'S OSCAR TIME', 'MONEY BACK IF HE WALKS' and 'WE WILL REFUND ALL LOSING BETS ON THE OSCAR PISTORIOUS TRIAL IF HE IS FOUND NOT GUILTY', became the most complained about non-broadcast ad ever. The ASA upheld the 5,525 complaints for causing serious or widespread offence and bringing advertising into disrepute. See the history of advertising regulation in the UK, available at www.asa.org.uk/About-ASA/Our-history.aspx (accessed 29 June 2015).

90 ASA's rulings (adjudications) are published in its website every Wednesday. They usually remain there for five years; available at www.asa.org.uk/Rulings/Adjudications.aspx (accessed 1 July 2015).

91 ASA Adjudication on Cadbury Trebor Bassett Services Ltd, 28 March 2007. Complaint Ref: A07-22497. The notes quoted below were taken from the adjudication published online in 2007. However, this is no longer available in the ASA's website. Instead, some details can be found in the ASA's Ad Bank, compilation of offensive advertising, available at www.asa.org.uk/News-resources/~/media/Files/ASA/Adcheck/Ad%20Banks/Offensive/Offensive%20advertising.ashx (accessed 3 July 2015); and in the ASA's Annual Report 2007, 'The top 10 most complained about ads of 2007', available at www.asa.org.uk/Newsresources/~/media/Files/ASA/Annual%20reports/ASA_CAP_annual_report_07.ashx. See also Sweney (2007).

even more excited, and he then ran out on to the street shouting 'Mastication for the Nation'.

The third TV ad showed a white, middle-aged woman at a women's meeting speaking in rhyme about the Trident gum in a Caribbean accent, when she was supposed to have spoken about late summer chutneys. She raised up both her arms and shouted 'Mastication for the Nation' at the end of her speech.

The fourth and last TV ad showed a white man, at what appeared to be a parrot-fanciers club meeting, speaking in rhyme about the Trident gum in a Caribbean accent. He raised up his right arm and shouted 'Mastication for the Nation' at the end of his rhyme.

The complaints raised a number of issues revealing that the viewers made connections between the advert and historical undervaluing, mocking and ridiculing of the accent and the mannerisms of the black communities in the UK. The viewers, including members of the Ligali Organisation (Chapter 4, IV), argued that the TV ads were offensive and racist, because they believed they showed offensive stereotypes and ridiculed black or Caribbean people and their culture. Another complainant argued that the cinema ad was offensive and racist, because he believed it promoted the stereotype of black Caribbean people having particular accents and mannerisms and some viewers challenged whether the TV ads were offensive and insensitive because 'Trident' was the name of the Metropolitan Police's 'black-on-black' gun crime initiative.

Cadbury's defence revealed its own, its research company's and the Broadcast Advertising Clearance Centre's lack of understanding of the harm caused by demeaning stereotypical adverts. Cadbury said it had undertaken research before launching the advert. It pointed out that the percentage of the sample who had found the ads offensive, when prompted, was in line with the general population score for previous research performed by the research company Millward Brown, and also that spontaneous comments about offence had been few and limited to the African Caribbean population! According to their research, Cadbury found the ads were likely to result in a polarised reaction and about one in five of the British African-Caribbean sample had found the ads offensive. Moreover, Cadbury was disappointed because the advert had been researched and the Broadcast Advertising Clearance Centre had ensured it was acceptable. With regard to the name of the brand, Cadbury said it was a coincidence that the Metropolitan Police's 'black-on-black' gun crime initiative had the same name.

The most significant part of this adjudication for the purposes of this example is that without the active participation of organisations such as Ligali and the complaints of the viewers, the ASA would not necessarily have had the elements – and the pressure – to understand the harm. It was indeed the disadvantaged group's counter speech that in this case made the difference. The ASA had to understand, from the complaints received, that the depiction of the black man's extreme response to tasting the product had resulted in a 'significant minority of viewers' inferring that this exaggerated behaviour and strong accent were a humiliating and negative depiction of black Caribbean people. Complainants told the ASA: 'it portrays us as objects to be laughed at', 'this near driving miss daisy degradation of singing songs for the whites sickens me', 'this man's behaviour shows anything but a positive role as a black man', 'it is as if it is laughing at black people who campaign for equal rights' and 'depicting times of a Minstrel Show, or where black people used to have to do degrading things to entertain white people'.[92]

The ASA concluded that the ads should not be shown again since they breached the CAP (Broadcast) TV Advertising Standards Code rules 6.1 (offence) and 6.6 (harmful stereotypes). Regarding the cinema advert it was decided that it breached CAP Code clauses 5.1 and 5.2 (offence).[93] In sum, this case reveals various issues relevant in order to understand the concept of ED: (1) the group-based injury; (2) the need to consult with key/informed and interested parties as an essential part of the adjudication process, and counter speech facilitation; (3) that complaints tend to be taken more seriously and have stronger arguments when they come from the organised civil society representing a disadvantaged group; and (4) that the codes the industry has written and the research it has produced can be ignored and/or that a sensationalist ad is worth taking a risk.

The victory of this case, however, does not guarantee success in similar future adjudications. In fact, Cadbury allegedly breached the Advertising Codes (CAP Code) again in 2011 but the ASA did not uphold the complaints although there are significant concerns about the content of the ad being racist. The case concerned a press ad for Cadbury's Bliss range of dairy milk chocolate which ran the strapline 'move over Naomi, there's a new diva in town'. The ASA did not uphold the complaints, including one from the campaigning group Operation Black Vote which branded the campaign an insult to black women for comparing a black woman (model Naomi Campbell) to a bar of chocolate.[94] The ASA concluded that there

92 Some of these views were reported by Sweney (2007).
93 The ruling was made under the provisions of the Broadcast Committee of Advertising Practice (BCAP) Television Advertising Code, November 2004; and British Code of Advertising, Sales Promotion and Direct Marketing, 4 March 2003.
94 For the racist implications of comparing black people to chocolate, see Robertson (2013). The author explores cocoa advertising, from the late nineteenth to the late twentieth century, to reveal the racialised meanings created for and by the commodity. Although with an emphasis on respectful white consumption, images of black people have been employed in cocoa marketing at particular moments, and such raced imaginings of cocoa consumption have both reflected and fed into a broader culture of racism in the west.

were no grounds for investigation after assessing the four complaints and the ASA Council considered that the ad was likely to be understood to refer to Naomi Campbell's reputation for 'diva-style' behaviour rather than race. This, however, was not the view of either those who complained, the supermodel, nor of Cadbury's legal advisers, who directed the company to withdraw the campaign and to offer a public apology on its corporate website.[95] However, the apology to Campbell 'was issued after the Rev Al Sharpton, the US civil rights activist, raised the prospect of a global consumer boycott unless Cadbury responded to Campbell's complaint'.[96] The fact that this case generated consequences different from those ruled by the ASA further compromises the already fragile credibility of this authority. The ASA's uncertain ability to handle complaints of this sort – which ultimately depends on the views of the members of the Council – may well increase the already existing reticence to make complaints about discriminatory content before this authority.[97] This is not to suggest that complaints about alleged discriminatory content always have to be upheld, but that the ASA is in fact in a position to decide on matters on which it may not be well informed or competent and therefore it requires formal collaboration from other agencies in order to secure some checks and balances.

III Towards a better system of self-regulation against ED

Nordenstreng suggests that the media is not generally an independent power, but rather a continuation of more fundamental social forces, such as the State, capital or market forces and civil society or non-governmental and non-commercial people's activities.[98] This implies that the media follows, accomplishes and/or materialises the interests of these forces to a greater or lesser extent and therefore it is never fully independent. A model proposed in 1999 by Galtung illustrates this situation. The model is in the shape of a triangle that represents the three pillars of society: State or government; capital or market forces; and civil society or non-governmental and non-commercial people's activities. In this model, the media is not located at the apex of the triangle but rather floats somewhere between the pillars. Its place is not static; it sometimes finds its place close to the State, close to capital-driven markets or drifting towards the

---

95 See Sweney (2011).

96 Sherwin (2011).

97 The ASA Council is the jury that decides whether advertisements have breached the Advertising Codes. Led by ASA Chairman, Lord Smith of Fisbury, two-thirds of the 13-strong Council are independent of industry and the remaining members have a recent or current knowledge of the advertising or media sectors.

98 See Nordenstreng (2000), pp. 328–342.

civil society.[99] In the context of ED, as we have seen, economic interests are capable of determining ultimately the extent to which the civil society can or cannot influence the media. For example, advertisers may be attentive to consumer's positions on certain issues (e.g. misogyny or racism), but this is not necessarily funded on convictions of an ideological, moral or ethical nature. Instead this is frequently guided by the feared prospect of losing buyers for their products. Similarly, media outlets such as Facebook, newspapers and television channels may fear loss of revenue from advertisers if their editorial content, publications or programming offends consumers and these request companies to have their adverts removed from such sites. Therefore, principles or the 'real concerns' of the civil society may not in the end be 'free standing' influences in the media.

Speaking of the independence of the media, however, usually refers to its independence from government; self-regulation, to the degree it is permitted by law, is seen to guarantee both this independence and freedom of expression. In most countries self-regulation is often accompanied by some degree of State regulation in order to ensure that minimum standards of democratic order and human rights are protected.[100] For example, although the media is largely self-regulated in the UK, there are legal mechanisms to protect individuals and groups, should their rights be violated by the industry; for example, through the protection of freedom of expression enshrined in article 10 of the European Convention on Human Rights, the tort of defamation, copyright law and criminal law. However, even though most democratic countries recognise and prohibit hate speech, there isn't a straightforward equivalent legal provision to back the stereotyping/discriminatory content provisions included in the often labelled 'Harm and Offence' sections in the standards codes of the media. Therefore, adjudications involving discriminatory content that is not serious enough to be considered hate speech are dealt with only by media organisations that, as has been noted, do not necessarily have the required disposition to deal with discriminatory content, and exist primarily to represent the interests of the media industry.

99　Galtung (1999) cited in Nordenstreng (2002), p. 1.
100　See, Laitila (1995). The Audio Visual Media Services Directive, AVMSD 2010/13/EU, for example, encourages Member States to use co- and self-regulation. See also the work of the European Regulators Group for Audiovisual Media Services (which brings together heads or high-level representatives of national independent regulatory bodies in the field of audiovisual services to advise the Commission in the implementation of the EU's AVMSD); and the study on the independence of regulators by the Hans Bredow Institute for Media Research (2011). Their 'INDIREG' study, conducted on behalf of the European Commission includes the development of a tool for the self-assessment of independence and efficient functioning of the media regulatory bodies, based on formal and de facto criteria, such as status and powers, financial autonomy, autonomy of decision-makers, knowledge and accountability and transparency mechanism.

In cases of discriminatory content and since ED is not legally (statutorily) recognised, all that an ordinary complainant can do is accept the relevant regulatory authority's decision. Cases can be dismissed, adjudicated, upheld or not, at the total discretion of the media and in their own terms, despite the power imbalances between the civil society and the media industry. Therefore, complaint-based mechanisms such as those implemented in the UK (which put the onus on the victims to act), should at least be improved. For a complaint mechanism to be effective, the codes, guidelines, procedures and previous adjudications need not only to be accessible (e.g. online), but also effectively publicised so that the public at large actually know whether or not they can complain, what about, to whom and how to do it persuasively. People need to trust the system and have specialised institutional support that will understand their point of view and assist them during the complaint. People need to be sure they are not competing hopelessly against the economic and ideological power of the media. When complaint-based mechanisms are complicated and treat the complaints and complainants with disdain, people give up (Chapter 4) and therefore leave the media facilitating the free speech of only those with power.

I The duties and potential of the Equality and Human Rights Commission

If we accept that the harm of ED, although discreet is deeply connected to discrimination understood as a multifaceted problem, the redress of ED then requires and would actually justify the intervention, to the degree that it may be permitted by law, of the EHRC. Moreover, the EHRC has a statutory duty under the Equality Act 2006 to encourage and support the development of a society in which: people's ability to achieve their potential is not *limited by prejudice or discrimination*, there is respect for and protection of each individual's human rights, there is *respect for the dignity* and worth of each individual, each individual has an equal opportunity to participate in society, and there is *mutual respect* between groups based on understanding and valuing of diversity and on shared respect for equality and human rights (part 1, s. 3).[101] As we have seen, ED limits participatory parity, harms human dignity and is a manifestation of misrecognition (disrespect) and so, the potential involvement of the EHRC in the redress of ED would not go against its duty; quite the contrary, it could help carry it out more effectively.

The role of the EHRC is in general terms to: ensure people are aware of their rights; work with employers, service providers and organisations to help them develop best practice; work with policy makers, lawyers and the

101 Italics are the author's.

Government to make sure social policy and the law promote equality; and use its powers to enforce the laws already in place.[102] As explained in Chapter 3, the Public Sector Equality Duty (PSED), established in the Equality Act 2010, applies to public authorities carrying out public functions (schedule 19) and to persons who are not public authorities but who exercise public functions.[103] The requirements of the duty are essentially to meet the needs of those who work for them and use their services. The duty hence requires public authorities to have due regard for the need to tackle discrimination and promote equal opportunities. When designing and delivering their services, they should consider how they can make them fair for everyone. It will also ensure that decision making is based on real-life experience and evidence of need, rather than arbitrary assumptions and stereotypes.

The PSED consists of a general duty and specific duties set out in secondary legislation to accompany the Equality Act 2010. The general duty has three main aims which require those subject to the Equality Duty, in the exercise of their functions, to have due regard to the need to: eliminate unlawful discrimination, harassment and victimisation and other conduct prohibited by the Equality Act 2010; advance equality of opportunity between people who share a protected characteristic and those who do not; and foster good relations between people who share a protected characteristic and those who do not.[104] Crucially in the context of ED, the Equality Act 2010 describes fostering good relations as *tackling prejudice and promoting understanding* between people from different groups and it states that compliance with the duty may involve treating some people more favourably than others (s. 149 (4), (5) and (6), respectively). Tackling prejudice and promoting understanding are related to the aims and remedies pursued through the legal recognition and contestation of ED. The counter speech and the redefinition of maligned groups by themselves in response to ED are indeed ways of promoting understanding; and the facilitation/promotion of this counter speech can be a way to 'foster good relations'. Now, since the EHRC itself is a listed public authority and the regulators discussed in this chapter are all carrying out public functions and are subject to the PSED,[105] some collaborative work that could contribute to the redress of ED wouldn't be out of order. Moreover, as we noted in II, 2, Leveson's recommendations for the press regulator included intervention in cases of alleged 'discriminatory reporting' and also that such intervention 'should reflect the spirit of equalities

---

102 Equality Act 2006, part 1, sections 8, 9, 10, 11.
103 Equality Act 2010, part 11, chapter 1, section 149 (2).
104 Equality Act 2010, part 11, chapter 1, section 149.
105 Equality Act 2010, schedule 19; and Equality and Human Rights Commission (2015a), pp. 19–20.

legislation'.[106] As expressed by the EHRC, the media self-regulators we have explored – Ofcom, IPSO and the ASA – have all:

> [A] duty to seek to strike the proper balance when protecting freedom of expression conflicts with other duties, remembering the very high threshold that will apply in cases which involve the media, or engage the public interest and in particular political comment. For entertainment rather than politics, the threshold will be lower.[107]

The EHRC offers as an example of 'lower threshold' the case of a complaint which was upheld about some posters advertising the Channel 4 series 'Big Fat Gypsy Weddings'. The reasoning for upholding the complaint was that such adverts were 'irresponsible, offensive and reaffirmed negative stereotypes and prejudice against the Traveller and Gypsy communities, finding in effect that the advertiser's Article 10 rights would not be infringed by a ban on the posters'.[108]

The EHRC recognises that 'the use of inflammatory language based on individual characteristics does not help promote constructive and informed dialogue and can cause personal distress and damage community relations'.[109] However, it has also made it clear that it is not its role 'to judge in individual cases whether offensive comments may or may not be protected under Article 10 … [and that neither] is it for [the EHRC] to determine whether any particular comment reaches a criminal threshold'.[110] These things said, however, the EHRC can – because it is within the general powers it already has – contribute to the redress of ED by, for example: disseminating ideas or information, undertaking research, providing education or training and giving advice or guidance.[111] The specific way in which the EHRC could participate in the redress of ED is necessarily the subject of a discrete analysis, which should also necessarily include an analysis of the extent to which media self-regulatory agencies would be willing/urged to collaborate. Nevertheless, for the purposes of this discussion, we can draw some general principles which are consistent with the EHRC's remit and duties. For example, one of its key roles is to provide advice and guidance on rights, responsibilities and good practice, based on equality and human rights. The EHRC has in fact created a number of resources for the private and public sector, including schools, businesses and professional bodies. These resources have included, for

---

106 Leveson LJ (2012), *Summary of recommendations*, para. 38.
107 Equality and Human Rights Commission (2015a), p. 19.
108 *Ibid.*
109 *Ibid*, p. 18.
110 *Ibid*, p. 25.
111 See Equality Act 2006, part 1, section 13, General powers [of the Equality and Human Rights Commission].

example, toolkits such as 'Equal choices, equal chances', which is a set of free online education resources to help deliver careers and equality-related learning. The toolkit includes a series of activities and multimedia resources in themes such as identity and challenging stereotypes.[112] Similarly, the EHRC could produce toolkits on media literacy for children and the population at large.[113] As we noted in Chapter 5, education is paramount in redressing discrimination at a cultural level. Moreover, media literacy in turn can help enable citizens and the organised civil society to make articulate complaints, exercise their free speech and tackle prejudice through the appropriate channels.

The EHRC could also produce resources for itself and for the media regulators, explaining the harm created by demeaning and stereotypical representations and reminding them of the many commitments and recommendations derived from the UK's membership to and/or ratification of various international and European documents, many of which specifically concern the media (Chapter 5). Undertaking this sort of research and its publication wouldn't be entirely groundbreaking. In fact, in the aftermath of the *Charlie Hebdo* incident concerning the publication in Paris of cartoons which were in the view of many 'offensive' on religious grounds, the EHRC produced its *Legal Framework on Freedom of Expression*. This document explores the boundaries between freedom of expression, unlawful discrimination and harassment, and hate speech.[114] While useful in many regards, the research did not, however, include enough reference to the existing complaint-based mechanisms of the media self-regulatory bodies; and neither did it mention the way in which people could use them to challenge discriminatory content that does not reach the criminal threshold. A later guidance produced in August 2015 marks another step forward, reinforcing the view about the potential role of the EHRC in the redress of ED. This guidance is aimed at the television broadcasting industry and focuses on two important aspects that can contribute to the redress of ED: 'increasing diversity both on and off screen'. These aspects have

112 See the 'Equal choices, equal chances' toolkit, available at www.equalityhumanrights. com/private-and-public-sector-guidance/education-providers/primary-education-resources/resource-toolkit (accessed 2 July 2015).

113 For a notion of 'media literacy', see, for example, Recommendation 1466 (2006) on 'Media education'. According to the Council of Europe, media education can be defined as teaching practices which aim to develop media competence, understood as a critical and discerning attitude towards the media in order to form well-balanced citizens, capable of making their own judgements on the basis of available information. It enables them to access the necessary information, to analyse it and be able to identify the economic, political, social and/or cultural interests that lie behind it. Media education teaches individuals to interpret and produce messages, to select the most appropriate media for communicating and, eventually, to have a greater say in the media offer and output.

114 Equality and Human Rights Commission (2015b), pp. 3, 16.

been discussed in Chapters 4 and 5, and will be further discussed in Chapter 8. The guidance was produced in conjunction with Ofcom in response to the under-representation of women, disabled people and people from ethnic minority backgrounds. It provides clarity about the initiatives and actions that are permissible by law to tackle under-representation (e.g. positive action, tie-back provisions, storing information on protected characteristics on databases, occupational requirements, targets and quotas and procurement). With this guidance, the EHRC confirms that it has a role to play in the matters that this book has identified as 'discrimination at a cultural level'; that it is possible to 'do something' to redress ED; and that television broadcasting has a unique role in 'shaping and reflecting our society values'.[115] However, as it has been noticed and will be further explained, the EHRC can and needs to do more to contribute to the redress of ED.

As things stand now and given that the industry creates its own codes and adjudicates in its own terms, research is very much needed in order to find out how much people actually know that they can complain, whether or not they know how to do so and whether or not they would trust the industry. In fact, the ASA's research on 'Public perceptions of harm and offence in UK advertising' found out that '[while] there was an underlying expectation that media self-regulation happens and should continue to happen ... the details of how this works were unfamiliar to almost all participants'.[116]

Information about the regulators of the media is available online. However, finding this information requires some knowledge about the industry; about the importance and the content of their standards codes; and about the existence of different complaints procedures. It is also vital to keep up-to-date because all this information can change at the total discretion of the industry and at whichever intervals it decides. Moreover, it is also unfair that access to information and to complaint mechanisms mostly relies on and largely depends on the efficiency of the website, and on people having access to and knowing how to use the internet. There are, of course, postal addresses and telephone numbers but so far these haven't been effectively publicised either. There are various regulatory authorities; although similar, they all have specific procedures, deadlines and codes that indicate the type of content that can be the object of a complaint. Ordinary people have to be aware of and master all these details in order to be able to make a good case, because otherwise complaints can simply be dismissed. It therefore appears fair that in the same way that the industry represents itself and protects its interests, consumers,

---

115 *Ibid*, p. 5.
116 Ipsos MORI (2012), p. 17.

including the organised civil society, should be properly advised and their interests should be protected.

Even though the EHRC does not have the power to adjudicate, and although it has said that it is not for it to determine whether any particular comment reaches a criminal threshold, the EHRC considers that 'those in the public eye and in positions of influence, in particular, should act responsibly in relation to use of language when discussing sensitive issues'.[117] Therefore the EHRC can make recommendations of this sort which can in effect contribute to the raising of awareness about ED and in turn contribute to its redress. However, more is needed. Advice about existing complaint-based procedures and about the existing standards codes, including help with their interpretation and guidelines could, for example, be offered by the Equality Advisory Support Service (EASS). The EASS was commissioned by the Government in 2012 to replace the EHRC Helpline, which is now closed; it is now the EASS which has taken the role of advising and assisting individuals on issues relating to equality and human rights, across England, Scotland and Wales. The EASS could therefore contribute to the redress of ED by providing relevant information – and explaining it – to people of different backgrounds and abilities. This information should include, for example, basic notions about self-regulation, information about the appropriate media outlet or regulatory body in charge of dealing with complaints, guidance about the relevant standards codes and about the types of content they can make a complaint about. Moreover, the EASS could also have a database of civil society organisations which work in the area of equality and discrimination and who may be interested in assisting those who wish to complain about ED in the media.

A free and 'independent' media is paramount for democracy and, therefore, media self-regulation should be taken seriously. However, this does not only mean advocating media's independence and respecting the rules the industry has set for itself; taking self-regulation seriously should also mean: promoting the rights the industry has arranged for the consumers (e.g. to make complaints), making sure the industry does provide the remedies it has the power to offer, and that, in general terms, regulators meet the needs not only of those who work for them but also of those who use their services.

IV Conclusions

Given that there are two valuable interests at stake – free speech and non-discrimination – media self-regulatory bodies and the EHRC or similar bodies need to work collaboratively for the redress of ED. While the

117 Equality and Human Rights Commission (2015a), p. 25.

protection of freedom of expression requires minimal or no content censorship at all, the regulators have a duty to tackle prejudice and to promote understanding between people from different groups and, therefore, they should create the appropriate channels so that the targets of ED can themselves contest discriminatory speech through more speech.

The intervention of the EHRC or similar bodies may include: carrying out research and promoting existing 'rights' to challenge ED; providing information and advice for the consumers; and elaborating specific guidelines for the media regulators. These should in turn be responsive to the advice and guidelines and also seek specific advice when necessary, including training for their staff. These principles could therefore ensure that there are *appropriate and efficient channels* to challenge discriminatory images and messages that do not reach hate speech laws thresholds; and the existence and effective use of these channels can in turn contribute to the politicisation of culture and to the development of a society where prejudice and discrimination do not hinder people's participatory parity.

V References

Barendt, Eric (2005), *Freedom of Speech*, 2nd ed., Oxford: Oxford University Press.

Equality and Human Rights Commission (2015a), *Legal Framework on Freedom of Expression*.

Equality and Human Rights Commission (2015b), *Thinking Outside the Box: Supporting the Television Broadcasting Industry*.

Galtung, Johan (1999), 'State, capital and civil society: the problem of communication', in Vincent, Richard, Nordenstreng, Kaarle and Traber, Michael, *Towards Equity in Global Communication*, Cresskill, NJ: Hampton Press.

Halliday, Josh and Wintour, Patrick (2012), 'David Cameron accused of dismissing Leveson report too quickly', *Guardian*, 30 November, available at www.theguardian.com/media/2012/nov/30/david-cameron-accused-prejudging-leveson (accessed 25 June 2015).

Hans Bredow Institute for Media Research, ed. (2011), *INDIREG: Indicators for Independence and Efficient Functioning of Audiovisual Media Services Regulatory Bodies for the Purposes of Enforcing the Rules in the AVMS Directive*, Study conducted on behalf of the European Commission.

Ipsos MORI (2012), *Public Perceptions of Harm and Offence in UK Advertising*, research conducted on behalf of the Advertising Standards Authority, July.

Laitila, Tiina (1995), 'Codes of ethics in Europe', in Nordenstreng, Kaarle, *Reports on Media Ethics in Europe*, University of Tampere, Publications of the Department of Journalism and Mass Communication, Reports B 41.

Leveson LJ (2012), *An Inquiry into the Culture, Practices and Ethics of the Press: Executive Summary and Summary of Recommendations*, London: The Stationery Office.

Mason, Rowena (2012), 'Leveson Inquiry recommendations likely to be adopted – Cameron', *Telegraph*, 7 October, available at www.telegraph.co.uk/news/politics/conservative/9592592/Leveson-Inquiry-recommendations-likely-to-be-adopted-Cameron.html (accessed 25 June 2015).

Media Standards Trust (2013), *The Independent Press Standards Organisation (IPSO): An Assessment*, available at http://mediastandardstrust.org/wp-content/uploads/downloads/2013/11/MST-IPSO-Analysis-15-11-13.pdf (accessed 24 June 2015).

Nordenstreng, Kaarle (2000), 'Mass communication', in Browing, Gary, Halcli, Abigail and Webster, Frank, eds, *Understanding Contemporary Society: Theories of the Present*, London: Sage.

Nordenstreng, Kaarle (2002), 'Media ethics in Europe: in search of core values', *International Colloquium on Media Ethics*, Centre Africain de Perfectionnement des Journaistes et Communicateurs (CAPJC), Tunis, 6–7 February.

Robertson, Emma, (2013), 'Race and the advertising of cocoa', in Hund, Wulf, Pickering, Michael and Ramamurthy, Anandi, eds, *Colonial Advertising and Commodity Racism*, Zurich: Lit Verlag.

Sancho, Jane and Wilson, Andy (2001), *Boxed In: Offence from Negative Stereotyping in TV Advertising*, report by ITC, Qualitative Consultancy.

Sherwin, Adam (2011), 'ASA says Cadbury was not racist when it compared Campbell to a chocolate bar', *Independent*, 21 June, available at www.independent.co.uk/news/media/advertising/asa-says-cadbury-was-not-racist-when-it-compared-campbell-to-chocolate-bar-2300278.html (accessed 1 July 2015).

Sweney, Mark (2007), 'Trident gum ad spat out', *Guardian*, 28 March, available at www.theguardian.com/media/2007/mar/28/advertising.uknews (accessed 1 July 2015).

Sweney, Mark (2011), 'Cadbury's Naomi Campbell ad not racist, rules watchdog', *Guardian*, 20 June, available at www.theguardian.com/media/2011/jun/20/cadbury-naomi-campbell-ad-not-racist (accessed 1 July 2015).

Sweney, Mark (2015), 'Ipso rival Impress to seek recognition under royal charter', *Guardian*, 20 May, available at www.theguardian.com/media/2015/may/20/ipso-rival-impress-to-seek-recognition-under-royal-charter (accessed 24 June 2015).

Tomlinson, Hugh (2014), 'The new UK model of press regulation'. Media Policy Brief 12, LSE Media Policy Project.

Chapter 8

Everyday discrimination as a legal wrong

I Introduction

The previous chapters have explored the various degrees and ways in which the harm created through the images and messages identified in this book as *everyday discrimination* (ED) has been acknowledged in international and regional documents, in criminal law and anti-discrimination law (ADL) statutes, as well as in the standards codes of media regulatory authorities. Making use of the findings of the previous chapters, including the strengths and weaknesses of existing provisions, this chapter specifies what ED consists of, and in so doing establishes its aims; corrects some of the flaws and gaps identified in current responses to discriminatory speech; and addresses the claims raised by the targets of ED.

Although the philosophical and theoretical principles argued in this book may serve to articulate, explain and understand the harm created by discriminatory images and messages wherever they are produced, ED in this book refers primarily to discriminatory images and messages in the media because they have been largely ignored by the law, mainly in response to freedom of expression considerations. However, it is possible to redress the harm they create without infringing freedom of expression; and it is necessary to recognise more clearly and legally the predicament in which they leave their targets and society as a whole. In order to contribute to these effects, the first part of this chapter specifies those defining characteristics of ED which are helpful in determining when a media product can be considered discriminatory. The second part indicates the ways in which ED is manifested and should therefore represent the issues that the recognition of ED seeks to redress. Finally, the third part illustrates the importance of a legal recognition of the harm created by ED and argues for its contestation on a level playing field as a means to redress the harm.

II Defining characteristics of ED

The printed and audiovisual production and reproduction of images and messages that use demeaning stereotypes, ridicule, malign or disparage people on the grounds of their belonging to a disadvantaged group are forms of discrimination 'through expressive means'; the term ED has been used in this book to give the harm they create a name, introducing it as a legal wrong, a form of discrimination, and therefore claiming it should be justiciable.

It is not, however, always straightforward to differentiate between, for example, ED and reflecting 'reality'; between ED and good faith criticism; or between ED and 'just' humour. Circumscribing the scope of ED is therefore a first step in addressing this form of discrimination from a legal point of view. The defining characteristics of ED that this section proposes are inspired by the findings of the previous chapters regarding the concerns expressed by the civil society; the issues raised in international and regional instruments targeting both the cultural aspects of discrimination and hate speech; and the strengths and weaknesses of existing hate speech regulations and of the 'harm and offence' provisions within the standards codes of the media regulatory authorities in the UK. No single element is more important than any of the others. In fact they may overlap. Together, they limit the scope of ED and serve to prevent the potential abuse or misuse of the protection that may be offered through the recognition of ED in any particular jurisdiction.

The defining characteristics of ED are: (1) it is a public act; (2) the historical, social, economic or political context determines whether an image or message is discriminatory and therefore captured by the concept of ED; (3) the targets of ED are disadvantaged groups; (4) ED is an intangible harm, a manifestation of disrespect; and (5) ED is a specific harm that forms part of a wider system of discrimination.

First, ED is a *public act*. This means that ED is harmful precisely because the demeaning image or message is made public. The environment is thus 'littered'; the targeted group's self- and social-esteem is being assaulted thereby compromising participatory parity. It is for this reason that the mass media (internet, television, radio, press and advertising) are particularly important because they make speech public to a wide audience. ED is therefore different from private conversations, harmful as they are.

ED causes pain; it is an affront to the feelings of the individual member of the targeted group. ED singles out members of certain categories of people, it may be highly embarrassing and distressing, particularly when the image or the message is seen by a member of the targeted group in the company of others who do not share the maligned trait. The latter constitutes the second dimension of the harm, this is to say the damage to the target's social standing and reputation as a member of the belittled group.[1] This is not to suggest that members of other groups will instantly and uncritically adopt a negative stereotype about the target group, but that they are being put in a position which unfairly allows them to 'judge' the standing of the member of the target group who in turn may feel the need or indeed be 'requested' to prove the discriminatory image or message to be wrong. Likewise, the 'public act' element means that ED needs to be, to a certain extent, permanent; be it printed, performed or reproduced in a way that makes it available to an audience that will be 'invited' to laugh at, believe or adopt a certain stereotype or demeaning concept about a group of people. Therefore, while intimidating its targets, ED makes the 'audience' feel in a position of power, which may include an ambivalent or latent relief of not being one of those targeted.

ED focuses on the media in particular because given its resources, immediate availability, reliance on the protection of free speech and the unequal power relations between the members of the public and the media industry, it is a distinct agent in the production and reproduction of discriminatory images and messages. Moreover, focusing on the media in particular allows for focused attention on what it is necessary to modify in the specific context of the media (e.g. complaint-based mechanisms, codes and guidelines to avoid ED and adjudication/conciliation processes).

Second, the *context* determines whether an image or message constitutes ED. This is to say that understanding and determining the harm of ED requires a context-specific approach and that context is paramount in determining whether or not an image or a message is discriminatory. Context for the purposes of ED means the historical issues and events that have led to the misrecognition and disrespect of certain identities (e.g. ideas about male superiority and the ideology of imperialism). Also it means that discriminatory expression is aggravated and often takes place precisely because of current social, political and economic circumstances (e.g. the rise of Islamophobia since the terrorist attacks in New York in 2001 and London in 2005; the economic, social and political issues associated with 'legal and illegal' immigration; and the financial crisis that started in 2007). The severity of discriminatory expression and/or the existence of discriminatory images and messages are therefore determined by their context. In broadcasting scenarios, the British Office of Communications Broadcasting Code understands context as including, but not being limited to: the editorial content of the programme, programmes or series; the service on which the material is broadcast; the time of broadcast; what other programmes are scheduled before and after the programme or programmes concerned; the degree of harm or offence likely to be caused by the inclusion of any particular sort of material in

---

1 See Parekh (2006), p. 313.

programmes generally or programmes of a particular description; the likely size and composition of the potential audience and likely expectation of the audience; the extent to which the nature of the content can be brought to the attention of the potential audience, for example by giving information; and the effect of the material on viewers or listeners who may come across it unawares.[2]

This understanding of context is aimed at elucidating whether or not the broadcasting of potentially harmful material is justified and provides elements for understanding the necessary contextual approach to potentially discriminatory images and messages against editorial content and times of broadcasting. This is, then, another dimension of context that can also help determine whether an image or message is discriminatory.

Regarding hate speech, context is also paramount in determining the meaning of the words or the intentions of the actor. According to a comparative hate speech study by the Pro Bono Publico programme of the Law Faculty of the University of Oxford, 'it appears that [there are] five contextual factors ... [including] historical and cultural associations; the identity of the speaker; the identity of the target; the setting and the audience; [and] the prevailing social conditions'.[3] These are not exhaustive and have been drawn only from some of the cases explored by the researchers. However, these factors coincide with various of the points raised in this book so far for the identification of ED and can indeed be useful to rescue and challenge content that may not 'fully' reach the criminal threshold but that is nevertheless discriminatory.

Power relationships are the bottom line of the contextual approach to ED; 'the emphasis on context urges attention to the medium, means of dissemination, and relationships between speaker and audience – race, religion, education and class'.[4] For example, speaking of the harm inflicted through the sexual objectification of women makes sense when placed against its context, that is to say, the historical undervaluing of women and what is coded as feminine, women's economic disadvantage and exploitation, the glass ceiling, harassment in the workplace, rape, domestic violence and so on. This means that a history of violence or persecution against a particular group – power relationships – can be a meaningful indicator of the disadvantage of such groups. It is for this reason that historical and contemporary power relationships matter when it comes to evaluating whether an image or a message is discriminatory. This evaluation should also include information about, for example, the

---

2 The Ofcom Broadcasting Code, 28 February 2011, Section 2, Harm and Offence, 2.3.
3 McConnachie *et al* (2012), pp. 10–17.
4 Abel (1998), p. 277.

group's degree of access to public positions, their standing in courts or involvement in public life, etc.[5]

The necessary contextual approach to ED is an element that can also help to determine which groups are more likely to be the targets under specific circumstances since ED cannot be understood as affecting everyone at all times.[6] Therefore the importance of context and what it involves needs to be more clearly included in the regulation of discriminatory media content and it also needs to be fully researched and assessed by complaints adjudicators.

Third, ED is a *disadvantaged-group-based issue*. Different communities at different points in history have been discriminated against. Without the element of disadvantage – which is often the product of the context – it would be inaccurate to speak about ED. For example, according to Parekh:

> Given the deep streak of anti-Semitism and anti-black racism in western societies (as indeed in many others), and given the need to counter the malicious stereotypes to which they have both been subjected for centuries with disastrous results, Jews and blacks would seem to qualify for anti-libel laws in most western countries. In the light of the increasing Islamophobia in West European countries, Muslims too might perhaps fall in this category.[7]

The decision as to whether one group is or is not the target of discriminatory images and messages depends on the context and cannot be determined in the abstract. For example, Muslims in western countries would not in the abstract constitute a disadvantaged group. However, the need to address Islamophobia and its increasing production of discriminatory images and messages has to do with contemporary economic, social, political and international events. For example,

> reform of domestic law was urged by the United Nations Human Rights Committee in the immediate aftermath of 11 September 2001. It expressed concern that, since recent terrorists attacks, persons have been the object of attack and harassment on the basis of religious beliefs.[8]

---

5 See the complaints made against the Trident advertisement referred to in Chapter 7, II, 3. The viewers made connections between the advert and historical undervaluing, mocking and ridiculing of the accent and the mannerisms of the black communities in the UK.

6 See, for example, Abrams and Houston (2006).

7 Parekh (2006), p. 316. Parekh argues that, like individuals, communities too can be objects of libel.

8 Cram (2006), p. 97.

The targets of ED are disadvantaged groups. Even though individuals feel the harm, this is so because of their group membership, as it is the case with other forms of discrimination such as unequal pay, 'every act of discrimination is done because of group membership, such as on the basis of sex or race or both, meaning done either with that conscious thought, perception, knowledge, or consequence'.[9] For example, it is individual women who are paid less, but this unequal pay is rooted in the negative value of women as a group. This is to say that discriminatory images and messages do not target individuals as such, but individuals as members of particular communities, as sharers of a specific cultural, racial or religious background and bearers of traits associated with it.[10] Parekh understands the harm in this way:

> Since individuals are not free-floating atoms but communally embedded, their identity is at once both personal and communal, and their self-respect is tied up with and partly grounded in respect for their community.[11]

The concept of ED, unlike other provisions addressing discriminatory speech, does acknowledge that discriminatory images and messages are group-based harms and also that discriminatory speech can happen on many and combined grounds.[12] A contextual analysis is necessary in order to determine which groups can be affected depending on the circumstances. The concept of ED is thus different, because it is not limited to the protection of certain grounds (as many hate speech laws do; see Chapter 6); and it urges an evaluation of the context in order to identify whether or not a particular group is in a disadvantaged position and should therefore be protected. This, however, on many occasions, will rely on the effective campaigning and lobbying of those affected and their supporters (which is in fact the way in which hate speech legislation has increased the number of characteristics protected).[13] In sum, the targets of ED are *disadvantaged groups* and the discriminatory speech of ED constitutes a specific form of disadvantage which forms part of a systemic chain.

---

9 MacKinnon (1994), p. 21.
10 See Parekh (2006), p. 313.
11 *Ibid*, pp. 313–314.
12 See Chapter 7, II, 2. It was noticed that the press is clear in protecting individuals but not groups.
13 Some identity groups, however, seem to gain sympathy and have their demands met more easily than others. Known tensions of this sort include the disadvantage of lesbian women and bisexual people compared to gay men in popular culture. See Guasp (2013), p. 22; and the invisibility of black women when struggles concentrate on either gender or race. See, for example, Crenshaw (1989).

Fourth, the images and messages of ED constitute *intangible harms*, 'misrecognition'; this means that discrimination occurs even where there exists no economic or material manifestation. This kind of harm, like harassment for example, is often trivialised and is more difficult to determine than physical harm or damage to property. There may also be fear of fraudulent litigation and concerns related to the difficulties in the payment of damages (if an economic sanction were appropriate). Physical injuries or damage to property are generally acceptable for legal actions and they are more easily proved. Although the law has shown that it is capable of addressing intangible harms (e.g. the legal recognition of defamation and harassment),[14] whenever there is no tangible harm, legislation tends to be more cautious. The risk of false claims (e.g. opportunistic claims from the powerful or on the basis of undemocratic values) is real and should not be underestimated; however, it would be unfair to deny recognition on this basis.

ED constitutes an intangible harm to the self- and social-esteem of its targets and results in status subordination. As Delgado has put it, referring to words that wound, in this sort of harm: 'Not only does the listener learn and internalise the messages contained in racial insults, these messages also color our society's institutions and are transmitted to succeeding generations.'[15] Ignoring intangible harms 'may deflect attention away from the subtle ways in which hateful expression [and discrimination] serve to oppress its targets'.[16] Indeed, according to Cram, the toleration of hateful expression (and discriminatory expression can also be added) promotes an ideology that encourages and maintains disrespect and hostility towards 'minority' groups and their members.[17] Likewise, ignoring intangible harms underestimates the potential that discriminatory images and messages have in maintaining relations of oppression and domination. Labelling any attempt to change or to criticise the *status quo* as 'political correctness gone mad' is another symptom of the underestimation of the harm, but also a conservative reaction against the challenging of imagery and symbols that inform discrimination in all of its manifestations, and as Abel has put it, 'what is denigrated as political correctness today may be taken for granted tomorrow'.[18] He reiterates the importance of recalling how many forms of status degradation long taken for granted have been delegitimated. For Abel,

> Racist, anti-Semitic, and sexist slurs that routinely infected daily discourse have been banished to the margins of deviance. The rants of

14 See the UK Defamation Act 1996.
15 Delgado (1993), p. 90.
16 Cram (2006), p. 136.
17 *Ibid.*
18 Abel (1998), p. 277. See also Williams (1995).

shock jocks titillate precisely because audiences know that such language is harmful and have largely abandoned it themselves. Indulgence in crude stereotypes by politicians or the mass media has become sufficiently rare to provoke public outcry, which usually compels retraction and apology.[19]

It is difficult to agree with Abel's thoughts about the sufficient rarity of crude stereotypes. As we have seen, ED and stereotyping – as ideological tools – are in constant 'movement'; they may diminish or intensify in different contexts (Chapter 4). However, what I want to rescue from Abel's quote is his emphasis on change and the dynamics of culture and the opportunity for its contestation. The possibility of 'public outcry', or complaint, has taken a long time to be acknowledged and it is still quite fragile and haphazard, and is relatively unknown in contemporary, largely democratic societies (Chapter 7). Complaining is still very costly. It may involve ridicule because of one's opposition to things considered 'just humour' or 'ignorance' and also the exclusion of the person – who complains – from certain positions or privileges when she is seen as a troublemaker. The 'rarity' of stereotypes or of other forms of ridicule is unlikely to be unprompted. It requires either changes in the social, economic or political circumstances that allow demeaning representations to flourish; or people gaining consciousness about the harm they create and therefore initiating complaints. However, for effective complaint mechanisms to be in place, the first step is the recognition of the harm, which is something that up to the present day remains elusive; law does not back it and access to redress is 'hit and miss'. The concept of ED is therefore aimed at the better understanding and recognition of the harm created through demeaning and stereotypical representations in order to effectively contest them and politicise culture.

The intangible harm associated with the concept of ED is generally 'misrecognition', in the form of disrespect with the resulting status degradation. Indeed, respect as Abel puts it is 'a central goal in the eternal resistance to subordination. Just as bourgeois revolutions sought political equality and proletarian movements aspired to transform relations of production, so identity politics strives for dignity'.[20] The goal of the protection against ED is to contest the means of reproduction and symbols – a struggle for recognition. The acknowledgement of discriminatory images and messages in the media – ED as a specific form of discrimination – would in part have this effect, namely: making the contestation of symbols possible and thus transforming the cultural patterns of representation and interpretation that lead to status subordination (Chapter 2). Unlike other

19 Abel (1998), p. 282.
20 *Ibid*, p. 245.

provisions against discriminatory speech, the concept of ED acknowledges that the harm of discriminatory speech is intangible (not necessarily economic or a threat to physical integrity or property); often subtle and unintended, but nevertheless a harm in and of itself.

Fifth, even though ED inflicts a discrete harm, it *forms a part of a wider system of discrimination*. It is not a matter of taste, decency or mere offence. Discriminatory expression is highly unlikely to exist in a world where there were no gross inequalities of income, economic exploitation or status subordination. ED is possible – and harmful – precisely because of the existence of oppression and subordination, and in fact, discriminatory images and messages are often both the cause and the consequence of such oppression. Redressing ED does not by itself put an end to other discriminatory behaviours or practices, but neither will addressing other forms of discrimination bring spontaneous redress to discrimination at a cultural level. That said, discriminatory images and messages, and indeed the cultural aspects of discrimination in general, have been largely ignored by ADL, as if discrimination existed in a cultural vacuum. As Parekh has put it:

> Discriminatory treatment of and hostility against a section of our fellow-citizens, which we rightly disapprove of, do not occur in a cultural vacuum. They grow out of and are legitimised by a wider moral climate which is built up and sustained by, among other things, gratuitously disparaging and offensive remarks, each individually perhaps good-humoured and tolerable but all collectively contributing to the dehumanisation or demonization of the relevant groups.[21]

ED could be said to be a part of a chain of cumulative damage. In fact, discriminatory expression is built on the historical subordination of certain groups while at the same time contributing to its reproduction. For example, in the case of racism, Delgado refers to racial slurs as an injury that 'calls upon the entire history of slavery and racial discrimination to injure the victim'.[22] In this sense, the wrongdoer would be jointly guilty along with all others, past and present, who have perpetuated racism. This is important especially because discriminatory images and messages are often trivialised by the argument that they are little harms when compared to 'real discriminatory practices'. There are two opposing views on this matter. On the one hand is the argument that the contribution that ED or similar practices make to racism, for example, is small and could not

21 Parekh (2006), p. 314.
22 Delgado (1993), p. 105.

possibly cause further significant damage because 'minority' group members are or should be inured to such treatment.[23]

On the other hand, the arguably more convincing view is that discriminatory speech is built on an existing disadvantage of those already harmed by various discriminatory practices and this makes the act more, not less, reprehensible. This means that ED and related practices (racial insults, epithets and name calling in Delgado's argument) are substantially exploiting an apparent susceptibility which makes the harm not only a part of a wider system of discrimination, but a particularly abusive one in itself.[24] This is possibly the most clarifying characteristic of ED – namely, it is a kind of harm that targets those who have been persistently discriminated against; it keeps relations of inferiority and superiority 'in their place', building on, reinforcing, justifying and maintaining status subordination.

III Manifestations and underpinnings of ED

ED is materialised in a product (e.g. an advert, an image or a comment in a TV or radio programme) that harms the self- and social-esteem of a disadvantaged group (misrepresentation). However, the concept of ED also includes the exclusion of certain groups from appearing in mainstream media, which reinforces stereotypes and does not reflect the 'diverse' composition of society (under-representation). Moreover, ED can also exist in the ways in which news is reported (coverage). These are the kind of issues about which targeted groups complain (Chapters 4 and 7) and they coincide with concerns raised in international instruments (Chapter 5).

ED, however, is in part the result of the broadcasting structures themselves.[25] This means that negative images and messages are the outcome; for example, not only of widespread racism and sexism, but are also linked to the way in which the media is structured; for example, in their policies of recruitment, promotion, decision-making processes, sponsors' demands and the 'culture' that all these people and processes together generate. Therefore, the redress of ED also requires the active participation of disadvantaged groups 'behind the scenes'; that is, in the workforce of the media industry, in decision-making bodies, as journalists and managers.

I Misrepresentation, under-representation and coverage

ED as *misrepresentation* means the actual image, message or advert which discriminates by stereotyping, subordinating and thereby harming the self- and social-esteem of disadvantaged groups. For example, in order to sell

23 *Ibid.*
24 *Ibid.*
25 See Hall (1971; 1997).

products, racist adverts take advantage of the historical undervaluing and ridiculing of certain races and the traits associated with them. Advertisers use this systemic undervaluation to catch attention, often through shock, while at the same time reproducing and sustaining disrespect and relations of domination.[26]

It could be argued that the media only reflects reality as it is, not as it should be. Broadcasters may maintain that they should not be held responsible for reforming attitudes and behaviours. Moreover, even when there is a commitment to present a more positive image – for example of women – advertising agencies may argue that they do not have a mandate to change the world but a responsibility to work in a changing world and reflect those changes in commercials.[27] There are a number of problems with these views. On the one hand, there is a huge profit, especially for advertisers, made from the disadvantage of certain groups. Indeed, profiting from disadvantage is also seen in real life. However, this makes the problem more and not less severe; for example, even though women are indeed harassed in real-life workplaces, this should not give advertisers licence to use women's harassment as a 'witty' way to sell underwear, body lotions and the like.[28] On the other hand, even though it is true that the media is not the only agency responsible for 'bad attitudes', it can certainly reflect society in a more accurate way. The media does not only reflect reality, *it chooses* which part of reality to reflect. Furthermore, as we noted in Chapter 7, regulators in the UK *are* subject to the Public Sector Equality Duty and therefore have a duty, among other things, to tackle prejudice and promote understanding; and in the words of the EHRC, the regulators we have explored – Ofcom, IPSO and the ASA – all have '[A] duty to seek to strike the proper balance when protecting freedom of expression conflicts with other duties'.[29]

Under-representation as a manifestation of ED inflicts two distinct but interrelated harms. On the one hand, it excludes certain identities from appearing in media products, as if they were not part of society; and on the other, their limited presence in media products is often stereotypical, and thus the few images available misrepresent them. For example, if only a small number of people from disadvantaged groups appear, and when they do, they appear in demeaning stereotypical roles, such random appearances do little favour to the targeted group in the sense that their participation is limited and negative. The number of times disadvantaged

---

26 See the examples in Chapter 7, II, 3.
27 See Sancho and Wilson (2001), p. 7.
28 Brands such as Dolce & Gabbana, Donna Karan and Noxzema have used 'gang rape', stalking and street harassment, respectively, to sell their products. See some critical views by the Sexual Assault Prevention and Awareness Centre, University of Michigan, available at https://sapac.umich.edu (accessed 16 July 2015).
29 Equality and Human Rights Commission (2015a), p. 19.

groups appear is as important as the roles they occupy. For example, white people, as the dominant majority in western countries, have an advantage; they appear most of the time and in a variety of roles (good, bad, lazy, hardworking, etc.); this is why the negative portrayals do not have the same damaging effect that they have when it comes to 'minorities' or dis-advantaged groups.[30] As Rosenfeld has put it:

> The paucity of minority viewpoints over the airwaves is detrimental ... [but negative] stereotyping seems a worse affront to equal respect than a mere failure to afford sufficient opportunities for self-expression. Also, the combination of negative stereotypes and gross under-representation of minority view points skews the information presented to the broadcast audience as a whole in a way that fosters and perpetuates prejudice against minorities.[31]

Moreover, the concern does not stop with what appears in the media, but continues with the impact such *repeated* images have on shaping and influencing attitudes and opinions. The continuous exposure to demeaning stereotypes about disadvantaged groups is not just a biased and partial reflection of reality, but an injury in and of itself. Therefore, protection against ED should challenge both the limited appearance of targeted groups and the kind of roles they occupy. The Equality and Human Rights Commission (EHRC) in the UK has shown concern about the 'lack of diversity on and off screen'. However, a guidance it produced in this regard only focuses on the legal measures that may be permissible in order to increase numbers which in itself is not enough if the kind of roles that under-represented groups occupy remain in the main stereotypical or sub-ordinated on and off screen.[32]

ED in *coverage* can be found in the way in which news is reported; however, it should be distinguished from the coverage or the exposure of racism, sexism and so on. Similarly, it is appreciated that, on occasion, a journalist or broadcaster may have little or no control over statements made by interviewees in live-to-air interviews. Moreover, media organisations have some latitude in the dissemination of the racist and hateful views of others as part of their role in facilitating debate on matters of public interest.[33] The Council of Europe, for example, has noted that national law and practice in the area of hate speech should take due account of the role

---

30 Certain 'white minorities', however, such as Eastern Europeans and working-class people in the UK are often disadvantaged groups and targets of ED, as their identity not as white but as 'foreign' and/or 'poor' makes them targets of demeaning stereotypes. See Chapter 4, II.

31 Rosenfeld (1991), p. 626.

32 See Equality and Human Rights Commission (2015b).

33 See Cram (2006), p. 123.

of the media in communicating information and ideas which expose, analyse and explain specific instances of hate speech and the underlying phenomenon in general, as well as the right of the public to receive such information and ideas. To this end, national law and practice should distinguish clearly between the responsibility of the author of expressions of hate speech, on the one hand, and any responsibility of the media and media professionals contributing to their dissemination as part of their mission to communicate information and ideas on matters of public interest, on the other.[34] Special care, however, needs to be exercised where a media outlet is at risk of being used for the propagation of hateful expression, particularly in situations of political and armed conflict.[35] Indeed, the media needs to report on incidents of racial hatred and other issues related to hateful expression. However, the manner and style in which such incidents are reported are equally important. As Banton has put it, the influence of the mass media is at least twofold: it influences the viewer's or reader's own attitudes, and it conveys signals about opinions in the peer group.[36] This is relevant because most people are concerned to keep in line with the expectations of those who are important to them or in a position of power and authority, be it individuals or institutions. For example:

> Television producers and at least some newspaper journalists may be more inclined than some others to see white prejudice as a problem which, if unchecked, is likely to cause increasing social conflict and economic cost in the future. They therefore try to persuade their audience that the matter is serious: to do so they turn their spotlights onto instances of conflict, prejudice and discrimination; thereby drawing a portrait of racial relations which looks worse than do the statistical data.[37]

It follows from this that the issue is not to argue against reporting racism, but to insist that the way in which it is reported matters, can actually contribute to racism and should therefore be contestable. For example, in the early years of affirmative action in US universities, there was a considerable backlash, nurtured in a significant part by the way in which affirmative action was commented on and presented.[38] The statistical analysis offered in the *Shape of the River*, a study of an enormous database called

---

34 See Committee of Ministers Recommendation No. R (97) 20 on 'Hate speech', Principle 6.
35 See Cram (2006), p. 123.
36 See Banton (1992), p. 353.
37 *Ibid*, p. 355.
38 It has been argued that the success of the California proposition banning all affirmative action was determined by a misleading presentation. Louis Harris polls suggest that a fairer presentation of the proposition would have led to its defeat. See Dworkin (2002), p. 398.

College and Beyond (C&B), refutes the most common misconceptions – often nurtured by tabloid headlines – about affirmative action in universities. One of these misconceptions, for example, is the acceptance of unqualified black people over their white counterparts. *The Shape of the River* showed that

> five of the C&B schools, which were otherwise representative of them all, retained full information about all their 1989 applicants, and more than 75 percent of the black applicants had higher math SAT scores, and more than 73 percent had higher verbal SAT scores, than the national average of white test-takers.[39]

Another common ground for attack and resentment was the emphasis on an increased racial tension and animosity within those white applicants who were not accepted. The study shows that 'those white students who were not admitted to their first-choice school, and might well be expected to blame their failure on racial preferences, do not disapprove of seeking racial diversity any more than their initially more successful classmates do'.[40] Arguably, part of the backlash in the US – and abroad, perhaps – was that the media tended to focus on rejected applicants as plaintiffs in lawsuits against affirmative action and sensationalist news was more available than factual coverage. On the other hand, misinformation can also have global effects; as Banton recalls,

> television reports of the black riots in the United States cities in 1967 were thought to have influenced white British ideas about possible dangers in Britain. What are called 'race relations' are perceived to have international as well as domestic implications.[41]

Following these findings, the protection against ED should also cover the possibility to contest *coverage*. In fact, this issue has been identified since 1997 in the Appendix for the Recommendation No. R (97) 21, of the Council of Europe on 'The media and the promotion of a culture of tolerance'. The Appendix called the media to reflect on a series of matters that are related to *coverage* and that can help to prevent discriminatory reporting. Some of these are: reporting factually and accurately on acts of racism and intolerance; reporting in a sensitive manner on situations of tension between communities; avoiding derogatory stereotypical depiction of members of cultural, ethnic or religious communities in publications and programme services; treating individual behaviour without linking it to a

---

39 See Bowen *et al.* (1998), quoted in Dworkin (2002), p. 391.
40 *Ibid*, p. 398.
41 Banton (1992), p. 355.

person's membership of such communities when it is irrelevant; depicting cultural, ethnic and religious communities in a balanced and objective manner and in a way which also reflects their own perspectives and outlook; alerting public opinion to the evils of intolerance; deepening public understanding and appreciation of difference; challenging the assumptions underlying intolerant remarks made by speakers in the course of interviews, reports, discussion programmes; and considering the influence of the source of information on reporting and the diversity of the workforce in the media enterprises, including the extent to which it corresponds to the multi-ethnic, multicultural character of its readers, listeners or viewers. These issues should be included as 'coverage guidelines' within the codes of media self-regulatory bodies, thus allowing for the public to complain should they be breached. The last issue, however, is closer to the 'transformation of the media structures' which is discussed next.

2 Lack of participation: behind the scenes under-representation of targeted groups

This is an issue closely related to institutional discrimination and employment discrimination, which may contribute to the lack of disadvantaged groups' viewpoints/interests being represented in mainstream media.[42] Therefore, it is not a direct manifestation of ED but it is crucial to it, it works as its background support or underpinning. With regard to the human composition of the media industry, various points of concern should be considered. A most significant one is the relationship that exists between disadvantaged groups' employment and 'diversity' in broadcast and programming. In this regard, Worthy has identified both the need to employ more disadvantaged groups and also the diversification of ownership of the media as a means to attack stereotypical portrayals of disadvantaged groups by diluting the control of white males over media programming. These views are to an extent captured by the concept of 'media pluralism', which embraces a number of aspects, such as diversity of ownership, variety in the sources of information and in the range of content available. Although definitions may vary, media pluralism tends to seek the presence of a range of sources, voices and perspectives so that no single 'media actor' has an overwhelming influence over the economic, social or political agendas. Allowing the contestation of discriminatory images and messages can therefore contribute to media pluralism by ensuring that opinions, definitions and voices that are not currently heard

42 For institutional discrimination, see Chapter 3, III, 2. For legal measures to tackle the 'lack of diversity on and off screen', see Equality and Human Rights Commission (2015b).

get prominence.[43] Similarly, Banton has argued that only when there are journalists from disadvantaged groups, and employment in the mass media reflects the composition of society as a whole, will a satisfactory balance be struck in reporting.[44] This is important as well in the sense that under-representation in media products cannot be said to be tackled simply by reporting about 'minorities' issues' – 'minorities' view points' need also to be heard. That said, a few disadvantaged groups' presence 'behind the scenes' does not in itself guarantee the elimination of stereotypes and the subordination of disadvantaged groups through images and messages. Members of disadvantaged groups can of course hold oppressive views about themselves and about others given that no one is immune to the various forces that drive and nurture discrimination. Moreover, if the conditions within the media are hostile, members of disadvantaged groups are likely and may even be required to collude (Chapter 3, IV). This is in part the reason why another important aspect for any project aiming to tackle misrepresentation through media reform should be the introduction and implementation of codes and guidelines concerning the representation of disadvantaged groups, and to avoid reporting, which contributes to prejudice and discrimination. ED is a team practice; it depends on producers, spaces available and the media industry's 'culture', its formal and informal rules, everyday practices and values; therefore, reforming the whole media is necessary for effectively challenging ED.

The media is not the embodiment of free speech, but a tool for freedom of expression. In this regard, it is worth noting that on a variety of occasions, the international community has called on governments to involve the media positively in development and social issues (Chapter 5). For example, at least since 1995, the Platform for Action of the Beijing Conference on Women had called on national and international media

---

43 See Worthy (1996), p. 531. See also the Council of Europe, Recommendation Rec (2007) 2 on 'Media pluralism and diversity of media content', 31 January 2007; and Council of Europe, Recommendation No. R (99) on 'Measures to promote pluralism', 19 January 1999. Also relevant is the work of the Centre for Media Pluralism and Media Freedom; in particular, the Report on the simplification and test implementation of a media pluralism monitor, 2014. Available at http://cmpf.eui.eu/Home.aspx (accessed 15 July 2015).

44 See Banton (1999), 45. This sort of interaction is also visible in relation to the 'culture' and lack of diversity in companies, and the kind of products they deliver including their adverts. Some declarations of those who criticised the Cadbury advert that compared the black model Naomi Campbell to a chocolate bar (Chapter 7) make this clear. The declarations included views about racism in Cadbury as a company itself. Campbell said 'they [Cadbury and other multinationals] should avoid causing offense in the first place which is better achieved by having greater diversity at board and senior management level'. See, Sweney (2011). Similarly, Lee Jasper, who was senior equalities adviser to Ken Livingston when he was Mayor of London said 'This issue is not just about the insult to Naomi Campbell. It's about how these companies treat black people in general. Part of the problem is that they don't see it as offensive.' See Kisiel (2011).

systems to promote increased and balanced participation by women and men in production and decision-making (at 240). Indeed, the Strategic Objective (J.1) was to increase the participation and access of women to expression and decision-making in and through the media and new technologies of communication. A similar call is found in the Council of Europe Recommendation No R (84) 17 on 'Equality between women and men in the media'. The measures recommended in this context are: encouraging adoption by media organisations of positive action programmes to improve the situation of women, particularly at decision-making levels and in technical services; ensuring application of the principle of equal treatment between women and men as a result of rules laid down for the recruitment, training, remuneration, promotion and any other conditions of employment of persons employed in the media; and encouraging the presence of women in an equitable proportion in media supervisory and management bodies (at 6, 8 and 9).

In the UK similar calls are currently pressing when it comes to black, Asian and minority ethnic people (BAME) because the media continues to be an unwelcoming environment. For example, as revealed by the latest *Creative Skillset 2012 Employment Census*, there has been a decline in the participation of BAME in the creative media industries in Britain. Their participation declined from 7.4 per cent of the total workforce in 2006 to 5.4 per cent in 2012.[45] The way in which the media is structured – and governed – is important.[46] The human composition of the media can generate a culture of belonging – or not – both inside the industry and outside through the images and messages it spreads. It can create and replicate relations of either parity or subordination because the media is, to a large extent, the main channel for the interpretation of events and the communication of ideas (including the selection of those events and ideas). When the least powerful groups – be it economically, socially or politically – are under-represented, their powerlessness is reflected and even manufactured in media products, thereby influencing the way in which they are deemed and treated. BAME people have on no few occasions turned to the development of 'their own' media and while this can be empowering and help them, among other things, to overcome the damage done to their self-esteem, it can also create forms of cultural enclavism and even

---

45 Brooks *et al* (2012), p. 4.
46 The concept of governance seems to be the most appropriate in the media context. At least in so far as media's regulation and its everyday operation requires cooperation; it generally involves a range of interactions among stakeholders who need to solve common/collective problems and their decision-making leads to the creation, reinforcement or reproduction of social norms and institutions. See Hufty (2011).

fundamentalisms.[47] These are issues whose complexity cannot be addressed in this section; indeed, the point at this stage is only to stress that mainstream media should be *really* open and available for all to participate. In fact, part of the redress of ED requires precisely that those who may not seek by themselves or who may not come across BAME people's 'own media' and own definitions, will nevertheless be provided with the information BAME people produce – through mainstream media – thereby tackling prejudice, promoting understanding and uncovering the unfairness of ED.

These things said, however, while 'diversity' in the media workforce and decision-making bodies cannot alone guarantee that there will be less discriminatory images and messages, the exclusion or limited opportunities for disadvantaged groups to take part in mainstream media is an indicator of structural arrangements that facilitate misrepresentation and complicate its contestation, given that media professionals – when belonging to dominant groups – are not spontaneously inclined or even culturally determined to understand the harm in the same way as the targets of systemic discrimination.

IV The legal recognition of ED

Regulation of speech is often greeted with suspicion. Libertarians warn that any speech restraint steps onto the slippery slope leading inexorably to totalitarianism.[48] Other objections consider speech regulation to be misguided, costly, ineffective or counterproductive; that it sets arbitrary boundaries and is often over- or under-inclusive (Chapter 6). Other critics consider that the law is ill-equipped to deal with the dynamics of cultural expression. This is to say that the injury that may be caused through speech depends on the speaker's identity or motive, an audience's response, and the relationship between them, yet the law is unable to account for such variables.[49] Similarly, legal prohibitions on speech may offer those who breach them free publicity and even a place in martyrdom. This is especially the case for expressions that seek visibility and impact through shock.

The objections outlined above should not be seen as deterrents for legal intervention but as issues that need to be taken into account in speech regulation. In other words, the difficulties that regulation entails should not prevent the recognition of real injuries, nor prevent the *search*

47 See Chapter 2, V, 3; and in particular Sunstein (2007), pp. xi–xii. Sunstein makes reference to the risks of a situation in which like-minded people speak or listen mostly to one another. Democracy is at risk whenever people sort themselves into enclaves in which their own views and commitments are constantly reaffirmed.

48 See Abel (1998), p. 245.

49 *Ibid*, p. 199.

for more appropriate ways to take action against them. The dangers of speech regulation are real; however, lack of intervention on this basis is a decision taken at the expense of the targets of discriminatory expression, and indeed is a form of regulation that supports the *status quo*. In sum, no legal provision comes without problematic implications and there must be something we can do because the law should be skilful and imaginative enough to deal with existing problems – rooted in rights – without worsening or creating other disparities. Dismissing real harms cannot be an acceptable answer.

Legal intervention with regard to ED is necessary for various reasons. To a certain degree, the law has the function of establishing what is and is not acceptable in society. It is true, as Delgado points out, that 'laws will never prevent violations altogether, but they will deter whoever is deterrable'.[50] The law has a 'teaching function'; it is indeed part of the social structures and arrangements that can either reinforce or prevent behaviours that harm participatory parity. The expected outcome is that if we change the social arrangements that permit these behaviours we can in turn change attitudes at least of those who unintentionally have taken part in injustice and are willing to reconsider their behaviours and see things from the point of view of the injured party. The law cannot of course by itself change attitudes, beliefs and prejudices, but it certainly has the duty to respond to the claims made by the targets of ED and create the institutional channels needed for altering deep-seated values and social attitudes. Moreover, by overlooking the fact that not everyone has the means to exercise their free speech, the law has for a long time favoured the speech of some – more often than not the powerful. When the law is perceived to serve the interests of only some people, its power to regulate conduct declines. This is to say that the targets of ED have been let down and have not been protected by the law in the same way as those with power have been protected when arguing for freedom of expression (e.g. arguably discriminatory, sexist or racist media owners, editors and multinational corporations advertising their products). Therefore, although probably unintentionally, but clearly because some interests matter more than others, the law has been partisan of the interests of some while ignoring others. For a long time, ED has been trivialised and its redress practically left to the will of media's regulators.

Legal intervention with regard to ED makes a political point, as does its absence. According to Cram, 'the response that dominant forces within a community give to hateful expression – their willingness to act against more overt forms of hatred – will assume symbolic importance to beleaguered minorities'.[51] This means that legal restraints represent the

50 Delgado (1993), p. 96.
51 Cram (2006), p. 110.

community position on the issues expressed by the speaker and its favour of participatory parity. On the contrary, if there is no will to protect groups from the harm done through speech, the whole community suffers in the sense that even if the message is resisted by both the victims and dominant group members, 'victim-group members may come to view all dominant group members with suspicion whilst the latter experience an ambivalent relief that they do not belong to the target group and thereby become distanced from victims'.[52]

The legal recognition of ED can empower its targets and relieve the sense of powerlessness caused by having no means of coping with the harms caused by the media. This means, as Delgado suggests in the context of racial insults, that

> victims must be able to threaten and institute legal action, thereby relieving the sense of helplessness that leads to psychological harm and communicating to the perpetrator and to society that such abuse will not be tolerated either by its victims or by the courts.[53]

That said, the recognition of ED *is not* aimed at putting people in prisons, imposing high fines or censorship. The legal recognition of the harm created through ED is aimed at making the 'marketplace of ideas' real and promoting participatory parity. This means that dissenting voices from oppressed groups can openly and powerfully complain about the media's discriminatory speech. It is the counter speech of the targets of ED that the law needs to promote by ensuring that the people have the means to successfully challenge ED and have their counter speech heard. Public apologies, right of reply, modification or withdrawal of the discriminatory materials can be ways to achieve this aim.

Legally acknowledging ED takes the claim from the 'private' to the 'public' sphere. In the context of racist speech, Matsuda points out, that the choice of public sanction, enforced by the State, is a significant one. She suggests that it is not an 'accident' that certain injuries are left to private individuals to absorb and resist by themselves; for example, she refers to the law's paucity – and slowness – in redressing the harm caused to certain categories of people such as women, children, 'people of colour' and 'poor' people; and for this reason, Matsuda affirms that a legal response to racist speech is a statement that victims of racism are valued as members of our polity, and on the contrary, the absence of law 'is itself another story with a message, perhaps unintended, about the relative value of different human lives'.[54]

52 *Ibid.*
53 Delgado (1993), p. 95.
54 Matsuda (1993), p. 18.

In the UK, even though there are a variety of provisions addressing various forms of discriminatory speech, and indeed in various ways recognising the harm as a form of discrimination, the harm done through demeaning and stereotypical representation in the media hasn't been recognised by anti-discrimination law (ADL) and access to redress does not appropriately protect the interests of those discriminated against. The law has been more active at a criminal law level. However, the thresholds of hate speech provisions are such that ED cannot be legally challenged. Moreover, the recognition of potential for harm on different grounds in hate speech legislation has been piecemeal, largely depending on effective campaigning and lobbying, thereby begging the question as to whether some identity groups are more 'popular' than others. Criminal law provisions tend to have such high thresholds that they become almost unenforceable unless the accused pleads guilty. Moreover, hate speech legislation is framed in terms of stirring up hatred and, hence, it follows a consequentialist approach instead of recognising a harm in and of itself which is what the concept of ED pursues. Legally recognising ED can correct these flaws in hate speech legislation and its inclusion within ADL statutes means introducing an alternative mechanism to deal with speech whose seriousness hate speech provisions would ignore, and so behaviours considered too trivial to deserve legal action would no longer be sent to legal limbo. In this way, the recognition of ED constitutes a response to the requirement made in some regional instruments about the need to have alternative non-criminal mechanisms against hate speech.[55]

Finally, ED needs to be legally recognised for two essential reasons. One is that there are two valuable interests at stake, free speech and non-discrimination; and the second is that it is a well-known requirement that any limitation to free speech should be provided by law. For example, article 10 (2) of the European Convention on Human Rights, establishes that formalities, conditions, restrictions or penalties in the context of freedom of expression need to be prescribed by law; and the International Covenant on Civil and Political Rights, article 19 (3) takes a similar approach. Redressing ED, for example through adjudication or conciliation procedures with the participation of media self-regulatory authorities and members of equality commissions and the organised civil society, can indeed be considered a formality, condition or restriction of free speech and therefore should be provided by law.

I Facilitating counter speech

The analysis in Chapter 7 about the way in which harms similar to that of ED are addressed in the UK makes apparent that while there are

---

55 See Council of Europe Recommendation No R (97) 20 on 'Hate speech'.

important freedom of expression considerations and therefore there should be little or no government intervention, there are also disadvantaged groups' interests at stake and these should also be protected and represented. Therefore, it was contested that an active involvement of the EHRC was in order; and as things stand now, there is much the EHRC could do and which is among its existing duties (e.g. advice for the targets on how to complain effectively, and guidelines and training for the media about the Public Sector Equality Duty in general and about discriminatory speech in particular). The involvement of both media self-regulators and equality commissions in the UK and elsewhere is therefore a principle that can be fine-tuned to any jurisdiction that decides to contest discriminatory speech transmitted through the media and which does not reach the criminal thresholds established in hate speech laws. The participation of both media self-regulatory bodies and equality commissions (or bodies of that sort) is necessary for the redress of ED because there are two valuable interests at stake – freedom of expression and non-discrimination. Moreover, the adjudication/conciliation processes should include the participation of interested parties that have expertise in issues of discrimination against disadvantaged groups.

The legal recognition of ED is aimed at promoting, securing and facilitating the counter speech of the targets of discriminatory images and messages. It can be said that counter speech is legally protected through the right to free speech. However, this legal protection is insufficient given the power imbalances between the media and the targets of this discriminatory practice. The exact way in which the redress of ED can take place in any particular jurisdiction needs to be specifically tailored. However, there are principles that can be taken as blueprints. For example, the redress of ED should include a dialogue between the victims and their supporters and the offenders. The power imbalances between ordinary people and the mass media are balanced through the legal recognition of ED together with the participation of interested parties and equality commissions during the adjudication/conciliation process. The dialogue requires parties to be prepared to critically examine their own fears, interests, judgements and assumptions, and to be willing to modify and even abandon them.[56] The adjudication process should therefore be a meeting where none leaves 'happy' or 'angry', but thinking. Leaving a meeting feeling 'happy' may mean that the problem was not understood, was superficially addressed or that someone has 'got away' with something, possibly unduly. Feeling angry after such a meeting has the potential to intensify hostilities; therefore, the expected outcome is that participants

---

56 See Parekh (2006), p. 311.

leave thinking critically and having a better understanding of all the issues at stake.[57]

Those who have a complaint about ED should be given the right to express their grievance and the accused should be allowed to offer an account. This means that the free speech of the media should be held accountable and the counter speech of the target (the grievance) should be promoted in order to make free speech a right for all and not just for those who have economic power, whose interests are represented and who have the means to get heard. In other words, what is intended through protection against ED is to make counter speech real through the contestation of discriminatory images and messages. It is the opportunity for those afflicted to express their disagreements, with the guarantee that the offenders will listen. It is an opportunity to put forward information that exposes stereotypes and prejudice. It is also an opportunity to define oneself (in contexts where one is mostly defined by others), thereby politicising culture, tackling prejudice and promoting understanding. Without the exposure of a critique of the speech of the powerful, free speech stops being a right and becomes a privilege, one more commodity in the market not accessible to all. A protected opportunity to contest discriminatory speech is the least that democratic countries can guarantee against the harm created by ED. Following the metaphor of the 'marketplace of ideas',[58] the right to complain amounts to offering the victim the opportunity to bring their product to the market and remind the media that they do not hold the monopoly on free speech. It is to tell the economic powers and advertisers that their exercise of free speech forms a part of a much bigger democratic process that also involves the protection and promotion of counter speech, especially of those who are disadvantaged. It implies making speech accountable – through speech. In a way, it is like putting a stop to what somehow has become like the children's game in which one in a group rings a doorbell and then they all run away knowing that they have done something wrong and that they can avoid being accountable. Speech should be a cycle and therefore should always expect potential feedback from the audience.

Free speech doctrine is more often than not mounted around fear of the Government's control and censorship of dissident voices. However, when it comes to ED the fear should not be so much of government but of the monopoly of communications, transnational corporations and the profit hunger of the advertising industry. For example, in most liberal

---

57 These ideas are inspired by the work done by InterCultural Iceland in the field of education, see www.ici.is/en (accessed 16 January 2015).

58 The metaphor was invoked by Justice Oliver Wendell Holmes in the dissenting opinion of *Abrams v United States* 250 US 616 (1919): 'The best test of truth is the power of the thought to get itself accepted in the competition of the market.'

societies the press is privately owned and, thus, independent from the Government. However, it is not independent from commercial interests. This in turn gives room for the promotion of the political, social and economic interests and agendas of the press proprietors, which can result in biased reporting, and in the election of some issues as 'news' and the exclusion of topics which are not seen by the proprietors as important.[59]

When it comes to the media against a disadvantaged group, the classic counter speech argument does not work unconditionally. As Polelle has put it: 'The need for a remedy arises because classic counter speech as a remedy is largely illusory in an age of multibillion dollar media megacorporations which are on the verge of becoming the media landlords of the marketplace of ideas.'[60] The power imbalances between the public in general and the mass media makes it naive to suggest that the best response to bad speech is just more speech without guaranteeing that this will in fact be possible. This is precisely the reason why protection against ED needs to be legally established, authorising the involvement of equality commissions and interested parties in adjudication/conciliation processes, as well as requiring the production of codes and guidelines aimed at preventing discriminatory images and messages. A free marketplace of ideas does not in fact function in the context of the media in the same way that it may function in the public square, where all citizens have or should have equal access.[61]

The adjudication/conciliation process should therefore be a 'counter speech meeting' aimed at ensuring some sort of political deliberation *among peers*. As Parekh describes it, political deliberation:

> is a multidimensional activity and serves several purposes. It depends on mutual understanding between different groups, sensitizes each to the concerns and anxieties of the others, leads to an unconscious fusion of ideas and sensibilities, encourages them to explore common areas of agreement, and plays a vital community-building role. Since it requires participants to defend their view in a manner intelligible to others, it encourages them to appreciate the contingency of and thus to take a critical view of their beliefs.[62]

This is a process of persuasion in which the parties meet each other in equal circumstances and with equal voice. The outcome depends on each case because every case is different, depending on the context of the alleged discriminatory image or message, and the disadvantaged groups

---

59 See Parekh (2006), p. 319.
60 Polelle (2003), p. 214.
61 *Ibid.*
62 Parekh (2006), p. 307.

may experience the harm to various degrees of intensity at different points in time. Provided that all interests are represented, however, the final decision ensures more legitimacy than it does when a case is only adjudicated by media self-regulatory bodies alone, and the power imbalances between the media and the targets are redressed when the latter are supported by well-organised interested parties. This is to say that better decision-making is achieved when fewer people feel excluded from the process, and this in turn may result in greater societal cohesiveness when the participants connect to each other and acquire empathy with each other's concerns.[63]

2 Who complains?

Anyone should be able to complain about demeaning stereotypical representation or other forms of status subordination through images and messages in the media. In the same way that we should expect anyone to assist someone who is being physically assaulted, we should expect our fellow citizens to act when someone's dignity is being wounded. In other words, our silence in the face of injustice makes us accomplices and we should all have the right not to have things we oppose done in our name. Moreover, in the case of racism, for example, although black people are at the receiving end and in fact white people may 'benefit' from racism in many ways, both white and black people can be agents of ED; and ultimately, it should be a right for everyone to complain because everyone's environment is 'being littered'. These things said, however, targeted groups, especially when organised, are in a better position to make more effective complaints; and indeed as seen in Chapter 7, Leveson's recommendations included that:

> The Board [press regulator] should have the power ... to hear complaints *whoever they come from*, whether personally and directly affected by the alleged breach, or a *representative group affected* by the alleged breach, or *a third party seeking to ensure accuracy* of published information. In the case of third party complaints the views of the party most closely involved should be taken into account.[64]

The participation and involvement of the organised civil society working against discrimination are needed at all stages. This is to say, in the production of the codes and guidelines, assisting in the evaluation of the complaints and in the decision making about possible sanctions. Complaining is difficult, exhausting and sometimes demeaning in the face of what is normally powerful, resourceful groups and individuals. It takes

63 See Cram (2006), p. 4.
64 Leveson LJ (2012), *Summary of recommendations*, para. 11. Italics are the author's.

time, energy, commitment and a great deal of confidence. The targets of discriminatory speech are more often than not victims of other forms of discrimination as well, and this can make complaining more taxing given their devalued social standing. Peer assistance and support for targeted groups is therefore not just extra help but indeed an essential element in a complaint-based mechanism. It is an element of empowerment to know, first, that one can complain and, second, that one is not alone. As Abel has put it, 'The very act of challenging hurtful speech begins to redress the status inequalities speech constructs, just as passivity affirms and encourages them.'[65]

The redress of ED is fundamentally aimed at empowering its targets and for this reason the remedial process can no longer be solely controlled by media regulatory bodies or 'professionals'. Those afflicted need support from other members of their subordinated category and allies in the same way that advertisers and licensees rely heavily on the organisations that represent them and protect their interests. The lack of support for those who complain about discrimination in the media is in fact allowing the media not only to adjudicate as they please, but also to set the rules of recognition or the lack of it at a cultural level.

Support from the organised civil society and from equality commissions is therefore essential; just as trade unions assist workers in complaints where their interests as a group are threatened, the targets of discrimination in the media must count on the support of their peers, especially of those who openly oppose subordination since the status of them all is lowered through the mass dissemination of disrespect. As shown in the research undertaken by Banton, 'Members of the ethnic majority are inclined to minimise the significance of complaints of insult or discrimination from minority members; they often think that complainants are unduly sensitive.'[66] Or, as Matsuda puts it, 'To white men racist speech is horseplay, prank, a joke but for the targets is a harm.'[67] Many white men may rightly disagree with this; however, the issue remains that disrespect is more clearly understood by those who have experienced it, and in this sense it is not surprising that complaints are dismissed or considered too petty when those who make the decisions do not belong to a disadvantaged group or have no sympathy, given their personal interests and loyalties. That said, not all members of disadvantaged groups acknowledge the need to complain. It is not uncommon for victims of disrespect who have internalised their oppression, and are either used to it or have learned to live with it, not to complain or even 'justify' their own subordination.[68]

---

65 Abel (1998), p. 263.
66 Banton (1999), 42.
67 Matsuda (1993), p. 21.
68 See generally on this point, Fanon (1986).

Moreover, there are those who actively participate in the misrecognition of their own group, unwittingly or as a means to get social acceptance. Complaints therefore need to be encouraged because, on the one hand, very often both the targets and the agents are not conscious of the problem; and on the other hand, because there is no institutional support to bring a complaint in fair terms. Likewise, complaints need to be encouraged because confronting 'social superiors' requires both emotional and institutional support. More so is this the case when the injury is not physical but dignitary. As Abel has put it, 'if physical injuries go unreported (rape, hate crimes, spousal abuse), it is to be expected that there will be fewer coming from purely dignitary harms'.[69]

Support and encouragement are also needed, given the strong likelihood that those who complain will be blamed or have their motives impugned by those they accuse; especially when the latter have power. In sum, complaints can come from the targets of ED or other individuals or groups, but in any case the active participation and collaboration with the organised civil society working against discrimination is necessary at all stages.

3 Remedies

ED is an injury inflicted through speech – images or messages. Allocating responsibilities for this discriminatory practice is not always straightforward. ED is teamwork; it may require actors, writers, spaces available, broadcasters, producers, designers, etc. In the UK, it is the responsibility of the licensees and advertisers to follow the codes written by the industry and, therefore, they and generally those with editorial control are held responsible with regard to discriminatory content. But the redress of ED should be aimed at repairing the damage done to its targets; and the targets themselves are best placed to propose the sanction that they believe to be appropriate. Often, what those afflicted seek is a right of reply, correction or withdrawal of the material, explanations, annotations and apologies (Chapters 4 and 7). This is not to suggest that alleged victims of ED should always get what they demand, but is to say that *their claims should be heard*; and that, if consistent with democratic values and equality legislation, their counter speech, their response to 'bad speech', should be promoted and publicised. Ultimately this means that in the same way that speech is protected, so should both counter speech and the means necessary for its production.

Abel agrees with most liberal authors that the best antidote for degrading speech is more speech, but of a particular kind:

---

69 Abel (1998), p. 262.

only an apology can rectify the status inequality constructed by harmful words. To achieve this, the social settings within which respect is conferred should encourage victims to complain through an informal process that evaluates speech in context and makes offenders render an apology acceptable to both victim and community.[70]

ED can essentially be remedied in this way because the aim is to challenge the *misrecognition* of the targeted group and to repair the status degradation by making it possible for people to complain on a level playing field against the media. Economic compensation is unlikely to effectively repair dignitary injuries and it is not the best compensation when it comes to groups as opposed to individuals. Moreover, as Abel has put it, 'accepting money may taint the victim as greedy, so punishment of offenders can transform outcast into martyr'.[71]

The harm that needs to be redressed is status degradation, which – in the words of Abel – can be just as harmful as contusions, and recognising its importance avoids the fatal flaw in consequentialist justifications for regulation – the unanswered (and perhaps unanswerable) empirical questions about the behavioural effects of speech. Words in this sense do not provoke fights, they *are* fights, and the remedy, provided that the injury is performed through speech, should also be speech, a protected kind of speech.[72] It is striking that even though speech is specially protected given its recognised value for society, the feasibility of counter speech is largely ignored and the harm that speech may inflict is largely seen as a price worth paying. What this means in the end is that the speech of some is protected at the expense of the misrecognition of others.

Speech can harm, but it also can heal. To do so, offenders need to acknowledge the injury and apologise in a way that is acceptable to the victim. The law can make this possible. First, by recognising the harm: status degradation (misrecognition), as a legal wrong; a form of discrimination. Second, by providing a remedy through adjudication/conciliation processes involving equality commissions, media self-regulatory bodies and interested parties in order to facilitate an opportunity to complain on a level playing field and initiate a dialogue with the offender. Third, the sanctions should be speech-oriented. This means an apology, right of reply, modification of the material and in some cases withdrawal; all this of course judged on a case-by-case basis. It is difficult to determine a proportionate sanction in the abstract; however, having all interests represented is a step towards that direction and promises more legitimacy than a procedure

---

70 *Ibid*, pp. 245–246.
71 *Ibid*, p. 270. Nevertheless, right of reply, public apologies, modification or withdrawal of the material can indeed have an economic cost that the offender should pay.
72 *Ibid*, pp. 264–265.

where not all interests are represented. These are therefore only principles that jurisdictions willing to address ED recognising and respecting all interests at stake could adopt and adapt to their particular contexts.

V Conclusions

The concept of ED rescues expressions that hate speech legislation does not cover. The *harm* in relation to ED is generally the misrecognition of the target group and the concomitant damage to the self- and social-esteem of its members. ED, however, is manifested in many recognisable ways, all of which can and should be identified and challenged. This book argues that the *legal wrong* that best recognises the harm created by ED is discrimination because the expressions of ED target those who have been persistently discriminated against; they keep relations of inferiority and superiority in 'their place', building on, reinforcing, justifying and maintaining status subordination.

Redressing ED requires that all interests at stake are evenly represented and protected and, therefore, *the remedy* should be provided through adjudication/conciliation processes involving equality commissions, media self-regulatory bodies and interested parties in order to facilitate the opportunity to complain on a level playing field and initiate a dialogue with the offender. Public apologies, right of reply, modification or annotations are all possible ways to enable the restoration of participatory parity and for maligned groups to put forward their own definitions of themselves, thus politicising culture. But for all these principles to be engaged it is necessary that the law recognises this harm and lays the legal foundations for effectively challenging bad speech with more speech.

VI References

Abel, Richard L. (1998), *Speaking Respect: Respecting Speech*, Chicago, IL: University of Chicago Press.

Abrams, Dominic and Houston, Diane M. (2006), *Equality, Diversity and Prejudice in Britain: Report for the Cabinet Office Equalities Review 2006*, Centre for the Study of Group Processes, University of Kent.

Banton, Michael (1992), 'The declaratory value of laws against racial incitement', in Coliver, Sandra ed., *Striking a Balance: Hate Speech, Freedom of Expression and Non-discrimination*, London: Article XIX.

Banton, Michael (1999), 'The causes of, and remedies for, racial discrimination', Commission on Human Rights, Fifty-fifth session. Sessional open-ended working group to review and formulate proposals for the World Conference against Racism, Racial Discrimination, Xenophobia and Related Intolerance, E/CN.4/1999/WG.1/BP.6.

Bowen *et al.* (1998), *The Shape of the River: Long-term Consequences of Considering Race In College and University Admissions*, Princeton, NJ: Princeton University Press.

Brooks, David, Campbell, Mike, Connolly, Milo; Heyer, Neil and Flintham, Neil (2012), *Creative Skillset Employment Census of the Creative Media Industries*, Creative Skillset.

Cram, Ian (2006), *Contested Words: Legal Restrictions on Freedom of Speech in Liberal Democracies*, Aldershot: Ashgate.

Crenshaw, Kimberlé (1989), 'Demarginalizing the intersection of race and sex: a Black feminist critique of antidiscrimination doctrine, feminist theory and anti-racist politics', *University of Chicago Legal Forum*, vol. 140.

Delgado, Richard (1993), 'Words that wound: a tort action for racial insults, epithets, and name calling', in Matsuda, Mari, Lawrence III, Charles R., Delgado, Richard and Crenshaw, Kimberle Williams, eds, *Words that Wound: Critical Race Theory, Assaultive Speech, and the First Amendment*, Boulder, CO: Westview Press.

Dworkin, Ronald (2002), *Sovereign Virtue: the Theory and Practice of Equality*, Cambridge, MA: Harvard University Press.

Equality and Human Rights Commission (2015a), *Legal Framework on Freedom of Expression*.

Equality and Human Rights Commission (2015b), *Thinking Outside the Box: Supporting the Television Broadcasting Industry*.

Fanon, Franz (1986), *Black Skin: White Masks*, New York: Pluto Press.

Guasp, April (2013), *Gay in Britain: Lesbian, Gay and Bisexual People's Experiences and Expectations of Discrimination*, Stonewall.

Hall, Stuart (1971), 'Black men, white media', BBC television debate on racial images, as quoted in *The Chronicle*, independent internet magazine focusing on the black African Caribbean experience in Britain and the African Diaspora, www.thechronicle.demon.co.uk (accessed 19 August 2008).

Hall, Stuart, ed. (1997), *Representation, cultural Representation and Signifying Practices*, Milton Keynes: Open University Press.

Hufty, Marc (2011), 'Investigating policy processes: the governance analytical framework (GAF)', in Wesimen, U. and Hurni, H., eds, *Research for Sustainable Development: Foundations, Experiences and Perspectives*, Bern: Geographica Bernesia.

Kisiel, Ryan (2011), 'Naomi Campbell's outrage as "racist advert" likens her to a chocolate bar', *Mail Online*, 3 June, available at www.dailymail.co.uk/news/article-1392182/Naomi-Campbells-outrage-racist-advert-likens-chocolate-bar.html (accessed 15 July 2015).

Leveson LJ (2012), *An Inquiry into the Culture, Practices and Ethics of the Press: Executive Summary and Summary of Recommendations*, London: The Stationery Office.

MacKinnon, Catharine (1994), *Only words*, New York: Harper Collins.

Matsuda, Mari (1993), 'Public response for racist speech: considering the victim's story', in Matsuda, Mari, Lawrence III, Charles R., Delgado, Richard and Crenshaw, Kimberle Williams, eds, *Words that Wound: Critical Race Theory, Assaultive Speech, and the First Amendment*, Boulder, CO: Westview Press.

McConnachie, C., *et al.* (2012), *Comparative Hate Speech Law: Memorandum*. Research prepared for the Legal Resources Centre, South Africa, Oxford Pro Bono Publico, University of Oxford.

Parekh, Bhikhu (2006), *Rethinking Multiculturalism: Cultural Diversity and Political Theory*, Houndmills: Palgrave.

Polelle, Michael (2003), 'Racial and ethnic group defamation: a speech-friendly proposal', *Boston College Third World Law Journal*, vol. 23, no. 213.

Rosenfeld, Michel (1991), '*Metro Broadcasting Inc. v. FCC*: affirmative action at the crossroads of constitutional liberty and equality', *University College Los Angeles Law Review*, vol. 38.

Sancho, Jane and Wilson, Andy (2001), *Boxed In: Offence from Negative Stereotyping in TV Advertising*, report by ITC, Qualitative Consultancy.

Sunstein, Cass (2007). *Republic.com 2.0*, Princeton, NJ: Princeton University Press.

Sweney, Mark (2011), 'Cadbury apologises to Naomi Campbell over "racist" ad', *Guardian*, 3 June, available at www.theguardian.com/media/2011/jun/03/cadbury-naomi-campbell-ad (accessed 15 July 2015).

Williams, Jeffrey, ed. (1995), *PC Wars: Politics and Theory In the Academy*, London: Routledge.

Worthy, Patricia (1996), 'Diversity and minority stereotyping in the television media: the unsettled First Amendment issue', *Hastings Communications and Entertainment Law Journal*, vol. 18, no. 509.

Chapter 9

Weaknesses and potential of anti-discrimination law in redressing *everyday discrimination*

I Introduction

In order to provide elements with which to begin theorising about the potential recognition of *everyday discrimination* (ED) within anti-discrimination law (ADL) this chapter explores various intertwined themes. The first section outlines why it is appropriate for ADL to intervene; the second section looks at some problems that such intervention would need to address; and the third section offers some insights regarding the conceptual ability of the law to incorporate discriminatory speech as a justiciable harm. The fourth section argues that the recognition of harassment as dignitary harm within ADL may be used as a precedent for the legal recognition of ED; finally, the fifth part outlines existing remedies within ADL and shows that neither the ability of the law to innovate in order to respond to existing harms nor the development of appropriate remedies are closed.

This chapter draws on literature, ADL legislation and jurisprudence from different jurisdictions (UK, EU law, Canada and South Africa). However, it is not the intention to analyse ADL within these jurisdictions. The chapter only explores some concepts at a doctrinal level from jurisdictions where they have been most saliently developed (the protection of human dignity in South Africa and Canada) in order to show that ADL may have the conceptual space to accommodate ED. If the principles and concepts that show space for ED in ADL are present and/or adopted in a particular context, then they could help justify the recognition of ED as a justiciable harm. This is a fair approach because to a large extent ADL – as much other law – in many jurisdictions is the result of 'borrowing'; of international and regional shared commitments and concerns; and the problems and claims of those afflicted are similar regardless of frontiers. Indeed, identity groups that face discrimination constantly share information, ideas and support each other's claims, and therefore, it can be expected that similar rationales and methods will be demanded and used in different jurisdictions.

II The role of anti-discrimination law

The narrative of discrimination suggests that discriminatory behaviours are 'justified' or performed because of the person's identity, this is to say that 'the chief mischief of discrimination is that a person is subjected to detriment because she is attributed with stereotypical qualities based on a denigratory notion of group membership'.[1] ED is a practice by which such stereotypical qualities are assigned, perpetuated and disseminated, thus denigrating certain groups. The targets of ED often feel discriminated against; they have challenged it for the harm it inflicts and for its connections to other discriminatory practices (Chapter 4). Media regulatory bodies acknowledge that messages and images can be discriminatory (Chapter 7); and, to various degrees, international instruments regard the harm caused by ED as an integral part of discrimination (Chapter 5). However, ADL has been for the most part silent both doctrinally and at a legislative level.

Demeaning stereotypical representations float in the popular imagery as discrimination and, indeed, they have a great deal in common with other discriminatory practices; they target disadvantaged groups and hinder participatory parity. Moreover, as explored in Chapter 3, discrimination is a multifaceted problem that exists at various interacting levels: structural, cultural, institutional and personal. In this scheme, demeaning and stereotypical images and messages are a manifestation of discrimination at a cultural level.

However, while this chapter argues that ED ought to be included within the legal structure of ADL, there is much to be said for law acknowledging misrecognition harm without the need to put it into the discrimination 'box'. For example, speaking of 'misrecognition through messages and images in the media' would express the injury in a more specific way than speaking of discrimination. As Hunter has put it,

> it may be preferable for feminists, rather than attempting to appropriate liberal concepts in the pursuit of our own causes, to introduce new descriptions of women's disadvantages – concepts of our own that may be more persuasive of the existence of a problem, and hence more normatively effective.[2]

A problem with discrimination is that it is inherently a comparative concept; for example, when it requires equivalence between men and women or among all women.[3] Misrecognition is not an issue of comparison,

---

1 Fredman (2002), p. 16.
2 Hunter (2008), p. 82.
3 *Ibid*, p. 84. See also Bamforth *et al* (2008), p. 275.

however, it is about social relations of subordination and status degradation; and thus, its redress does not require a levelling out of treatment, or the achievement of a certain standard, but respect for one's identity. Feminists have encountered this problem in the past. Sexual harassment, for example, constitutes a discrete harm that could find no comfortable 'home' in existing legal constructs until it was put into ADL statutes. So, even though discrimination fails to express accurately the problem of demeaning and/or stereotypical representation, ADL is one way to make the harm intelligible in the existing legal framework. Moreover, experiences of status degradation are often referred to as discrimination; and discrimination, as a broad concept, has the capacity to refer to systemic injustice based on a disadvantaged identity. The legal recognition of discriminatory speech as a form of discrimination aims at the transformation of ADL by making it acknowledge the cultural dimension of discrimination. The concept of ED incorporates into ADL the political and philosophical rationale behind the concept of misrecognition (disrespect) and translates it into legal terms, thus legitimating claims of discrimination at a cultural level that need to be individually assessed and redressed because, although being part of a bigger system, they cause harm in and of themselves.

III Some problems in anti-discrimination law

Some of the problems that ADL would meet in redressing ED are not, however, necessarily particular to ADL, but to the liberal understanding of the law in general. That said, the issues that are discussed in the next sections particularly affect the potential of ADL to redress ED. Three main problems can be identified; first, law's underlying assumption that the State is neutral and impartial; second, law's liberal inclination to be focused mainly on the individual rather than groups; and third, its tendency to protect business- or market-oriented concerns. These are not insurmountable obstacles, but they constitute assumptions that need to be challenged should they exist in a particular jurisdiction in order to facilitate the expansion of the protection of the law to also include protection against ED.

I State's neutrality

The neutrality of the State and the law has been widely challenged. This is particularly clear in ADL, where intervention or lack of it has often been characterised more as a political decision than as a commitment to neutrality.[4] Compelling State interests and the demands of society have made

4 See Lacey (1998), pp. 188–220.

State intervention, in many settings, a necessary tool to redress the disadvantage experienced by many groups in contemporary broadly democratic societies.

Neutrality means that the State should not show a preference for any group. This is in fact the idea of neutrality that originally informed the principle of formal equality and the idea of equality as consistency. However, when the State, through the law, without justification fails to intervene in order to redress injustice or is silent, even though it has the capacity to do otherwise, it is making a political decision that legitimates the *status quo*.[5] It could therefore be argued that, where there exists discrimination and deep-seated relations of domination, the decision of the State not to intervene cannot be considered to be neutral since it is a political decision that supports existing dominant groups in the maintenance of their positions of superiority over those groups which are subject to discrimination and prejudice.[6] Redressing discrimination requires and has received State intervention at many levels (Chapter 3); intervention at the legal level through ADL in order to redress cultural aspects of discrimination such as ED is one crucial aspect of this process.

2 Individualism and group harms

Discrimination is not only a question of individual justice. ADL's ultimate subject differs from the legal subject of the prevailing liberalism. The legal subject for ADL is disadvantaged (dominated) groups as opposed to the 'abstract' (male, white, with some wealth) individual of classic liberalism. Ignoring group membership obscures the nature of the problem that ADL needs to redress and, on the contrary, having disadvantaged groups in mind 'introduces into the courtroom the historical realities of racism and sexism, which could no longer be marginalized on the legal agenda by being divided up into individual pathological acts of discrimination of no general political significance'.[7]

Rights in the western world were historically thought to serve individuals, in practice men, and to protect their property. It is therefore not surprising that it has been so difficult to put the position and experience of oppressed groups explicitly on the legal agenda, despite all the efforts made so far by various social movements. Groups should be the ultimate legal subjects of ADL. Ignoring group membership means to compare the individual member of a group with the mainstream (privileged individual) norm; to put the blame only on individual prejudice rather than on institutions and social structures as well; and to give remedy to individual

5 See *ibid*, p. 29.
6 See Fredman (2002), p. 129.
7 Lacey (1998), p. 38.

complaints rather than aiming at having an effect on the whole group that is potentially harmed.

For the purposes of ADL, groups should be better understood as a set of relationships. Understanding groups as relations is most important at least in two different senses. One is that people have affinities with more than one group – one can be black, lesbian, Catholic and so forth; the second is that groups are not aggregates of people united by one characteristic. Being black in Britain, for example, means no problem at all if taken in isolation; it is the social relations and interactions that can turn skin colour into a disadvantage. The same happens with being a woman. It is the relations that matter and the way in which they produce social disadvantage. Understanding disadvantaged groups as the subject of ADL is nevertheless controversial. It has been argued that 'the recognition of group difference for remedial purposes always threatens to reproduce the harm of the production of group difference we set out to remedy in the first place'.[8] This assertion, however, harbours problematic assumptions. First is the consideration of 'group difference' as the problem that needs to be tackled. Difference is not the problem. As stated above, being a woman or being black means no disadvantage if taken in isolation. It is the social relations of domination that disadvantages such groups, and it is these that need to be tackled. Second, considering disadvantaged groups the subject of ADL does not amount to rendering them subjects of special protection, benefits or compensation. It *is not* redressing a group's 'inherent status of need' that should constitute the aim of ADL, but remedying the structural, cultural and institutional patterns that lead to unfavourable treatment of some people on the grounds of their group membership; to some extent this has been acknowledged in contemporary ADL work, where institutional change and the transformation of structures that *create* disadvantages are the focus of attention (Chapter 3). However, for example, media regulatory bodies do not always understand the group nature of discrimination. IPSO, for example, although recognising the potential for discrimination through the press, addresses the issue in an individualistic manner (Chapter 7).

The relevance of understanding groups as the legal subject for the purposes of ED is that discriminatory speech harms the self- and social-esteem and respect accorded to the individual members of a disadvantaged group. A discriminatory image or message that stereotypes, ridicules and/or denigrates on the grounds of, for example, race, gender or religion sends the same message to all the individuals that share the despised trait and to the society as a whole, thus affecting their social standing as a group. Therefore, given that the discriminatory material inflicts a group harm, the remedies should relieve the whole group, for example, through

8 Ford (2003), p. 4. See also Fiss (1976).

modification or withdrawal of discriminatory material, apologies or right of reply.

3 The protection of business or market oriented concerns

Protection against ED through ADL is or can be complicated where the development of ADL is dependent on and/or dictated by market interests or constraints and when tackling disadvantage is not its primary directive. For example, in the UK, important provisions in the Equality Act 2010, such as: the public sector duty regarding socio-economic inequalities (s. 1),[9] the dual discrimination provision (s. 14) and the gender pay gap reporting measures (s. 78) will not be taken forward. The last two were not taken forward largely because, the Government argued, the cost they would represent for businesses. On 23 March 2011 it published the Plan for Growth which included the announcement of a decision not to bring forward the dual discrimination provision. This was as part of the Government's drive to reduce the cost of regulation on all businesses in order to create the 'right conditions' for increased competition, job creation and sustainable growth. Therefore, people who have experienced discrimination because of a combination of protected characteristics (e.g. a black woman or a Muslim man) will need to bring one or more *single* characteristic claims.[10] A similar rationale has been given with regard to s. 78, which requires employers to publish information relating to the gender pay gap. The Government said that it will not implement the measure while it is working with business on how best to support increased transparency on a voluntary basis.[11]

Market constraints affecting ADL are nothing new; the European Union (EU) provides a good case study that illustrates the ways in which some anti-discrimination provisions were generated. The EU was established in order to create a common market; therefore, the redress of race discrimination or discrimination against women was not among its priorities. It was for this reason that human and social rights were excluded. It was not until issues of unequal payment became unfair for the market that the Union began taking sex discrimination into account. The problem was not the unfairness of the fact that women in certain jurisdictions were paid less than men, but the economic disadvantages that unequal payment

---

9 This duty would have allowed, for example, health trusts and local authorities to target their services at people who lived in deprived areas.
10 See HM Treasury (2011), pp. 1, 18, 53.
11 See the Equality and Human Rights Commission's announcements on the progress and state of the Equality Act 2010, last updated 6 May 2015, available at www.equalityhuman-rights.com/legal-and-policy/legislation/equality-act-2010/what-equality-act (accessed 21 July 2015).

brought to the Union.[12] For some this could nevertheless be an equality achievement; however, the process and reasons for its achievement are paramount in determining its further success and the future of other equality rights. This is so because the same market-oriented process can have a different outcome. If discrimination against women becomes beneficial for the market, then, this market-oriented logic would keep discrimination in place. This can also happen on other grounds. In fact, it has been argued that, 'the refusal [of the EU] to accept responsibility was previously based, not in the view that race discrimination was separate from the economic goals of the Union, but that it was functional to those goals'.[13]

Another indication that anti-discrimination provisions were initially caught in the net of market/economic constraints is that, with exceptions, they are mostly focused on the employment context. Equality in access to and in the conditions of employment is necessary; however, it is only one sphere of social life where discrimination exists and, indeed, discrimination in employment does not exist in a cultural vacuum. Nevertheless, as explored in Chapter 3, ADL's scope has been steadily extended to cover other areas and levels of discrimination including the institutional. However, the rationale for securing equality rights should be independent of economic constraints; and on the contrary should be focused on challenging such economic constraints which are often those that create discrimination by disadvantaging certain categories of people. Furthermore, on a different level, as noted in Chapters 6 and 7, economic powers (e.g. multinational corporations, media outlets and advertisers) have indirectly but in effect regulated content not on an ethical basis of attending to human rights or equality legislation, but attending to their fear of loss of revenue if they either 'offend' consumers or companies. This is problematic and therefore a 'stronger' version of ADL is needed in order to secure the advancement of equality rights in a principled manner as opposed to it being subject to or hindered by lucrative interests.

IV Conceptual ability of anti-discrimination law

ADL has potential to address and redress ED; its theory, evolution, jurisprudence and statutes allow the inference that ADL is able – if only theoretically – to recognise the harm inflicted through ED as a discriminatory practice. The following sections explore the potential of ADL (primarily focused in the UK but similar potential may exist in other jurisdictions) through four intertwined themes. The first is the 'expansiveness' of equality rights; the second is the move of ADL from formal to substantive

---

12 See Fredman (2001), p. 216.
13 *Ibid*, pp. 217–218.

equality; the third is ADL's aim to redress disadvantage; and the fourth is the protection of human dignity as a value that informs the equality principle. The proposition that ADL has conceptual ability to incorporate ED is inspired by elements from different jurisdictions. These elements help construct one possible way in which ADL, in any particular jurisdiction that may adopt and adapt these elements, can start addressing ED. For example, Canadian and South African jurisprudence on human dignity and their emphasis on redressing disadvantage offer valuable elements for jurisdictions willing to interpret the protection of human dignity in a way that can authorise/justify the legal recognition and redress of ED.

I The expansiveness of equality rights

As we saw in Chapter 3, ADL in the UK has steadily moved from its formal equal treatment origins to a more expansive and nuanced understanding of the problem of discrimination. This movement suggests that the protection and remedies against discrimination are always 'under construction' and responsive to social demands. Similarly, the grounds on which discrimination is acknowledged to exist have also expanded. In the UK, the characteristics initially protected were race and sex, whereas the Equality Act 2010 now protects nine characteristics.[14] Discrimination was mostly protected in the area of employment, whereas relatively new developments have extended its scope to goods such as housing, healthcare and education.[15] In this regard, the expansiveness of the scope of ADL has included not only material goods but also 'dignitary harms' such as harassment.[16]

While the expansiveness of equality rights is not free from flaws, the intention here is to point out that equality rights are cumulative – because disadvantage and inequality are also cumulative – and have little by little responded to many social demands. Even though ED has to some extent been acknowledged by the media regulatory bodies in the UK, the rationale and manner of its inclusion in standards codes has not been sufficiently explored and indeed the adjudication processes that follow complaints made in this context do not evenly represent all the interests at stake (Chapter 7). Therefore, the expansiveness of equality rights in attention to the many areas where discrimination exists prompts/motivates seeking redress for visibly existing discriminatory practices that have yet to be formally recognised by ADL.

---

14 Bamforth *et al* (2008), pp. 565–1161. The protected characteristics are age, disability, gender reassignment, marriage and civil partnership, pregnancy and maternity, race, religion or belief, sex and sexual orientation.

15 *Ibid*, pp. 5–17.

16 *Ibid*, pp. 448–516. I have discussed the 'expansiveness' of the principle of equality, including the constitutional command to not discriminate, in Pérez Portilla (2007).

2 From formal to substantive equality

The changes and improvements in anti-discrimination provisions reveal, on the one hand, that we cannot understand the aim of anti-discrimination laws by reference to a straightforward equal treatment principle;[17] and that the concept of substantive equality is better suited to deal with contemporary demands against discrimination. There are various ways in which formal and substantive equality have been explained and differentiated. For example, formal equality can be seen as a starting point, mainly working as a promise of consistency. This is not to suggest that formal equality is not important; it has the vital function of 'prevent[ing] the formation of different categories of citizens with differing rights and status, and to guarantee the equality of all before the law'.[18] However, in contemporary societies this notion of equality is not enough. It fails to recognise the disadvantage experienced by some groups and the structural arrangements that sustain inequality. The substantive approach, on the other hand, rejects an abstract view of justice and instead insists that justice is only meaningful in its interaction with society, where:

> The unfortunate reality is that it is women rather than men who have suffered cumulative disadvantage due to sex discrimination.... Once this is accepted, it becomes clear that to adopt a symmetrical approach, whereby unequal treatment of men is regarded as morally identical to discrimination against women, is to empty the equality principle of real social meaning.[19]

Substantive equality therefore deals with the phenomenon of structural discrimination rather than simply focusing on individual treatment; according to Hunter, substantive equality acknowledges that treating people as if they were the same as a norm from which they actually differ in significant ways is just as discriminatory as penalising them directly for their difference, and it suggests that dominant norms themselves need to be changed.[20] Following Fredman, substantive equality addresses the interaction between recognition and redistribution, focusing not on status per se, but 'on those groups for whom status differentiation is correlated with disadvantage';[21] and this considering as well that discrimination extends beyond individual acts of prejudice. Therefore, for Fredman, substantive equality must also include some positive duties. This means that equality

17 See, for example, important developments such as indirect discrimination and the duties to make adjustments for disabled persons (Chapter 3).
18 O'Cinneide (2008), p. 84.
19 Fredman (2002), p. 128.
20 See, Hunter (2008), p. 4.
21 Fredman (2008), p. 178.

requires more than restraint. In addition, 'it calls for a duty on the State to take positive measures to promote equality, including, where appropriate, allocation of resources'.[22]

Similarly, according to Cowen, advocate of the High Court of South Africa:

> A substantive view of equality encompasses an approach to analysis or evaluation of impugned conduct or law. This approach requires a court to have regard to the context, and its relationship to systemic and structural forms of domination within a society, with a view to remedying disadvantage and subjugation.... A substantive equality approach therefore permits, and reveals the justifications for, positive steps to be taken to redress patterns of disadvantage.[23]

The Canadian understanding of substantive equality is similar. There, substantive equality implies the recognition of structural differences and disadvantages between groups and requires that the experience of non-dominant groups should be incorporated into the formulation of legal norms in order to overcome disadvantages and produce substantively fair results.[24]

These understandings of substantive equality make it possible to suggest that, wherever they are adopted, they can, if only theoretically, give ADL the potential to address and justify the inclusion of ED as a discriminatory practice given that, as we have argued in the previous chapters (Chapters 3 and 8 in particular), ED is a form of disadvantage in itself and a part of systemic and structural discrimination.

3 Redressing disadvantage

The previous section revealed that the adoption of a substantive model of equality requires the redress of disadvantage. Disadvantage means that we live in an 'unequal world', where there are gross inequalities in, for example, wealth, health and social status. Disadvantage is often referred to as an outcome of historic patterns of discrimination such as apartheid in South Africa, religious discrimination in Ireland, Nazism in Germany or the legacy of slavery. However, it also refers to subtler, but equally insidious forms such as homophobia found in most contemporary

---

22 *Ibid*, p. 177. See also Fredman (2007), pp. 218–234.

23 Cowen (2001), p. 37. See also *President of the Republic of South Africa v Hugo* 1997 (4) SA 1 (CC), 41. The reasoning of the court led to the need to implement a conception of equality which is both substantive and remedial. This means, an analysis of the discrimination claim that takes full account of the context and is able to respond to difference.

24 See Graycar and Morgan (2008), p. 107. The authors make reference to *Andrews v Law Society of British Columbia* [1989] 1 SCR 143, where the Supreme Court of Canada laid the framework for what would come to be seen as a jurisprudence of substantive equality.

societies;[25] and it can also be generated by contemporary social, economic and political conditions that generate stereotypical ascriptions that malign some groups.

Disadvantage is visible in many ways, including chronic under-representation in particular types of work or positions of power, inequitable access to the benefits of employment or State provision of services, or the imposition of inordinate costs on those who attempt to maintain religious or cultural preferences which conflict with those of the dominant group. This is often also referred to as 'structural discrimination'.[26]

Doctrinally speaking, the dominance approach has been used to refer to these patterns of disadvantage. This approach not only maps the existing inequalities and social disadvantages, but also puts them into context and identifies the social reality that nourishes them. In this approach it is inaccurate, for example, to speak about sex inequality because the reality is that what is happening is discrimination against women.[27] This makes clear another characteristic of disadvantage/domination, namely its relational nature. This means that, as we saw earlier, it is social relations – relations of dominance – that disadvantage women as a group. Similarly, racism in this view is not

> about objective characteristics, but about relationships of domination and subordination, about hatred of the 'Other' in defence of the 'Self', perpetrated and apparently legitimated through images of the 'Other' as inferior, abhorrent, even sub-human.[28]

Disadvantage can also be structural and, as such, it combines two elements: first, an appreciation that there are patterns of disadvantage or that there are groups that seem to be disproportionately and persistently in worse positions; and second, that there are certain permanent arrangements, practices, institutions and social structures that produce this outcome.[29] ED is an example of the combination of these two elements. On the one hand, the images and messages of ED misrepresent the groups they target, thus keeping them in the 'worse positions' in the cultural imagery, affecting their social standing as a group; and on the other, ED is a practice that finds support in current legal and institutional arrangements that allow the media to produce the disadvantage of some groups without significant challenge. The redress of ED through ADL would therefore be plainly justified if a substantive model of equality were adopted.

25 See Fredman (2002), p. 19.
26 Fredman (2001), p. 235.
27 See Lacey (1998), p. 25. See also MacKinnon (1987), pp. 40–41.
28 Fredman (2001), p. 216.
29 See Collins (2003), p. 17.

4 The protection of human dignity

As we saw in Chapters 5 and 6, both at a doctrinal and legal level, the harm created through discriminatory and hate speech is often related to or understood as harm to the dignity of the individual members of the target groups. Moreover, as we noted in Chapter 3, the protection of human dignity is a constant in most jurisdictions that have enacted ADL and so, given the convergence of these factors, this section looks into what human dignity has been considered to involve within ADL in some of the jurisdictions where the protection of human dignity has been more salient. The analysis that follows is only conceptual, and is aimed at the better understanding of the conceptual ability of ADL to incorporate harms such as ED by appealing to the protection of human dignity.

The equality principle is informed, and its scope determined, by a set of values which vary depending on the jurisdiction. Thus, for example, in the jurisprudence of Canada and South Africa, the protection of human dignity is particularly salient and in these jurisdictions the court's interpretation of 'dignity' is a guiding principle for equality rights. It helps to determine when and how equality rights are violated and who should be protected under certain circumstances. However, the interpretations these jurisdictions have made can also offer lessons about the risks of an ADL that focuses solely or more prominently on dignitary harms to the detriment of redistributive claims. Moreover, while the protection of human dignity is common in guiding equality rights in largely democratic societies; it is nevertheless controversial and its interpretation is neither unanimous nor is it 'set in stone'. There are both pessimistic and optimistic views about the adequacy of dignity as a guiding principle of the equality guarantee. On the one hand, for example, McCrudden points out both the lack of consensus on what dignity means and its continuous use as 'placeholder'. He argues that at the moment, there is probably no single coherent interpretation in any one jurisdiction.[30] On the other hand, Small and Grant see dignity as the end of the legal enquiry, not an intuitive reaction to the facts based on some abstract notion. What this means in each case will differ, not simply in whichever way satisfies the demands of the judicial designer but based on a structured assessment of context.[31]

As pointed out by McCrudden, there is no consensus on the interpretation of dignity; however, there are some patterns of its meaning in ADL. These patterns do not offer an 'all purpose recipe'; nevertheless, they do offer insights about some of the problems that should be addressed by ADL and justifications for so doing. But even these can be contentious.

---

30 See McCrudden (2006), pp. 45–46.
31 See Small and Grant (2005), p. 51.

The priority given to dignity over material disadvantage in some Supreme Court of Canada jurisprudence, for example, has been problematic in so far as it has allowed the court to ignore distributive claims if these are argued not to demonstrate harm to human dignity. As explained by Fredman, in *Gosselin v Quebec*,

> the claimant challenged the policy of providing welfare recipients under 30 years old only one-third of the basic line benefits available to those over 30 unless they participated in a designated work activity or education programme. In practice, there was a significant shortfall in places available, and those which were available were relatively short-term. Thus many young people, including the claimant experienced real poverty.[32]

This means that if taken alone a purely status-based interpretation of dignity could well undermine the distributive dimension. At the same time, the importance of this aspect of equality should not be lost.

> There are some situations in which it [dignity] is the most salient reason for an equality claim. Sexual harassment, racist abuse, humiliation of

---

32 *Gosselin v Quebec* 2002 [SCC] 84, para. 61 (McLachlin J). See Fredman (2007), p. 220. A similar example is *Law v Canada* (Minister of Employment and Immigration), [1999] 1 SCR 497, paras 99, 107, 108. This case created the test for establishing equality rights claims under section 15 of the Canadian Charter of Rights and Freedoms (CCRF). The case involved a 30-year-old widow without dependants who was denied survivors benefits under the Canadian Pension Plan (CPP), which are usually given to those over 45, or to the disabled, or to those with dependants at the time of death. The question before the court was whether the CPP regulations infringed s. 15 of the CCRF on the ground that they discriminate on the basis of age against widows and widowers under the age of 45, and if so, whether this infringement was demonstrably justified in a free and democratic society. The court recognised that a measure excluding childless widows under 45 from survivor's benefits imposed a disadvantage on them. However, Iacobucci J concluded that the law *was not discriminatory* because it did not reflect or promote the notion that they are less capable or less deserving of concern, respect and consideration or perpetuate the view that people in this class are less capable or less worthy of recognition or value as human beings or as members of Canadian society (italics are the author's). The Supreme Court of Canada has found difficulties arising from the attempt in *law* to employ human dignity as a legal tool. The court has noted that, as critics have pointed out, human dignity is an abstract and subjective notion that, even with the guidance of the four contextual factors, cannot only become confusing and difficult to apply; it has also proven to be an additional burden on equality claimants. Those four contextual factors are: (1) pre-existing disadvantage, if any, of the claimant group; (2) degree of correspondence between the differential treatment and the claimant group's reality, (3) whether the law or program has an ameliorative purpose or effect; and (4) the nature of the interests affected. See, *R. v Kapp*, 2008 SCC 41, [2008] 2 SCR 483 para. 19, 21, 22. Other similar cases include *Miron v Trudel* [1995] 2 SCR 418; *Egan and Nesbitt v Canada* [1995] 2 SCR 513; and *Canada v Hislop* [2007] 1 SCR 429.

old people, and homophobic bullying at schools are all examples of situations in which the primary claim is based on dignity.[33]

ED is also one of those situations, and this book echoes the importance of protecting human dignity through ADL in cases like these while also recognising the risk of an interpretation of dignity that may result in an obstacle to socio-economic claims.

Similar to the jurisprudential need to redress disadvantage, in South Africa and Canada, the value of dignity is relevant to and should be understood in a context of *substantive equality*. In South Africa, this implies that the Court,

> have regard to the context of the alleged violation, including its social and historical context, and its relationship to systemic and structural forms of domination within a society, with a view to remedying disadvantage and subjugation.[34]

Now, as we noted from the outset, the protection of human dignity is primarily understood as a guiding principle of the equality guarantee. The Supreme Court of Canada has declared that the fundamental values enshrined in the Canadian Charter's equality guarantee are the protection and enhancement of human dignity, the promotion of equal opportunity and the development of human potential based upon individual ability.[35] More specifically, the purpose of the equality guarantee has been declared as the need:

> To prevent the violation of essential human dignity and freedom through the imposition of disadvantage, *stereotyping*, or political or *social prejudice*, and to promote a society in which all persons enjoy equal recognition at law as human beings or as members of Canadian society, equally capable and equally deserving of concern, *respect* and consideration.[36]

In declaring the purpose of the equality guarantee, the Supreme Court is also outlining ways in which human dignity is violated, such as the imposition of disadvantage, stereotyping and political or social prejudice, which as we have seen, are characteristic of ED. More specifically in *Law v Canada*, Iacobucci J, writing for a unanimous court, described not only the

---

33 Fredman (2007), pp. 225, 230.

34 Cowen (2001), p. 37.

35 *Miron v Trudel* [1995] 2 SCR 418, 489.

36 Iacobucci J. in *Law v Canada* (Minister of Employment and Immigration) [1999] 1 SCR 497, para. 51. This purpose had been similarly declared before in *Miron v Trudel* [1995] 2 SCR 418; *Egan v Canada* [1995] 2 SCR 513; *Vriend v Alberta* [1998] 1 SCR 493; and *Andrews v Law Society of British Columbia* [1989] 1 SCR 143. Italics are the author's.

meaning of dignity but also ways in which it is harmed and enhanced; and in so doing, he incorporated many of the elements that this book has put forward for the recognition of ED through ADL:

> Human dignity means that an individual or group feels self-respect and self-worth. It is concerned with physical and psychological integrity and empowerment. Human dignity is harmed by unfair treatment premised upon personal traits or circumstances which do not relate to individual needs, capacities and merits. It is enhanced by laws which are sensitive to the needs, capacities and merits of different individuals, taking into account the context underlying their differences. Human dignity is harmed when individuals and groups are marginalized, ignored or devalued, and is enhanced when laws recognise the full place of all individuals and groups within Canadian society.[37]

This definition demonstrates that the harm created through ED can be constructed as harm to human dignity understood in this way and, therefore, this concept can inspire a way to legally justify the redress of ED through ADL in a jurisdiction which chooses to legally recognise this harm. ED can be said to harm human dignity given that, on the one hand, discriminatory speech hinders the feelings of self-respect and self-worth of its targets, affecting their psychological integrity and empowerment; and on the other, ED marginalises, ignores and devalues the members of disadvantaged groups through misrepresentation, under-representation and lack of participation in the media industry (Chapter 8). The definition is nevertheless problematic regarding its emphasis on merit. Merit usually requires meeting a standard and individuals may be unable to meet this due to historical disadvantages or personal attributes:

> merit leans towards a standard: the individual must conform, but if diversity and difference are to be accepted as fundamental to human dignity, then it is merit that should be adjusted to accommodate difference, in order to ensure that merit criteria do not mask or perpetuate disadvantage.[38]

Human dignity is therefore understood as encompassing feelings of self-respect and self-worth. These feelings – immaterial goods – cannot be distributed fairly; they are the product of social relations (Chapter 2). They arise where there is participatory parity and are hindered through

---

37 *Law v Canada* (Minister of Employment and Immigration), [1999] 1 SCR 497, para. 53, citing with approval the statement of Lamer CJ in *Rodriguez v British Columbia (Attorney General)* [1993] SCR 519 para. 554.
38 Small and Grant (2005), p. 39.

relations of domination and discrimination. Self-respect and self-worth are created or destroyed within and by social relations, which are in themselves subject to a range of historical, cultural, institutional and structural forces. The production and reproduction of ED is an example of these social relations that ADL should redress.

In South Africa, 'dignity' is mainly a value that guides the equality guarantee in response to the history of humiliation and degradation of the previous apartheid regimes.[39] There are various dispositions that make this clear. Probably the most significant one is section I of the Constitution, which states that 'the new South African State is founded on the values of human dignity, the achievement of equality, and the advancement of human rights and freedoms'. In South Africa, the meaning of dignity as a concept is determined at a general level and determinable at a historical level through understanding what had been denied to people under apartheid.[40] Determining a violation to human dignity requires *a contextual analysis* to decide whether there is discrimination on a ground that is not specified and/or whether the alleged discrimination is unfair; for this, the Court considers:

> various (non-exhaustive) factors, including the position of the complainants in society, whether they have suffered in the past from patterns of disadvantage, whether the discrimination in the case under consideration is on a specified ground or not, as well as the nature of the provision or power and the purpose sought to be achieved by it. These factors go to an overall determination of the extent to which the discrimination has affected the rights or interests of the complainants and whether it has led to an impairment of their fundamental human dignity or constitutes an impairment of a comparably serious nature.[41]

This emphasis on context in order to understand and assess discrimination resonates/coincides with one of the defining characteristics of ED, which is that the historical and/or social context determines whether an image or a message is discriminatory and therefore is captured by the concept of ED (Chapter 8) and so, this is another example of the existence of aims and methods used in ADL which coincide with the aims and methods apposite for the redress of ED. Similarly, discrimination on unspecified grounds is determined on the basis of whether the impugned treatment is based on characteristics or attributes which have the potential to impair fundamental human dignity, or have a similar effect.[42] For

39 See Fredman (2002), p. 17.
40 See Cowen (2001), p. 54.
41 *Harksen v Lane NO* 1998 (1) SA1 (CC); 1997 (11) BCLR 1489 (CC) para. 51.
42 See Small and Grant (2005), p. 32; and Cowen (2001), p. 36.

example, in *Larbi-Odam and Others v Member of the Executive Council for Education*, the court held that differentiation on the ground of citizenship in the appointment of teachers had the potential to impair the fundamental human dignity of the applicants. The factors that weighed in this case included the fact that non-citizens are a minority, lacking political power, and that individuals had no control over their citizenship. In addition, attention was drawn to evidence of threats and intimidation against schools considering the appointment of foreign teachers and the history of disadvantage suffered by black people deprived of citizenship in apartheid South Africa, citizenship based on race.[43]

In fact, the protection of human dignity is often found in clauses against discrimination, supplementing the list of protected characteristics.[44] However, even when it is not explicit, the protection of human dignity is nevertheless influential in extending the anti-discrimination clause to cover analogous grounds. In Canada, for example, such an extension is justified as follows: 'Equality means that our society cannot tolerate legislative distinctions that treat certain people as second-class citizens, that demean them, that treat them as less capable for no good reason, or that *otherwise offend fundamental human dignity*.'[45] Therefore, the protection of human dignity is relevant when determining whether discrimination on an unspecified ground is unfair and therefore whether a non-listed ground should be deemed a reasonable ground that should be protected against discrimination.[46]

43   *Larbi-Odam and Others v Member of the Executive Council for Education (North West Province) and Another* 1998 (1) SA 745 (CC); 1997 (12) BCLR 1655 (CC). As explained by Small and Grant (2005), p. 58.
44   See, for example, the South African Prevention, Prohibition and Elimination of Unfair Discrimination Act's definitions in chapter 1, section 1. Definitions (1) 'prohibited grounds'.
45   *Egan v Canada* [1995] 29 CRR (2d) 79, 104–105. The Supreme Court established that sexual orientation constitutes a prohibited basis of discrimination under section 15 of the Canadian Charter of Rights and Freedoms.
46   In Canada there are various cases exemplifying that the grounds of discrimination (enumerated in section 15 of the Canadian Charter of Rights and Freedoms) are not exhaustive. *Vriend v Alberta* [1998] 1 SCR 493 is an example in which sexual orientation was given – via dignity analysis – a previously denied protection. The Supreme Court of Canada unanimously held that the Alberta Government's omission of sexual orientation from the Individual Rights Protection Act (IRPA) violated section 15 of the Canadian Charter of Rights and Freedoms. The Court found that there was a psychological harm, which may ensue from this state of affairs 'fear of discrimination will logically lead to concealment of true identity and this must be harmful to personal confidence and self-esteem'. Cases like this often combine arguments of dignity and disadvantage. Regarding citizenship, an example can be found in *Andrews v Law Society of British Columbia* [1989] 1 SCR 143; other cases are *Egan and Nesbitt v Canada* [1995] 2 SCR 513; this is a case about the denial of spousal allowance based on opposite sex definition of 'spouse'; and *Canada v Hislop* [2007] 1 SCR 429, referring to statutory distinctions restricting same-sex spouses' eligibility for and access to arrears of Canadian Pension Plan survivor benefits in violation of section 15.

So far, various examples have been shown of ways in which jurisprudential interpretations of dignity in the context of ADL coincide with the rationale of ED that has been built in this book. Moreover, these interpretations offer some optimism about the conceptual ability of the law to accommodate harms such as ED and tools to further develop the concept. The risks of an ADL mainly focused on the protection of human dignity have also been noted; particularly when the protection of human dignity is used in order to grant or deny material goods such as welfare benefits. However, it has also been noted that there are cases which saliently address status-based inequalities and which may not necessarily, or in principle, be directly linked to material or economic claims (e.g. both South Africa and Canada have recognised that prohibition of same-sex marriage harms the dignity of gay men and lesbians).[47] The distinction between economic and status-based inequalities is not necessary because they are opposing claims, but because no dimension should undermine the other. Fredman, for example, argues that a full understanding of equality needs to incorporate both recognition and redistribution. Based on a deeper understanding of substantive equality, which constitutes the conceptual framework for the inter-penetration of redistributive and recognition issues, corresponding legal measures need to be constructed to reflect these principles. Fredman suggests two main ways in which this can be done, the most promising being positive duties to promote equality and justiciable socio-economic rights.[48]

This book has argued for recognition – against being routinely maligned or disparaged in stereotypic cultural representations, and in favour of giving more prominence to claims based on dignity, particularly regarding discriminatory media content. This project, although daring, is not antithetical to existing initiatives aimed at balancing freedom of expression and non-discrimination. For example, as noted in Chapter 5, the idea that human dignity is harmed with no direct reference to material or economic claims but through various kinds of demeaning representation has been made

---

47 The Canadian courts have interpreted section 15 of the Charter as requiring the State to recognise same-sex partnerships as equal to heterosexual marriages. See, for example, *M v H* (1999) 171 DLR (4th) 577; and *Halpern v Canada (A.G.)* (2003) 225 DLR (4th) 529. The Constitutional Court in South Africa has also given recognition to same-sex marriages. See *Minister of Home Affairs and Another v Fourie and Another* (CCT 60/04 [2005] ZACC 19; 2006 (3) BCLR 355 (CC); 2006 (1) SA 524 (CC) (1 December 2005)). Other cases in which dignity is the most salient claim are *Vriend v Alberta* [1998] 1 SCR 493; and, in the UK, *I v United Kingdom*, App. No. 25680/94 (Eur Ct HR, July 11 2002).

48 See Fredman (2007), pp. 218–234.

clear in documents from the Council of Europe[49] and the European Union,[50] and is often present in hate speech legislation (Chapter 6).[51] Moreover, the idea that discriminatory speech (expression that subordinates and harms the self- and social-esteem and respect accorded to disadvantaged groups) in the media can harm human dignity is also recognised in the standards codes of the media industry (Chapter 7).[52]

ED harms human dignity in the sense outlined in the Canadian and South African jurisprudence. It harms the self- and social-esteem of disadvantaged groups and does not exist in isolation; it is part of systemic discrimination, past and present, and perpetuates status subordination. In this sense, ED can also be understood as a form of disadvantage; it reinforces and perpetuates the demeaning stereotypical ascriptions that often inform the unfair treatment given to its targets. For these reasons, it is possible to suggest that ADL, when guided by the protection of human dignity and based on a model of substantive equality which requires the redress of disadvantage, has the potential to justify the inclusion of ED as a discriminatory practice. Moreover, the contextual analysis observed by the courts in order to determine the grounds on which discrimination should be prohibited provides guidance for a principled inclusion of grounds to be protected against ED that are not included in hate speech laws.

V Harassment and ED

The acknowledgement of the harm of harassment is an example in which the law takes into account a problem that, like ED, was considered by many as trivial. Sexual harassment is a concept which reconstructs, from a

49 See, for example, Council of Europe Recommendation CM/Rec(2009)5 on 'Measures to protect children against harmful content and behaviour and to promote their active participation in the new information and communications environment'. This document establishes that it is a priority for the Council of Europe to protect freedom of expression and *human dignity* in the information and communications environment by ensuring a coherent level of protection for minors against harmful content and developing children's media literacy skills.
50 See, for example, EU Recommendation (2006/952/EC) on the 'Protection of minors and human dignity and on the right of reply in relation to the competitiveness of the European audiovisual and on-line information services industry'. The Recommendation recalls the Charter of Fundamental Rights of the EU, in particular article 1, which refers to the inviolability, respect and protection of human dignity.
51 See, for example, German Criminal Code, Section 130; South Africa's Promotion of Equality and Prevention of Unfair Discrimination Act 2000, Chapter 2 Prevention, Prohibition and Elimination of Unfair Discrimination, Hate Speech and Harassment, section 10. Prohibition of hate speech; and, as an example from the European Court of Human Rights, see *Erbakan v Turkey* judgment of 6 July 2006, 56.
52 See, for example, the Ofcom Broadcasting Code 21 March 2013, section 2; and the UK Code of Broadcast Advertising, 1st edition, 1 September 2010, section 4.8.

feminist perspective, behaviour conventionally regarded as acceptable and even favourable to women, as unacceptable, oppressive and illegal.[53] For women, harassment used to be a problem without a name. It was and still is a threat to women who trespass the boundaries of their perceived 'natural' place (the home), and instead go to the workplace, a male-dominated area. As Andrea Dworkin has suggested, harassment occurs in places where the oppressed are not welcome: schools, the workplace and positions of power. We do not see them there because they do not belong there.[54] Pornography in the workplace is, as she puts it, 'a way to drive women out of the workplace ... it is indeed, like "Get out nigger"'.[55] Sexual harassment is therefore a consequence of both the structural assumption that a woman's place is in the private sphere, the home, and of the cultural norms governing male and female sexual roles and behaviour.[56] Moreover, sexual harassment of women not only undermines a woman's dignity, but also her efforts to function in a 'different' role.[57]

Sexual harassment, like ED is a part of social injustice. It used to have no name, but its targets knew what it felt like.[58] Harassment, however, cannot only be sexual; it can also happen to other dominated groups (including harassment based on combination of grounds, e.g. against black women). In this view,

> once the mischief of sexual harassment is framed in terms of power and dominance, which are aimed at policing and enforcing gender stereotypes, it is also possible to see a continuity between the harm of sexual harassment and other forms of discriminatory harassment.[59]

In EU law, for example, harassment *related to* race, religion, sexual orientation, disability and age is prohibited in employment as well as in some other areas such as public services and the provision of private goods and services.[60]

---

53 See Lacey (1998), p. 29.
54 See Dworkin (1997), p. 202.
55 *Ibid*, p. 199.
56 See Houghton-James (1995), p. 17.
57 See Epstein (1996), p. 405.
58 See MacKinnon (1979), p. 27.
59 Bamforth *et al* (2008), p. 473.
60 *Ibid*. See Directive 2000/78/EC of 27 November 2000 ('The Employment Directive' on age, disability, religion or belief and sexual orientation); Directive 2000/43/EC of 29 June 2000 ('The Race Directive' on race and ethnic origins); Directive 2002/73/EC of 23 September 2002 (amending the Equal Treatment Directive of 1976, hence 'The Amended Equal Treatment Directive on sex, gender re-assignment and marital status'); and Directive 2006/54/EC of 5 July 2006, which consolidates several directives related to equal treatment as well as certain case law developments.

Directive 2006/54/EC on the implementation of the principle of equal opportunities and equal treatment of men and women in matters of employment and occupation (recast) defines harassment as: 'where unwanted conduct related to the sex of a person occurs with the purpose or effect of violating the dignity of a person, and of creating an intimidating, hostile, degrading, humiliating or offensive environment'. Sexual harassment, on the other hand, is defined as: 'where any form of unwanted verbal, non-verbal or physical conduct of a sexual nature occurs, with the purpose or effect of violating the dignity of a person, in particular when creating an intimidating, hostile, degrading, humiliating or offensive environment'. Discrimination under this directive includes both conduct and also any less favourable treatment based on a person's rejection of or submission to such conduct.[61]

The core concept of discriminatory harassment in all the directives refers to unwanted conduct 'related to' the prohibited ground.[62] This category is broader than the common wording of direct discrimination provisions that require conduct to be performed 'on the grounds of' the prohibited ground because it eliminates the element of causation. 'As a matter of language it seems clear that requiring conduct to be on a particular ground imposes a more stringent demand than requiring it to be related to that ground.'[63] To some degree it could be argued that this wording separates out the notion of harassment from discrimination. Ellis, for example, considers that '[a]lthough deemed to be types of discrimination, the new torts of harassment and sexual harassment do not reflect the accepted concept of discrimination, not least in containing no element of actual or hypothetical comparison'.[64] However, even though there are

---

61 See Directive 2006/54/EC, article 2. This is a recast directive that coalesces previous directives and case law on equal treatment for women and men in employment. Some of the antecedents to the inclusion of sexual harassment in EU law can be found in Rubenstein (1988). See also Ellis (2005), pp. 237–239.

62 For a comprehensive analysis of the implications of the wording 'related to' and its interpretation and application in UK harassment legislation, see Barmes (2007).

63 *Ibid*, p. 453. However, authors such as Ellis have pointed out that in some respects it is arguable that their requirements are actually more stringent than simply demonstrating unlawful discrimination in the usual ways (harm and causation). Ellis refers to problems related to elements such as 'unwanted' (presumably subjective condition), 'violating the dignity' (a phrase which will no doubt eventually have to be explained by the ECJ and may come to contain an objective element) and the purpose or effect of 'creating an intimidating, hostile, degrading, humiliating or offensive environment' (again perhaps at least partially an objective matter). See Ellis (2005), pp. 239–240.

64 Ellis (2005), p. 239.

arguments about the inadequacy of including harassment in ADL,[65] the wording 'related to' and the absence of comparison together with the language of 'dignity' of the individual rather than 'unequal treatment' to justify the concern with harassment, show the potential of ADL to adapt its requirements in order to tackle in more appropriate ways behaviours which, although they are discrete, form a part of systemic discrimination. As Barmes has put it:

> The larger context of subordination or mistreatment is invoked in the individual interaction. This is why it is arguably right to treat the merest connection between harassment and some aspects of identity as sufficient to turn harassing conduct into a discrimination act.[66]

Likewise, the lack of a comparative approach reinforces the expectation that alleged harassers will not escape liability if they treat everyone equally badly.[67]

Although not without pitfalls which cannot be discussed here in detail,[68] these examples taken from EU law are indicative of the evolution of ADL. It is worth noting that there is an emphasis on dignity and respect as important elements in addressing discrimination, and not only with regard to material goods, where dignity analysis can be problematic. The conduct need not, according to the directives, be directed specifically against the victim, although of course it is also prohibited where it is so directed; it is enough, for example, if a generally homophobic atmosphere, or an atmosphere antipathetic to a particular religion, prevails in a workplace.[69]

The creation of a hostile environment is harassment. This environment is created through both printed materials and verbal expressions. For

65 See Dine and Watt (1995). The authors explain that 'sexual harassment has little to do with discrimination [understood by the authors as disparate treatment] and issues of differential treatment are irrelevant in sexual harassment claims. In essence [sexual harassment] is a form of bullying based on the popular perception that sexual behaviour is a private matter.... Sexual harassment is no joke and a conviction in a criminal court is a good way to make that point. Not only is it imperative that adequate and workable complaints procedures are established in workplaces, but that sexual harassment is made properly actionable both inside and outside the *narrow confines of employment law*', p. 363 (italics are the author's). In the present author's research, harassment and ED are discrete harms; however, they form a part of systemic discrimination. They do not occur independently from other discriminatory practices; they can be both their drivers and byproducts while at the same time inflicting a harm in and of themselves. In this view both harassment and ED can be considered to be discriminatory practices.

66 Barmes (2007), p. 461.

67 *Ibid*, p. 460. See also *Brumfitt v Ministry of Defence* [2005] IRLR 4 for an example of this issue.

68 For these pitfalls, see Bamforth *et al* (2008), pp. 473–481; and Ellis (2005), pp. 113–114.

69 Ellis (2005), p. 240.

example, sexual harassment through literature refers to the display of sexually explicit materials such as promotional calendars, pin-up photographs and magazines. The implications here are, first, that these materials offend in and of themselves; and second, that they motivate sexually harassing behaviour.[70] In its verbal forms, harassment can include anything from passing but persistent comments about a woman's body or body parts to all sorts of stereotypical messages and 'jokes' about the cultural beliefs and traits of targeted groups.

Harassment is an example in which the group-based nature of discrimination is explicit. This is especially the case in harassment 'through expressive means', which bears some resemblance to ED. Images and messages that stigmatise, ridicule, abuse and objectify women are humiliating to any woman – they send a message to every woman and man. In the same sense, racial harassment that uses offensive and gross generalisations and stereotypes based on race transgresses the dignity of all the individuals within the targeted group.

In the case of harassment, as in other cultural aspects of discrimination (Chapter 3), issues of internalisation of subordination and collusion take place. Complaining about it is often a considerable burden because of the material difficulty and potential financial cost when set against the resources of institutions who frequently defend these complaints in Employment Tribunals. In addition, and significantly as a function of the former, the stress created for complainants in such circumstances makes proving a case very difficult. Moreover, for many people it is just 'easier' to tolerate it and keep going with the 'hope' of being accepted and liked. Indeed, for many people harassment is no more than a condition of work.

The remedies for harassment in the UK comprise the traditional financial compensatory remedies such as awards for injury to feelings.[71] Even though harassment can indeed have an economic impact on the victim and this must be compensated, financial remedies cannot in themselves redress the dignitary harm created. Directive 2006/54/EC establishes that employers and those responsible for vocational training should be encouraged to

---

70 See Becket (1994), p. 252.
71 See Selwyn (2011), pp. 178–179. The award will usually fall within three bands, depending on the frequency and nature of the wrongful act. An award may also be made for psychiatric illness suffered as a result of sex discrimination and/or harassment (*HM Prison Service v Salmon* [2001] IRLR 425, [2001] Emp LR 1035). There is no limit on the amount that can be awarded, which can include aggravated damages if the injury was inflicted by conduct that was high-handed, malicious, insulting or oppressive (*HM Prison Service v Johnson* [2007] IRLR 951, (2007) 151 SJLB 1165) and such damages should not be aggregated with or treated as part of the damages awarded for injury to feelings (*Scott v Commissioners of Inland Revenue* [2004] EWCA Civ 400, [2004] ICR 1410, [2004] IRLR 713, [2004] 148 SJLB 474, [2004] *Times*, 19 April).

take preventive measures against harassment and sexual harassment.[72] Such preventive measures can include the production of policies alerting the public and making statements that harassment would not be tolerated. Training courses for all staff – including managers and supervisors – and apologies for the victims could also be part of the remedy. Eliminating harassment is indeed included in the general equality duty in the UK, which makes it clear that redressing harassment requires not only reactive but also proactive measures. In this way, harassment also bears a resemblance to ED. Indeed they are behaviours that support and reinforce each other. They are reflections of relations of domination. Both are possible because there are some agents who can perpetrate them without fear of being challenged. Both are deeply rooted in culture (a culture of oppression), while also re-creating such a culture. They are, however, so embedded that they are often perceived as normal and unchangeable, as just 'the way life is'. Victims of harassment in the workplace often report severe consequences, such as diminishing work performance, the quantity and quality of their work, ability to work with others, attendance record, emotional distress, physical stress, anger, fear, anxiety, depression, guilt, humiliation, embarrassment, etc.[73] Indeed, 'psychologists and social workers report that severe/chronic sexual harassment can have the same psychological effects as rape or sexual assault'.[74] Moreover, these effects are aggravated by the lack of real opportunity to challenge this behaviour since there is often too much to lose. The victims of harassment face a double hazard. On the one hand, they fear that their complaint will be ignored or simply not believed. On the other hand, they experience fear of being blamed, considered unprofessional or even to have 'asked for it'.[75]

Harassed women experience disrespect and status devaluation which hinder their participation as peers in society. Harassment, be it in the workplace or at school, does not stop there; the harm can last a lifetime; it follows the victim; and its toleration tells women how they are perceived and how they ought to be treated. Harassment, the same as ED, is not an isolated phenomenon but part of a much bigger picture of domination. Sexual harassment of women 'is not incidental, nor tangential to women's inequality, it is a crucial expression of it and a central dynamic in it'.[76] Harassment is a reflection of relations of domination. It is usually men who

---

72 See also the proposals made by Rubenstein (1988) and the Commission of the European Communities Recommendation of 27 November 1991 (and annexed Code of Practice) on the protection of the dignity of women and men at work, 92/131/EEC, OJ [1992] L49/1.

73 See Epstein (1996), p. 405.

74 Koss (1987).

75 See MacKinnon (1979), p. 49.

76 *Ibid*, p. 31.

harass women, heterosexual and homophobic people who harass gay people and so on. In the case of racial harassment:

> Explicitly racist material seeks to confirm existing racism and to convert the doubting. What is pleasurable here is recognising ugly (foreign, black, Jewish) and knowing yourself to be different from this – this material encourages its audiences to feel white and proud. What is relished by the viewer is a sense of superiority rather than a sense of lack. This kind of fun is only available to some people. The 'ugly' aren't supposed to feel good about seeing themselves like this.[77]

The causes and consequences of harassment have a great deal in common with the causes and consequences of ED. The acknowledgement of the existence of harassment first as a harm in and of itself which did not require economic or material harm to 'legitimise' it, then as a legal wrong captured by ADL, demonstrates the possibilities for the recognition of ED within ADL. There is a problem, there are complaints, and there are theoretical and jurisprudential elements to justify its consideration as discrimination and provide a remedy. Therefore, harassment is a precedent that indicates that discriminatory images and messages are not something that our peers in society should be expected to tolerate and that it is possible to legally address and redress wrongs of this sort. Discriminatory images and messages disseminated through the media are a central dynamic in discrimination and examples that clearly show that justice goes beyond the redistribution of material goods and that it also requires the procurement of relations of respect among peers. The recognition of harassment in ADL (in the UK and Europe) is an example that shows that equality and the elimination of discrimination cannot be achieved if we tolerate and learn to live with disrespecting, stereotyping or humiliating other human beings. The acknowledgement of the existence of harassment and ED also has an emancipatory element because it has been ultimately people – the targets – who have created these concepts, and provided the principles to legally challenge the harm they create.

VI Remedies

Practically, ADL's enforcement and the procurement of remedies must be country-specific. They are complex and encounter a variety of problems

---

77 Becket (1994), p. 88.

that cannot be discussed here.[78] In the UK, where discrimination is found, there is a range of *individual* remedies available such as: monetary compensation for most types of cases, awards for injury to feelings (especially in harassment cases), re-instatement or re-engagement (unfair dismissal cases) and recommendations (to obviate or reduce the adverse effect on the complainant).[79] The redress of the collective nature of the problem of discrimination in the UK has taken the form of 'equality duties' and although insufficiently enforced, there are also mechanisms such as contract compliance as a technique for using the financial power of the public sector to achieve the goals of Discrimination Law in the private sector (forms of positive action).[80] The development of these remedies over time demonstrates that further development is not closed. The redress of ED therefore can draw upon these already existing remedies for discrimination, while at the same time tailoring them to the specific harm that ED creates. As has been noted in Chapters 7 and 8, the most appropriate remedies for ED – and which indeed the targets often pursue – are public apologies, right of reply, modification or withdrawal of the material. These ED-specific remedies are not antithetical to those already in place in the UK in so far as they can be considered compensatory (aiming to put the victim into the position he or she would have been had the wrong not occurred). Now, given that ED happens through the media and therefore there are freedom of expression considerations, it has been argued that remedying ED through the promotion of more speech is in principle justified through the right of reply, which is legally permitted and promoted at EU level.[81] Moreover, remedies such as public apologies, right of reply, modification or withdrawal of the material can indeed strengthen ADL. In the same way that institutional discrimination requires remedies other than the individual ones, the redress of discrimination at a cultural level

78 See Fredman (2002), pp. 161–195. Some of these flaws are problems associated with the fact that, on the one hand, the lack of social, political and economic power of individuals from target groups makes it difficult for them to access individual remedies under existing Discrimination Law structures; and, on the other, the adversarial and adjudicative nature of individual remedies for discrimination is not suited to address the collective and structural aspects of inequality.

79 See Bamforth *et al* (2008), pp. 1165–1253.

80 In the UK this has been insufficiently enforced, especially as compared with jurisdictions such as the US and Canada. Contract compliance allows the public sector to use its economic power to negotiate clauses in private contracts which can promote some of the central goals of ADL; for example, by making the award of public contracts to private companies conditional on meeting certain criteria such as non-discrimination and equality standards. Collective remedies and extra legal strategies in the UK are explored in Bamforth *et al* (2008), pp. 1254–1288. Positive action is included in the Equality Act 2010 (ss. 158, general, and 159, recruitment and promotion). Positive action is legal and entirely voluntary; it can be taken to overcome disadvantage, meet a need or encourage participation in a certain activity.

81 See Chapter 2, V, 2, including footnotes 103–105.

demands different and specific remedies aimed at contesting and repairing the self and social deprecation (harm to human dignity) created through demeaning and stereotypical images and messages in the media. Media regulatory bodies have already contemplated these kinds of remedies; however, they could be imposed in a fairer way by having all interests represented in conciliation procedures, to which ADL is no stranger.[82]

If the principles proposed in this book were accepted, the specific form of adjudication or conciliation will depend on the particularities of each jurisdiction and crucially on the powers conferred to bodies such as equality commissions and on the possibility of imposing obligations on media regulatory authorities. These aspects are necessarily the subjects of specific research. The point here is simply to illustrate that the conceptual space exists in ADL to accommodate the concept of ED and that appropriate remedies can be legally established and justified.

VII Conclusions

If we agree that discrimination is a multifaceted problem that exists and is reinforced at various interactive levels, including the cultural, then it becomes apparent that the eradication of discrimination requires action at all such existing levels. Discriminatory images and messages in the media are forms of discrimination at a cultural level which ADL has the potential to redress. The evolution of ADL demonstrates that its development, although not without problems – mainly associated with individualistic approaches and economic constraints – is not closed and that ADL is capable of recognising harms and creating new strategies for the redress of specific forms of discrimination. This chapter has provided some theoretical arguments which break ADL's silence about demeaning and stereotypical representation in the media. Thus, it provides grounds and meaning for the recurrent associations made between hate/discriminatory speech, harm to human dignity and discrimination generally.

VIII References

Bamforth, Nicholas, Malik, Maleiha, O'Cinneide, C. and Bindman, Geoffrey (2008), *Discrimination Law: Theory and Context*, London: Thomson, Sweet & Maxwell.

---

82 In the UK, conciliation is mostly used in unfair dismissal cases generally, and also in cases that involve claims of discrimination. However, it has been noted that disadvantaged social groups will often lack the power to negotiate fair settlements and that additional support from agencies or trade unions may be necessary. Bamforth *et al* (2008), pp. 1209, 1252.

Barmes, Lizzie (2007), 'Constitutional and conceptual complexities in UK implementation of the EU harassment provisions', *Industrial Law Journal*, vol. 36, no. 4.

Becket, Jane (1994). 'In and out of view: visual representation and sexual harassment', in Brant, Clare and Lee Too, Yun, eds, *Rethinking Sexual Harassment*, New York: Pluto Press.

Collins, Hugh (2003), 'Discrimination, equality and social inclusion', *The Modern Law Review*, vol. 66.

Cowen, Susie (2001), 'Can dignity guide South Africa's equality jurisprudence?', *South African Journal of Human Rights*, vol. 17.

Dine, Janet and Watt, Bob (1995), 'Sexual harassment: moving away from discrimination', *Modern Law Review*, vol. 58, no 3.

Dworkin, Andrea (1997), *Life and Death*, The Free Press.

Ellis, Evelyn (2005), *EU Anti-Discrimination Law*, Oxford: Oxford University Press.

Epstein, Deborah (1996), 'Can a "dumb ass woman" achieve equality in the workplace? Running the gauntlet of hostile environment harassing speech', *The Georgetown Law Review*, vol. 84, no. 399.

Fiss, Owen (1976), 'Groups and the Equal Protection Clause', *Philosophy and Public Affairs*, vol. 5, no. 2.

Ford, Richard (2003), 'Unnatural groups: a reaction to Owen Fiss's "Groups and the Equal Protection Clause"', *Issues in Legal Scholarship*, vol. 2, no. 1, article 12.

Fredman, Sandra (2001), 'Equality: a new generation?' in *Equality Law: Reflections from South Africa and Elsewhere*, *Acta Juridica*, Faculty of Law, University of Cape Town.

Fredman, Sandra (2002), *Discrimination law*, Oxford: Oxford University Press.

Fredman, Sandra (2007), 'Redistribution and recognition: reconciling inequalities', *South African Journal of Human Rights*, vol. 23.

Fredman, Sandra (2008), *Human Rights Transformed: Positive Rights and Positive Duties*, Oxford: Oxford University Press.

Graycar, Reg and Morgan, Jenny (2008), 'Equality rights: what's wrong?', in Hunter, Rosemary, ed., *Rethinking Equality Projects in Law: Feminist Challenges*, Oxford: Hart.

HM Treasury (2011) *The Plan for Growth*, Department for Business Innovation and Skills.

Houghton-James, Hazel (1995), *Sexual Harassment*, Cavendish Publishing Limited.

Hunter, Rosemary (2008), 'Alternatives to equality', in Hunter, Rosemary, ed., *Rethinking Equality Projects in Law*, Oxford: Hart.

Koss, Mary (1987), 'Changed lives: the psychological impact of sexual harassment', in Paludi, Michele, ed., *Ivory Power: Sexual Harassment on Campus*, University of New York Press.

Lacey, Nicola (1998), *Unspeakable Subjects*, Oxford: Hart.

MacKinnon, Catharine (1979), *Sexual Harassment of Working Women*, New Haven, CT: Yale University Press.

MacKinnon, Catharine (1987), 'Difference and dominance: on sex discrimination', in *Feminism Unmodified*, Cambridge, MA: Harvard University Press.

McCrudden, Christopher (2006), 'Human dignity', University of Oxford Faculty of Law, Legal Studies Research Paper Series, Working Paper No. 10.

O'Cinneide, Colm (2008), 'The right to equality: a substantive legal norm or vacuous rhetoric?', *UCL Human Rights Review*, vol. 1, no. 1.

Pérez Portilla, Karla (2007), *Principio de igualdad: alcances y perspectivas*, 2nd ed., México: Porrúa-UNAM.

Rubenstein, Michael (1988), *The Dignity of Women at Work: A Report on the Problem of Sexual Harassment in the Member States of the European Communities*, Commission of the European Communities.

Selwyn, Norman (2011), *Selwyn's Law of Employment*, 16th ed., Oxford: Oxford University Press.

Small, Joan and Grant, Evadné (2005), 'Dignity, discrimination and context: new directions in South African and Canadian Human Rights Law', *Human Rights Review*, vol. 6, no. 2.

Chapter 10

Conclusions

It is not a coincidence that the harm associated with discriminatory speech has taken so long to be legally recognised. Certain injuries, as recalled by Matsuda, have been left to private individuals to absorb and resist by themselves. She spoke of the law's paucity in redressing the harm caused to certain categories of people such as women, children, 'people of colour' and 'poor' people. In this view, a legal response to discriminatory speech is a statement as much as it is its silence; and both entail 'a message, perhaps unintended, about the relative value of different human lives'.[1] It takes power and/or empowerment to get 'heard'.

The ideas in this book interrupt the passivity in ADL's theory regarding the constant associations made in public discourse, policy and even in some legal documents between demeaning or stereotypical representation in the media and discrimination. The book has referred to images and messages that can be insidious, subtle, widely available, 'normalised', and which do not reach the thresholds established in hate speech laws. Naming the harm facilitates pointing it out and can start relieving the sense of hopelessness generated by not even having the means to express the injustice felt. Giving the harm a name also means refusing to accept or learn to live with those expressions and facilitates contesting their definition of the status order of society. *Everyday discrimination* (ED) describes the normality, spontaneity and omnipresence of demeaning and stereotypical images and messages, and contends that they indeed constitute a form of discrimination. The images and messages of ED, together with the 'lack of diversity' within the media industry, promote the disadvantage of their targets, they are one form that inequality takes and a link in the chain of systemic discrimination; they keep relations of inferiority and superiority in 'their place', building on, reinforcing, justifying and maintaining status subordination without significant challenge.

ED has been analysed from various angles, including theoretical positions, policy, local, regional and international legislation, as well as,

1 Matsuda (1993), p. 18.

crucially, the targets' point of view. A variety of principles have been delineated in order to challenge ED. These principles are in harmony with existing legal frameworks and institutions within broadly democratic societies and indeed they support and reinforce freedom of expression values. However, the path is not smooth, not least because the tensions between freedom of expression and equality/non-discrimination and their political, cultural and economic context have tended invariably to generate controversy. Nevertheless, and even in the event of blatant disagreement with the arguments and principles put forward in this book, they entail a series of reasonable and crucial questions to which the choice of legal inactivity in response to ED will need to respond.

I Reference

Matsuda, Mari (1993), 'Public response to racist speech: considering the victim's story', in Matsuda, Mari, Lawrence III, Charles R., Delgado, Richard and Crenshaw, Kimberle Williams, eds, *Words that Wound: Critical Race Theory, Assaultive Speech, and the First Amendment*, Boulder, CO: Westview Press.

Index